The Triumph of Voting Rights in the South

A recipient of

The Julian J. Rothbaum Prize

whose sponsor advocated
the highest standards of scholarship
in all disciplines

The Triumph of Voting Rights in the South

CHARLES S. BULLOCK III

AND

RONALD KEITH GADDIE

UNIVERSITY OF OKLAHOMA PRESS : NORMAN

Library of Congress Cataloging-in-Publication Data

Bullock, Charles S., 1942–
The triumph of voting rights in the South / Charles S. Bullock III and Ronald Keith Gaddie.
p. cm.
Includes bibliographical references and index.
ISBN 978-0-8061-4079-7 (hardcover : alk. paper) 1. African Americans—Suffrage—Southern States. 2. United States. Voting Rights Act of 1965. 3. Minorities—Suffrage—Southern States. 4. Linguistic minorities—Suffrage—Southern States. 5. Elections—Southern States. 6. Voting—Southern States. 7. Southern States—Politics and government—1951– I. Gaddie, Ronald Keith. II. Title.
JK1924.B85 2009
324.6'208996073075—dc22

2009009377

The paper in this book meets the guidelines for permanence and durability of the Committee on Production Guidelines for Book Longevity of the Council on Library Resources, Inc. ∞

1 2 3 4 5 6 7 8 9 10

Contents

List of Illustrations		vii
List of Tables		ix
Acknowledgments		xiii
Introduction		3
Part I	The Original Seven Section 5 States	
	1. Mississippi	29
	2. Alabama	58
	3. Georgia	78
	4. Louisiana	111
	5. Virginia	141
	6. South Carolina	164
	7. North Carolina	190
Part II	The 1975 Amendment States	
	8. Texas	221
	9. Florida	253
Part III	Southern States Not Covered by Section 5	
	10. Tennessee	285
	11. Arkansas	304

Part IV Conclusions
12. A Comparative Analysis of the Impact of the Voting Rights Act in the South 323
13. Assessing the Voting Rights Act in Political Context 342

Epilogue: The 2008 Presidential Election 365

Appendix A. Analytic Methods for Estimating Racial Voting Patterns 375
Appendix B. Voter Registration and Turnout by Race and Ethnicity 379

Notes 387
Index 417

Illustrations

FIGURES

1.1.	Black elected officials in Mississippi, 1969–2001	38
2.1.	Black elected officials in Alabama, 1969–2001	65
3.1.	Black elected officials in Georgia, 1969–2001	88
3.2.	Black percentage of the Democratic primary turnout, 1990–2006	107
4.1.	Black elected officials in Louisiana, 1969–2001	120
5.1.	Black elected officials in Virginia, 1969–2001	145
5.2.	Proportionality in black legislative representation in the southern states, 2007	149
6.1.	Black elected officials in South Carolina, 1969–2001	173
7.1.	Black elected officials in North Carolina, 1969–2001	198
8.1.	Black elected officials in Texas, 1969–2001	230
9.1.	Hispanic elected officials in Florida, 1984–2004	261
9.2.	Black elected officials in Florida, 1969–2001	262
10.1.	Black elected officials in Tennessee, 1969–2001	292
11.1.	Black elected officials in Arkansas, 1969–2001	311

MAPS

I.1. V. O. Key, Jr.'s South 7

13.1. Possible preclearance coverage using the Norwood Amendment trigger 347

E.1. Counties won by Obama-Biden in 2008 367

Tables

1.1.	Racial makeup of the Mississippi legislature, 1963–2007	42
1.2.	Results of Mississippi statewide elections, 2003	43
1.3.	Racial preferences for Democratic candidates in select Mississippi races, 1992–2004	50
1.4.	Estimates of racial preferences for Congress in Mississippi, 2000–2004	51
1.5.	Estimates of racial preferences for select statewide Mississippi offices and Confederate flag referendum, 2000–2003	52
2.1.	Changes in registration in Alabama counties with low black registration in 1964	61
2.2.	Racial makeup of the Alabama legislature, 1965–2007	68
2.3.	Alabama statewide elections, 2000 and 2006	72
2.4.	White and black support for major Democratic Party candidates in Alabama, 1992–2004	73
2.5.	Estimates of white support for Democratic candidates in contested Alabama elections, 1994–2006	75
2.6.	Estimates of white support for Alabama's Democratic congressional candidates, 1998–2004	76
3.1.	White and nonwhite registration, 1962 and 2004, and turnout, 2004, in thirty Georgia counties	81

3.2.	Official registration and turnout in Georgia, 1996–2006	86
3.3.	Racial makeup of the Georgia General Assembly, 1963–2007	92
3.4.	Change in black voting-age population and registration in majority-black districts after first 2001 senate plan in Georgia	97
3.5.	Racial voting patterns in black-white contests for Georgia's 5th Congressional District	99
3.6.	Racial voting patterns in Georgia congressional contests involving African American candidates, 1992–1998	101
3.7.	White support for white Georgia Democratic house candidates, 1992–1998	102
3.8.	Racial preferences for Democrats in Georgia, 1992–2006	103
3.9.	Success of Democratic statewide candidates in Georgia, 1998–2006	104
4.1.	Official registration by race in Louisiana, 1964–1967	113
4.2.	Black voter registration and turnout in Louisiana, 1965–2008	118
4.3.	Racial makeup of the Louisiana legislature, 1965–2007	124
4.4.	OLS estimates of racial voting patterns in Louisiana congressional elections	128
4.5.	Estimates of black and white voter preferences, Louisiana BESE and PSC elections, 1998–2004	132
4.6.	Estimates of white voter and black voter preferences in Louisiana statewide constitutional offices and U.S. Senate, 1995–2004	135
5.1.	Racial makeup of the Virginia General Assembly, 1965–2007	148
5.2.	OLS estimates of white support for Democratic candidates in Virginia, 1986–2001	154
5.3.	Estimates of racial support for Democratic Party candidates in Virginia Congressional District 3, 1992–2004	155
5.4.	Estimates of white support for Democrats in statewide constitutional offices in Virginia, 1985–2005	157
5.5.	OLS and EI estimates of support for black candidates in Tidewater region state legislative general elections	159
5.6.	Support for black candidates of choice, controlling for opponents, in Virginia general elections	160
6.1.	Registration and turnout by race in South Carolina, 1972–2006	170
6.2.	Racial makeup of the South Carolina legislature, 1965–2007	176

6.3. Turnout in South Carolina primaries, 1984–2008 179
6.4. Estimates of white support for white Democratic U.S. House candidates in South Carolina, 1992–1998 183
6.5. Estimates of white voter support (%) for Democratic candidates in South Carolina, 1998–2006 184
7.1. Change in two North Carolina congressional districts' racial makeup 201
7.2. Racial makeup of the North Carolina General Assembly, 1965–2007 204
7.3. Estimates of support by race for African American candidates in North Carolina congressional and statewide contests, 1982–1998 211
7.4. White support (%) for white North Carolina Democratic U.S. House candidates, 1994–1998 213
7.5. Congressional election results for Democratic candidates in North Carolina, 2000–2002 215
7.6. EI statewide election results in North Carolina, 1996–2004 216
8.1. Spanish surname voter registration in Texas, 1992–2006 229
8.2. Latino-majority congressional districts in Texas, 2002 and 2004 233
8.3. Estimates of Hispanic and Anglo voter preferences for Henry Bonilla in Texas Congressional District 23, 1992–2002 234
8.4. Black-access districts, Balderas (2002) and HB-3 (2004), in Texas 236
8.5. Latino and African American Texas state legislators, 1965–2007 238
8.6. Candidate race and ethnicity, minority preferences, and statewide election outcomes in Texas, 1992–2006 241
8.7. Ecological regression (EI) estimates of racial voting patterns in select Texas congressional primary elections, 1992 245
8.8. Ecological interference (EI) estimates of the predominant minority voting behavior in Texas congressional districts 248
9.1. Racial and ethnic voter registration in Florida, 1994–2008 259
9.2. Florida congressional districts, black and Latino population, and Section 5 coverage 265
9.3. Latino and African American state legislators in Florida, 1967–2007 266

9.4. Hispanic population in Section 5 counties in Florida 269
9.5. Statewide Democratic candidate support by voter race or ethnicity, Florida, 1992–2006 275
9.6. Estimated Republican candidate support by race and ethnicity in select Florida counties, 1998 and 2000 277
9.7. Estimates of racial and ethnic preferences, statewide and legislative general elections, Collier County, Florida, 2002 278
9.8. Estimates of racial and ethnic preferences, statewide and legislative general elections, Hillsborough County, Florida, 2002 279
10.1. Racial makeup of the Tennessee General Assembly, 1965–2007 294
10.2. Estimated white voter support for Democrats for president, U.S. Senate, and governor, 2000–2006, and U.S. House, 2000, in Tennessee 299
10.3. Racial preferences for Democratic candidates in Tennessee, select races, 1992–2006 301
11.1. Racial makeup of the Arkansas General Assembly, 1965–2007 313
11.2. Democratic vote share in Arkansas statewide elections, 2002 and 2006 317
11.3. Estimates of white and black voter support for Democrats in contested Arkansas congressional elections, 1996, 2000, 2004 318
11.4. Black and white voter support for Democratic candidates in Arkansas, 1996–2004 319
12.1. Voter registration 326
12.2. Estimates of voter turnout among citizens in 2004 328
12.3. African American elected officials, 2001 330
12.4. African Americans in congressional, state, and local office 332
12.5. Summary of state rankings 339
E.1. Vote share and racial support for southern Democratic candidates in 2008 369
E.2. Proportion black, white, and Latino in the 2008 electorate 370
B.1. Voter registration data by race and ethnicity 380
B.2. Voter turnout data by race and ethnicity 383

Acknowledgments

This book was made possible by our friend Edward Blum of the American Enterprise Institute. Prior to the 2005–2006 debate over the renewal of the Voting Rights Act, Edward contacted us and asked if we would be interested in evaluating the advances in minority voter empowerment in the sixteen states covered by Section 5 of the Act. He then secured funding through the American Enterprise Institute and his own Project on Fair Representation, and also obtained supplemental funding from the Searle Freedom Trust for studies of voting and black political empowerment in three non–Section 5 states: Arkansas, Oklahoma, and Tennessee. This initial project resulted in a series of brief monographs submitted to the U.S. House of Representatives and U.S. Senate Judiciary Committee as part of the formal record on renewal of the Voting Rights Act. Edward also facilitated Gaddie's testimony before the U.S. Commission on Civil Rights, the U.S. House of Representatives Judiciary Subcommittee on the Constitution, and the U.S. Senate's Judiciary Committee.

As we went about building on the reports prepared in 2005 and 2006, the questions directed to Gaddie by Senators Edward M. Kennedy, John Cornyn, and Tom Coburn influenced our thinking about the Act and are reflected in this volume. This volume goes beyond our earlier work to include materials from subsequent elections and a brief examination of the political success of President Barack Obama.

At the University of Oklahoma Press, publisher John Drayton, editor-in-chief Chuck Rankin, acquisitions editor Jay Dew, and manuscript editor Emily Jerman all provided ongoing encouragement and support for the project, and influenced the content and presentation to produce a superior product. Errors of commission or omission reside with the authors. The reviewers for the Press provided timely and helpful criticism and suggestions for revision. We are especially grateful to Professor Tom Brunell of the University of Texas at Dallas for his extremely careful, surgical reading of the book and the care he took in guiding us toward needed revisions.

Some of the arguments and thoughts in this volume originally appeared in the *Fordham Urban Law Journal*,[1] *New York University Journal of Legislation and Public Policy*,[2] and *Georgetown Journal of Law & Public Policy*.[3]

Finally, our thanks go out to all of our colleagues around the country who have acted as expert witnesses and researched the politics of the South and minority empowerment, and also to all the lawyers we have worked both for and against in voting rights and redistricting lawsuits over the years. The South this book describes is a product of all of our efforts to feed the facts of race and politics into the judicial crucible, to create, what we hope, is a better and more civil truth.

Charles S. Bullock III
Athens, Georgia

Ronald Keith Gaddie
Norman, Oklahoma

The Triumph of Voting Rights in the South

Introduction

This Mr. Chairman, is perhaps the negroes' temporary farewell to the American Congress; but let me say, Phoenix-like he will rise up some day and come again.

GEORGE H. WHITE, JANUARY 29, 1901

It is the single most important piece of civil rights legislation, other than the constitutional amendments, in the history of the country.

MAYNARD JACKSON, TWO-TIME ATLANTA MAYOR

The most successful civil rights law in history.

EDWARD M. KENNEDY

The Voting Rights Act of 1965 represented a landmark departure in the century-long pursuit of voting rights in the United States. "The Act," as it is often simply referred to, became law in August 1965, four months after President Johnson's call for a voting law that would be sufficient to accomplish what three previous civil rights acts (1957, 1960, and 1964) and two constitutional amendments had been unable to achieve: to allow voters, regardless of race, to register and vote, free from political intimidation and violence, without having to overcome unnecessary obstacles.

Most of this statute is permanent and applies nationwide. Congress considered other parts, however, to be so extraordinary when first enacted that they were made subject to sunset provisions. The extraordinary nature of the legislation is founded in the description of these "emergency provisions," which allowed the national government to intercede in the historical and traditional conduct of state and local elections. The degree of intervention was unprecedented since the departure of the last Union forces from the South in 1877, and Georgia historian Numan Bartley aptly termed the 1965 effort to deliver on the promise of the Fourteenth Amendment the "second Reconstruction" of the South.[1]

The initial sunset was five years out from enactment. In 1970 Congress extended the short-term provisions for another five years, and in 1975 a seven-year extension passed. In 1982 and then most recently in 2006, these temporary provisions were extended for a quarter of a century. As a means of federal preemption of state authority, the Voting Rights Act (VRA) stands as a model of temporary legislation designed to address fundamental failings to protect individual rights. Political scientist Charles Lamb observes that "the Voting Rights Act of 1965 and its extensions gave the federal government unparalleled powers to protect the voting rights of blacks, poor whites, and other minority groups."[2]

The original VRA targeted the South, where arbitrary implementation of election law; physical, psychological, and economic intimidation; and a century of custom compounded the effects of an economic and social environment that kept black voters subjugated. Many southern communities denied black citizens access to the ballot, and those who sought to register had to overcome significantly higher hurdles than other potential voters. In parts of the South, African Americans who sought to vote put their lives on the line. Only a significant national government effort could bring states that had long denied suffrage to black citizens into compliance with the guarantees of the Fifteenth Amendment.

This book describes the advances in access to the ballot since the advent of the second Reconstruction, the translation of that access into representation, and the evolution of the politics of the southern states as it relates to the role of the minority electorate. The picture we paint is one of sometimes substantial if not unimagined progress in voting rights arising from the implementation of Section 5, and later, Section 2, of the Voting Rights Act. Progress is uneven, but as the following chapters document, both in voting and descriptive representation, progress is undeniable and most evident where the Act has been in force the longest.

DEFINING THE SOUTH

Scholars have perceived voting rights to be a persistent, southern problem. V. O. Key, Jr.'s seminal 1949 work *Southern Politics in State and Nation* started out as a study of the southern poll tax.[3] Key quickly grasped that the South's problems were not as simple as the poll tax, and *Southern Politics* grew into an intense study of the complex interplay of race, agrarianism, populism, capitalism, and political tradition in the South. The first lesson Key imparted to three generations of southern-politics scholars is that to talk of the South requires a definition of the South.

The problem confronted when defining the South is choosing dimension(s). The South can be thought of in a variety of ways: as a cultural entity, defined by heritage, tradition, faith, or speech pattern; as a product of the distinct social structures of race, caste, and segregation; in political terms, as a one-party political bastion defending segregation and states' rights; or in more historical terms, as the source of rebellion. James Street, the noted twentieth-century North Carolina journalist, observed that traces of Dixie can be detected as far west as Oklahoma, as far north as New Jersey and Delaware, and across the Ohio River in the Butternut counties of southern Indiana and Illinois. Florida, even in the 1940s, emitted what he characterized as a "faintly tropical" rebel yell, though the characterization alludes to the question of whether Florida was indeed, even back then, southern.[4]

In *The Mind of the South*, W. J. Cash argued that the white South was defined by a preoccupation with the status of black people.[5] The South was built on an agricultural economy, and the foundation of that economy was at first slavery and then the subsequent caste system of tenant farming and economic segregation. This system perpetuated contradictory views of blacks both as children who must be looked after in a paternalistic fashion and as a physical threat that must be held down and controlled by whites.

For Cash, this love-hate relationship of whites toward blacks permeated all aspects of southern culture. It reinforced segregated institutions and economic subjugation of blacks. Writing at about the same time as Cash, John Dollard, in a Depression-era study of a small Deep South town, described firsthand the formalized multitiered system of race and class that structured all aspects of small-town and rural southern society.[6] The long-standing formal relationships and ritual surrounding race promoted the colorful yet spiteful politics of demagoguery and vilification that propelled the careers of ancient southern demagogues such as "Pitchfork Ben" Tillman of South Carolina and Theodore Bilbo of Mississippi.

To determine just how "southern" a state is, political science relies on a physical concept of the South based largely on political factors such as the decision of states to secede and other race-related events. The generally accepted physical definition comes from V. O. Key, who argued for a South defined by the act of secession.[7] Key contended that secession, Civil War, and the subsequent Reconstruction experience defined southern politics and also shaped subsequent attitudes toward race relations. Using this typology, a South emerges that is quite expansive, stretching from Alexandria, Virginia, in the Northeast to El Paso, Texas, in the Far West (see map I.1). This South (indicated in gray) encompasses eleven states—Alabama, Arkansas, Florida, Georgia, Louisiana, Mississippi, North Carolina, South Carolina, Tennessee, Texas, and Virginia. This definition excludes two stars from the Confederate flag (Missouri and Kentucky) and also the former Indian Territory (Oklahoma), where the Five Tribes fought alongside the Confederacy.[8] It is this definition of the South, a political-geographic definition, that is the accepted standard in the subfield of southern politics and that we use here. Virtually every major work on southern politics since V. O. Key has subscribed to this definition.[9]

CONDITIONS IN THE SOUTH

When John Kennedy became president in 1961, the South had been erecting obstacles to black political participation for almost a century. In the immediate aftermath of the Civil War and the ratification of the Fifteenth Amendment, voting by black men had been widespread in the South.[10] Participation remained fairly extensive through the end of the nineteenth

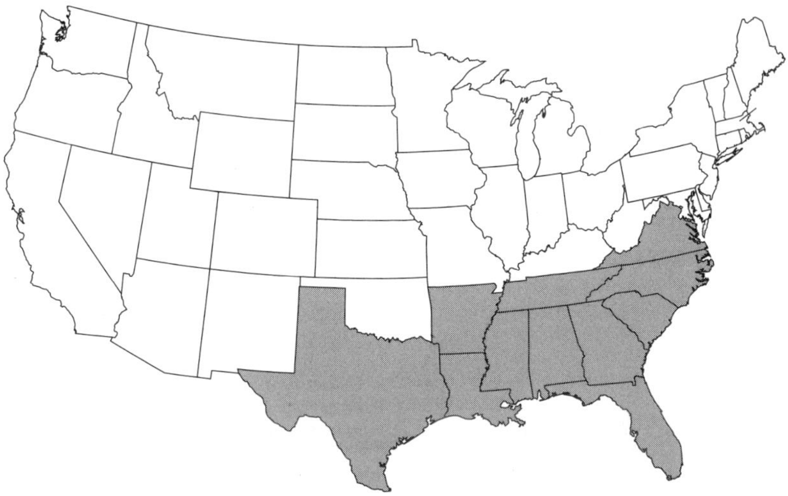

Map I.1. V. O. Key, Jr.'s South.

century.[11] Following ratification of a new constitution by Mississippi in 1890, southern states became increasingly thorough in their efforts to remove African Americans from the registration rolls. The Mississippi Constitution instituted a literacy test along with an understanding requirement.[12] It also called for a poll tax, a technique that had been used in Georgia since the 1870s,[13] and disfranchised prospective voters for a variety of illegal activities. The latter were chosen with an eye toward what white legislators believed to be crimes particularly likely to be committed by African Americans. The constitution also established a longer residency requirement for registration on the assumption that African Americans were more mobile than whites.

The U.S. Supreme Court failed to intervene and strike down these provisions of the Mississippi Constitution.[14] Once the high court gave its approval to the new restrictive techniques, other states added new requirements to voter registration. Use of the poll tax and literacy requirements became widespread across the South, and voter participation fell further, among both blacks and whites, but especially among the black population.[15]

Given the widespread illiteracy among both races in the South, states provided ways by which illiterate whites could nonetheless register to vote. One technique, the "grandfather clause," gave a pass to whites whose ancestors had been registered voters. The time period for which one's ancestors needed to have been registered excluded most blacks. The "fighting grandfather" exemption allowed individuals unable to pass a literacy test to register if their ancestors fought for the *state's* armed forces during the Civil War. Some states exempted from the literacy requirement individuals who met a real property–ownership threshold. When Georgia adopted a literacy requirement in 1908, it exempted those whose ancestors had served in the armed forces of the Confederacy or the United States, or who had good character, or who owned at least forty acres or property valued at more than five hundred dollars.[16]

One of the most effective techniques for eliminating black political influence was the white primary, which limited participation in the Democratic primary to white voters. Since the Democratic Party dominated politics to the exclusion of Republican alternatives in most of the South for decades after the end of Reconstruction, the winner of the Democratic nomination invariably ascended to public office. Thus, the white primary excluded African Americans from participating in the decisive elections.

Gradually, the federal courts began dismantling the palisades that kept blacks out of the voting booth, first invalidating the grandfather clause in 1915.[17] After a generation of litigation, the Supreme Court struck down the white primary, noting that even if a party and not the state operated it, its central position in determining who would hold political power made it subject to the federal Constitution.[18] Most states, led by North Carolina, voluntarily did away with the poll tax. Nonetheless, despite these steps that removed some obstacles, relatively few southern African Americans voted when President Kennedy urged Americans to explore new frontiers. According to the U.S. Commission on Civil Rights, in 1959 just "25 percent of the nearly five million Negroes of voting age" in the South were registered to vote.[19]

CONGRESS ACTS TO PROVIDE ACCESS TO THE BALLOT

In response to continuing low levels of black participation in the South, Congress finally adopted legislation designed to facilitate black registration. In 1957 Congress enacted the first civil rights legislation since Reconstruction. Although this legislation appears timorous in retrospect, after generations of congressional inaction, it constituted a breakthrough. The 1957 Civil Rights Act authorized the attorney general of the United States to sue local election officials on behalf of blacks who had been unfairly denied registration. This important feature shifted the financial burden associated with bringing suit against local registrars from disappointed prospective voters to the federal government with its limitless resources. The statute also provided access to a critical resource—legal talent—since the South had few African American attorneys and, in the racially charged atmosphere, white litigators often hesitated to stick their necks out on behalf of blacks. These early suits often involved going through registration records to build a case that illiterate whites had been allowed to register while more educated blacks had been rejected. This research required personnel that the federal government could muster but that might well stretch the financial resources of African Americans or even groups representing their interests.

Only slowly did federal attorneys bring suit under the 1957 Civil Rights Act. By 1960 only a handful of lawsuits had been filed. Even federal authorities often encountered obstacles on the way to the courthouse, such as those thrown up by an Alabama judge who took personal control of local registration records just ahead of federal authorities' arrival.[20] The local judge refused to release the records to the authorities, the first act in what became a tidal wave of media attention ultimately generated by George Wallace. Consequently, on the eve of the 1960 presidential election, in which both parties courted African American votes outside the South, Congress approved a new Civil Rights Act. This legislation directed local registration officials to maintain records for at least twenty-two months after an election and, if requested, to turn these documents over to federal authorities.

The 1957 and 1960 Civil Rights Acts had only a modest impact on black registration in the South. Estimates of the number of southern blacks registered to vote inched up from 1.24 million in 1956 to 1.46 million four years later and 1.48 million in 1962.[21] The U.S. Department of Justice brought lawsuits against fifty Deep South counties in this period to enjoin them from discriminating against potential black voters. While John Kennedy's letter to Coretta Scott King expressing concern about the imprisonment of her husband, the leader of the Civil Rights Movement, is often credited with winning over black voters, fewer than one in three African American adults in the South voted in 1960, and in Mississippi and Alabama, black voters were nearly nonexistent.[22]

President Kennedy did not rush to introduce civil rights legislation, though his administration was formulating a new proposal at the time of his assassination. His successor, Lyndon B. Johnson, used the murder of the popular young president to urge Congress to act quickly on what became the 1964 Civil Rights Act. This sweeping legislation addressed discrimination in public accommodations, schools, employment, and voting. Title I of the Act focused on registrars who rejected black applicants for trivial errors on their applications. By making completion of the sixth grade in an American school presumptive of literacy, the measure shifted the burden of proof from the prospective registrant to the registrar, who now had to demonstrate that a person with at least a sixth-grade education was illiterate. The 1964 statute also required that literacy tests be conducted in writing and that the results be made available to the applicant.

By the time of the 1964 election, black registration in the South exceeded two million, or about 43 percent of those eligible to register. Following his landslide victory, President Johnson, who had benefited from overwhelming black support, decided to root out the remaining obstacles to voter registration. In salty language, Johnson directed his attorney general, Nicholas Katzenbach, "I want you to write me the goddamndest, toughest voting rights act that you can devise."[23]

THE 1965 VOTING RIGHTS ACT

The 1965 Voting Rights Act (VRA) targeted jurisdictions that had histories of voting discrimination. On the basis of criteria to be described shortly, the most important provisions of this new legislation singled out the bulk of the South but ignored the rest of the nation. The Act pinpointed for special coverage Alabama, Georgia, Louisiana, Mississippi, South Carolina, Virginia, and about forty counties in North Carolina. Congress took a dual-track approach as it sought to eliminate existing barriers and prevent future ones.[24] First, to root out techniques then used to restrict black political participation, the VRA banned tests and devices—such as literacy tests, good character tests, and understanding tests—as prerequisites to registration in these jurisdictions.

Another portion of the statute—and this portion has become the most controversial—barred the targeted jurisdictions from adopting new requirements designed to impede black registration or voting. This came in response to widespread attitudes best expressed by Mississippi's segregationist governor James Coleman, who had boasted, "Any legislature can pass a law faster than the Supreme Court can erase it."[25] To prevent the southern jurisdictions subject to Section 5 of the VRA from throwing up new roadblocks to black participation—obstacles that would require time and money to challenge in court—lawmakers barred the immediate implementation of new laws relating to elections by covered jurisdictions.[26]

The legislation's key provision, one that has been renewed four times, is Section 5, which requires selected jurisdictions to obtain approval from the federal government before carrying out any changes that impact elections. Before a covered jurisdiction can implement a new districting plan, change the rules under which an election is held, move a voting precinct, or annex territory to a municipality, the federal government must approve the proposal. Approval can come from one of two sources: the attorney general of the United States can preclear the proposed change, or the jurisdiction can seek a declaratory judgment from the District Court for the District of Columbia. If a jurisdiction pursues the judicial route, the attorney general of the United States serves as the defendant.

The preclearance requirement applies only to jurisdictions that had low levels of voter participation in the past. Section 4 of the 1965 Act included a "trigger" that identified jurisdictions subject to Section 5. The trigger had two parts. It applied to jurisdictions that had a test or device as a prerequisite for voter registration and in which less than half of the voting-age population had registered or cast ballots in the 1964 presidential election.

The test most frequently covered by the 1965 trigger was a literacy requirement (understanding tests and good character tests were also included). The poll tax, however, was not included and its elimination came by other means. The Twenty-fourth Amendment to the Constitution had removed the tax from federal elections in 1964, and a year after adoption of the Voting Rights Act, the Supreme Court banned poll taxes as prerequisites for voting in nonfederal elections.[27]

The primary consequence for jurisdictions subject to Section 5 is that they must secure federal approval before implementing changes in election laws. There are other consequences that allow greater initiative by the national government. Federal officials can be sent to Section 5 jurisdictions to sign up eligible voters improperly rejected by local registrars. Four days after the passage of the Act, the first federal registrars arrived in nine counties or parishes in Alabama, Mississippi, and Louisiana. Officers were initially swamped by anxious blacks who often believed that the examiners would only be present for a day or two at most.[28] This provision resulted in the enrollment of thousands of African Americans in the Deep South in the first few years of the legislation's existence. Within two years of the enactment of the 1965 measure, federal agents signed up fifty-eight thousand new voters in Mississippi along with another sixty-five thousand in Alabama and twenty-five thousand in Louisiana.[29]

A longer-lived result of Section 5 coverage has been that it makes jurisdictions eligible for having federal observers sent in to monitor Election Day activities. The observers cannot intercede or overrule the behavior of poll workers, but they can report any irregularities that they observe. Over the forty years of implementation, federal observers have been dispatched to scores of counties in the covered jurisdictions.

Although jurisdictions can go to court to secure approval for proposed changes, the vast bulk of the preclearance activities have played out with the attorney general. The attorney general has sixty days from receipt of a proposal to grant or deny approval. Should the attorney general not respond within the sixty-day window, Department of Justice (DOJ) approval is presumed. The time for consideration can be extended if DOJ asks the jurisdiction for additional information. Such a request stops the clock, and upon receiving the requested information, the attorney general has another sixty days in which to decide.

The submitting jurisdiction has the burden of proving that the proposed change will not leave African Americans worse off.[30] If the attorney general is not convinced that the proposed change has neither a discriminatory purpose nor effect, the proposal will be rejected. The submitting jurisdiction receives a letter indicating the problems identified by the attorney general. A disappointed jurisdiction can at that point turn to the District Court for the District of Columbia and seek its approval. Alternatively, jurisdictions can go directly to the court in the District of Columbia and seek a declaratory judgment that the proposed change is not discriminatory.

Requiring Section 5 jurisdictions to secure pre-approval of certain types of legislation from the federal government and authorizing federal authorities to register voters constituted major changes in the distribution of powers within the federal system. In 1965, Congress recognized the extraordinary nature of its action and, consequently, limited Section 5 to half a decade.

RENEWING THE VOTING RIGHTS ACT

By 1970 when Section 5 was scheduled to expire, two-thirds of the South's adult blacks had registered to vote.[31] Nonetheless Congress believed that the attitudes that had justified the preclearance requirement remained widespread, and therefore, to prevent backsliding by unreconstructed southerners, it extended Section 5 for another five years.

The 1970 Voting Rights Act introduced a second trigger. The new trigger applied to jurisdictions that had a test or device as a prerequisite to registration and in which less than half of the adult population had registered or voted in the 1968 presidential election. This trigger added to the existing jurisdictions three boroughs of New York City, two counties in California, ten townships in New Hampshire, and eight Arizona counties. The new trigger identified no additional southern jurisdictions. The 1970 Voting Rights Act also banned literacy tests nationwide. The initial statute had banned literacy as a requirement for voting only in jurisdictions subject to Section 5. The 1970 Act extended the life of Section 5 for another half decade.

Rather than allow Section 5 to expire in 1975, Congress extended the provision for another seven years in order to cover the redistricting that would be conducted after the 1980 census. The 1975 extension of the Voting Rights Act included a third trigger. The new trigger extended the preclearance requirement to Texas and other jurisdictions with large numbers of Hispanics, Native Americans, and Native Alaskans. Latino leaders, impressed by the impact the first two versions of the Voting

Rights Act had had on expanding political participation opportunities for African Americans, wanted areas with concentrations of Latinos made subject to preclearance.[32] The original 1965 Act has also caused the administration of alternative literacy standards for foreign-language speakers, especially in New York City. Beyond an enhancement of Puerto Rican registration in Manhattan, no gains were evident in Latino suffrage from the use of an alternative literacy test prior to 1972.[33] The 1975 trigger extended the preclearance requirement to jurisdictions in which (1) at least 5 percent of the population belonged to a single-language minority group, (2) all of the election materials in 1972 had been printed only in English, and (3) less than half of the voting-age population had registered or voted in that year's presidential election. The new legislation treated providing only English instructions for voters in jurisdictions having substantial numbers of non-English speakers as analogous to a literacy test. This third trigger extended preclearance to Texas, Arizona, Alaska, five Florida counties, two South Dakota counties, three California counties, two New York boroughs, and two Michigan townships.[34]

The 1982 law did not introduce an additional trigger but required that jurisdictions subject to preclearance continue to obtain federal approval for any changes for another quarter century. The 1982 Act adopted language intended to make it easier for jurisdictions covered by Section 5 to "bail out," that is, to remove themselves from that section. That opportunity proved to be illusory. As reported in the Virginia chapter, only a handful of jurisdictions have completed the bailout process.

Rather than wait until 2007, Congress extended application of Section 5 for another quarter century in 2006. As in 1982, the 2006 statute did not introduce a new trigger mechanism, although Rep. Charlie Norwood (R-Ga.) offered an amendment during the House debate that would have updated the triggers. Norwood argued that election data from 1964, 1968, or 1972 do not accurately reflect the participation opportunities for African Americans in the twenty-first century and would be even less reflective of race relations in 2031 when the 2006 extension comes to an end. Norwood and his supporters noted that for the jurisdictions covered by the 1965 Voting Rights Act, the election returns which brought them under coverage would be sixty-six years old in 2030 when very few people who had voted at the time of the initial statute would be alive. Rather than to continue relying on aging election data, Norwood proposed implementing a dynamic trigger that would cover any jurisdiction in which less than half of the voting-age citizens had voted in any of the three most recent presidential elections.

While the members of the House who voted for the Norwood Amendment came chiefly from the South and were overwhelmingly Republicans, some voting-rights experts also expressed concern about continued usage of election data now decades old. In testimony before congressional committees, several law-school professors pointed out that in the initial challenge to the Voting Rights Act, the Supreme Court had acknowledged the unprecedented nature of the preclearance provision but had upheld it in light of the extraordinary conditions that it sought to correct. In 1969, in the first case to consider the new statute, Chief Justice Warren wrote, "This may have been an uncommon exercise of congressional power, as South Carolina contends, but the Court has recognized that exceptional conditions can justify legislative measures not otherwise appropriate."[35] When addressing other kinds of issues, the Supreme Court has indicated that the remedy must be commensurate with the problem.[36] In light of these views of the Court and with its more conservative makeup in the early twenty-first century, some Section 5 supporters worried that a failure to update the trigger mechanism might result in it being struck down.[37] A challenge that raises the issue of whether the federal oversight authorized in Section 5 has been extended too long came before the Supreme Court in 2009 (*North Austin Municipal Utility District No. One v. Holder* 557 U.S._2009). The high court failed to rule on the constitutionality of Section 5, focusing on the narrower statutory concern brought by the plaintiff, and found in favor of the plaintiff jurisdiction. As discussed in the concluding chapter, potential future litigation of Section 5 looms.

THE 2006 DEBATE

During the 2006 congressional debate on the renewal of Section 5, all sides praised the success of this legislation. Democrats and Republican, liberals and conservatives, those who wanted to see the provision extended without change as well as those who thought amendments were in order all pointed with pride to the advances in African American political strength since the mid-1960s. One of the most powerful statements came from Rep. Melvin Watt (D-N.C.), one of the first two African American members of Congress from the Tar Heel State since 1901. Watt's district, the 12th Congressional District, had been the source of significant litigation throughout the 1990s, but both the district and Watt endured. Speaking in support of the renewal of the Act, Watt observed that

> there are those who argue that the Voting Rights Act has outlived its usefulness, that it is outdated, and that it unfairly punishes covered jurisdictions for past sins. Yet I stand here as living proof of both the effectiveness of and continuing need for the Voting Rights Act. . . . When George White said his temporary farewell [in 1901], he likely did not think it would be so long. . . . Although the successes of the Voting Rights Act have been substantial, they have not been fast and furious. Rather, the successes have been gradual and of recent origin.[38]

House Judiciary Committee Chair James Sensenbrenner (R-Wis.) had fought against delaying actions for nearly nine months related to minority-language ballot provisions of the Voting Rights Act. The Wisconsin Republican summed up the conclusions of the Judiciary Committee in an address to the House:

> The extensive record of continued abuse compiled by the Committee over the last year echoes that which preceded congressional reauthorization of the VRA in 1982, and which led me to make the following observation during the Committee's consideration of VRA reauthorization legislation then: "Testimony is quite clear that this Act . . . has been the most successful civil rights act that has ever been passed by the Congress of the United States. . . . The overwhelming preponderance of the testimony was that the Voting Rights Act has worked. It has provided the franchise to numerous people who were denied the right to vote for one reason or another. It has provided a dramatic increase in the number of minority elected officials in covered jurisdictions. I think that very clearly demonstrates the need for an extension. . . . The hearings also very clearly showed that the creativity of the human mind is unlimited when it comes to proposing election law changes that are designed to prevent people from voting.[39]

The Act would pass the House overwhelmingly, though four amendments were considered, including one to update the trigger mechanism as described earlier. Another amendment, which garnered nearly two hundred votes, would have stripped minority-language ballot provisions from the renewal. When the Act came up for final passage, fewer than three dozen Republicans cast dissenting ballots.

A week later the Senate took up the legislation. Conservative senator Jeff Sessions (R-Ala.), while more circumspect about the need for blanket renewal of the Act, nonetheless spoke for the legislation. His support was the equal to Watt's appeal to history:

> The results of the Voting Rights Act of 1965 were some of the best things that ever happened to Alabama . . . [v]oter registration rates for Blacks and Whites in Alabama are now virtually identical. In fact, in the last presidential election, according to the Census Bureau, a larger percentage of African Americans voted than Whites in the State of Alabama. Now, that was the goal of the act—to have this kind of progress occur. In fact, over the past 15 years, Alabama has not had a single court find the State guilty of violating the 15th amendment or the very broad protections afforded by section 2 of the Voting Rights Act. . . . The people of Alabama understand that these changes in our State are good, and they do not want to do anything that would suggest that there is any interest in moving away from the great right to vote. We want to reauthorize the Voting Rights Act.[40]

Sessions's support was not without caveat. The junior senator from Alabama spoke not just for the progress of Alabama. He also rose to advance the more controversial aspect of the renewal debate, the prospect for revision of the Act. In doing so, Sessions sounded a need for careful conversation regarding the nature of the renewal of the Act, noting that "[h]ow we reauthorize the act is something that is worthy of discussion. . . . The witnesses we have heard in the Judiciary Committee over the past couple of months have had many different ideas, and after hearing from them, I am concerned that we should have listened more carefully to the recommendations."[41]

Sessions's caveat was met by the powerful symbolism of history and the living proof of voting-rights progress in the form of descriptive representation and the sacrifices of decades passed. The statement of freshman

Sen. Barack Obama (D-Ill.), the second African American to represent Illinois in the U.S. Senate, captured the content and spirit of the emotional appeal of the Voting Rights Act renewal, and reminded listeners of a different Alabama than the one described by Senator Sessions:

> [T]he most striking evidence of our progress can be found right across this building, in my dear friend, Congressman John Lewis, who was on the front lines of the civil rights movement, risking life and limb for freedom. And on March 7, 1965, he led 600 peaceful protestors demanding the right to vote across the Edmund Pettus Bridge in Selma, Alabama . . . [b]lacks and whites, teenagers and children, teachers and bankers and shopkeepers—a beloved community of God's children ready to stand for freedom. . . . I wonder, where did they find that kind of courage? When you're facing row after row of state troopers on horseback armed with billy clubs and tear gas . . . when they're coming toward you spewing hatred and violence, how do you simply stop, kneel down, and pray to the Lord for salvation? But the most amazing thing of all is that after that day—after John Lewis was beaten within an inch of his life, after people's heads were gashed open and their eyes were burned and they watched their children's innocence literally beaten out of them . . . after all that, they went back to march again. . . . They awakened a nation's conscience, and not five months later, the Voting Rights Act of 1965 was signed into law. And it was reauthorized in 1970, 1975, and 1982. Now, in 2006, John Lewis, the physical scars from those marches still visible, is an original cosponsor of the fourth reauthorization of the Voting Rights Act, and he was joined last week by 389 of his House colleagues in voting for its passage.[42]

The effectiveness of Section 5 was praised on all sides. But the meaning of the success was the subject of different interpretations. Democrats and civil rights leaders pointed to past accomplishments as a basis for arguing that Congress dare not modify the current requirements. Speakers in this camp warned that modification of Section 5 would open the door to backsliding on the part of the covered jurisdictions. Nancy Pelosi (D-Calif.), soon to become Speaker of the House, observed that "[w]ithin months of the Voting Rights Act's passage, a quarter of a million new African American voters had been registered. A quarter of a million new voices that had been silenced could finally be heard. They, along with millions to follow, changed the world with a vision of justice, equality, and opportunity for all."[43]

After noting the numbers of minorities who had been elected to Congress, Representative Pelosi warned against efforts to limit the length of the extension of Section 5 to a decade. "Make no mistake, the ten-year limitation on key VRA provisions seriously undermines its effectiveness," she said.[44]

In contrast, legislators who wished to shorten the proposed renewal period from twenty-five years down to a decade or who wanted to replace the triggers that relied on electoral data from the 1960s and 1970s with more contemporary figures used the success already achieved as a launching pad for arguing that modifications were appropriate to reward those jurisdictions that had fully complied with the statue. For example, Rep. Lynn Westmoreland (R-Ga.) said on the House floor:

> It is true when the Voting Rights Act was first passed in 1965 Georgia needed Federal intervention to correct decades of discrimination. Now, 41 years later, Georgia's record on voter equality can stand up against any other State in the Union. Today black Georgians are registered to vote at higher percentages than white Georgians, and black Georgians go to the polls in higher percentages than white Georgians. One-third of our state-wide elected officials are African Americans, including our Attorney General and the Chief Justice of our Supreme Court. Plus, African American representation in the State legislature closely mirrors their representation in Georgia's population.[45]

The deck of testimony was decidedly stacked toward a blanket renewal in the House. Nathaniel Persily of the University of Pennsylvania observes that of forty-six witnesses called before the House Judiciary Committee Subcommittee on the Constitution, only three advocated revising the Act.[46] On the Senate side, however, Persily notes a more balanced evidentiary record, though the Senate accepted the blanket renewal of the Act approved by the House of Representatives in July.[47] The Voting Rights Act temporary provisions were renewed, including the 1972-based trigger, through 2031.

One change was in the wind, however, and that was a legislative correction of the judiciary's interpretation of how the Section 5 non-retrogression standard might be satisfied. Congress undid the Supreme Court's broader interpretation of Section 5 in *Georgia v. Ashcroft*, echoing the previous renewal in 1982, when the Congress corrected the Court's interpretation of *Mobile v. Bolden*[48] (discussed in the following section) and dramatically increased the potential reach and impact of the nationally applied Section 2.

SECTION 2

Our discussion thus far has focused on Section 5, but the emergency provision is not the only portion of the Voting Rights Act that has contributed to the growth in the numbers of minority elected officials. In 1982, Congress not only extended Section 5 for a quarter century but also rewrote Section 2. Prior to this time, Section 2 had been viewed as nothing more than a restatement of the Fifteenth Amendment guarantee of the right to vote regardless of race.

In 1980, the Supreme Court overturned a lower court decision that had invalidated the electoral system of Mobile, Alabama. For decades, a commission had governed Mobile. This approach, pioneered by Galveston, Texas, as it sought to rebound from the 1900 hurricane, combines legislative and executive functions. In commission cities, voters use citywide elections to choose individuals to head the major offices in the city. One individual would be elected mayor, another might be chosen as the head of public safety, another might head up the public utilities department, and yet another might lead the school system. The commissioners, as a body, serve as the city council for the community. Since each commissioner has citywide responsibilities, all run at large. Since it continued to elect commissioners at large, Mobile did not need to secure approval from the Department of Justice (DOJ) for decennial redistricting plans. Indeed, since Section 5 deals only with proposed changes, it had no impact on Mobile's electoral system.

A lower court had struck down Mobile's at-large electoral system because although the city was more than one-third African American, no blacks had ever won a seat on the commission. The Supreme Court overturned this lower court decision because plaintiffs failed to prove that the city had intended to discriminate either when it adopted the commission format with its at-large elections or in maintaining that system.[49]

Section 2 is permanent and applies nationwide. Nonetheless, when the Act came up for renewal in 1982, Congress rewrote Section 2 to eliminate the need to prove intent and thereby legislatively reverse the *Mobile* decision. This approach offended Sen. Orrin Hatch (R-Utah), who observed, "I do not believe a community ought to be labeled a civil rights violator unless there is some wrongful motivation on its part."[50] Henceforth all that a plaintiff need show to prevail is that the effect or result of the existing electoral system limited minorities to less chance to elect their candidates of choice than enjoyed by whites. In urging rewriting of Section 2 to eliminate the need to prove intent to discriminate, the head of the DOJ's Voting Rights Section argued the impossibility of demonstrating motive, noting that "[the Justice Department] is not dealing with dummies. They're not about to be so blatant that you can trace intent."[51]

Beginning in the 1980s, hundreds of jurisdictions that used at-large elections or multimember districts faced challenges. Although the rewritten version of Section 2 specifically stated that jurisdictions had no obligation to have minorities represented on their governing bodies in roughly the same proportion as in the population, communities in which minorities were substantially underrepresented—and especially if no minorities had been elected—were likely to be sued by private plaintiffs. When plaintiffs won, the remedial action involved drawing single-member districts. Invariably one or more of these single-member districts had a sufficient concentration of minority voters that if they voted together, they could elect their preferred candidate. This has facilitated the election of scores of African Americans to local collegial bodies such as city councils, county commissions, and school boards.

In the early 1990s, the Department of Justice incorporated Section 2 into its reviews of redistricting plans submitted pursuant to Section 5. Prior to this, Section 5 reviews had hinged on whether the submitting authority was guilty of retrogression. If the new plan left minorities no worse off than under the status quo then DOJ would approve the submission. But once DOJ included Section 2 in its preclearance evaluations, it required that jurisdictions draw additional majority-minority districts when possible. Thus while Section 5 had been a negative power that allowed DOJ to block plans that would have reduced the prospects for electing minorities, Section 2 became a positive tool used to force jurisdictions to create additional opportunities for minorities. In the most high-profile examples, DOJ used Section 2 as a goad to force Georgia, Louisiana, and North Carolina to draw additional districts that in 1992 sent African Americans to Congress.

By mid-decade, the Supreme Court had stepped in and began undoing some of the changes demanded by DOJ pursuant to Section 2. As detailed in the North Carolina chapter (chapter 7), the court first expressed its displeasure with that state's long, narrow 12th Congressional District that in some places was no wider than two lanes of I-85. Writing for the Court, Justice Sandra Day O'Connor fretted that the precision with which the state had separated blacks and whites in order to fashion a majority-black district reminded her of South African apartheid.[52] Two years later the Court fleshed out its reasoning in a challenge to the additional majority-black congressional district DOJ had demanded in Georgia. In *Miller v. Johnson*, the Court acknowledged that while race was to be considered in drawing districts, if race overshadowed other factors such as compactness, contiguity, and adherence to political boundaries, then the plan violated the Equal Protection Clause of the Fourteenth Amendment.[53] Subsequent litigation successfully challenged majority-black congressional districts drawn predominately on the basis of race in Louisiana, Florida, Virginia, and Texas, and a New York majority-Hispanic district.

Ultimately the Supreme Court went further than simply overturning some of the actions required by DOJ as a result of its reliance on Section 2. In a school district case from Louisiana the Court chastised DOJ for incorporating Section 2 into Section 5 reviews. The Supreme Court underscored its decision from *Beer v. United States* that retrogression provided the *only* basis for rejecting redistricting plans.[54] Thus, in *Reno v. Bossier Parish School Board*, the Supreme Court removed Section 2 from the arsenal of instruments available to DOJ when reviewing a districting plan.[55] As part of the 2006 renewal of the Voting Rights Act, Congress reversed the Supreme Court's decision and authorized inclusion of Section 2 considerations in future Section 5 reviews.

DATA

To assess voting-rights progress in the South, we focus on three dimensions of participation: voter registration and participation in elections, the ability to elect representatives from the minority community to public office, and observed differences between black and white preferences in election outcomes.

In an ideal world, assessments of the impact of the Voting Rights Act on minority participation would rely on tabulations indicating rates of registration and turnout by race. However, most states do not collect these data. Official state figures will be presented for the states that provide that kind of information (Florida, Georgia, Louisiana, North Carolina, and South Carolina). For purposes of comparability across all eleven states, we rely on the results of the post-election participation surveys conducted by the U.S. Census Bureau. The biennial census surveys ask large samples of adults whether they registered and if so whether they voted in the preceding general election. Since these estimates rely on self-reports, they are subject to inflation.[56] Social pressures to participate in the electoral process are such that some non-registrants will tell an interviewer that they have registered and some who stayed at home will report that they went to the polls. The self-report data are far from perfect, but for most states these are the only estimates of participation by a racial group. These data are useful for comparisons across time and across jurisdictions on the assumption that the incidence of overreporting of participation will be roughly equal across time and place.

Beginning with the 1980 presidential election, the Census Bureau provides estimates of voter participation for each state for whites and blacks. In some jurisdictions, separate figures are provided for those with Spanish surnames. Since 1998, the Census Bureau estimates have provided additional groupings. Figures became available for non-Hispanic whites and, less often, non-Hispanic blacks. However, in order to maintain comparability, the figures that we present by state will include the white and black estimates for the entire time period, and for years where separate figures for non-Hispanic whites are available, these too are examined.

Figures on black office holding rely heavily on the surveys conducted by the Joint Center for Political and Economic Studies. Beginning in 1969 and for many years after, the JCPES carried out annual surveys. Later the surveys became biennial before ending in 2001. In discussing statewide offices, and congressional and state legislature seats, we update the Joint Center data to bring them up to the present. Figures on numbers of objections registered by the Department of Justice to propose changes in election laws come from DOJ.

The estimates of racial voting patterns come from three sources. Where available, we have relied upon the work of others. Some of this is published research, while other estimates come from expert reports submitted as evidence in voting-rights litigation. Augmenting the figures of others are estimates that we have made using methodologies that are standard in voting-rights litigation—ecological regression analysis and the ecological inference technique. These methods are generally accepted and universally applied when evaluating racial and ethnic participation and voter preferences. Appendix A to this book offers a detailed description of these techniques and their application to assist the reader who is interested in understanding how voting experts derive such estimates. However, for the reader interested in results rather than methodology, the ecological regression or EI estimates in our tables, should be read as estimates of the level of support for a candidate from a racial or ethnic group, presented as a proportion (from 0 to 1) or as a percentage (from 0 percent to 100 percent) of the vote cast by the group.

Where available, exit polls conducted for high offices are used as a source of racial voting preferences. Exit polling usually gathers information on presidential, senatorial, and gubernatorial elections. Because of problems with the 2002 surveys, the results of those exit polls were never released and that is why exit poll data for that year are missing in most instances.

A NATURAL EXPERIMENT

A variety of factors influences the changes in African American political participation and office holding. Many people, beginning with President Johnson, expected that the Voting Rights Act would promote black political participation. One of the issues to be examined after the review of change in individual states is whether states subject to Section 5 for longer periods and more extensively covered by it have experienced greater changes than have states never subject to this requirement or states that were only partially covered or that came under coverage more recently. Toward this end the eleven states will be compared on a number of dimensions, including minority voter registration and participation, differences in black and white voter preferences, and the success of minority candidates in securing election. Offices considered here range from local positions up through seats in the state legislature and Congress as well as statewide positions. The chapters for Florida and Texas, the two southern states with sizable numbers of Hispanics, contain materials on mass and elite participation among Latinos.

The Voting Rights Acts have not affected politics in the eleven southern states equally. Section 5 has covered most of the states since its inception in 1965. Two states, Florida and Texas, became subject to Section 5 only with the 1975 amendments that extended coverage to language minorities. In Florida and North Carolina Section 5 covers only selected counties. Section 5 has never covered Arkansas and Tennessee.

The book is organized to assess progress in each state in succession, starting with those states that have been covered the longest by Section 5, then those states picked up by the 1975 amendments, and then the two southern states not subject to preclearance. The concluding chapters present a comparative assessment of voting-rights progress across the southern states. They also explore a variety of issues that arise regarding racial progress in political participation, and how race interacts with party in assessing voting progress and participation in the new, modern, two-party South.

PART I

The Original Seven Section 5 States

CHAPTER 1

Mississippi

The theme throughout V. O. Key, Jr.'s classic study of southern politics is that concerns of race determine the nature of the region's politics. "In its grand outlines the politics of the South revolves around the position of the Negro," he writes. ". . . [I]n the last analysis the major peculiarities of southern politics go back to the Negro. Whatever phase of the southern political process one seeks to understand, sooner or later the trail of inquiry leads to the Negro."[1] He goes on to note that "it is the whites of the black belts who have the deepest and most immediate concern about the maintenance of white supremacy."[2]

Key was but one of many observers of the southern political scene who saw in Mississippi the region's politics taken to extremes. Race had a greater influence in Mississippi than elsewhere in the South because it was the last state in the South in which African Americans constituted a majority of the population, as blacks made up 49.2 percent of the state's residents as recently as 1940. Even as the state's white population edged ahead of its black population, sixty of Mississippi's eighty-two counties had black majorities in 1940.[3]

Key introduces his Mississippi chapter with the following: "On the surface at least, the beginning and end of Mississippi politics is the Negro. He has no hand in the voting, no part in the factional maneuvers, no seats in the legislature; nevertheless, he fixes the tone—so far as the outside world is concerned—of Mississippi politics."[4] As the state with the highest black percentage, Mississippi strove more than its neighbors to perpetuate white supremacy.[5] Efforts to deny African Americans any semblance of equality extended into the latter half of the twentieth century with the brutal 1955 lynching of Emmett Till, a young visitor from Chicago, who showed off to his Mississippi cousins by flirting with the wife of a white storeowner; the execution of three civil rights workers during Freedom Summer in 1964;[6] and the assassination of Medgar Evers, the head of the state's National Association for the Advancement of Colored People (NAACP), in 1963. White Citizens Councils, formed to oppose school desegregation and other steps toward equality, began in Mississippi and spread across the South. Local Mississippi chapters soon had eighty thousand members.[7]

During much of the twentieth century leading Mississippi politicians castigated the national government for seeking to protect the state's black citizens. After a particularly racist campaign, the U.S. Senate refused to seat the reelected Theodore Bilbo for the racial appeals he had made during the course of his 1946 campaign. And while many white southerners objected to federally mandated school desegregation, Mississippi took its resistance further than other states. In neighboring Alabama, George Wallace went through the charade of standing in the schoolhouse door to prevent integration at the University of Alabama, but once the television cameras had been packed away, he stepped aside and allowed desegregation to proceed. In contrast, when desegregation came to Ole Miss, a night of rioting erupted that left two dead, and more federal soldiers were sent to Oxford, Mississippi, than had fought for the Union at Manassas in 1861.[8]

African Americans eager to participate in the political system faced more obstacles than elsewhere in the South. With traditional avenues closed, civil rights activists set up an alternative structure in 1964 and held private caucuses to choose delegates to the Democratic National Convention. These delegates went to the convention in Atlantic City as members of the Mississippi Freedom Democratic Party (MFDP). They appealed to the credentials committee pointing out that they would support the election of Lyndon Johnson while they charged that many of the official delegation would not work to elect Johnson and might actually vote for Republican Barry Goldwater. The MFDP rejected a compromise that would have given it two seats. Four years later, a biracial MFDP delegation was seated in place of the white delegation sent by the state party.

MFDP suspicions about the loyalty of Mississippi Democrats proved accurate. The 1964 presidential election sledgehammered the Deep South states away from their moorings in what had been the solid Democratic South. Given the choice between southern Lyndon Johnson, who had just pushed the 1964 Civil Rights Act through Congress, and Senator Goldwater, one of the few Republicans to oppose that legislation, the Deep South joined the Republican's native Arizona to provide the challenger's only Electoral College votes. Once again Mississippi proved more extreme than its neighbors. Although Mississippi cast fewer votes than any of Goldwater's other states, it gave him his largest margin of victory, 303,910. The Republican's 87.1 percent of the Mississippi vote was 17 percentage points greater than his second-best showing. The explanation for why the state with the largest black population gave barely 10 percent of its votes to the Democratic nominee is, of course, that on the eve of the Voting Rights Act the Magnolia State rarely permitted African Americans access to the ballot.

Most African Americans had been barred from the ballot in Mississippi for decades. In keeping with Key's proposition that the communities having the highest percentages of blacks led efforts to disfranchise African Americans, Mississippi initiated the efforts that removed most southern blacks from voter rolls. As the nineteenth century drew to a close, Mississippi purged its registration rolls of blacks. The state adopted a new constitution in 1890 that required voters to be able to read or, if illiterate, to be able to explain portions of the constitution when read to them, which gave local registrars vast discretion. The 1890 constitution also implemented a poll tax, devised an extensive list of crimes for which a voter could be disfranchised, and extended the residency requirement for registering to vote. Kousser estimates that these new conditions for registering reduced black turnout by more than two-thirds and white turnout by approximately one-third.[9]

More than three generations later, Mississippi remained the most adamant opponent of African American political participation. Following the passage of the 1965 Voting Rights Act, when it became clear that the federal government would promote black access to the ballot box, Mississippi adopted stratagems to minimize the expanding black electorate's influence. The state enacted legislation that: (1) allowed counties to appoint rather than elect county school superintendents, (2) permitted counties to shift from single-member districts to at-large elections for county commissioners, and (3) substantially increased the number of signatures to get on the ballot as an independent candidate. Civil rights attorneys challenged each of these changes, arguing that they should not be allowed to take effect until approved by federal authorities pursuant to Section 5 of the Voting Rights Act. Attorneys for the state of Mississippi had argued that Section 5 applied only to legislation dealing specifically with registering to vote. When the U.S. Supreme Court reviewed these new statutes, it expanded the scope of Section 5. Chief Justice Warren's majority opinion in the case, *Allen v. State Board of Elections*,[10] held that "we must reject a narrow construction that appellees would give to Section 5. The Voting Rights Act was aimed at the subtle as well as the obvious state regulations that have the effect of denying citizens of their right to vote because of their race."[11] As a consequence of the Supreme Court decision, all matters relating to the conducting of elections that take place in states subject to Section 5, including redistricting, must be submitted for review either to the attorney general of the United States or the district court in the District of Columbia.

BLACK REGISTRATION AND TURNOUT

Incomplete estimates reported by the Civil Rights Commission state that in 1964, Mississippi had only 28,500 registered black voters compared with 525,000 whites.[12] The Commission on Civil Rights provided figures for fewer than half of the Mississippi counties. Of those counties for which figures are available, Warren County had the highest percentage (22.7) of its adult black population registered to vote before enactment of the new law. Only four other counties had as much as 10 percent of their black adults registered. At one extreme, in Humphreys County, where blacks outnumbered whites by a margin of almost two to one, none of the 5,561 adult African Americans were on the voting rolls. In Holmes

County, where blacks made up more than 60 percent of the adult population, 20 of 8,757 adult blacks had managed to register. In Claiborne, where blacks made up more than two-thirds of the population, 26 of 3,969 African Americans had gotten onto the registration rolls. Just south of Memphis, in Tunica County, the nation's poorest until casinos were built starting in 1990, 1,407 of 2,011 adult whites but only 38 of 5,822 blacks had signed up to vote.

As in the rest of the South, implementation of the Voting Rights Act spurred black registration. Two years following enactment, the share of the black voting-age population registered to vote in Mississippi burgeoned from 6.7 to 59.8 percent.[13] Of the 181,233 blacks who signed up to vote, almost a third got added to the rolls by federal examiners dispatched to the Magnolia State under the authority of the Voting Rights Act. Within the first two years, federal examiners signed up voters in thirty-one of the state's eighty-two counties. In Hinds County, where Jackson is located, more than 10,000 black voters registered with federal examiners. In some counties, most of the black voters signed up with the federal officials. For example, 7,230 of 7,526 blacks registered by 1967 in LaFlore enrolled with federal examiners. In Madison County, federal officials added 6,586 of the 7,037 black registrants

Commission on Civil Rights data indicate that by the fall of 1967, ten Mississippi counties had more black than white voters registered, although in some of these counties, the number of voters for which race was not given might mean that more whites than blacks were actually on the registration list. In some counties, blacks had gone from having virtually no one registered to dominating the registration rolls. For example, in Claiborne County, prior to the Voting Rights Act, only 26 blacks were registered to vote, but by 1967 the number had swelled to 3,092 so that African Americans constituted more than 60 percent of the registrants, a number more consistent with the potential electorate.

In appendix B, Census Bureau estimates for registration and turnout in Mississippi and all other Southern states from 1980 through the 2006 midterm election are reported. These data have been placed together in an appendix, which will be periodically referenced throughout the volume, to facilitate comparison by the reader. Although some unregistered individuals will tell a pollster that they registered, these census figures still remain the best estimates for Mississippi.[14] With five exceptions from 1980 through 2006, Mississippi whites reported registering at higher rates than blacks. The greatest disparity came in 1980 when 85.2 percent of the voting-age whites, compared with only 72.2 percent of blacks, reported registering. Disparities have narrowed, and in the five most recent elections through midterm 2006, the differences never reached 4 percentage points. Three of the five instances in which black registration exceeds that for whites came in the two most recent presidential elections covered in the table. In 2004, 76.1 percent of blacks compared with 72.3 percent of whites registered, reversing the 1998 pattern when 75.2 percent of whites and 71.3 percent of blacks registered.

Excluding the Hispanic component of the white population—a figure the Census Bureau began reporting for states in 1998—does not change the direction of any of the racial comparisons. In the presidential years, the degree to which blacks register at higher rates than whites narrows. In the midterm elections, the gap between black and non-Hispanic whites is greater than in the initial comparison except in 2006, when the black advantage narrows once Hispanics get removed from the white component.

Materials in the bottom set of rows in the voter registration table in appendix B permit comparison between the registration rates in Mississippi and the non-South. Throughout the quarter century, African American registration has been greater in Mississippi than in the rest of the nation. In all but two years (1988 and 1996), Mississippi's black registration ran at least 10 points above that for the non-South. Not only has the reported rate of registration of Mississippi African Americans exceeded that of blacks elsewhere, it has exceeded nonsouthern white registration for every year except for 1996. Eliminating non-Hispanic whites increases registration rates for nonsouthern whites, but the only year in which their registration rate exceeds that of Mississippi African Americans remains 1996. After 2002 the differences are less than 3 percentage points. The evidence shows that racial disparities in Mississippi registration rates have largely been eliminated. Black Mississippians are at least as likely to register as citizens in other parts of the country.

Census Bureau estimates of turnout over the same quarter century appear in the second table of appendix B. In all but three elections, white Mississippians report voting at higher rates than African Americans. The rate at which white participation exceeds that for blacks varies but has an upper range of 11.4 points in 1980 and 10.5 points in 1996. The difference is less than 4 percentage points in 1982, 1984, 1988, 1990, 1998, 2000, and 2002. In 1984, blacks report voting at higher rates than whites, but the difference is a negligible 0.4 points. In the two most recent elections, however, blacks turn out at substantially higher rates than whites, with the difference exceeding 10 points in 2006. Comparing figures for African Americans with non-Hispanic whites results in slightly higher turnout for whites, but in 2004 and 2006, non-Hispanic whites still voted at lower rates than did Mississippi blacks.

The last set of rows in the table provides comparative data for the non-South. In most years black turnout in Mississippi exceeds that for the rest of the country. In every presidential year except 1996, Mississippi blacks reported voting at higher rates than nonsouthern blacks. In 1992 the difference is 8 percentage points, while in 1984 and 2004 it exceeds 10 percentage points. In four of the midterm elections, Mississippi's African American turnout exceeds that in other parts of country. The figures are higher in Mississippi in 1982, 1994, 2002, and 2006, while the figures are identical in 1998. In the midterm years in which Mississippi turnout is higher, the differences are modest except in 2006 when half Mississippi's blacks but only 38 percent of African Americans outside the region voted. In 1986 and 1990, when turnout is higher among nonsouthern blacks than Mississippians, the differences are between 4 and 6 percentage points.

When the voting rate for Mississippi blacks is compared with *whites* outside the South, Mississippi African Americans come close to equaling the turnout rate for nonsouthern whites in presidential years except in 1996 and actually exceed the white rate outside the South in 1984 and 2000. The Mississippi black turnout rate of 66.8 percent in 2004 exceeds white voting outside of the South for any year in the time series. In midterm elections, however, nonsouthern whites invariably go to the polls at higher rates than do Mississippi blacks. Mississippi's lower midterm turnout reflects the state's electoral cycle. Mississippi holds elections for state officers in odd numbered years so that in midterm elections only federal offices appear on the ballot. When Mississippi blacks are compared with non-Hispanic whites outside the South, the comparison is less favorable for Mississippi African Americans. In 2000, non-Hispanic whites in the North and West voted at a rate 3.1 percentage points above Mississippi blacks, while in 2004, the difference shows a modest half-a-percentage-point advantage to non-South whites.

African American participation in Mississippi has come to rival that for whites and frequently exceeds that for blacks or whites outside of the South. This constitutes a remarkable turnaround given the extraordinarily low levels of black participation permitted by the dominant white society forty years ago.

One interpretation of the enthusiastic participation of African Americans after breaking through the decades-old barriers blocking participation is that Mississippi blacks treasure the franchise more than citizens elsewhere. Efforts to create access have led to efforts to convert registration into mobilization, not only verifying the expectations of racial-voting scholars, but also more recently obliterating the differences in participation rates between blacks and the higher socioeconomic status (SES) white population.

AFRICAN AMERICAN OFFICE HOLDING

During Reconstruction, Mississippi's predominantly black population succeeded in electing many of its own. Until Edward Brooke (R-Mass.) defeated Endicott Peabody in 1966, the only two African Americans to ever serve in the U.S. Senate came from Mississippi. The Magnolia State also elected blacks as lieutenant governor, secretary of state, Speaker of the house, and president of the senate in the immediate aftermath of the Civil War.

As African Americans again became participants in the Mississippi political system, they found the state's Democratic Party as closed to them as the county registrar's office had been for most of the twentieth century. Consequently, many of the earliest black candidates ran not in the primaries sponsored by the official Democratic Party but under the banner of the Mississippi Freedom Democratic Party or as independents. As noted earlier, the Supreme Court rebuffed state efforts to complicate the task of running as an independent.[15] While MFDP candidates' only successes—and these were limited—came at the local level, their presence affected the outcome of several higher offices. Thad Cochran, now the third-most-senior Republican in the U.S. Senate, owes his political career to black candidates who split the Democratic vote. Cochran won his initial election to the House with 48 percent of the vote. Then, in 1978, he became the state's first Republican senator in the twentieth century with 45 percent of the vote since Charles Evers (brother of the assassinated civil rights leader) took 23 percent of the vote away from the Democratic nominee. Another Republican who benefited from third-party black candidacies was Jon Hinson, who held on to a congressional seat with 39 percent of the vote in 1980 when Lester Burl McLemore, a black political scientist, placed ahead of the Democratic nominee.

When the Voting Rights Act was first adopted, the only black officeholders in Mississippi served in Mound Bayou, an all-black town.[16] The 1969 tabulation of African American elected officials in the state found sixty-seven, most of whom served in virtually all-black communities.[17] Mound Bayou had an African American mayor and ten African American members of its council. Fayette also had an African American mayor, as well as five council members, a constable, two justices of the peace, and two election commissioners who were black. Winstonville had a black mayor and five black council members.

With the extension of the franchise, black Mississippians began winning offices in communities other than those in which their race was concentrated. By the early 1980s, as figure 1.1 illustrates, more than four hundred African Americans held public office at the state. In the mid-1980s, the number exceeded five hundred, and in the early 1990s, it passed the seven hundred mark. In the most recent enumeration done by the Joint Center for Political and Economic Studies, almost nine hundred African Americans held office in the Magnolia State, the largest number for any state. There are more than four hundred African American municipal officers and well over one hundred school board members. The 2001 survey found blacks holding almost two hundred county posts including approximately one hundred of the state's 410 county commission seats. According to a more recent enumeration, additional African Americans have won county commission posts and now total 127 commission seats, or 31 percent, which approximates the black share of the voting-age population.[18]

African Americans have also made gains in winning judicial offices. During the 1990s, the method by which Mississippi chose its trial-court

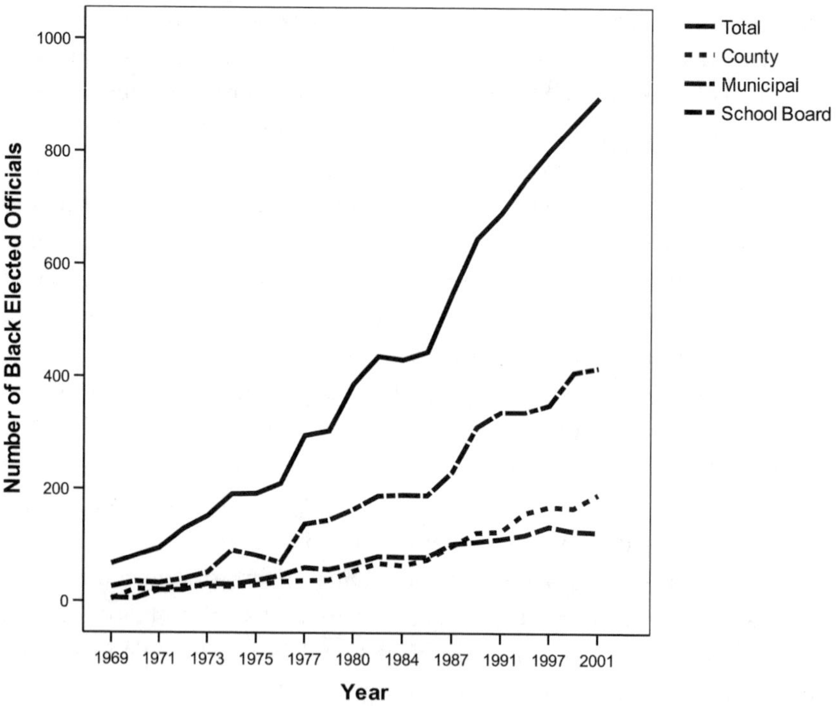

Figure 1.1. Black elected officials in Mississippi, 1969–2001. *Source:* Various volumes of the *National Roster of Black Elected Officials* (Washington, D.C.: Joint Center for Political and Economic Studies).

judges came under attack. Plaintiffs sought to have judicial circuits broken into subregions, some of which would be majority black in population. The logic behind these demands was analogous to the challenges that had been filed across the nation beginning in the mid-1980s when the target had been county commissions, school boards, and city councils elected at large. Plaintiffs contended that in these at-large arrangements candidates preferred by minority voters could be defeated by the greater number of white voters. However, if the at-large format were replaced by single-member districts and if some of those districts had a predominately minority electorate, then at least in those areas minorities would be able to select their candidates of choice. After plaintiffs prevailed in their challenges to the Mississippi judiciary, the numbers of black judges being elected increased. As of 2005, blacks held 16 percent of the forty-nine circuit-court judgeships, 18 percent of the forty-five chancery judgeships, and 19 percent of the twenty-six county-court judgeships.[19]

African Americans in Congress

For much of its history, Mississippi allocated one of its congressional districts to the Delta—the rich bottomland along the Mississippi River extending from the northwestern corner of the state south to Vicksburg. Most counties in this productive farming region have high concentrations of African Americans. Slow population growth during the 1950s cost Mississippi a congressional district. The Delta district had been about 60 percent black in 1962, but the new configuration extended it eastward into the Hill Country where the bulk of the population is white.[20] Following *Wesberry v. Sanders*[21]—in which the Supreme Court demanded that congressional districts have equal populations—the state made further adjustments. The plan adopted in 1966 divided the Delta among three districts that ran east and west across the state.[22] The new 2nd District in the northern part of the state was 51 percent black in its total population, but with the voting-age population (VAP) only 44 percent black, civil rights lawyer Frank Parker characterized it as a "phantom majority-black district."[23] Whites constituted a majority of the registered voters.

The post-1980 redistricting redrew the 2nd District to be 54 percent black in population, with a 48 percent black VAP. Estimates placed the share of the registered voters who were African American at 40 percent.[24] Robert Clark, who had broken the color line in the Mississippi house, won the Democratic nomination but lost the open congressional seat in the general election by fewer than three thousand votes.

After a mid-decade adjustment of congressional boundaries in response to a voting-rights challenge, the 2nd District became blacker with African Americans constituting 58 percent of the total population and 53 percent of the VAP. This new configuration sent Mike Espy, the first African American to represent Mississippi since 1883, to Congress with 52 percent of the vote. Espy became the first African American to represent a predominately rural congressional district in the post–civil rights era. Barone and Ujifusa underscore the critical nature of this redistricting by pointing out that had Robert Clark competed in the district that Espy won, Clark would have been elected in 1982.[25]

Espy continued to represent the district until tapped by President Clinton to serve as secretary of agriculture. In the special election to replace Espy, African American Bennie Thompson won the runoff with 55 percent of the vote. Thompson led a field with multiple Democrats including Espy's older brother. In the runoff, Thompson consolidated the African American vote in what was now a 63 percent black district to defeat the primary front-runner, white Republican Hayes Dent. Unlike Espy, Thompson made little effort to attract white votes in his initial election. Given the smaller proportion of black voters in the district that first elected Espy, had he ignored white concerns and not tried to expand his support from the white community, he would have been left in a precarious position. But by the time Thompson won the special election, the district had been reconfigured to make it substantially blacker. Thompson's initial election fits with the theoretical understanding offered by David Canon, who hypothesized that in an election that involves a white opposing multiple blacks in a majority-black district, the black nominee will probably be radical as opposed to moderate.[26] This is because white voters will have rallied to the white candidate. In districts in which only African Americans candidates compete, the white vote will usually fall in behind a moderate so that the more radical African American candidate loses to a biracial coalition.

Thompson, who holds one of three Democratic seats in Mississippi's congressional delegation, has compiled a liberal voting record.[27] He has consistently voted with the Democratic leadership in the House, a stand that would probably defeat a southerner with a less heavily minority constituency. As an outspoken representative of black concerns, Thompson was slow to reach out to white voters and consequently, although now in his ninth term, he continues to draw credible challengers. A black Republican nominee managed more than 40 percent of the vote in 2002 and 2004 in what is now a 63.2 percent black district.[28] In 2006 Thompson successfully overcame a primary challenge from another of Mike Espy's relatives, and became chairman of the powerful U.S. House Homeland Security Committee in the 110th Congress.

African Americans in the State Legislature

Robert Clark, the first African American to benefit from the Civil Rights Movement and enter the Mississippi legislature, joined the state house in 1967. Eight years passed before a second African American took a house seat. On through the 1970s, as Mississippi waged a lengthy courtroom battle to maintain its traditional districting practices, which made extensive user of multimember districts, black representation remained miniscule.[29] Finally, with the adoption of single-member districts and creation of numerous majority-black districts, black representation almost quadrupled to 15 house members as shown in table 1.1. During the 1980s, black representation in the 122-member house increased gradually, and then under a new districting plan drawn to accommodate population shifts during the 1990s, the number of African American house members increased by more than 50 percent to 31. Black representatives increased gradually during the 1990s so that by the turn of the new century, African Americans held almost 30 percent of the house seats.

The first African American to reach the state senate did so only after the resolution of the long-running legal challenge. Throughout the 1980s, the fifty-two–member upper chamber had a pair of African American members. That number rose to ten, as shown in table 1.1, with a new districting plan in 1992. As a consequence, African Americans held 19 percent of the seats in the senate during the 1990s. With the new century and a new redistricting plan, an eleventh African American senator won office, boosting the share of seats held by blacks above 20 percent.

In the Democratically controlled Mississippi legislature, African Americans have attained powerful positions. Robert Clark[30] became Speaker Pro Tempore in 1991, and blacks have chaired important committees since 2003.[31] In 2006, African Americans chaired four of the twenty-nine committees in the senate. In the house, African Americans chaired ten of nineteen committees. Among the committees chaired were the powerful house Ways and Means Committee and the committees dealing with Medicaid and universities and colleges.

Frank Parker, a civil rights attorney who litigated voting challenges in Mississippi for many years, argued that in order for African Americans to win Magnolia State legislative seats, districts needed to be at least 65

TABLE 1.1. Racial makeup of the Mississippi legislature, 1963–2007

	Senate	% Black in Senate	House	% Black in House
1963	0	0.00	0	0.00
1967	0	0.00	1	0.82
1971	0	0.00	1	0.82
1975	0	0.00	4	3.28
1979	2	3.85	15	12.30
1983	2	3.85	18	14.75
1987	2	3.85	20	16.39
1991	4	7.69	21	16.94
1992	10	19.23	30	24.19
1995	10	19.23	31	25.41
1999	10	19.23	35	28.69
2003	11	21.15	36	29.51
2007	11	21.15	35	28.69

Source: David A. Breaux, Stephen D. Shaffer, and Hilary B. Gresham, "Mississippi: Emergence of a Modern Two-Party State," in *The New Politics of the Old South,* 3rd ed., ed. Charles S. Bullock III and Mark Rozell (Lanham, Md.: Rowman and Littlefield, 2006), 110.

percent black. Parker reasoned that this proportion of black residents in total population was needed to offset racial differences in age, registration, and turnout rates.[32] Writing a decade after Parker, Orey continued to support the notion that the election of black legislators in Mississippi often requires districts to be almost two-thirds black in total population.[33] This is a higher concentration than thought to be necessary for black electoral success elsewhere. Requiring a high concentration of African Americans suggests an inability of black candidates to attract much of the white vote. If almost two-thirds of a district's population needs to be black for an African American to be elected, the number of seats that might go to black legislators is restricted.

African Americans in Statewide Office

No African American has won a statewide constitutional office in Mississippi. In the 2003 election, African Americans contested two offices for the Democratic Party. Democrats nominated Barbara Blackmon for lieutenant governor, and Gary Anderson carried the Democratic banner forward in

TABLE 1.2. Results of Mississippi statewide elections, 2003

	Candidate	Vote	Percent
Governor	Haley Barbour-R	470,404	52.6
	Ronnie Musgrove-D*	409,787	45.8
Lt. Governor	Amy Tuck-R*	542,129	61.0
	Barbara Blackmon-D	329,454	37.1
Sec'y of State	Julio Del Castillo-R	201,765	23.5
	Eric Clark-D*	610,461	71.0
Att'y General	Scott Newton-R	325,942	37.3
	Jim Hood-D	548,046	62.7
Treasurer	Tate Reeves-R	447,860	51.8
	Gary Anderson-D	403,307	46.6
Auditor	Phil Bryant-R*	587,212	76.3
	No Democratic Party candidate		
Insurance Comm.	Aaron DuPuy-R	211,859	24.8
	George Dale-D*	610,341	71.4
Agriculture Comm.	Max Phillips-R	274,097	32.1
	Lester Spell-D*	564,283	66.1

Source: Mississippi Secretary of State.

*Incumbent.

Black candidates in **boldface.**

the race for treasurer. Anderson lost by 5 percentage points as reported in table 1.2. Blackmon, who challenged Amy Tuck, the incumbent who had initially been elected lieutenant governor as a Democrat before changing parties, managed only 37 percent of the vote.

The 2003 elections were good to the Republican Party as it won half of the eight statewide contests—the first time the GOP has held more than two constitutional offices in Mississippi.[34] Democrats did not even put forward a candidate to challenge auditor Phil Bryant. On the other hand, Democrats re-elected the secretary of state, insurance commissioner, and agriculture commissioner, and won the post of attorney general, taking more than 60 percent of the vote in each of those contests. While Blackmon and Anderson got the fewest votes of the seven Democratic nominees, Anderson got a slightly larger share of the vote than repudiated incumbent governor Ronnie Musgrove. Although Anderson was more experienced than his Republican opponent, having directed the state's Department of Finance and Administration, he was unable to match Tate Reeves in fund-raising.[35]

While no African American managed to win a state office in 2003, the nomination of two blacks by the Democratic Party marked an advance for black political ambitions. In 1999, the one African American to seek statewide office ran a poor second in the Democratic primary when challenging incumbent Agriculture Commissioner Lester Spell.

In 2007, Gary Anderson ran for insurance commissioner and was the only African American on the statewide ballot. He lost by more than sixty thousand votes as he attracted less than a quarter of the white vote. Despite losing, Anderson won the third-highest vote share given any Democrat, which suggests that while he attracted relatively few whites, he may have done better than most Democrats who lost seven of the eight offices they sought in the increasingly Republican state.[36]

Mississippi elects three Supreme Court justices from three districts. Currently the nine-person Supreme Court has one African American. The district that elects the African American jurist has a 46 percent black voting-age population.[37] The first black to serve on the court, Reuben Anderson, who ascended to the bench in 1985, was the first African American graduate of the University of Mississippi law school. An African American—but only one—has served on the high court for the last generation.

Since 1995, Mississippi has had a second appellate court, the Court of Appeals, whose ten members are elected from five districts. One of the five districts is majority black and both of the judges it elects are African Americans.[38]

With Mississippi accounting for the nation's highest percentage of black population, one would expect Barack Obama to have done well in the presidential primary there, and he did, winning the Magnolia State with 61 percent of the vote. Democratic efforts at maximizing African American registration and turnout in the general election led some to see this state, which has not voted for a Democratic presidential nominee since 1976, as in play in 2008. (A brief analysis of the 2008 general election results for Mississippi and the other states appears in the epilogue.)

FEDERAL MONITORING

The remarkable change in the role of African Americans in Mississippi would not have occurred but for the vigilance of the Department of Justice (DOJ), which has rejected 169 proposed changes in the Magnolia State's electoral environment. This is the third-largest number of objections, ranking behind Texas and Georgia. Those other states, however, have far more counties and municipalities than Mississippi, and thus more jurisdictions that may fail to meet DOJ expectations. As noted earlier, efforts in Mississippi to minimize the impact of the Voting Rights Act and to perpetuate discriminatory practices led to the lawsuit that vastly broadened the scope of the VRA so that it regulated far more than changes directly aimed at voter registration and turnout.[39]

During the first decade in which Section 5 operated, DOJ sent twenty-five objections to Mississippi. In the next decade, DOJ held up sixty-seven proposed changes, and from 1985 to 1995, it rejected another sixty-six changes. Recently the incidence of objections has declined in Mississippi as elsewhere. Since 1995 the state has encountered only eleven objections. This small number of objections has been interpreted as evidence that Section 5 is operating as intended—that is, its presence deters discriminatory actions.[40] It was doubtlessly this history of submission and rejection that in 1981 led Thad Cochran, then the junior senator from Mississippi, to critically observe that the Voting Rights Act compelled "local officials [to] have to go to Washington, get on their knees, kiss the ring and tug their forelock to all these third-rate bureaucrats."[41]

Mississippi has averaged only one objection a year since 1995, but one of these played a prominent role in the 2006 congressional debate about extending the Voting Rights Act's Section 5. Many members of both houses of Congress pointed to the actions of a Mississippi town as evidence that Section 5 needed to be extended for another quarter century and that the scope of its coverage should not be altered. The action that attracted so much attention was the decision by the town of Kilmichael to cancel a municipal election. The city council acted after candidate filing had ended and it appeared that African Americans, who now constituted a majority among registered voters, were on the verge of winning most of the offices including that of mayor. Although DOJ was slow to respond, not getting an objection off until more than half a year after cancellation of the election, it demanded an election. Two years later, when the election was finally held, blacks won three council seats and the mayor's office.[42]

Canceling an election was extraordinary. A review of all DOJ objections issued since 1995 turns up only one similar objection, and that involved Grenada, Mississippi. Nevertheless, the audacity of suspending a regularly scheduled election just as blacks appeared poised to make gains convinced a number of legislators that jurisdictions subject to Section 5 could not yet be trusted to treat minorities fairly and therefore must continue to be monitored by federal authorities.

In addition to garnering objections, Mississippi has frequently been asked to provide more information for proposed changes submitted to DOJ. From 1990 through 2005, DOJ requested more information 474 times. Approximately a quarter of these involved redistricting plans and another quarter involved voter-registration procedures. Approximately one-sixth of these involved polling places or precincts. Once more information was provided, DOJ approved the proposal 60 percent of the time, which accounted for 284 of these submissions. In fifty-five instances, DOJ objected upon receiving fuller information. In forty-four cases, the jurisdiction proposing the change withdrew it.[43]

THE CURIOUS CASE OF NOXUBEE COUNTY

The vestiges of race and tradition die hard, and the final irony of the Voting Rights Act in Mississippi is the use of Section 2 to defend the voting rights of white voters from a local black majority. In February 2005, the United States Department of Justice brought a voting-rights challenge against the chairman of the Democratic Party of Noxubee County, Mississippi; the county's registrar; the county's election commission; and the county.[44] Noxubee County is more than 70 percent African American and displays racially polarized voting. The United States alleged that the county's Democratic Party chair, Ike Brown, led a concerted effort to deny or abridge the voting rights of white voters in Noxubee County. Two years later, in 2007, the federal court held that Brown, still acting as head of the Democratic Party in Noxubee County, and the county had engaged in a variety of activities to dilute or deny the white vote. The laundry list sounds familiar to anyone who has studied the implementation of Jim Crow. Brown (or those working with him) recruited candidates for office who did not meet residency requirements for the county to oppose white candidates. White voters were excluded from party meetings and caucuses, and systematically refused the opportunity to work as poll workers. Black voters were moved on the voting rolls to vote outside their residential voting district, in order to vote against white candidates in other districts. In at least one instance, a poll worker took ballots from black voters in line and marked them on their behalf.[45] There was systematic manipulation and falsification of absentee ballots to dilute white votes, and access to absentee ballots was denied to white students and teachers who worked or studied outside the district, described by federal authorities as "racially disparate." Absentee ballots were accepted or rejected on the basis of race, with yellow sticky notes used to indicate white ballots. About 20 percent of all ballots in Noxubee County were cast via absentee, making these ballots critical to determining election outcomes. ABC News, reporting on the story in December 2005, quoted a white resident of Macon, Mississippi, observing, "I think we're getting a little dose of our ancestors' medicine, if you want to know the truth."[46]

The federal court ruled in favor of the plaintiffs in Noxubee County. The decision represented a fundamental expansion of the application of Section 2—an act designed to protect black voting rights was used to end black discrimination against white voting rights. The court's opinion indicates that there is nonetheless a different standard applied to denial of white voting rights. The district court observed that the U.S. Supreme Court has made clear that the essence of Section 2 is to challenge election law, structures, or a practice that "interacts with social and historical conditions to cause an inequality in the opportunities" to participate and elect preferred representatives.[47] The trial court states that "such interaction simply does not exist when dealing with the voting rights of historically privileged white voters who as a group do not suffer the effects of past discrimination,"[48] making a results test insufficient when discrimination against white voters is at issue. A higher intent standard needed to be met, and the court found that the standard was met and a remedy required, because "no one could reasonably argue that an election official's racially motivated decision to count the votes of black voters while rejecting those of white voters is discrimination that cannot be countenanced under any view of Section 2."[49]

Noxubee County presents a curiosity. Black elected and party officials, chosen by black voters empowered by the Voting Rights Act, engaged in the very practices used in the past to deny the vote to African Americans. Evidently, in the politics of Noxubee County and possibly elsewhere in the South, the legacy of corrupt practices looms larger than race. These traditions, which are part of the broader political culture, transcend race to create an accepted practice among political leaders and their supporters in which voters have no value or opinions other than those given to them by political leaders. This assumption rejects the most basic tenet of democratic theory and individual rights, namely that the vote is a right and investment of the individual to be determined by the individual and not by the agents of the party or the state.

RACIAL VOTING PATTERNS

Mississippi does not maintain voter-registration data by race. Therefore, efforts to use statistical techniques to estimate racial voting patterns must match precinct returns with precinct-level data showing the voting-age population by race or rely on county data.

Regardless of the unit of analysis, the result is consistent: elections in Mississippi are historically highly polarized. Estimates of voting behavior by race in some heavily black counties such as Bolivar and Madison show that during the 1970s and on into the mid-1980s, only infrequently could black candidates attract as much as 10 percent of the white vote even though they got substantial majorities among African American voters.[50]

American University political historian Allan Lichtman conducted an extensive racial-polarization analysis for selected counties and for numerous judicial contests in the 1980s, but the elections of greatest interest for the purposes of this study are two congressional elections and a Supreme Court contest. An examination of the ecological regressions for those contests contained in Lichtman's report shows that the electorate was highly polarized in the two congressional elections. The Democratic nominees, Robert Clark in 1984 and Mike Espy in 1986, got an estimated 95 percent and 97 percent of the black vote respectively, while the Republican candidate, incumbent Webb Franklin, got approximately 93 percent of the white vote in 1984 and 88 percent in 1986. The primary for the Supreme Court position is one of the few Lichtman analyzed that is not racially polarized.[51] The estimates indicate that black candidate Reuben Anderson took an overwhelming share of the black vote (85 percent) but also polled a majority of the white vote (58 percent).

To some extent, the differences in candidate preferences reported in the congressional elections have a partisan basis. Polling data in table 1.3 illustrate the intense party divisions between Mississippi blacks and whites. In statewide exit polls from 1992 through 2004, the white and black preferences have differed. The black vote is in lockstep for Democrats, with 86 to 100 percent of all respondents saying they voted for Democrats. The white vote, meanwhile, is always majority Republican (the reciprocal of the Democratic vote reported in table 1.3), though the exit poll responses vary from 50.6 percent of white respondents voting Republican for the U.S. House in 1992 to 89.5 percent reporting ballots for incumbent U.S. senator Thad Cochran in 1996.[52] In two recent major statewide contests for which there are exit polls at the time of our writing—governor in 2003 and president in 2004—whites voted 77 percent and 83 percent Republican while more than 90 percent of blacks voted Democratically.

Ordinary least squares regression estimates of black and white support for congressional candidates between 2000 and 2004, as reported in table 1.4, reveal racially structured preferences when both major parties offer candidates. However, white Democratic incumbents attract substantially more of the white vote than other Democratic candidates, regardless of race. In nine of the thirteen congressional races examined in the table, the Republican candidate received at least 81.7 percent of the white vote. In four cases, which involved white Democratic incumbents Ronnie Shows (District 4, 2000) and Gene Taylor (District 5, 2000; District 4, 2002, 2004), the Democrat received at least 40 percent of the white vote, and Taylor always got more than 60 percent of the white vote. Black incumbent Bennie Thompson received an estimated 17.1 percent, 18.3 percent, and 11.4 percent of the white vote in three wining efforts in his majority-black Delta district. Thompson's showing is in line with that of white Democrats who have challenged Republican incumbents but well below white Democratic incumbents. Among white Democrats, incumbent Ronnie

TABLE 1.3. Racial preferences for Democratic candidates in select Mississippi races, 1992–2004

	Office	Black	White
1992	President**	92.7	27.7
1992	U.S. House	88.9	49.4
1994	U.S. Senate*	98.0	—
1994	U.S. House	100.0	—
1996	President*	94.9	23.0
1996	U.S. Senate**	69.2	10.5
1996	U.S. House	86.4	12.7
2000	U.S. Senate**	86.5	9.0
2000	President	95.7	17.4
2002	U.S. Senate	—	1.3
2002	U.S. House	—	27.9
2003	Governor	94.0	23.0
2004	President**	92.9	15.9

Sources: Mississippi exit poll data from Voter News Service (VNS) and, after 2002, the National Elections Pool.

Note: 2002 VNS exit polls are considered to have questionable external validity.

*Democratic incumbent running.

**Republican incumbent running.

Shows got only 10.5 percent of the vote when he had to face fellow incumbent Chip Pickering (R) in 2002 after the two incumbents got thrown together as a result of the state losing a congressional district. Only the eight-term Gene Taylor with his moderate voting record has managed to attract majority support from white voters in recent years.[53]

Black ballots go overwhelmingly for the Democratic candidate when one appears on the ballot. Roger Wicker in 2002 is the only Republican with a Democratic opponent to attract more than 30 percent of the black vote from 2000 to 2004. In the absence of the Democratic Party cue, however, black congressional voters are less cohesive. In 2004 Wicker drew only a Reform Party opponent (Barbara Dale Washer, a white retired school teacher). Wicker pulled an estimated 53 percent of the black vote. In the 3rd District, Chip Pickering secured 47.1 percent of a fractured black vote against two independents. But, in the presence of two-party competition and in the absence of Democratic incumbents, white and black voters have sharply different congressional preferences.

TABLE 1.4. Estimates of racial preferences for Congress in Mississippi, 2000–2004

	District	Candidate/Party	Black	White
2000	1	Wicker-R*	18.6	82.9
		Grist-D	81.4	17.1
	2	**Thompson-D***	>100.0	17.1
		Caraway-R	<0.0	82.9
	3	Pickering-R*	15.7	95.8
		Thrash-D	84.3	4.2
	4	Shows-D*	>100.0	41.4
		Lampton-R	<0.0	58.6
	5	Taylor-D*	97.5	78.7
		McConnell-R	2.5	21.3
2002	1	Wicker-R*	39.6	83.6
		Weathers-D	60.4	16.4
	2	**Thompson-D***	88.5	18.3
		LeSueur-R	11.5	81.7
	3	Pickering-R*	23.2	89.5
		Shows-D*	76.8	10.5
	4	Taylor-D*	80.6	76.7
		Mertz-R	19.4	23.3
2004	1	Wicker-R*	53.0	95.7
		Washer-Ref.	47.0	4.3
	2	**Thompson-D***	91.6	11.4
		LeSueur-R	8.4	88.6
	3	Pickering-R*	47.1	96.3
		Giles-I	34.5	3.4
		Magee-I	18.4	0.3
	4	Taylor-D*	71.6	63.1
		Lott-R	28.4	36.9

Source: Ordinary least squares (OLS) estimates.

*Incumbent.

Black candidates in **boldface.**

Recent Mississippi statewide elections exhibit the same stark, race-party-incumbency structure. Of seven statewide elections from 2003 analyzed in table 1.5, three exhibited pronounced party preferences by race. Republican candidates for governor, lieutenant governor, and treasurer captured 70.3 percent, 83.6 percent, and 67.7 percent of the estimated white vote, but less than 19 percent of the black vote. All three candidates prevailed, and the

TABLE 1.5. Estimates of racial preferences for select statewide Mississippi offices and Confederate flag referendum, 2000–2003

	Office	Candidate/Party	Black	White
2000	President	Bush-R	3.7	82.2
		Gore-D	96.3	17.8
2000	U.S. Senate	Lott-R*	15.4	94.4
		Brown-D	84.6	5.6
2001	Flag referendum	Old flag (Confederate)	8.5	89.5
		New flag (Reform)	91.5	10.5
2003	Governor	Barbour-R	18.8	70.3
		Musgrove-D*	81.2	29.7
	Lt. Governor	Tuck-R*	18.3	83.6
		Blackmon-D	81.7	16.4
	Sec'y of State	Clark-D*	87.1	66.2
		Del Castillo-R	5.2	28.4
		Blackburn-I	7.6	5.4
	Att'y General	Hood-D	85.8	54.0
		Newton-R	14.2	46.0
	Treasurer	**Anderson-D**	82.9	32.3
		Reeves-R	17.1	67.7
	Insurance Comm.	Dale-D*	97.7	65.7
		DuPuy-R	2.3	34.3
	Agriculture Comm.	Spell-D*	95.9	56.7
		Phillips-R	4.1	43.3

Source: Ordinary least squares (OLS) estimates.

*Incumbent.

Black candidates in **boldface.**

Latino candidate in *italics.*

candidates for lieutenant governor and treasurer bested black, Democratic opponents. Contests for secretary of state, insurance commissioner, and agriculture commissioner featured white, Democratic incumbents who won the majority of white ballots along with most black ballots. The attorney general contest to succeed popular incumbent Mike Moore was won by a white Democrat (Hood) who carried 54 percent of the white vote. Hood's success and Governor Ronnie Musgrove's failure stand in contrast to the prevailing pattern of race-party-incumbency structure.

The pattern observed in the three 2003 races where Republicans won had been evident in 2000. George Bush and Trent Lott, running for president and

U.S. senator, respectively, commanded levels of white and black support similar to what was observed in 2003 contests for governor, treasurer, and lieutenant governor. The same pattern appears in the 2001 state flag referendum, which pitted a flag featuring a Confederate battle flag against a new flag that eliminated the Saint Andrew's cross. Whites massively favored the old flag while more than 90 percent of blacks wanted a change.

David A. Breaux, Stephen D. Shaffer, and Hilary B. Gresham document the precipitous decline of Democratic identification among Mississippi whites and the stability of party identification among Mississippi blacks since 1981.[54] Their figures come from surveys of Mississippi voters conducted by the polling operation at Mississippi State University.[55] The quarter-century time series shows relatively little variation in the party identification of black Mississippians. The range in Democratic Party identifiers among blacks is from a low of 77.2 percent in 2002 to a high of 90.4 percent in 2000. In all but two years, more than 80 percent of the African Americans identified with the Democratic Party. Never did more than 13.4 percent identify themselves as Republicans, and in six of the fourteen years, Republicans could claim the loyalty of fewer than one in ten blacks. The drop in Democratic identifiers in 2002 is attributable to a record-high incidence of blacks identifying themselves as independents (10.4 percent). African Americans' intense loyalty to the Democratic Party is reflected in the exit poll and regression estimates presented in tables 1.3 through 1.5.

In the early 1980s, most whites joined the vast majority of blacks in identifying with the Democratic Party. However, after 1990, fewer than 40 percent of white Mississippians thought of themselves as Democrats. In 2002, white Democratic identifiers dropped below 30 percent, and in 2004, only 22.2 percent of the white sample identified as Democrats. As the Democratic identifiers have decreased, Republican Party members have risen. In 1982, a third of the whites saw themselves as Republicans, but a decade later, 56 percent of whites identified with the GOP. For the remainder of that decade, the Republican percentage hovered around 55 percent, but then in 2002 it leapt to almost two-thirds of the sample where it remained in 2004.

As has occurred across the South, Mississippi conservatives have all but abandoned the Democratic Party, with barely one in ten still calling themselves Democrats.[56] Increasingly a white, conservative Republican

Party squares off against a black, liberal Democratic Party. With two-thirds of whites now identifying with the GOP, it is well positioned to win statewide contests even though it does not command majority support in the state. A 2004 poll showed Mississippi voters tilting toward the GOP by a 46.8 to 42.3 percent margin.[57]

White realignment first materialized in delivering the state to Republicans in presidential elections. Mississippi has cast its Electoral College votes for a Democrat only once since 1956, and that one time came more than a generation ago when the state helped elect Jimmy Carter president in 1976. Even then Carter's Mississippi victory was his narrowest in the South, a 14,463-vote plurality.

As Republican strength has grown among white voters, the GOP has added high-profile offices to its list of successes. In 1978, Thad Cochran won a Senate seat, the first Republican statewide victory other than a presidential election. A decade later, Republicans took Mississippi's other Senate seat. The GOP achieved its first gubernatorial victory in 1991 when Kirk Fordice defeated incumbent Ray Mabus by a 51 to 48 percent margin. Fordice won reelection, and in 2003 Haley Barbour scored the third Republican gubernatorial victory in the last four elections.

According to Census Bureau estimates, African Americans cast 36 percent of the votes in the 2004 presidential election. If 85 percent of that black vote goes to a Democrat, then the Republican nominee needs approximately 70 percent of the white vote to win. If 90 percent of the black vote goes to the Democrat, a Republican would need at least 72 percent of the white vote for victory, and with 95 percent black cohesion, almost three-fourths of the white vote would be needed for a GOP victory.[58] With two-thirds of white Mississippians now identifying themselves as Republicans, the GOP is within striking range of a persistent statewide majority if it mobilizes its partisans.

Democratic incumbents, especially those for less visible statewide offices as well as legislative candidates, can often secure sufficient white votes to win. Although we do not have estimates of the vote split in the 1999 gubernatorial election, the outcome demonstrates a situation in which the Democratic nominee eked out barely enough white votes for a plurality.[59] The more common pattern, however, as revealed in tables 1.3

through 1.5, is for the Republican to attract more than three-fourths of the white vote and to claim victory.

When incumbency ceases to be a factor, it is difficult to distinguish in Mississippi whether an election is structured by a racial issue, a candidate's race, or partisanship. White voters are so overwhelmingly Republican and black voters so overwhelmingly Democratic that any statewide or congressional election assumes a racial/partisan structure once one controls for incumbency.

An analysis of state legislative voting is not part of this presentation, but it is likely that the reason for continued Democratic control of both chambers through 2008 hinged in part on the attractiveness of Democratic incumbents.[60] Democrats linked to the national party have encountered increasing difficulty in finding favor with white Mississippians. Still, enough voters remain satisfied with the Democratic state legislator whom they know and who takes policy positions in line with those of the state's white voters even if in conflict with the policy stands of national Democrats. White congressional Democrats from the state struggle to balance the expectations of their electorate and their colleagues in the Congress; Democratic state legislators do not face that kind of cross pressure. White Democrats in the Mississippi legislature can stake out moderate positions like Gene Taylor has done in Congress or position themselves even further to the right without fear of displeasing their party's leadership, and by so doing, these local Democrats continue to win elections. Consequently, a biracial coalition of Democrats continues to dominate the Mississippi house. As of the 2008 election, the Mississippi house had thirty-five black Democrats, forty-one white Democrats, and forty-six white Republicans. By 2008, Democratic control of the state senate had shrunk to the narrowest of margins with eleven black Democrats, sixteen white Democrats, and twenty-five white Republicans, and the Republican lieutenant governor has given several of the chamber's most powerful posts to his fellow partisans. After the 2003 elections, state senator James Shannon Walley (D-Leakesville) changed parties to give control of the chamber to Republicans, by creating a tie broken by Republican lieutenant governor Amy Tuck. In the 2007 elections Democrats won back the chamber by a 28–24 seat margin until a party change by state senator Nolan Mettetal to the

Republicans narrowed the Democratic majority to 27–25. The biracial Democratic coalition that controls the lower chamber continues to push for progressive legislation and scores some victories even over the opposition of Republican chief executives.[61]

CONCLUSION

Mississippi has had the longest journey from out of the darkness of segregation and racial subjugation. The state entered the 1960s with the lowest rates of black voter registration and participation, and the most unabashedly violent and vehement efforts to keep blacks from the ballot box. One would be hard-pressed to note a more recent, more extreme example of the blatant absence of democratic opportunity in the United States than the Mississippi that immediately preceded the passage of the Voting Rights Act.

By the beginning of the twenty-first century, proportionally more blacks than whites had registered to vote in Mississippi, and Mississippi blacks have registered to vote and turned out at rates well ahead of African Americans outside the South for two decades. Once implementation of the Voting Rights Act knocked down racial barriers to the ballot, African Americans in Mississippi enthusiastically embraced political opportunities.[62] White Mississippians often vote at higher rates than blacks, though the difference in self-reported turnout is typically less than 5 points and in the most recent election examined in appendix B blacks actually voted at higher rates than whites. Increases in black voter participation are not consistent across the state, though majority black counties are less likely to exhibit low voter participation—a result consistent with the trends of voter participation revealed by survey data.

Mississippi leads the nation in the black percentage in its population, yet the state is home to fewer African Americans than New York City. More blacks hold public office in the Magnolia State (nearly nine hundred) than anywhere else in the United States, and a black person is more likely to be represented by or to get to vote for a black officeholder in Mississippi than anywhere else in the United States. Since 1986, an African American has been elected from the majority-black Delta congressional district. Black representation is approaching proportionality on county commissions and in the state house of representatives, though the black proportion in the state senate still lags.

Advances in black office holding have come even though party voting is starkly divided along racial lines, with statewide and congressional elections often featuring 80–20 divisions of both races in opposition to each other's preferences. These divisions are affected more by incumbency than by candidate race, and are reflective of the wholesale movement of the respective races into separate parties, and an increasing tendency to vote those party preferences up and down the ticket. The political future of Mississippi is likely one of an increasingly Republican white electorate up and down the ticket that predominates in white communities, and of a homogenous black electorate that predominates in the Black Belt and in certain urban and rural quarters where black-white coalitions are possible due to lingering local white preferences for Democrats.

CHAPTER 2

Alabama

Alabama prides itself as being the "Heart of Dixie." On the steps of its old Capitol is marked the spot where Jefferson Davis took the oath of office to become the president of the Confederate States of America. With this heritage, perhaps it should not be surprising that the state produced some of the most intransigent opponents to racial change. Many of the most dramatic confrontations faced by the Civil Rights Movement took place in Alabama.

Had a competition been staged in the 1960s to identify the leading opponent to racial fairness, multiple claimants to the title would have called Alabama home. From Birmingham came Police Commissioner Bull Conner, who attacked peaceful civil rights protestors with water cannons and police dogs. Conner's policemen stood idly by while a mob burned the Freedom Riders bus. His city became known as "Bombingham" as a result of the number of blasts set off by Klansmen. In one particularly horrible event on a Sunday morning at a church, a cell of Klansmen detonated a bomb that killed four little girls. From Montgomery came the operators of the municipal bus system that asked Rosa Parks to vacate her seat for a white person and to move to the back of the bus. That action sparked the bus boycott that lasted more than a year and propelled the newly arrived young minister Martin Luther King, Jr., into the national spotlight. From Selma came Sheriff Jim Clark, who repeatedly clashed with the black citizens trying to register to vote in his rural county. And then there was four-time governor George Wallace, who, after losing in 1958 to the more racially conservative John Patterson, vowed, "Well boys, no other son-of-a-bitch will ever out-nigger me again."[1] Wallace lived up to that pledge and stood in the schoolhouse door in a vain effort to block desegregation of the University of Alabama. He used his multiple gubernatorial and presidential campaigns to stir up racial passions not only in Alabama but across the nation.

Long before the racial obstructionists of the 1960s, Alabama had adopted the full range of techniques designed to limit African American political participation. Just after the turn of the twentieth century, the state embraced the literacy test, a cumulative poll tax, and white primary. It also imposed a lengthy residency requirement before a person could vote and denied the ballot to those guilty of petty crimes.[2] The effectiveness of the discriminatory practices included in the 1901 Alabama Constitution was such that the number of black registrants is estimated to have plummeted from an initial 180,000 to no more than 3,000 in 1903.[3]

After the Supreme Court invalidated the white primary, Alabama added the Boswell Amendment to its constitution. This amendment—one of nearly eight hundred additions to the nation's longest constitution[4]—sought to discourage black participation in the Democratic primary. It required literacy or that an individual own real estate or personal property valued at three hundred dollars or more.[5] Prospective voters had to demonstrate their ability to not only read and write but also to interpret the constitution to the satisfaction of the local registrar. They also needed to demonstrate good character.

BLACK REGISTRATION AND TURNOUT

The Boswell Amendment and the actions of Governor George Wallace and other Alabama racists proved so intimidating that at the time of the Voting Rights Act (VRA) adoption, Alabama had a smaller share of its voting-age African American population registered than any state other than Mississippi. As of 1964, only 19.3 percent of the black adult Alabamians had registered to vote.[6] In contrast, 69 percent of the age-eligible whites had signed up to participate in elections. In seventeen of Alabama's sixty-seven counties, fewer than 10 percent of the black voting-age population appeared on the voting rolls in 1964. In two counties having a total of more than eleven thousand black adults, not a single African American had been permitted to register. One of these counties, Lowndes, later became the site where the black panther was first adopted as an emblem for black political mobilization when Stokely Carmichael, the leader of the Student Nonviolent Coordinating Committee, launched an unsuccessful effort to elect blacks to local office.[7]

Change came quickly. Less than two years after passage of the Voting Rights Act, more than half of Alabama's black adults had signed up to vote. Federal officials sent to the state pursuant to the VRA helped increase black registration from 19.3 to 51.6 percent by signing up 60,316 African Americans. Of all African Americans registered to vote as of 1967, almost a quarter had signed up with federal election examiners. This included more than 19,000 registered by federal officials in Jefferson County (Birmingham) along with another 9,000 in Montgomery County. In Dallas County, the site of the famous Selma march where state patrolmen clubbed John Lewis and other marchers as they set out for Montgomery, federal examiners enrolled 8,972 African Americans. Before the passage of the new law, only 320 of the 15,115 age-eligible blacks had registered in Dallas County. In Lowndes County, where no blacks appeared on the voter rolls before the legislation, federal examiners added 2,730 so that blacks constituted a majority of the registrants. In Wilcox County, the other county with no registered blacks prior to the legislation, federal examiners signed up 3,666 new voters, and by 1967, more blacks than whites had registered in that county.

Table 2.1 shows the increases in African American registration in counties in which fewer than 10 percent of the age-eligible blacks were registered prior to passage of the Voting Rights Act. In fourteen of the seventeen counties, more than half the black adults had registered by 1967. At the upper end, in Greene County, black registration had increased from 5.5 to 79 percent. Other remarkable gains occurred in Marengo, where black registration shot up from 3.8 to 74.7 percent; in Perry, where the increase was from 5.6 to 74.2 percent; and in Dallas, where it rose

TABLE 2.1. Changes in registration in Alabama counties with low black registration in 1964

	1964 registration (%)		1967 registration (%)		Number registered by federal authorities	
	White	Nonwhite	White	Nonwhite	White	Nonwhite
Autauga	78.6	1.4	>100	65.5	275	1,017
Barbour	96.9	7.8	>100	63.7	0	0
Butler	86.6	5.1	96.1	38.1	0	0
Choctaw	99.4	6.3	>100	76.4	0	0
Dallas	65.7	2.1	91.2	70.4	75	8,972
Elmore	93.7	8.3	>100	60.6	192	1,558
Geneva	70.8	4.7	94.9	38.0	0	0
Greene	>100	5.5	>100	79.0	49	2,053
Hale	>100	3.9	>100	68.4	34	3,570
Lowndes	>100	0.0	>100	59.1	23	2,730
Marengo	>100	3.8	>100	74.7	193	4,890
Monroe	>100	6.6	>100	51.4	0	0
Perry	87.4	5.6	>100	74.2	87	2,731
Pike	>100	5.2	>100	65.4	0	0
Russell	54.6	7.6	93.6	40.1	0	0
Sumter	>100	5.5	>100	50.5	9	12
Wilcox	>100	0.0	>100	62.1	11	3,666

Source: U.S. Commission on Civil Rights, *Political Participation* (Washington, D.C: Government Printing Office, 1968), 224–227.

from 2.1 to 70.4 percent. In the two counties in which no African Americans had managed to get onto the registration rolls prior to the Voting Rights Act, more than 59 percent had signed up to vote within two years of its passage. Despite these remarkable gains, black registration lagged that for whites. Even before the VRA several of these counties had more white registrants than white adults as a result of not purging registration rolls to eliminate those who had died or moved away.

Alabama does not maintain registration or turnout data by race, leaving the surveys done by the U.S. Bureau of the Census as the best source (appendix B). With two exceptions, the rates at which Alabama whites reported registering between 1980 and 2006 exceed those for blacks. The two exceptions are 1986, when approximately one percentage point more blacks than whites reported being registered, and 1998, when the difference was less than a percentage point. The largest disparities tended to come in the early 1980s, with the greatest difference occurring in 1982 when 70.2 percent of whites compared with 57.7 percent of African Americans had registered. Two years earlier, the difference had been 11 percentage points. From 1988 through 1996, white registration rates ran 6 to 10 percentage points above black registration.

Racial differences have narrowed over time so that in the 2000 and 2004 presidential elections, the rate at which whites reported registering is less than 3 percentage points greater than for blacks. A larger disparity existed in 2002, when 73.7 percent of whites—contrasted with 67.6 percent of blacks—said that they had signed up to vote, but in 2006 the difference had closed to 1.2 points.

Latinos have not migrated to Alabama in large numbers. Consequently, when registration rates among whites, exclusive of Hispanics, are considered, the figures differ little from the white adult population that is used throughout the time series. Once Hispanics are excluded, the figure for white registration in 1998 goes from being slightly less than that for blacks to slightly more. In the next two election years for which data are available, the non-Hispanic white registration figure is approximately one-half percentage point higher than the white figure. In the two most recent elections in the table, non-Hispanic whites registered at a rate less than 3 percentage points higher than blacks.

Except for 1982, Alabama blacks always registered at higher rates than blacks living outside of the region. The advantage in favor of African Americans in the Yellowhammer State has increased over time. In the five most recent years surveyed, Alabama African Americans registered at rates at least 9 percentage points higher than nonsouthern blacks, with the greatest gap in the entire time series coming in 2006 when 71.8 percent of Alabama blacks but only 53.6 percent of nonsouthern blacks had registered to vote. Not only do Alabama African Americans report registering at higher rates than blacks outside the South, in every year surveyed, beginning with 1990, Alabama African Americans have reported registering at higher rates than whites outside of the South. Even with the exclusion of Hispanics, the rate at which blacks registered in Alabama narrowly exceeds that for whites in the non-South in 1998, 2000, and 2006. In 2002 and 2006, the two figures are essentially equal. The problem of much lower African American registration in Alabama than the rest of the nation was corrected as early as 1980, and the state has avoided a relapse.

Self-reported figures on turnout gathered by the U.S. Bureau of the Census and presented in the second table of appendix B indicate that, in all but three years, a higher proportion of Alabama's age-eligible whites than blacks participated in the election. Two of the greatest differences come in the first two elections when approximately 10 percentage points more of the white than black adults voted. These early disparities are matched in 1994 with white turnout at 64.3 percent compared with 53.5 percent for African Americans. The most recent decade has witnessed greater equality, with 2002 being the only recent year in which white turnout exceeded black turnout by as much as 4 points.

In 1986, a larger share of the black than white population reported voting. In 1998, the figures are the same for both groups with 51.6 percent of the age eligible having voted. In 2004, black turnout exceeded white turnout by 1.7 percentage points. The two previous presidential elections for which results have been tabulated (2000 and 2004) had differences of less than 4 percentage points in white and black turnout.

Excluding non-Hispanic whites from consideration raises the figure for white turnout by less than a single percentage point. Despite the slight increase in the white registration figure, even without Hispanics, it remains below the figure for blacks in 2004 while edging just above the black figure in 1998.

Recall that one of the keys for making Section 5 of the Voting Rights Act applicable to a jurisdiction was that less than half of its voting-age citizens had voted in 1964. In that year, only 36 percent of Alabama's adults cast ballots. Four years later, perhaps spurred on partly by the independent candidacy of its favorite son George Wallace, Alabama turnout surged to 52.9 percent of the adults.[8] Most Alabamians did not participate in another presidential election until 1984, when slightly more than half (50.9) voted. While Alabama participation rates dipped below 50 percent in 1988 and again in 1996, when Alabama turnout stood at 47.7 percent, that was only 1.2 percentage points lower than the nation as a whole. In 2004, 54.8 percent of Alabamians voted, a figure less than 1 percentage point below the national figure.

When compared to the self-reported turnout rates for the non-South, African American turnout in the non-South exceeded that for Alabama in four of the first five years. The greatest difference, 7.3 percentage points, occurred in 1982. Beginning in 1990, Alabama blacks reported voting at higher rates than blacks living outside of the South. The largest difference came in 1994 when 53.5 percent of Alabama African Americans but only 40.2 percent of those living outside the region voted. The most recent election, in 2006, shows a gap of almost 10 points. Nonsouthern whites usually vote at higher rates than Alabama African Americans. In three of the seven mid-term elections, however, Alabama blacks went to the polls at higher rates than nonsouthern whites, although this most recently occurred in 1998.[9] Excluding Hispanics from the white turnout rate in the non-South shows nonsouthern whites continuing to vote at lower rates than Alabama blacks in 1998. For the other years, excluding Hispanics results in a substantially higher white turnout rate in the non-South compared to that of Alabama blacks.

Alabama turnout has increased in a dramatic fashion. As figures reported by Patrick Cotter demonstrate, from 1936 through 1952, Alabama turnout in presidential elections ran roughly 40 percentage points below the national figure. Since 1980, Alabama turnout has been within 4 percentage points of the national figure and in 1992 exactly equaled the national figure. In 2004, Alabama participation lagged that of the nation by less than one percentage point.[10] The low levels of participation that made Alabama subject to Section 5 of the VRA ceased being a problem more than a generation ago.

AFRICAN AMERICAN OFFICE HOLDING

In 1969, Alabama had seventy African American public officials, half of whom held municipal offices. Black office holding tripled in the next eleven years and reached 238 in 1980 with half holding municipal offices while just over 10 percent each served either on school boards or in county positions. By 1984, more than three hundred African Americans had been elected in Alabama, and that number reached 448 in 1987. Successful challenges to at-large elections brought pursuant to Section 2 resulted in the creation of many single-member district plans for local

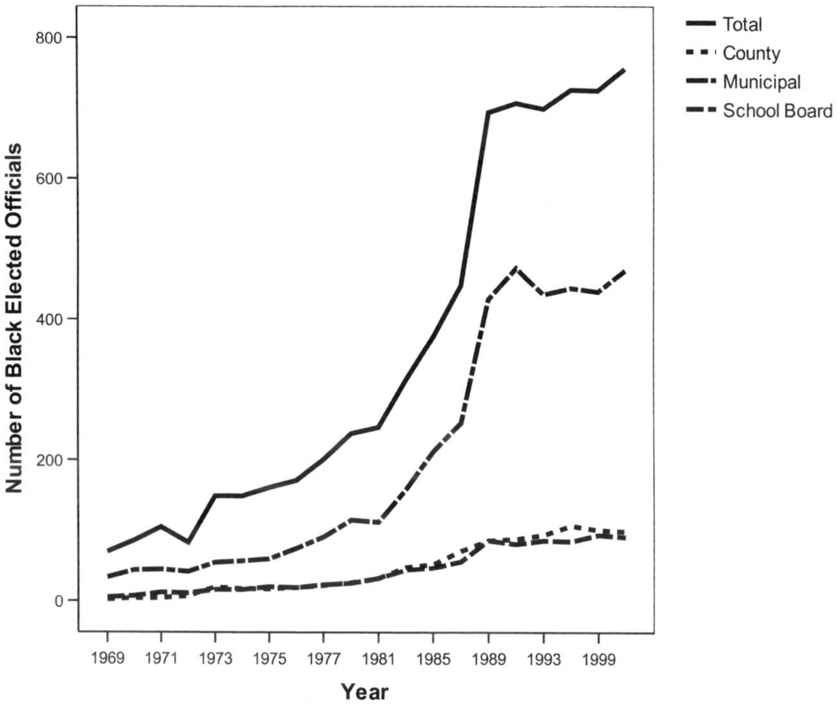

Figure 2.1. Black elected officials in Alabama, 1969–2001. *Source:* Various volumes of the *National Roster of Black Elected Officials* (Washington, D.C.: Joint Center for Political and Economic Studies).

collegial bodies. By 1989, the numbers of African American officials had jumped to almost seven hundred. Thereafter, the number of black officials grew slowly, reaching 756 in 2001 (see figure 2.1). Of that number, 470 held municipal offices while fewer than 100 served in county government or on school boards. Only Mississippi has a greater number of African Americans holding public offices than Alabama.

Scores of jurisdictions in Alabama got caught up in an open-ended lawsuit challenging discriminatory electoral rules. *Dillard v. Crenshaw County* was filed in the mid-1980s and expanded to include seventeen county commissions, twenty-eight county school boards, and 144 cities.[11] As a consequence of this litigation (which persisted for decades), many jurisdictions that elected their public officials at large had to adopt procedures that make it easier for blacks to win public office. While most of the defendants that have either lost or chosen to settle have moved to single-member districts with one or more of the resultant single-member districts having a black majority, several jurisdictions have adopted innovative electoral formats. These innovations have included both cumulative and limited voting. Use of either of these approaches allows a jurisdiction to continue to elect all members of its collegial governing body at large but makes it easier for minorities to win at least one position.

With cumulative voting, electors can cast as many votes as there are seats to be filled, but the format also allows them to cast more than one of their preferences for a single candidate. Indeed, in a jurisdiction that elects five members to its governing board, a voter would be allowed to cast all five of his or her ballots for a single individual. If a single African American candidate ran and most black voters cast all five of their preferences for that individual, that person would stand a good chance of being elected even if African Americans constituted less than 20 percent of the electorate. Under a more typical at-large arrangement, where there might be five separate contests for the five seats, the black preferences in each of the five contests could easily be overwhelmed by white voters.

With limited voting, voters register preferences for fewer candidates than the number of seats on the board to be filled. Thus a board might consist of five commissioners, but a voter could express preferences for no more than three. Since voters cannot express as many preferences as there are seats to be filled, strategic voting by minorities will enable them to fill at least one position, where under a traditional voting arrangement with each voter registering preferences in five separate contests, the minority preference could be defeated. In most of the communities that have adopted either cumulative or limited voting, African Americans have succeeded in winning elections.[12] While these innovative changes contribute only a few of the new black officeholders elected beginning in the mid-1980s, they do play some role.

African Americans in Congress

When the legislature failed to enact a redistricting plan following the 1990 census, a federal court imposed a congressional map largely designed by

Republicans. That map contained a 67 percent black district that linked the African American populations in Birmingham and Montgomery with a large swath of the rural Black Belt. When the white Democratic incumbent opted not to seek reelection, the open seat drew a large field in which two African American state senators led in the Democratic primary. In the runoff, Earl Hilliard bested his colleague by a scant 670 votes.

Hilliard represented the 7th District for the duration of the configuration adopted in 1992. However, under the map adopted in 2001 that excluded Montgomery, Hilliard failed to maintain his hold on the 61.7 percent black district. He fell to Artur Davis, who is a generation younger and had served as an assistant U.S. attorney. Davis, who had been held to a third of the vote when he challenged Hilliard in 2000, increased his vote share to 43 percent in the Democratic primary. The incumbent, who had won with 58 percent in the 2000 primary, slumped to only 46 percent two years later. In the decisive runoff, Davis—with strong financial backing from supporters of Israel, who were motivated by what they perceived to be Hilliard's opposition to the Jewish state—polled 56 percent of the vote. Davis built a biracial coalition in the face of strong support for the incumbent from the Congressional Black Caucus.

African Americans in the State Legislature

African Americans arrived in the Alabama legislature a bit later than in most southern states. The first black members won seats in the 105-member house of representatives in 1970. When the state undertook a major redistricting prior to the 1974 election, the black percentage jumped from two to twelve, where it remained throughout the decade. As shown in table 2.2, during the 1980s African Americans comprised approximately one-sixth of the house. The redistricting efforts of the 1990s created twenty-seven majority-black seats and boosted the black proportion of the house to just over a quarter of the membership. Those figures, which have remained unchanged for a decade, are almost identical to the black share of the total population of the state. Members of both chambers in Alabama serve four-year terms.

Table 2.2 also shows the black presence in the thirty-five–member state senate, where the first African Americans took seats in 1975. The

TABLE 2.2. Racial makeup of the Alabama legislature, 1965–2007

	Senate	% Black in Senate	House	% Black in House
1965	0	0.00	0	0.00
1967	0	0.00	0	0.00
1969	0	0.00	0	0.00
1971	0	0.00	2	1.90
1973	0	0.00	2	1.90
1975	2	5.71	13	12.38
1977	2	5.71	13	12.38
1979	3	8.57	13	12.38
1981	3	8.57	13	12.38
1983	3	8.57	15	14.29
1985	5	14.29	19	18.10
1987	5	14.29	19	18.10
1989	5	14.29	18	17.14
1991	5	14.29	19	18.10
1993	5	14.29	19	18.10
1995	8	22.86	27	25.71
1997	8	22.86	27	25.71
1999	8	22.86	27	25.71
2001	8	22.86	27	25.71
2003	8	22.86	27	25.71
2005	8	22.86	27	25.71
2007	8	22.86	26	24.76

Source: Data compiled by the authors.

1980s redistricting saw black membership in the senate go to 14 percent, and with the new mapping early in the next decade, which produced eight majority-black districts, blacks made up almost 23 percent of the senate, a figure that approximates the African American share of the voting-age population in the state.

Rather than seeking to increase the number of districts likely to elect African Americans during the negotiations over the post-2000 redistricting, the state legislature's Black Caucus sought to maintain a system in which the Democratic Party would be a majority.[13] The experiences of Georgia and South Carolina might have informed this decision. Efforts in Georgia and South Carolina to maximize the number of seats likely to elect African Americans subsequently opened the door for Republicans to take control either of the legislature or the state's congressional delegation.

The growing numbers of Republicans have meant that the Alabama Legislative Black Caucus now constitutes a substantial share of the Democratic membership of the legislature. In 2007, the eight African American senators held the balance of power between the twelve Republicans and fifteen white Democrats in the senate. In the house, African Americans held twenty-six seats while Republicans commanded forty-three, leaving white Democrats with thirty-six seats. As they have come to become a substantial minority within the legislative Democratic Party, and as individual legislators have acquired seniority, the Black Caucus members have also achieved positions of leadership.

Hastings Wyman, the longtime publisher of the *Southern Political Report*, observed the following about African American strength within the Alabama legislature in 2001:

> In the Alabama Senate, African American Henry "Hank" Sanders, who chairs the Finance and Taxation Committee, is among the upper chamber's most influential members. Black senators chair seven other senate committees, including Education; Health; Judiciary; and Industrial Development and Recruitment. The late Sen. Michael Figures served as President Pro Tem of the Senate. His widow, Vivien Figures, chairs the Education Committee. In the House, John Knight, an African American who chairs the Ways and Means Committee, is among the House's most influential members. Demetrius Newton serves as Speaker Pro Tem. African Americans chair three House committees: Education; Local Legislation; and State Government. However, "the most vocal and best watch-dog" among the black lawmakers, says an African American insider, "is State Rep. Alvin Holmes of Montgomery. He's the Al Sharpton and Jesse Jackson of the legislature. He doesn't get much legislation passed, but he keeps them honest, black and white."[14]

In 2007, blacks chaired eight of the twenty-four standing committees in the senate. In 2007, African American lawmaker Demetrius Newton served as Speaker Pro Tempore of the house. While all of the other leadership of the senate was white, Michael Figures had been president pro tempore of the senate before his death in the late 1990s. Black empowerment is evident not just in the very efficient translation of black votes into black seats within the chamber, but also in the translation of black seats into institutional power.

African Americans in Statewide Office

Alabama has had no African Americans elected to statewide constitutional offices, but African Americans have served on its Supreme Court. The first black justice, Oscar Adams, was appointed in 1980 and won reelection in 1982 and 1988. A second African American, Ralph Cook, won a full term on the Supreme Court in 1994 but lost a reelection bid in 2000. In 2000, two other African American judges who had been appointed to statewide appellate panels by Governor Don Siegelman (D) failed in reelection efforts (Judge John England on the Supreme Court and Judge Aubrey Ford on the Court of Criminal Appeals). Hastings Wyman believes that the poor performance of these three black candidates in 2000 discouraged an effort by former Tuskegee mayor and state legislator Rep. Johnny Ford to run for state auditor in 2002.[15] In 2006, England and Aubrey Ford attempted to regain the judicial seats they had lost six years earlier but had no greater success.

Black candidates for statewide judicial posts have fared poorly, but for most of the last decade, white Democrats have fared little better. Although Democrats held eighteen of nineteen appellate court positions in Alabama before 1994, going into the 2006 election Democrats held just one lonely seat on the state Supreme Court. Democratic voting shares have fallen into the very low 40s in many recent contests.

Results for statewide contests held in 2000 and 2006 appear in table 2.3. Of the dozen offices decided in 2000 statewide voting, Democrats triumphed in only the Place 3 seat on the Court of Appeals. Democrats did not even offer a candidate for Place 2 on the Supreme Court. Among the ten Democrats who lost were three African Americans. In the four contested positions for the Supreme Court, Ralph Cook turned in the strongest performance among Democrats, while John England had the third-best performance. The African American member of the Court of Criminal Appeals, Aubrey Ford had the poorest performance among the three Democrats competing for positions on that bench. While Ford ran last among the Democrats competing for the Criminal Appeals Court, his was not the weakest Democratic performance in that year. With 44.5 percent of the vote, Ford did better than Reese who lost Place 3 on the Court of Civil

Appeals with 43.9 percent of the vote and Al Gore who managed only 42.4 percent of the vote in his unsuccessful bid for the presidency.

Table 2.3 also contains the results for twenty statewide contests on the ballot in 2006. Overall, Democrats ran better in 2006 than six years earlier as they won five contests, including both seats on the Public Service Commission. A Democrat was also elected as commissioner of agriculture and lieutenant governor. In the judicial contests, however, the only successful Democrat was Sue Bell Cobb, who was elected as the first female chief justice of the Supreme Court. African American John England turned in the strongest performance of the unsuccessful Democratic nominees for the Supreme Court. Aubrey Ford had the second-strongest performance among three unsuccessful Democratic candidates for the Court of Criminal Appeals. As in 2000, the African American judicial candidates in 2006 did not do significantly worse than white Democratic nominees.

The ability of black candidates to win Democratic nominations received additional confirmation in 2008 when Barack Obama handily defeated Hillary Clinton in the presidential primary. On his way to garnering 56 percent of the vote, Obama attracted the support of 84 percent of the blacks along with a quarter of the white vote according to the exit polls. He did even better among black voters in the general election, with 98 percent of their votes, but support from whites fell to just 12 percent. Obama's experience paralleled that of several other recent black candidates who succeeded in winning the Democratic primary but came up short in the general election.

RACIAL VOTING PATTERNS

As in most of the South, voting in Alabama breaks down along racial/partisan lines, with the black vote solidly behind Democratic candidates and white voters divided but generally and increasingly favoring Republicans. These divisions in congressional elections are structured by incumbency. As described above, a few Democrats have prevailed for major statewide offices in recent years, although the trend statewide is toward the election of Republicans with heavy, white support. Democratic incumbents have proven no more effective than Democratic challengers in winning statewide contests.

TABLE 2.3. Alabama statewide elections, 2000 and 2006

	Democrat	Vote	Republican	Vote
2000				
Supreme Court				
Chief Justice	Yates	726,348	Moore	878,480
Place 1	**Cook**	742,946	Stuart	824,895
Place 2	No Democrat+		Lyons	889,895
Place 3	**England**	714,429	Woodall	846,297
Place 4	Laird	696,705	Harwood	845,141
Civil Appeals				
Place 1	Monroe	757,247	Pittman	771,416
Place 2	Steagall	735,650	Crawley	779,758
Place 3	Reese	676,390	Murdock	863,131
Criminal Appeals				
Place 1	Fry	746,552	Shaw	767,710
Place 2	**Ford**	673,750	Wise	840,282
Place 3	Cobb*	783,962	Martin	746,785
President	Gore	692,611	Bush	941,173
2006				
Governor	Baxley	519,827	Riley	718,327
Lt. Governor	Folsom*	629,208	Strange	610,982
Att'y General	Tyson	576,830	King	653,045
Sec'y of State	Worley	509,797	Chapman	693,334
Treasurer	Segrest	471,570	Ivey	724,861
Auditor	Clarke	531,717	Shaw	627,424
Comm. of Ag.	Sparks*	701,320	Lipscomb	485,275
Public Service Commissioner				
Place 1	Cook*	635,755	Rice	549,601
Place 2	Parker*	633,584	Hooper	550,435
Supreme Court				
Chief Justice	Cobb*	634,494	Nabers	596,237
Place 1	No Democrat		Lyons	763,898
Place 2	Kennedy	506,691	Woodall	665,610
Place 3	Johnson	495,846	Stuart	680,103
Place 4	**England**	532,837	Murdock	651,057
Civil Appeals				
Place 1	Vaughn	514,138	Moore	647,427
Place 2	Drake	543,644	Pittman	608,180
Place 3	McFerrin	525,491	Thomas	620,940
Criminal Appeals				
Place 1	**Ford**	515,889	Shaw	632,224
Place 2	Patton	505,680	Wise	643,492
Place 3	Paseur	552,703	Welch	600,287

Source: www.sos.state.al.us/downloads/election/2000/general/2000g-general.xls (accessed February 24, 2007).

Black candidates in **boldface.**

*Winning Democrats.

+A libertarian polled 225,969 votes.

TABLE 2.4. White and black support for major Democratic Party candidates in Alabama, 1992–2004

Year/Office	White	Black
1992		
President**	31.5	96.0
U.S. Senate*	61.9	97.9
1994		
Governor*	38.2	93.3
1996		
President*	32.2	91.1
U.S. Senate	32.8	86.9
1998		
Governor**	48.3	93.0
U.S. Senate	22.8	82.4
2002		
Governor*	23.9	97.0
U.S. Senate	16.7	93.8
U.S. House	19.5	75.8
2004		
President**	24.1	93.2
U.S. Senate**	19.8	81.5

Source: Exit polls, 1992–2004.

Note: 2002 Voter News Service (VNS) exit polls are considered to have questionable external validity.

*Democratic incumbent seeking reelection.

**Republican incumbent seeking reelection.

Exit poll data in table 2.4 show that by far the highest white vote for a Democratic candidate in the last decade went to Governor Don Siegelman, who got 48.3 percent in 1998. Four years later, when Siegelman's reelection bid narrowly failed, the questionable 2002 exit polls show his white vote down by half. In 2004, Democrats for president and the U.S. Senate failed to attract even a quarter of the white vote, and that puts them at the same level as Siegelman two years earlier. From 1992 to 1996 Democrats usually attracted about a third of the white vote. In statewide contests since 1992, Democrats invariably attracted at least 80 percent of the black vote and frequently drew more than 90 percent.

The role of partisanship is illustrated in the case of Richard Shelby. A Democratic congressman, Shelby commanded almost unanimous support from Alabama's black voters as a Democrat running for the U.S. Senate in 1992, but after switching to the GOP in 1994, he managed only one in six black votes in 1998 and slipped even further in 2004. His white vote swelled from 61.9 percent in 1992 to almost 80 percent twelve years later. His 1992 candidacy is the only recent effort by a Democrat to attract majority-white support, according to the exit polls.

Exit polls ask voters' preferences only for top-of-the-ticket contests. Through the application of regression analysis, estimates of racial support can be developed for a wider range of offices. Table 2.5 presents estimates since 1994 for selected statewide contests. According to data presented in table 2.5, most whites supported only one Democrat running for governor, lieutenant governor, attorney general, or the Supreme Court. Don Siegelman took 59 percent of the white vote when elected lieutenant governor in 1994. That year, incumbent Democratic governor "Little Big Jim" Folsom, Jr., managed just 43.2 percent support from whites in a losing effort. Siegelman achieved the second-highest white percentage reported in table 2.5 when he attracted 49.2 percent of the white vote in his successful gubernatorial bid.

There is a systematic decline in white voter support for Democrats running for the Supreme Court or major statewide offices. In the 1990s, Democrats could usually muster more than 40 percent of the white vote. Beginning with 2000, only three Democrats secured more than 40 percent of the white vote and some candidates fell below 30 percent.

Democrats seeking the three major statewide executive offices have averaged 41.4 percent of the white vote since 1994. In the one office to attract black candidacies, white Democrats running for the Supreme Court had averaged 34.8 percent while black Democrats running for the Supreme Court had averaged 36.8 percent (though just 33.8 percent since 2000). Democrats running statewide get less support among whites in Alabama. The difference observed in black candidate performance seems to be a function more of office and party than of race since Democrats, in general, are losing.

Incumbents have dominated recent congressional contests. The Democratic candidates in table 2.6 most likely to get at least 40 percent of the white

TABLE 2.5. Estimates of white support for Democratic candidates in contested Alabama elections, 1994–2006

	Office	% White	% Total
1994	Governor	43.2	49.4
	Lt. Governor	59.0	62.2
	Att'y General	37.0	43.0
	Supreme Court, S3	45.9	50.5
1996	Supreme Court, S1	43.0	47.2
1998	Governor	49.2	57.7
	Lt. Governor	42.9	49.6
	Att'y General	43.9	49.6
	Supreme Court, S1	44.6	49.7
	Supreme Court, S2	32.5	48.5
	Supreme Court, S3	34.2	52.2
2000	**Chief Justice, Supreme Court**	32.6	45.2
	Supreme Court, S1	38.3	47.4
	Supreme Court, S3	35.0	45.8
	Supreme Court, S4	37.6	45.2
2002	Governor	39.0	49.0
	Lt. Governor	44.0	51.5
	Att'y General	27.8	38.8
	Supreme Court, S1	36.6	46.3
2004	Supreme Court, S1	31.7	44.1
	Supreme Court, S2	26.9	40.0
2006	Governor	32.1	41.9
	Lt. Governor	42.5	50.7
	Att'y General	36.5	46.9
	Chief Justice, Supreme Court	43.4	51.5
	Supreme Court, S2	32.4	43.2
	Supreme Court, S3	31.4	42.2
	Supreme Court, S4	33.6	45.0

Source: Ordinary least squares (OLS) estimates.

Boldface indicates a black Democratic candidate.

vote are incumbents, who, with one exception, ran in Districts 4 and 5. The exception, African American Artur Davis, running in the majority-black 7th District, commanded an estimated majority of the white vote in his 2004 reelection bid. Democrats who challenged Republican incumbents have struggled to poll 20 percent of white vote. Davis proved to be far more attractive to whites than his predecessor, Earl Hilliard, had been in 2000.

TABLE 2.6. Estimates of white support for Alabama's Democratic congressional candidates, 1998–2004

	District	% White	% Total
1998	District 2**	15.1	31.0
	District 3**	26.2	42.0
	District 4**	49.1	56.0
	District 5*	71.0	70.0
	District 6**	20.8	28.0
2000	District 2**	14.2	69.0
	District 4*	40.8	61.0
	District 7*	5.0	75.0
2002	District 1	30.7	60.0
	District 2**	7.3	69.0
	District 3	32.7	50.0
	District 5*	77.0	73.0
2004	District 1**	28.2	37.0
	District 2**	5.8	28.0
	District 3**	19.3	39.0
	District 4**	27.1	25.0
	District 5*	72.1	73.0
	District 7*	50.2	75.0

Source: Ordinary least squares (OLS) estimates.

Boldface indicates that Democratic candidate is black.

*Democratic incumbent running.

**Republican incumbent running.

Thus Davis succeeded in assembling a biracial coalition while Hilliard had owed his office to strong black support in a racially polarized environment.

FEDERAL MONITORING

Between 1982 and 2006, the Department of Justice rejected forty-six proposals for changing election laws and procedures for Alabama. Jurisdictions in the state withdrew another 181 proposed changes after DOJ asked for further information.[16] The federal government has made extensive use of its authority under the Voting Rights Act to send observers in to monitor elections. Over the last forty years, observers have been present for 176 elections in twenty Alabama counties.[17] Fifteen of those counties have been visited by observers since 1982. Perhaps the national record for having had the greatest number of elections monitored goes to Hale County, which has had monitors on the scene for twenty-two separate elections. While, as noted earlier, federal officials did come in and register a number of voters in Alabama in the immediate aftermath of the adoption of the 1965 legislation, that authority has not been used recently in the state.[18]

CONCLUSION

Alabama in 1965 had nearly as far to go as Mississippi along the path of voting rights. The state has made tremendous strides in black voter participation and in descriptive representation. The gap between black and white voter participation has narrowed, and Alabama blacks are more likely to register and vote than their nonsouthern counterparts.

The effort at black voter mobilization has translated into significant gains in terms of descriptive representation. Dramatic gains are evident for school boards and city and county offices, though those gains often came in areas with predominantly black populations. Black state legislators are elected roughly in proportion to the eligible electorate. These black legislators have achieved positions of power and influence within their chambers. In an increasingly Republican state, black votes are necessary, but insufficient, to elect Democratic statewide officeholders.

Efforts to elect black statewide officeholders have been few and generally unsuccessful. One recent successful black statewide candidate—Ralph Cook for Supreme Court—joined white Democrats in being dismissed from the court by the growing Republican electorate. This defeat, while attributed by some observers to race, is consistent with the pattern of failure of a variety of white Democratic statewide candidates to attract sufficient white votes to marry to the united support provided by African American voters. The 2010 candidacy of Arthur Davis, for governor, will provide a stern test of the party/race thesis in Alabama.

CHAPTER 3

Georgia

Georgia has a long legacy of taking actions that have impeded black political participation. In 1871, the state became the first to enact a poll tax, and in 1877, it made the tax cumulative,[1] meaning that past unpaid poll taxes accumulate and an individual must pay the back taxes in order to vote. In the wake of an 1898 Supreme Court decision validating the Mississippi Constitution's restrictions on African American political participation, Georgia joined other southern states in adopting additional prerequisites for registration.[2] These requirements included a literacy test, which required voters to demonstrate their ability to read and write, a property test, an understanding clause, and a grandfather clause. Georgia also adopted provisions limiting participation in the Democratic primary to white voters.[3] Since no Republicans won any major offices in the state for almost a hundred years, the Democratic primary determined who would hold public office in Georgia, in all but a few mountain counties, until the early 1960s.

In 1945, the state legislature adopted a new constitution that abolished the poll tax. It was reluctant, however, to give up the white primary, even though the Supreme Court had banned it in Texas in the 1944 case of *Smith v. Allwright*.[4] In his last gubernatorial bid in 1946, three-time governor Eugene Talmadge ran on a platform that promised to maintain the white primary.[5] Despite his efforts, a number of blacks voted in that year's Democratic primary.[6] In 1947, the General Assembly sought to maintain an all-white primary by removing the state from the operation of the Democratic primary, but acting governor M. E. Thompson vetoed the legislation.[7]

Even with the elimination of the white primary and the poll tax in the 1940s, black registration rates remained low in Georgia into the early 1960s, as the literacy test coupled with frequently antagonistic local registrars discouraged black participation. In the period immediately preceding the enactment of the Voting Rights Act of 1965, only 27.4 percent of Georgia's nonwhite voting-age population was registered to vote, compared with 62.6 percent of the white voting-age population.[8] During this period, only Alabama and Mississippi had smaller proportions of their potential black electorate registered to vote. In thirty Georgia counties with substantial African American populations, less than 10 percent of the age-eligible blacks were registered in 1962. In four of these counties, the voting lists contained the names of fewer than ten nonwhites.[9]

Even though only 167,663 nonwhites had registered to vote in Georgia in 1962, the number of white registrants was high enough that 53.6 percent of the state's total voting-age population was registered, satisfying that portion of the Section 4 trigger. Despite its registration numbers, Georgia's low voter turnout rate made it subject to Section 5. In the 1964 presidential election, the vote cast equaled just 43.2 percent of the state's voting-age population, thus failing to exceed the 50 percent needed to avoid Section 5 coverage.

As in other southern states covered by Section 5 of the VRA, immediate and dramatic change followed the VRA's passage. By 1967, 52.6 percent of Georgia's nonwhite voting-age population had registered to vote.[10] Increased registration also extended to the white population, where just over 80 percent of the age-eligible population had registered to vote.[11]

Particularly dramatic increases in black registration occurred in the thirty Georgia counties that had most consistently rebuffed black political overtures. Table 3.1 reports the white and nonwhite registration rates, as of December 1962, for the thirty counties in which fewer than 10 percent of the age-eligible nonwhites were registered. In these counties, substantially larger shares of the white population were registered.[12] Surprisingly, in a number of the counties, the registration rolls included more names of whites than existed in the age-eligible white population counted in 1960 (indicated by ">100" in the percent column of table 3.1). While nonwhites found it difficult to register, comparable barriers did not dissuade whites.

Within two years after passage of the VRA, registration rates for nonwhites increased in each of these thirty counties. In all but four of the counties, more than 10 percent of the nonwhite adults had registered. In eight counties, a majority of nonwhite adults had signed up to vote. Baker County, with 71.7 percent of its nonwhite adults on the voting lists, led the way toward enfranchisement. The median level of nonwhite registration in 1967 was 28.25 percent, as compared to 5.6 percent in 1962, indicating that while some progress had been made, much remained to be done to extend suffrage to Georgia's black population. Chattahoochee County, one of the counties with very low registration in 1962, was the only one in which a higher proportion of nonwhite than white registrants had signed up to vote by 1967. Because of the large concentration of military personnel in that county, however, only 7.2 percent of the adult nonwhites and 6.3 percent of the whites had registered.

As shown in table 3.1, in each of the thirty counties with low rates of black registration in 1962, African American registration had become widespread by 2004. In every county except Chattahoochee, most adults had registered. The mean for the thirty counties in 2004 was 69.6 percent, and in eight counties, registration exceeded 75 percent.

In addition to this progress in African American voter registration, black turnout also increased in Georgia in the forty years after passage of the VRA. In every one of the thirty counties, at least a majority of registered black women voted in 2004. In the Atlanta suburbs of Fayette County, 88 percent of registered black women and 82 percent of registered black men participated. A higher proportion of black female registrants than white male registrants voted in Chattahoochee, Fayette, and Marion counties, and in a number of suburban counties the participation rates of black females almost equaled that of whites. Despite this evidence of success, the more common pattern was for black turnout rates to lag behind those for whites, especially in rural counties. Participation rates among African American men also invariably lagged behind those of black women, often with a disparity of more than 10 percentage points.

Table 3.1. White and nonwhite registration, 1962 and 2004, and turnout, 2004, in thirty Georgia counties

	1962 Nonwhite Registrants	% Registration 1962		% Registration 1967		% Black Registration 2004	% General Election Turnout 2004			
		Nonwhite	White	Nonwhite	White		Black Female	Black Male	White Female	White Male
Baker	24	1.9	>100	71.7	>100	76.5	77	69	81	79
Bleckley	45	3.3	73.9	20.8	>100	55.4	75	55	80	79
Burke	427	6.5	84.1	41.8	99.7	73.5	72	63	79	78
Calhoun	145	6	>100	24.6	>100	55.8	68	59	76	76
Chattahoochee	17	0.9	4.2	7.2	6.3	35.1	60	49	65	55
Early	261	8	92.9	20	>100	68.3	55	46	78	78
Echols	19	7.7	92.9	7.7	>100	63.7	51	41	66	62
Fayette	26	2.2	77	5.7	84.9	118.2*	88	82	88	85
Glascock	1	0.3	>100	6	>100	59.4	74	62	82	85
Harris	263	8.5	>100	36.1	>100	69.3	72	55	80	78
Houston	413	9.8	44	54.8	80.1	69.4	79	73	80	80
Jeff Davis	56	6.2	>100	65	>100	76.9	64	55	70	70
Jefferson	283	5.9	82	54.9	91.6	71.9	72	55	81	79
Lee	29	1.6	84.8	55	>100	65	76	64	82	79
Lincoln	3	0.2	>100	47.6	>100	67.7	71	62	80	81
McDuffie	251	9.2	87.5	41.4	98.6	61.6	69	61	80	78
Madison	55	5.6	77	26.4	80.1	57.8	78	66	80	80
Marion	55	3.4	>100	17.4	>100	83.4	74	60	76	72
Miller	6	0.6	>100	19.9	52.9	72	53	40	73	71
Mitchell	375	7.5	>100	29.7	95.1	52.9	69	57	80	79
Quitman	38	5.4	>100	25.6	>100	84.6	64	55	68	66
Seminole	11	0.9	>100	33.9	>100	66.9	57	48	72	71
Stewart	136	5.1	>100	26.4	>100	78.9	68	49	77	73

Table 3.1. White and nonwhite registration, 1962 and 2004, and turnout, 2004, in thirty Georgia counties (*continued*)

	1962 Nonwhite Registrants	% Registration 1962		% Registration 1967		% Black Registration 2004	% General Election Turnout 2004			
		Nonwhite	White	Nonwhite	White		Black Female	Black Male	White Female	White Male
Sumter	548	8.2	73.5	46.7	>100	65.8	68	55	80	80
Talbot	219	8.7	>100	25.9	>100	79.7	74	66	79	77
Terrell	98	2.4	96.6	53.9	>100	65	69	56	83	82
Treutlen	45	4.6	100	62.1	85.4	74.3	71	60	76	73
Warren	188	8.4	85.8	63.7	>100	73.7	70	58	85	81
Webster	9	0.9	98.8	26.8	>100	76.5	71	60	83	82
Worth	296	7.8	>100	25.8	85.8	59	62	56	80	78

Sources: U.S. Commission on Civil Rights, *Political Participation* (Washington, D.C.: U.S. Government Printing Office, 1968); www.sos.state.ga.us/ELECTIONS/voter_registration/credit_for_voting_reports.htm.

*Fayette County has experienced an influx of African Americans since 2000, which is reflected in the registration data.

Turning to the United States Census Bureau survey of registration and turnout (appendix B) offers a look at the self-reported participation rates from 1980 to 2006. By 1980, 59.8 percent of voting-age African Americans reported having registered compared with 67 percent of whites. During the 1980s, approximately 7 percentage points more whites than blacks were registered. By 1990, black and white Georgians had nearly identical registration rates: 57 percent of African Americans of voting age reported being registered, compared with 58.1 percent of whites. In 1994, a larger proportion of blacks (57.6 percent) than whites (55 percent) had registered. Blacks have reported registering at higher rates than whites in four of the seven most recent elections, including the two most recent presidential elections. In the 2002 midterm election, when more voting-age whites than blacks reported registering, the disparity was only 1.1 percentage points, but in 2006 the gap had grown to 4.2 points.

The figures for whites are comparable across the twenty-four–year period. However, in recent years Georgia has experienced a large Hispanic influx. The 2000 census reported almost half a million Hispanics in Georgia, but as of 2004 barely thirty thousand—approximately 27 percent of Hispanics eligible to vote—had registered to vote, suggesting that limiting voting data to non-Hispanic whites will result in a higher percentage of the white voting-age population being registered. Once Hispanics are excluded, white registration has exceeded that for blacks since 2002. In 2004, for example, 64.2 percent of blacks and 68 percent of non-Hispanic whites reporting registering, as compared to only 63.5 percent of all whites. Even after removing Hispanics from the estimates, however, higher proportions of blacks than whites reported registering in 1998 and 2000.

Comparing the registration rates in Georgia to those of nonsoutherners shows that from 1980 through 1994, blacks living outside the South invariably reported higher rates of registration that did Georgia blacks. In 1982, 1984, 1988, and 1992, the difference was approximately 10 percentage points. Beginning with 1996, however, self-reported registration rates among Georgia blacks have exceeded those of blacks outside the region.

These data show that even before the implementation of the Motor Voter Act in 1993 and the Help America Vote Act of 2002, both of which were designed to facilitate registration and participation, the disparity in black and white registration rates had largely been eliminated. In 2004, African Americans constituted 27.4 percent of all registered voters in Georgia and 27.2 percent of the Georgia citizen voting-age population.[13]

VOTER TURNOUT

The racial disparity in voter turnout in Georgia has also diminished. As shown in appendix B, in 1980 the Census Bureau estimated that 43.7 percent of age-eligible African Americans voted in the general election, compared with 56 percent of whites. In the midterm election of 1982, the racial disparity dropped to 8.2 percentage points. Voting trends between 1980 and 2006 indicate greater racial disparity in presidential than in midterm elections. Until 1996, at least 10 percent more whites than blacks voted in presidential elections, and even in 1996, white turnout exceeded the black figure by almost 7 percentage points. In contrast, in midterm elections, the greatest racial differences—which occurred in 1982 and 1994—have been approximately 8 percentage points. In 1990, almost identical percentages of black and white Georgians went to the polls.

Black voter turnout has continued to rise in the twenty-first century, particularly in presidential elections. Reported black turnout rates remained around 40 to 45 percent until 2000, when 51.6 percent of age-eligible blacks in Georgia reported voting. In the same election, only 48.3 percent of age-eligible whites reported voting. In the most recent presidential election included in the tables (2004), black participation rates again slightly exceeded those for whites. In midterm elections, which traditionally have lower turnout among both blacks and whites, black voter participation has not been so strong. The proportion of age-eligible blacks voting in midterm elections peaked in 1990 at 42.3 percent; after 1990, the number seesawed, dropping to 30.9 percent in 1994, rising to just over 40 percent in 1998, and then ebbing to between 38 and 39 percent in 2002 and 2006. Black turnout in a midterm election exceeded white turnout only in 1998.

Excluding data for Hispanic whites results in a higher turnout rate for non-Hispanic whites, although from 1998 to 2002, the increase was less than 2 percentage points. From 1998 to 2004, turnout rates for blacks and non-Hispanic whites in Georgia differed by fewer than 5 percentage points. In 1998 and 2000, black turnout exceeded the non-Hispanic white figure by at least 2 percentage points. In 2002, the non-Hispanic white turnout rate was 4.5 percentage points above the black rate, and in 2004 it was 3 points higher than the black rate. In the most recent election covered by the data, however, blacks fell 7.6 points behind non-Hispanic whites.

As is the case with registration rates, progress in voter turnout can also be evaluated by comparing Georgia to states outside the South. In 1982, for example, the difference between nonsouthern blacks and blacks in Georgia reached 16 percentage points, and it declined only slightly, to 13 percentage points in the next presidential election. In the five most recent elections through 2006, however, the reported participation rates for African Americans in Georgia and nonsouthern states have been essentially equal. These data suggest that much of the disparity in voter turnout of twenty years ago has been eliminated. In particular, in two of the five most recent election years covered in the table, the reported black participation rate in Georgia exceeded that for the state's non-Hispanic whites, while outside the South, black participation rates have approximated those for Georgia African Americans since 1998.

Data from the Secretary of State

A problem with self-reported political participation data, such as that compiled by the U.S. Census Bureau, is that respondents tend to give socially approved answers[14]—some individuals who were unregistered will tell a pollster that they had registered, and because of the heavy emphasis placed upon the civic duty of voting, a number of nonvoters will report that they went to the polls. Georgia is one of five states that maintains voter registration data by race, making it possible to have more accurate registration data concerning race. Since 1996, Georgia's secretary of state has conducted a postelection audit of voter turnout by going through voter sign-in sheets and cross-checking that information against the registration data showing the voter's race. Unlike the figures provided by the Census Bureau, these are not estimates but actual counts. As shown in table 3.2, the number of black registrants in Georgia increased by more than 265,000 between 1996 and 2006. In 1996, African Americans constituted 24.4 percent of all registrants, but by 2006 they accounted for 28 percent of registrants.

TABLE 3.2. Official registration and turnout in Georgia, 1996–2006

	Registration		Turnout		Turnout %	
	Black	White	Black	White	Black	White
1996	929,525	2,822,012	497,086	1,814,983	53.5	64.3
1998	971,847	2,867,910	415,839	1,382,647	42.8	48.2
2000	980,033	2,792,479	615,723	1,993,493	62.8	71.4
2002	962,720	2,695,306	458,640	1,536,635	47.6	57.0
2004	1,155,706	2,917,322	834,331	2,344,632	72.2	80.4
2006	1,198,259	2,963,854	512,495	1,553,839	42.8	52.4

Source: Georgia Secretary of State, www.sos.state.ga.us/elections/.

The Georgia secretary of state data demonstrate that black turnout has also increased. As reported in table 3.2, slightly fewer than 500,000 Georgia African Americans voted in the 1996 presidential election. Eight years later, the number of blacks voting for president increased by 337,000. During the same eight-year span, the share of all black registrants going to the polls in presidential elections grew from 53.5 percent to 72.2 percent. The number of additional blacks voting exceeded the number of new black registrants by almost half, indicating that a substantial number of blacks came to the polls who had previously registered but not voted. The number of blacks participating in midterm elections also grew, but just kept pace with increased registration so the turnout percentage in 2006 remained what it had been eight years earlier after having peaked at 47.6 percent in 2002. Yet while the percentage of black registrants who voted increased, black turnout trailed white turnout. As table 3.2 shows, the black turnout rate in 1996 was almost 11 percentage points less than the white turnout rate. The disparity shrank to 8.6 points in 2000 and was down to 8.2 percent in 2004, when 72.2 percent of black registrants and 80.4 percent of white registrants voted, but expanded to almost 10 points in 2006. The Census Bureau statistics for voter turnout, while calculated differently, also affirm higher white non-Hispanic turnout.[15] Despite the disparity between whites and blacks, the variation in the participation rates for both groups indicates that blacks are not subject to systematic discrimination at the polling place; in fact, the black turnout rate in 2004 exceeds the white turnout rate in previous years.

AFRICAN AMERICAN OFFICE HOLDING

Since the passage of the VRA, African Americans have become much more successful at winning elected offices in Georgia. When Congress adopted that legislation, the state had only three African Americans holding office. In 1969, thirty African Americans held office in Georgia, fourteen of whom served in the state legislature.[16] Another eight sat on city councils and three served on school boards. By 1973, the number of black officials in Georgia had risen to one hundred, and three years later it topped two hundred. By 1984, just over three hundred African Americans held public office in Georgia, with 170 serving on city councils and another fifty-eight serving on school boards.

The number of African American officeholders continued to grow through the 1980s, in part because of a 1982 amendment to the VRA's Section 2. As a consequence of this change, single-member district systems replaced many at-large systems, and the number of African American officeholders continued to grow (see figure 3.1). By 1987, the total number of blacks holding public office in Georgia was almost 150 percent higher than the 1984 figure. By 1991, more than five hundred blacks were serving in Georgia. After 1991, however, the growth rate slowed; in 2001, 611 African Americans held office in Georgia. As in previous years, approximately half of black office holders in 2001 served at the municipal level, with another hundred serving in county offices and a slightly larger number sitting on school boards. By some estimates Georgia currently has more than eight hundred black elected officials.[17] The next sections will review the growth in the number of African Americans in Congress, the state legislature, and statewide offices.

African Americans in Congress

Since 1972, when Georgia and Texas became the first southern states to elect an African American to Congress in the twentieth century, African Americans have succeeded by fashioning biracial coalitions in majority-white districts. The first African American politician to do so in Georgia was civil rights activist Andrew Young. Young was elected to the U.S. House in his second effort, two years after he won the Democratic nomination but lost in the general election to a Republican incumbent. Young triumphed in the 5th

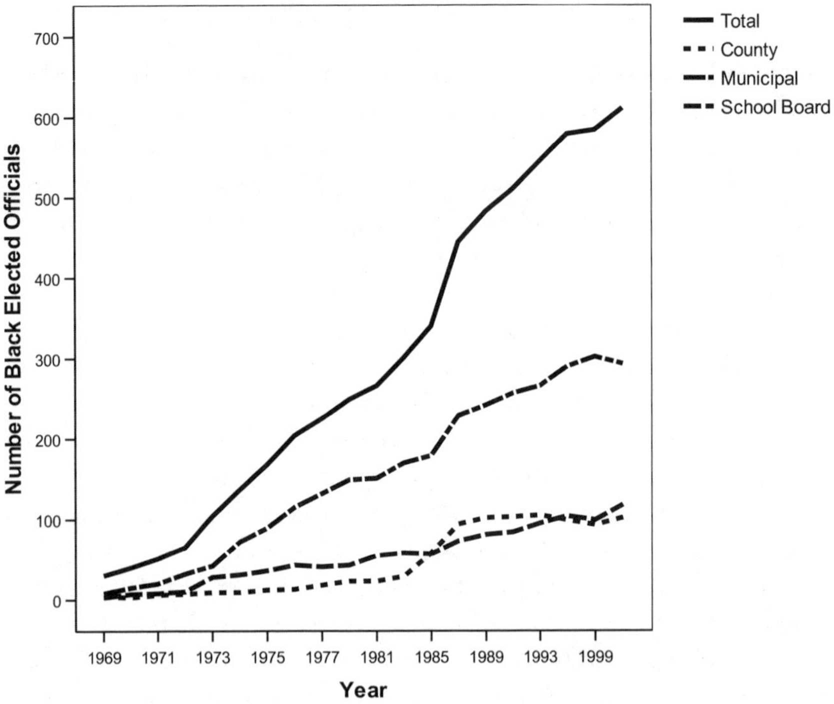

Figure 3.1. Black elected officials in Georgia, 1969–2001. *Source:* Various volumes of the *National Roster of Black Elected Officials* (Washington, D.C.: Joint Center for Political and Economic Studies).

Congressional District, which was 44 percent black. He won reelection in 1974 and 1976, taking two-thirds of the vote in the latter general election. After his third victory, Young resigned from Congress when President Carter named him U.S. ambassador to the United Nations.

In the special election following Young's resignation, white liberal Wyche Fowler led a field of twelve candidates with 40 percent of the vote. In the subsequent runoff, Fowler easily defeated civil rights hero John Lewis with 62 percent of the vote. Fowler held the 5th Congressional District seat for a decade, during which he defeated a number of African American challengers. He continued to win even after the district became 65 percent African American in 1982. As had been the case with his predecessor, Fowler succeeded by appealing to a biracial coalition.

When Fowler ran for the U.S. Senate in 1986, a large field of candidates—all but one of whom was African American—entered the 5th District Democratic primary. State senator Julian Bond led the primary with 47 percent of the vote while John Lewis polled 35 percent of the vote. Lewis prevailed in the runoff by winning more than 80 percent of the white vote. Bond attracted the bulk of the black vote, but Lewis's biracial coalition produced a 52 percent majority.

The 1992 elections sent two more African Americans to Congress: Sanford Bishop, from the 2nd District in southwest Georgia, and Cynthia McKinney, who won the 11th District, which stretched from Atlanta's eastern suburbs to Augusta and Savannah. With three African Americans in the eleven-person delegation, blacks achieved a level of representation in the House equal to their share of Georgia's 1990 population.

In 2002, David Scott became the fourth African American in Georgia's House delegation. With four African Americans in Congress at one time, Georgia had the largest number of black members, compared to its population, to represent any state in Congress. Other states that have had four African Americans serving in the House have much larger delegations than Georgia's thirteen seats.[18] When Scott joined Georgia delegation, African Americans' share of Georgia House seats (31 percent) exceeded the percentage of blacks in Georgia's 2000 population (29.5 percent).

A black majority in the population—to say nothing of a black majority among registrants—is not necessary for African Americans to win Georgia congressional seats. Of thirty-three congressional elections won by African Americans since 1972, fifteen occurred in districts in which less than half of the population was black. Of the eighteen contests won by African Americans in majority-black districts, eleven occurred in the 5th District. Sanford Bishop won six of his eight elections since 1992 when his district had a white majority. Even in the two elections when his southwest Georgia district had a black majority, most registrants were white. David Scott has also won in a district where blacks did not constitute a majority of either the population or the registrants. Three of Cynthia McKinney's six victories from 1992 to 2004 came in a district in which whites outnumbered blacks. The ability of African Americans to win congressional seats in districts in which most voters are white provides evidence that at least a share of the white electorate is quite willing to have a black representative.

When the Department of Justice (DOJ) reviewed Georgia's congressional districting plans in the early 1990s, however, it seemed to assume that African Americans could be elected only from majority-black districts. DOJ rejected the state's first two districting plans and demanded three majority-black districts.[19] DOJ's assumption was put to the test after the Supreme Court struck down Georgia's 11th District for violating the Equal Protection Clause of the Fourteenth Amendment to the U.S. Constitution.[20] The Court concluded that, in drawing this district, the General Assembly had violated the U.S. Constitution by relying predominately on race in determining the district's boundaries; the district's "irregular shape," with "several appendages drawn for the obvious purpose of putting black populations into the [d]istrict," subordinated traditional districting principles such as "compactness, contiguity, and respect for political subdivisions."[21] The *Miller* decision sparked widespread concern, especially in the minority community, that redrawing the majority-black districts to increase their white populations would end the careers of African American legislators.[22] The 1996 election proved those fears to be unfounded, as both Bishop and McKinney easily won reelection in their new majority-white districts, defeating white challengers in both the Democratic primary and the general election.

Some sought to discount these victories by attributing them to incumbency, asserting that had the seats been open, whites would have won.[23] The 2002 election provided a partial test of that proposition. Black state senator David Scott faced three experienced challengers, including another black state senator, a white state senator, and a former white congressional candidate who had most recently served as executive director of Georgia's Democratic Party. Not only did Scott turn back these qualified opponents, but he also managed to win a majority of the vote in the Democratic primary for this open seat, thus avoiding a runoff.

Not all black congressional candidates succeeded in 2002. While Scott won his majority-white district, an African American nominee lost in the 12th District, which had approximately the same racial composition. In that race, African American Champ Walker, a political novice, won the Democratic nomination in a runoff against another black contender. Walker, however, proved to be a deeply flawed candidate. He had been arrested multiple times, although never convicted, and he ran an inept campaign in which he performed poorly in some debates and avoided others. Walker's greatest strength—his father, Charles Walker—may have also proven to be his greatest liability. The elder Walker served as the majority leader in the state senate when the General Assembly drew the district in which his son ran, but suspicions of corruption had surrounded him, and the elder Walker was ultimately convicted on more than 125 federal charges. Champ Walker lost the general election, taking only 45 percent of the vote.

The 2001 redistricting also gave Georgia's 3rd District a substantial black minority. The population of this middle Georgia district, centered on Macon, was just under 40 percent black. The African American who ran in the district's Democratic primary finished third, winning only 11 percent of the vote. His low vote count suggests that he failed to unify the support of the black population, which constituted 35 percent of the district's registrants. At least a partial explanation for his lack of success may be that the most powerful black politician in the district, Robert Brown, who had been the vice chair of the Senate Reapportionment Committee, managed the campaign of the successful white Democrat Jim Marshall.

African Americans in the State Legislature

With his election in 1962, state senator Leroy Johnson became the first black southern legislator in modern times. A second black entered the fifty-four–member senate before passage of the 1965 VRA. As table 3.3 shows, increases in the number of seats held by African Americans in the senate came slowly as the institution had only two black members until after the redistricting following the 1980 census, when the number doubled to four. By 1985, blacks held more than a tenth of the seats in the senate which now had 56 seats. Gradual increases continued, and by 1997, the black delegation constituted almost a fifth of the senate—a figure that, aside from a dip in 2003, persisted through 2005. A twelfth African American won a senate seat in 2006.

The first African Americans in the state house of representatives since Reconstruction arrived following implementation of the one-person, one-vote districting plan in a 1965 special election. After that election, African Americans held seven out of 205 house seats, or roughly 3 percent. By 1975,

TABLE 3.3. Racial makeup of the Georgia General Assembly, 1963–2007

	Senate	% Black in Senate	House	% Black in House
1963	1	1.9	0	0.0
1965	2	3.7	7	3.4
1967	2	3.7	9	4.4
1969	2	3.6	12	6.2
1971	2	3.6	13	6.7
1973	2	3.6	14	7.8
1975	2	3.6	19	10.6
1977	2	3.6	21	11.7
1979	2	3.6	21	11.7
1981	2	3.6	21	11.7
1983	4	7.1	21	11.7
1985	6	10.7	21	11.7
1987	6	10.7	24	13.3
1989	7	12.5	25	13.9
1991	8	14.3	27	15.0
1993	9	16.1	31	17.2
1995	10	17.9	32	17.8
1997	11	19.6	33	18.3
1999	11	19.6	33	18.3
2001	11	19.6	36	20.0
2003*	10	17.9	39	21.7
2005*	11	19.6	39	21.7
2007+	12	21.4	43	23.9

Source: Charles S. Bullock III, "Georgia," in *The New Politics of the Old South*, 3rd ed., ed. Charles S. Bullock III and Mark J. Rozell (Boulder, Colo.: Rowman and Littlefield Press, 2007).

*The House has two Latino members and the Senate has one.

+The House has three Latino members.

African Americans held a tenth of the house seats, a chamber now reduced to 180 seats. African American representation in the house then stalled for a decade, before beginning a gradual rise in 1987. By 2001, blacks held a fifth of the house seats; following redistricting, their share increased to 21.7 percent. After the 2006 general election, blacks held almost a quarter of the house seats. In 2005, for the first time in modern memory, the house included a Republican African American. A special election in 2006 brought a second black Republican to the house.

Growing black representation in the General Assembly has occurred even as the number of Democrats in the legislature has decreased. The 2007 senate has more black Democrats (twelve) than white Democrats (ten), and the house has thirty-one white, forty-one black, and one Hispanic.

During the last session in which Democrats had majorities in both chambers (2002), blacks chaired seven of twenty-three standing committees in the senate including the Rules Committee—the chamber's most powerful—on which they had four of fourteen seats. A black also chaired the Reapportionment Committee, which redrew senate districts in 2001. In the house, blacks chaired six of thirty-three committees including the Rules Committee, which, like in the senate, serves a critical gatekeeping function since legislation must be placed on the Rules calendar to have any chance of being called up for consideration on the floor. In 2002, African Americans served as the majority leader of the senate, the Democratic caucus chair, and secretary in the house. In both chambers African Americans served on Governor Roy Barnes's leadership team.[24]

The end of Democratic control of the legislature early in the twenty-first century greatly reduced African American influence. Republicans chair all house committees, and the two black Republicans lack the seniority needed to lead a committee. The senate has a tradition of token bipartisanship with a few members of the minority party named to lead minor committees. In 2007, three senate committees had Democratic chairs, one of whom was black.

Although the triumph of the GOP has greatly curtailed the influence of blacks in the General Assembly, when Democrats maintained majorities in the face of a rising tide of Republicans, African Americans frequently secured support of their white Democratic colleagues and enacted their policy preferences. During the 1990s and into the early 2000s, the Legislative Black Caucus (LBC) could demand reciprocity since it provided the votes essential to the success of gubernatorial proposals. The LBC positioned itself to secure benefits by backing the Democrats who won the party primary and went on to lead the state.[25] The LBC got what it wanted in redistricting and pressured Governor Barnes to take the lead in replacing the state flag that had been adopted in 1956, most of which was devoted to the stars and bars of the Confederate battle flag. After an extensive review of roll call voting in the General Assembly from 1992 to 1999, Wielhouwer and Middlemass sum up: "We can confidently conclude that substantive representation of the African American community, here defined as legislative outcomes coinciding with LBC votes, was largely attained by the Georgia General Assembly during the 1990s."[26]

African Americans in Statewide Office

Robert Benham became the first African American to hold a statewide elective post in 1984 when Governor Joe Frank Harris named him to the Court of Appeals, the state's second-highest tribunal. African Americans have had a substantial measure of electoral success in statewide offices, particularly the state judiciary.[27]

Benham won reelection to his post and held it until being appointed to the Supreme Court of Georgia, when he was succeeded on the Court of Appeals by Clarence Cooper, a black superior court judge. In time Cooper became a federal district judge, and John Ruffin, another African American, succeeded him. Ruffin was subsequently returned to the bench without opposition twice. In 1999, Governor Roy Barnes appointed two African Americans, Yvette Miller and Herbert Phipps, to newly created seats on the Court of Appeals, and both Miller and Phipps have subsequently won reelection to the Court of Appeals with no opposition.

Benham again led the way for blacks in the Georgia judiciary when, in 1989, he was appointed to a vacancy on the state Supreme Court and became the first African American to serve on the state's highest tribunal. He won reelection in 1990 by defeating a white challenger. In 1992, Leah Sears became the first African American woman to serve on the Supreme Court when Governor Zell Miller appointed her to a vacancy. Benham and Sears have both repeatedly won six-year terms, sometimes by defeating white challengers and at other times by running unopposed. In her third victory, Sears defeated a white conservative who had strong support from Governor Sonny Perdue and from other leading Republicans. In June 2005, Governor Perdue tapped a third African American, Harold Melton, to the seven-person Supreme Court. Melton, who had been the governor's executive counsel, won election to the remainder of the term without opposition.

African Americans have won two of Georgia's constitutional offices. Former state representative Thurbert Baker had previously been appointed to an interim vacancy as attorney general of Georgia, and in 1998, he won a full term against a strong challenge from a Republican senator. He won reelections in 2002 and 2006. The second African American to win a constitutional office was Michael Thurmond, a former state legislator, who was elected as the state labor commissioner. Thurmond's victory came after he won the nomination in a Democratic runoff and then turned back a Republican opponent. Like Baker, Thurmond won additional terms in 2002 and 2006. In 2000, another African American, David Burgess, became the first African American to hold one of the five seats on the state Public Service Commission. Burgess won reelection in 2002 but lost a reelection bid in 2006.

Georgia elects thirty-four officials statewide: two U.S. senators, eight constitutional officers, seven members of the Supreme Court, twelve members of the Court of Appeals, and five members of the Public Service Commission. In 2007, eight of these thirty-four statewide officials were African American, resulting in a black share of statewide offices (23.5 percent) slightly less than the proportion of blacks in Georgia's voting-age population (27.2 percent). The proportion of black statewide officials had been 26.5 percent until Burgess lost in a general election runoff.[28] Of the fifteen statewide officials elected on partisan ballots, only three were Democrats in 2007 and two of those are African Americans.[29]

All the African Americans who have won statewide elections in Georgia have done so with substantial white support. The data in table 3.2 indicate that whites cast approximately three-fourths of the votes in a typical general election, making it impossible for an African American to win a majority by mobilizing only black support.

The successes enjoyed by black candidates in statewide contests have extended to Democratic presidential contests. Jesse Jackson led the field in 1988, and in 2008 Barack Obama got a larger share of the primary vote in Georgia (66 percent) than in any other state including his home state of Illinois. He managed this feat by taking 88 percent of the black vote along with 43 percent of the white vote, according to exit polls.

REDISTRICTING

In agreeing to reduce minority concentrations during the 2001 redistricting, members of Georgia's Legislative Black Caucus accepted the analysis prepared by David Epstein, the expert employed by Attorney General Thurbert Baker in anticipation of court challenges to the state's redistricting plans. Epstein concluded that African Americans had a reasonable chance of winning election in districts where blacks constituted no more than a large minority of the voting-age population (VAP).[30] Specifically, he estimated that a legislative district without an incumbent needed a 44 percent black VAP (BVAP) for African Americans to have a 50 percent chance of electing their preferred candidate.[31] Charles Walker clearly bought into Epstein's analysis. When asked about the black VAP needed for African Americans to have an equal chance of winning in Georgia, Walker testified, "Forty percent and above. Generally around the state, I would feel comfortable at a 45 percent BVAP level."[32] As the black VAP rises above 44 percent, the probability of electing a black candidate increases.

As shown in table 3.4, the 2001 redistricting substantially reduced the percentage of African American registrants in the majority-black districts. Both the senate plan adopted in 2001 and the one it replaced featured a dozen districts in which blacks constituted the majority of the population, but four of the reapportioned districts changed from being majority black to majority white among registered voters. Redistricting reduced the number of senate districts in which the black registration figure exceeded 55 percent from eleven to seven.

In the Section 5 preclearance hearing conducted by the District Court for the District of Columbia on Georgia's 2001 redistricting plans, the Department of Justice (DOJ) voiced no concerns about congressional or state house districts and accepted the reductions in black concentration in all but three senate districts.[33] DOJ even accepted District 15, in which the black VAP fell from 61.6 to 50.9 percent, and the drop from 63.1 to 51.5 percent in District 22. In both districts, more than 64 percent of the registrants had been black, while under the new plan, blacks accounted for about half the registrants. Even the three senate districts (2, 12, and 26) to which DOJ objected were subsequently approved once the U.S. Supreme

TABLE 3.4. Change in black voting-age population and registration in majority-black districts after first 2001 senate plan in Georgia

Senate district	Population deviation	Black % of voting-age population			Black % of registration	
		2001 plan	Pre-2001 plan	% change	2001 plan	Pre-2001 plan
2	–3.12	50.31	60.30	–9.99	48.42	62.38
10	–4.96	64.14	70.30	–6.16	63.06	69.81
12	–4.15	50.66	55.30	–4.64	47.46	52.48
15	–4.67	50.87	61.60	–10.73	50.25	72.69
22	–4.85	51.51	63.10	–11.59	49.44	64.07
26	–4.39	50.80	62.30	–11.50	48.27	62.79
35	–1.76	60.69	75.60	–14.91	64.73	81.00
36	–4.73	56.94	60.00	–3.06	58.65	61.39
38	–4.76	60.29	76.30	–16.01	60.38	75.33
39	–4.98	56.54	54.40	2.14	59.79	59.46
43	–4.79	62.63	88.40	–25.77	63.11	89.14
55	–4.97	60.64	71.90	–11.26	60.99	73.07
Average		56.34	66.63	–10.29		

Source: Computed from data provided by the Georgia General Assembly Reapportionment Office, accessed at www.georgia2000.org/.

Court found that the district court did not consider the correct factors in determining that the 2001 Georgia districting plans violated Section 5.[34]

Most black leaders who took a stand supported the redistricting plan at issue in *Georgia v. Ashcroft*. Attorney General Thurbert Baker pursued the appeal to the Supreme Court challenging the district court finding that three senate districts violated the VRA by reducing black concentrations. He persisted in this appeal even after Georgia's new governor, Sonny Perdue (R), ordered him to abandon it.[35]

Congressman John Lewis also supported reducing minority concentrations in legislative districts. Explaining why he did not object to the changes, even though the black percentage in his district dropped from 62 to 56 percent, Lewis said, "[Georgia] is not the same state it was. It's not the same state that it was in 1965 or in 1975, or even in 1980 or 1990. We have changed. We've come a great distance. . . . It's not just in Georgia, but in the American South, I think people are preparing to lay down the burden of race."[36] Elsewhere in his testimony, Lewis elaborated:

> I think many voters, white and black voters, in metro Atlanta and elsewhere in Georgia, have been able to see black candidates get out and campaign and work hard for all voters. And they have seen people deal with issues as, I said before, that transcend race: economic issues, environmental issues, issues of war and peace. . . . So there has been a transformation, it's a different state, it's a different political climate, it's a different political environment. It's altogether a different world that we live in, really.[37]

Robert Brown, an African American who served as vice chair of the Senate Reapportionment Committee, also agreed that major changes have taken place in Georgia in recent years. He testified that "[t]here has been some change from that rigid, 'if there's an African American on the ticket, there's an automatic "no" votes for whites.'"[38] Senator Brown also testified that his fellow African American senators strongly supported the redistricting plan. As he pointed out, "The Senate Plan would not have passed without [black] support."[39] Brown opined that a district with a 50 BVAP could likely be won by an African American even if the candidate was competing for an open seat and lacked the advantages of incumbency.[40]

Because the rate of white registration tends to exceed that of black registration and white registrants vote at higher rates than black registrants, it is likely that whites would constitute most of the voters in at least five of the previously majority-black districts in the 2001 plan. Therefore, the implication of the Epstein analysis, which was accepted by the Legislative Black Caucus, is that African American candidates can attract a sufficient share of the white vote to win in these districts. Indeed, evidence both from statewide elections and some congressional elections indicates that African Americans now enjoy a degree of success in Georgia even when the majority of the electorate is white. The blacks who have won statewide contests have succeeded at a time when blacks cast no more than a quarter of all votes, indicating a substantial white crossover vote for African American candidates.

RACIAL AND PARTY VOTING PATTERNS

The willingness of the Department of Justice to accept reductions in black concentrations in several districts in Georgia's 2001 redistricting plans

TABLE 3.5. Racial voting patterns in black-white contests for Georgia's 5th Congressional District

	Support for black candidate(s)	
	White voters (%)	Black voters (%)
1970 primary	23	99
1970 runoff	32	100
1970 general	19	100
1972 primary	39	100
1972 general	25	100
1974 general	55	100
1976 general	44	100
1977 primary	5	98
1977 runoff	4	96
1978 primary	6	34
1982 general	10	31

Source: Ordinary least squares (OLS) estimates computed by the authors from official election returns.

and the acceptance by the U.S. Supreme Court of even the districts that DOJ found to be problematic indicate that key federal authorities now believe that blacks can succeed in districts that are not dominated by African American voters. A chief consideration is that while in the past blacks were more willing to support a white candidate than white voters were to vote for a black candidate, the situation has changed dramatically.

Table 3.5 presents estimates of black and white support for African American candidates who ran for Congress in the 5th Congressional District from 1970 through 1982. Andrew Young, an African American, won the Democratic nomination in this predominantly white (44 percent black) district in 1970, although he lost the general election. From 1972 to 1976, Young won the seat with near-unanimous black support while garnering a substantial white vote, attracting a white majority in the 1974 general election. When Young left Congress, Wyche Fowler, a white Democrat, won a 1977 special election in a highly polarized environment. In his first election, Fowler won without black support, but the sharp decrease in black support for black candidates in 1978 indicates that Fowler, like his predecessor, fashioned a biracial coalition. During Fowler's tenure, white support for his black opponents dropped to 10 percent or less.

Today, black candidates can count on more support from the white electorate than white candidates receive from the black electorate, as shown in tables 3.6 and 3.7. Table 3.6 presents the post-1990 estimates of racial voting patterns in Georgia congressional races. African American candidates often poll 30 percent or more of the white vote and at least 90 percent of the black vote. The African American who ran poorest is Denise Freeman in 1998, who took on popular incumbent Charlie Norwood. While Freeman received strong support from African American voters, she polled little more than a fifth of the white vote. In recent years, African American candidates, with the notable exception of John Lewis in 1998, have been unable to attract a majority of white voters.

Table 3.7 shows, however, that white Democrats have also failed to carry the increasingly Republican white vote. In neither 1996 nor 1998 did any white Democratic candidate for Congress attract a majority of the white vote. In 1994, only one Democratic nominee got the bulk of the white vote, and in 1992, three white Democrats took a majority of the white vote. In the early 1990s, white voters responded differently to black and white Democrats, but by the end of the decade, most white voters found Democratic candidates, regardless of the their race, unacceptable. Consequently, success of Democratic candidates—both black and white—relies heavily on black support. The most recent evidence of importance of the black vote comes from the 2006 Democratic gubernatorial primary, in which the winner took the bulk of the black vote but only 41 percent of the white vote.[41]

Exit polls provide another perspective on racial voting patterns. Since 1992, Democrats have always taken at least 80 percent of the black vote while most whites invariably preferred Republicans. Table 3.8 shows that since 1992 no Democrat has managed more than 45.2 percent of the white vote, and that figure was achieved in the 2000 U.S. Senate election when former Democratic governor Zell Miller—as well as the other candidates—ran without partisan identification because it was a special election to fill a vacancy. Three of the successful Democrats, identified with a + in table 3.8, hovered just under 40 percent of the white vote, generally the minimum white vote needed for a Democratic statewide victory. Bill Clinton carried Georgia in 1992 by a margin of less than thirteen thousand votes, but his

TABLE 3.6. Racial voting patterns in Georgia congressional contests involving African American candidates, 1992–1998

		Whites		Blacks	
District	Black candidates	OLS	EI	OLS	EI
1992 primaries					
Georgia District 2	4 candidates, Democratic primary, open	26.3	32.3	88.7	83.9
Georgia District 11	4 candidates, Democratic primary, open	56.5	61.7	92.1	89.9
1992 runoffs					
Georgia District 2	Bishop, open	17.5	30.4	85.5	76.6
Georgia District 11	McKinney, open	21.2	35.0	97.7	86.3
1992 general election					
Georgia District 2	Bishop*	30.0	33.2	100.0	98.2
Georgia District 11	McKinney*	31.6	37.9	97.9	96.4
1994 general election					
Georgia District 2	Bishop*	40.4	42.7	99.5	94.7
Georgia District 11	McKinney*	23.8	32.5	99.8	94.4
1996 primary					
Georgia District 11	McKinney*	21.3	24.9	92.3	92.7
1996 general election					
Georgia District 2	Bishop*	37.4	37.7	100.0	97.1
Georgia District 4	McKinney*	30.7	32.1	100.0	99.2
1998 general election					
Georgia District 2	Bishop*	37.8	39.5	99.9	95.4
Georgia District 4	McKinney*	34.9	36.2	97.2	95.0
Georgia District 4	Warren**+	65.1	63.8	2.8	5.0
Georgia District 5	Lewis*	50.2	53.7	97.7	96.8
Georgia District 5	Lewis**+	49.8	46.3	2.3	3.2
Georgia District 10	Freeman**	17.5	23.7	90.5	80.8

Source: Charles S. Bullock III and Richard E. Dunn, "The Demise of Racial Districting and the Future of Black Representation," *Emory Law Review* 48 (Fall): 1209–1253.

Note: All candidates are Democrats unless otherwise indicated (+ indicates Republicans).

OLS = ecological regression; EI = ecological inference.

*Incumbent.

**Challenger.

TABLE 3.7. White support for white Georgia Democratic house candidates, 1992–1998

	White candidate	White support	
		OLS	EI
1992			
Georgia District 1	Christmas	36.9	35.4
Georgia District 3	Ray*	41.2	40.7
Georgia District 4	Steinberg	45.1	47.1
Georgia District 6	Center**	39.2	41.2
Georgia District 7	Darden*	55.6	56.0
Georgia District 8	Rowland*	57.7	53.7
Georgia District 10	Johnson	52.3	51.7
1994			
Georgia District 1	Beckworth**	18.3	18.2
Georgia District 3	Overby**	30.0	31.1
Georgia District 4	Yates**	41.9	41.8
Georgia District 6	Jones**	35.2	36.0
Georgia District 7	Darden*	45.5	44.5
Georgia District 8	Mathis	34.9	34.4
Georgia District 9	Deal*	57.3	57.1
Georgia District 10	Johnson*	29.7	30.1
1996			
Georgia District 1	Kaszans**	15.9	19.2
Georgia District 3	Chafin**	25.0	30.9
Georgia District 6	Coles**	36.9	41.1
Georgia District 7	Watts**	38.5	37.4
Georgia District 8	Wiggins**	34.7	38.1
Georgia District 9	Poston**	34.0	33.5
Georgia District 10	Bell**	32.0	31.9
Georgia District 11	Stephenson**	33.2	33.5
1998			
Georgia District 6	Coles**	22.7	25.2
Georgia District 7	Williams**	38.5	37.5
Georgia District 8	Cain**	21.6	22.9
Georgia District 11	Littman**	26.2	28.5

Source: Charles S. Bullock III and Richard E. Dunn, "The Demise of Racial Districting and the Future of Black Representation," *Emory Law Review* 48 (Fall): 1209–1253.

OLS = ecological regression; EI = ecological inference.

*Incumbent.

**Challenger.

TABLE 3.8. Racial preferences for Democrats in Georgia, 1992–2006

	Office	Black	White
1992	President+	89.8	30.9
1992	U.S. Senate+*	85.5	39.1
1994	Governor+*	91.4	45.0
1996	President*	92.0	29.5
1996	U.S. Senate+	86.8	39.6
1998	U.S. Senate**	88.3	30.3
1998	Governor+	87.6	39.7
2000	President	86.8	39.6
2000	U.S. Senate+*	91.7	45.2*
2004	U.S. Senate	87.0	23.0
2004	President**	88.0	23.0
2006	Governor**	81.0	27.0

Source: Voter News Service (VNS) and Voter Education Project (VEP) exit polls for various elections.

Note: Zell Miller served two terms as governor and four as lieutenant governor, and was well known as a Democrat while his leading opponent in the special election to fill the remainder of Paul Coverdell's (R) term was former Republican senator Mack Mattingly. However, since this was a special election, the partisan affiliation of the candidates did not appear on the ballot.

+Successful Democrats.

*Democratic incumbent running.

**Republican incumbent running.

victory with only 30.9 percent of the white vote became possible because Ross Perot siphoned off Republican votes.

Table 3.9 presents data showing the fate of Democratic candidates competing statewide over the last decade. In the past five elections through 2006, African Americans have had greater success in statewide contests than have white Democrats. The white Democrats shown in table 3.9 won 36 percent of the twenty-eight contests in which they participated; African Americans won or led in 73 percent of eleven contests for which they won nominations. David Burgess led in the 2006 Public Service Commission (PSC) election but failed to achieve the majority vote required under Georgia law. He lost in the largely ignored runoff

TABLE 3.9. Success of Democratic statewide candidates in Georgia, 1998–2006

	Office	Democrats' vote	Democrats' %	Result
1998	Senator	791,904	45.2	Lost
	Governor	941,076	52.5	Won
	Lt. Governor	990,496	56.4	Won
	Sec'y of State	983,905	56.6	Won
	Att'y General	883,932	50.9	Won
	Agriculture Comm.	1,085,694	62.8	Won
	Insurance Comm.	651,891	37.7	Lost
	School Supt.	794,324	46.0	Lost
	Labor Comm.	894,656	52.7	Won
	PSC (Hargis)	746,081	44.6	Lost
	PSC (McDonald)	638,054	49.6	Won
2000	President	1,116,230	43.2	Lost
	Senator	1,413,224	58.2	Won
	PSC (Burgess)	1,201,346	52.3	Won
	PSC (Boyd)	928,005	41.0	Lost
2002	Senator	931,857	45.9	Lost
	Governor	937,062	46.3	Lost
	Lt. Governor	1,041,227	51.9	Won
	Sec'y of State	1,225,232	61.1	Won
	Att'y General	1,093,734	55.6	Won
	Agriculture Comm.	1,138,705	57.4	Won
	Insurance Comm.	657,754	33.2	Lost
	School Supt.	859,653	43.0	Lost
	Labor Comm.	1,007,468	51.2	Won
	PSC (Sizemore)	913,119	47.5	Lost
	PSC (McDonald)	911,669	47.1	Lost
2004	President	1,366,149	41.4	Lost
	U.S. Senator	1,287,690	40.0	Lost
	PSC (Barber)	1,217,443	39.5	Lost
2006	Governor	811,049	38.2	Lost
	Lt. Governor	887,506	43.2	Lost
	Sec'y of State	862,412	41.8	Lost
	Att'y general	1,185,366	57.2	Won
	School Supt.	734,702	35.0	Lost
	Insurance Comm.	713,324	34.4	Lost
	Agriculture Comm.	1,168,371	56.0	Won
	Labor Comm.	1,127,182	54.8	Won
	PSC (Burgess)	994,619	48.8	Runoff required*
	PSC (Wise)	823,681	40.4	Lost

Source: Computed by the authors from election returns posted at www.sos.ga.gov/elections/.

Boldface indicates African American candidates.

*The black Democrat led the general election but, having failed to poll a majority of the vote, lost the runoff.

(only 215,092 votes cast statewide). However, even counting him as a loss, black Democrats won 64 percent of the time.

In 2006, Republicans made further gains in Georgia by winning the open posts of lieutenant governor and secretary of state. The incumbent African Americans won reelection as attorney general and labor commissioner and were two of the three Democrats successful in statewide contests. An African American lost in her bid to unseat the state school superintendent. White Democratic challengers came up short against the governor, insurance commissioner, and one of the Public Service Commission seats. White Democrats also failed in efforts to retain the offices of lieutenant governor and secretary of state for their party, leaving Agriculture Commissioner Tommy Irvin as the only white Democrat with a statewide victory.

The Georgia ballot contained three statewide races in 2004: the presidency, a Senate seat, and one seat on the Public Service Commission. The races for president and the Public Service Commission featured white Democrats while the Democratic Senate nominee was African American U.S. representative Denise Majette. Table 3.9 shows that the three Democrats, all of whom lost, polled remarkably similar vote shares, with John Kerry attracting 41.4 percent of the vote, Majette 40 percent, and the Democratic nominee for the Public Service Commission, Mac Barber, 39.5 percent.

In 2002, Democrats split the statewide results, winning five contests and losing six. A different pattern emerges, however, once we control for the race of the Democratic nominee. The white Democratic nominees won only three of nine contests in which they competed, while both of the black Democratic nominees won. The African Americans were incumbents, but incumbency cannot explain this result, as all but two of the white Democratic nominees were also incumbents. White Democratic incumbents won three contests and lost four, including the two at the top of the ticket for senator and governor.

In 2000, Democrats won two of the four contests in which all Georgians could vote, and one of the winners was the only African American nominee. White Democrats, vying for the three other spots, won only one. In 1998, African American Democrats won two of three contests, and white Democrats did approximately the same, winning five of eight contests.

The insurance commissioner race, the sole 1998 contest that was lost by an African American candidate, is somewhat anomalous. Not only did the candidate have to run against a Republican incumbent, but some questioned the seriousness of her campaign. African American Charles Walker, who was majority leader of the state senate at the time, said that she "did not have the support of the black community nor did she have a credible campaign. No one took her seriously. . . . [S]he never even campaigned. She never even put signs up. She didn't do anything."[42]

The increase in the number of blacks nominated by the Democratic Party for statewide offices may result in part from the heightened influence of black votes in Democratic primaries. As shown in figure 3.2, black influence now looms far larger in the Democratic primary than in the population or general elections. In the early 1990s, blacks cast less than a quarter of the votes in Democratic primaries. But in each of the last three general primaries, blacks have cast at least 45 percent of the Democratic ballots, and in the 2004 Democratic primary, blacks cast 47.2 percent of the votes. In the 2008 presidential primary, a solid majority of the vote came from blacks drawn to the polls by the Obama candidacy. African Americans now account for almost half of the Democratic primary votes in Georgia, even though they constitute only 27 percent of the state's registered voters. While outcomes vary across the state, it is likely that in districts at least 30 percent black, African Americans may cast the majority of the votes in the Democratic primary, so that their preferences can determine the Democratic primary winner. In 2006, African Americans won the Democratic nomination for four of ten statewide offices while in 2004 one of the two statewide Democratic nominees was black.

The politics of Georgia have undergone a dramatic transformation in all aspects of minority participation. African Americans have won hundreds of offices elected from constituencies of various sizes. In recent general elections, black statewide Democratic candidates have fared better than their white colleagues. Georgia's white electorate increasingly supports Republicans, but black Democrats are doing about as well as white Democrats in attracting white voters. White support is crucial to the success of black candidates. Without white support, African American candidates could not have achieved the notable success that they have enjoyed in recent years. As stated in the post-trial brief filed by Georgia's

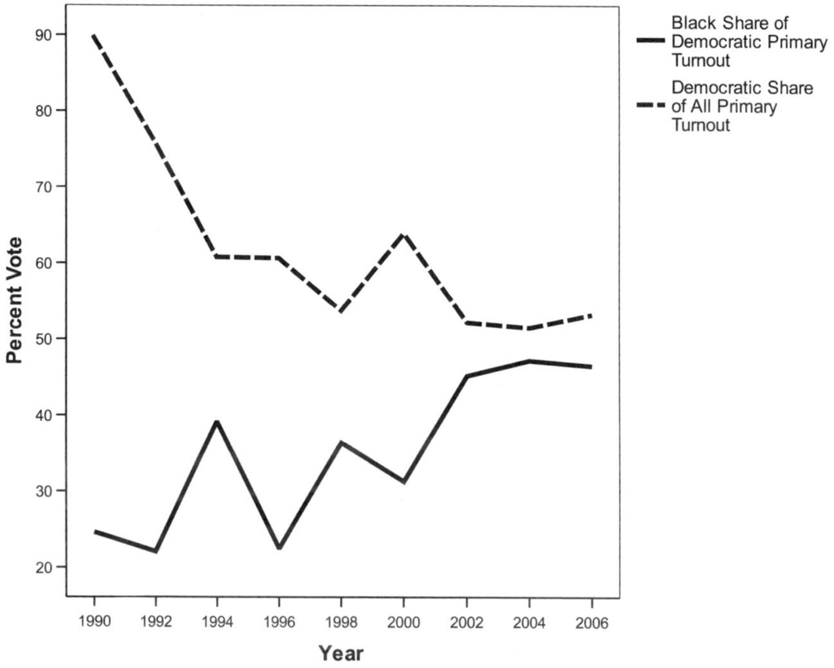

Figure 3.2. Black percentage of the Democratic primary turnout, 1990–2006. *Source:* Georgia Secretary of State, www.sos.state.ga.us/elections/.

African American attorney general Thurbert Baker in *Georgia v. Ashcroft*, "The [s]tate['s] racial and political experience in recent years is radically different than it was ten or twenty years ago, and that is exemplified on every level of politics from statewide elections on down. The election history for legislative offices in Georgia—House, Senate and Congress—reflect a high level of success by African American candidates."[43]

FEDERAL MONITORING

Despite the political advances made by the black community, the U.S. Department of Justice has rejected a relatively large number of changes in election laws adopted in the Peach State. During the first decade of Section 5, Georgia had more of its proposed changes in election laws rejected (forty-one) than any other state. During the next decade, only Texas, which has ninety-five more counties and far more municipalities, exceeded Georgia's sixty-eight denials of preclearance. From 1985 to 1994, Section 5 objections in Georgia declined to fifty-two, a number exceeded by Texas, Mississippi, and Louisiana. Since 1995 only ten submissions from Georgia have failed to meet with DOJ approval. Six of the most recent objections involved redistricting plans, with one of these being directed at the plan adopted by the majority-black Albany City Council. To put the incidence of recent DOJ objection in perspective, from 1990 to 2005, Georgia submitted 34,733 election law changes to DOJ, 139 of which Justice found to be objectionable for an approval rate of 99.6 percent.[44]

Georgia's recent experience with Section 5 illustrates the conflicts that began to emerge between DOJ and the federal courts, which share responsibility for administering Section 5. Six objections beginning in 1989 involved the creation of additional judgeships. DOJ objected to these new judgeships because the judges would be elected circuit-wide. DOJ wanted subdistricts created, some of which would have African American majorities in their populations. The state disagreed, and after it prevailed in a judicial challenge,[45] DOJ withdrew the objections.

Three other sets of objections involved Georgia's redistricting plans for congressional and state legislative districts in the early 1990s. Ultimately the Supreme Court ruled that DOJ had overstepped its bounds by forcing Georgia to subordinate traditional districting principles to considerations of race in order to meet DOJ demands that the state maximize the number of majority-black districts.[46]

Upon receipt of a proposed change, DOJ may seek more information from the submitting authority before ruling on the submission. DOJ asked for more information on 1,325 of the more than 34,000 submissions received from Georgia jurisdictions from 1990 to 2005.[47] Almost half of these requests involved annexations, 342 dealt with methods of elections, and 108 related to redistricting. Ultimately 44 of the 1,325 requests sparked an objection, but in 1,055 instances no objection followed. The submitting authority withdrew 90 proposals, which may indicate another 90 instances in which Section 5 prevented implementation of a change believed to disadvantage minorities.

CONCLUSION

In the years since the enactment of the VRA, black participation has reached unprecedented levels in Georgia, suggesting that the institutionalized racism that necessitated the VRA has been largely eliminated. In some recent years, the Census Bureau has estimated that African Americans and whites have registered and voted in elections at roughly comparable rates, although figures reported by Georgia's secretary of state show white registrants voting at higher rates than blacks. Nonetheless, the state figures also show growing black participation with black registration in 2004 equaling the black proportion among Georgia adult citizens. From 1996 to 2006, the secretary of state's data on actual registration reported in table 3.2 (not the general population survey estimates) show an increase in black registration of almost 25 percent, and in 2004, 72 percent of this enlarged black electorate went to the polls.

African Americans have also made impressive gains in office holding. In 2008 Georgia had four African Americans in Congress and fifty-five state legislators. Approximately a quarter of the statewide officials were black as of 2007, including two constitutional officers and three Supreme Court justices. As the success in winning statewide posts suggests, African Americans are now winning races even when blacks are not a majority of the population. Additionally, in a number of majority-white districts, black voters can determine the Democratic nominee. Finally, another factor facilitating the election of black candidates from majority-white districts has been the greater willingness of whites to vote for black candidates than vice versa.

Future prospects for black candidates in Georgia depend in part on the future of the Democratic Party. White voters increasingly identify with the Republican Party, and beginning with 1992, there have been few elections in which Republicans have not added to their ranks of elected officials in Georgia. African Americans now hold more state legislative, congressional, and statewide constitutional offices than do white Democrats, but Democratic candidates, both black and white, are increasingly failing to win elections at all levels. If these trends continue, African Americans may lose some of the statewide posts they held in 2008 as they did in 2006 when David Burgess lost his reelection bid for the Public Service Commission. Nevertheless, they are unlikely to lose congressional or state legislative seats in districts that have substantial black populations and may make additional gains as white Democratic incumbents step aside.

CHAPTER 4

LOUISIANA

At the very end of the nineteenth century, Louisiana adopted a series of requirements that substantially reduced black participation. Beginning in 1898, voters had to register and be able to mark a secret ballot. Marking a secret ballot required that voters be literate, and Morgan Kousser reports that in 1900, 61 percent of Louisiana's adult black males but only 18 percent of the white adult males were illiterate.[1] In the next year, the Bayou State adopted a poll tax and a literacy test. Kousser estimates that these restrictions reduced black turnout by 93 percent.[2] This reverses the trend prior to the adoption of the restrictive provisions of increasing black participation. Louisiana also adopted a white primary, but, unlike other Deep South states, did not seek to come up with ways to maintain it once the practice was struck down in *Smith v. Allwright*.[3]

The implementation of the Voting Rights Act has had a pronounced impact on political participation in Louisiana, and the initial goals of the Voting Rights Act have long since been achieved in the Pelican State. African Americans register and vote in large numbers and have done so for years. There are more than seven hundred black officeholders in the state, and blacks now hold almost a quarter of state legislative seats and two of the eight Board of Elementary and Secondary Education seats.

Party preferences in the state are generally structured by race, especially in national and major statewide contests. Whites prefer Republicans; blacks prefer Democrats. But, in lower-level contests, partisanship is generally less significant in structuring the contests than in major statewide contests and congressional elections. Often voters in both races rally behind one candidate, or no majority cohesion appears for any candidate. Black preferences can defeat the white choice, though this pattern does not extend to contests in which the black preference is an African American. Blacks frequently give 80 percent or more of their votes to a Democratic candidate, but a comparable level of white cohesion occurs only when an African American has made it to the runoff and the white vote goes to the African American's Republican opponent.

BLACK REGISTRATION AND TURNOUT

A generation after *Smith v. Allwright*, the U.S. Commission on Civil Rights reported official figures from the Louisiana secretary of state that showed 31.6 percent of the state's voting-age nonwhites registered to vote in the 1964 general election.[4] The range in the rates of black registration across the state varied widely, reaching as high as 93.8 percent in Evangeline Parish but falling to only 1.7 percent in Tensas, 1.9 percent in Claiborne, and 1.9 percent in West Feliciana parishes. The three parishes in which the smallest proportion of age-eligible African Americans were registered to vote had large black populations and two of them were majority black. In six parishes more than three-fourths of the age-eligible blacks were registered to vote prior to the Voting Rights Act.

Three years later, after the Voting Rights Act had been enforced for two years, 58.9 percent of the age-eligible African Americans in Louisiana had signed up to vote. Contributing to these numbers were 24,130 nonwhites registered by federal examiners sent into nine parishes pursuant to the Voting Rights Act. In Caddo Parish, where Shreveport is located, federal examiners enrolled almost 7,300 black voters, and in Ouachita Parish, they signed up almost 5,500.

Table 4.1 reports the changes in registration in the thirteen parishes in which less than 10 percent of the adult black population had registered in 1964. By 1967, the change had been dramatic in some parishes. West

TABLE 4.1. Official registration by race in Louisiana, 1964 and 1967

County	Nonwhite reg. 1964	White % reg. 1964	Nonwhite % reg. 1964	White % reg. 1967	Nonwhite % reg. 1967
Bossier	599	63.0	8.7	74.6	44.9
Catahoula	236	81.5	1.9	93.3	41.4
East Carroll	136	64.8	3.3	100.0	68.9
East Feliciana	182	38.7	3.0	50.7	38.9
Franklin	284	84.2	6.4	99.0	16.3
Madison	294	74.0	5.7	100.0	74.5
Morehouse	491	74.6	6.8	89.7	19.5
Plaquemines	96	88.3	3.3	100.0	47.9
Red River	96	100.0	4.4	100.0	64.8
Richland	381	74.8	8.3	93.8	21.7
Tensas	60	94.2	1.7	100.0	30.2
West Carroll	76	66.1	5.5	92.8	26.1
West Feliciana	85	47.8	1.9	100.0	98.2

Source: Louisiana Board of Elections.

Feliciana Parish had 98 percent of its voting-age blacks registered in 1967, up from less than 2 percent three years earlier. Contributing to this increase were 1,300 new voters signed up by federal examiners. Table 4.1 also shows that the share of the black adult population registered in 1967 in some other parishes such as Morehouse, Richland, and Franklin was far more modest with fewer than a quarter of the adult African Americans on the registration rolls.

When the percent of the adult black population registered in 1964 is regressed on the percent nonwhite in the adult population, the relationship is highly significant and negative (b = –.591).[5] When black registration in 1967 is regressed on the percent nonwhite in the adult population, the relationship is still negative (b = –.213), but it no longer meets conventional standards of statistical significance. Prior to the Voting Rights Act, we find a relationship in line with the V. O. Key, Jr., hypothesis that black population concentrations are associated with more repressive white behavior.[6] But after passage of the legislation and an 84 percent increase in black registration, the relationship weakened substantially.

Appendix B shows more recent figures on self-reported black and white registration as compiled by the U.S. Bureau of the Census. The self-reported registration rates are quite similar for African Americans and whites throughout the twenty-six–year time period. In 1980, almost three-fourths of the whites surveyed and just under 70 percent of the African Americans said they were registered. Throughout the remainder of the 1980s, black registration figures slightly exceed those for whites. The 1992 figures represent the last year in which a higher proportion of African Americans than whites had registered, with the disparity being approximately 6 percentage points as 82.3 percent of the African Americans compared with 76.2 percent of whites reported having registered to vote. Beginning with 1994, the rates of white registration have exceeded those for African Americans, although in most years the differences have been relatively small. The largest disparities come in the midterm years of 1994, 1998, and 2006, when approximately 7 percentage points more whites than blacks claimed to be registered to vote. In 2002, the difference drops to less than one percentage point, before expanding to 4 points in 2004. Except for the atypically low black rates in 1994 and 2006, more than 70 percent of the African American population has been registered. White registration figures have also been above 70 percent except for in 1982 when only 67.5 percent of the whites surveyed reported being registered.

The disparity increases when the comparison is between non-Hispanics whites and blacks. Excluding Latinos from the ranks of white registrants increases white registration by no more than half a percentage point in 1998 and 2000. In the next three elections, excluding Hispanics results in white registration rates rising by less than 2 points.

Throughout the time period, African Americans in Louisiana have reported higher registration rates than blacks outside the South. In the early 1980s, differences between the two groups were less than 10 percentage points. Beginning with 1988 the difference has exceeded 10 percentage points except in 1994 and 2004, and even in those years Louisiana African Americans voted at rates 7 points more than nonsouthern blacks. The most recent figures show that in 2006, Louisiana blacks were 13.3 percentage points more likely to register than were nonsouthern blacks. Louisiana black registration exceeds 70 percent in nine elections—a percentage never achieved by African Americans outside the region.

Not only do Bayou State blacks register at higher rates than blacks outside the region, they also have higher registration rates than nonsouthern whites. Even when Hispanics are excluded from the white figure, it comes up short of Louisiana's black registration prior to 2004.

Self-reported turnout (presented in appendix B) shows that in presidential election years, at least 60 percent of the African Americans of voting age in Louisiana participate. The high figure comes in 1992, when black Louisianans helped carry their state for Bill Clinton and 71.5 percent reported voting. Despite higher levels of participation, blacks turned out at lower rates than whites in five of the seven presidential elections between 1980 and 2006. Only in 1984 and 1992 did blacks vote at higher rates than whites. In the other years, white turnout exceeded African American turnout, with the largest difference occurring in 1988 when 67.5 percent of age-eligible whites and 61.5 percent of the African Americans voted. The only other instance in which the racial difference exceeded 5 percentage points took place in 1980, when 65.6 percent of whites and 60.1 percent of black adults went to the polls. In the three most recent presidential elections covered by the data, the differences ranged from 1.7 percentage points in 1996 to 3.2 percentage points in 2000.

Midterm election turnout is invariably lower, and in some instances, much lower. In 1982 and 1994, fewer than one in three adult Louisiana African Americans bothered to cast ballots—figures that were only modestly improved on in 2006. At the high end, almost 56 percent of Louisiana blacks reported voting in 1986 and 1990. Despite lower turnout rates, in three of the seven off-year elections, blacks voted at higher rates than whites. In 1998, the disparity was 10 percentage points, and in 1982, while only 32 percent of the blacks surveyed said they voted, whites had an even poorer showing with 23.6 percent turnout. In 1990, the rate at which blacks said they voted exceeded that for whites by more than 5 percentage points. White self-reported turnout outpaced that for blacks in 1986, 1994, 2002, and 2006. In none of these years did white voting exceed black voting by as much as 5 points. The largest difference occurred in 1994 when 35.6 percent of whites compared with 30.9 percent of blacks cast ballots. In 1986, the difference was only 1.7 percentage points as 57.5 percent of whites and 55.8 percent of African Americans voted.

One factor that accounts for the much lower turnout in many off-year elections when compared to presidential-year elections is that Louisiana does not choose its state officers in the midterm off-year. Louisiana state elections come in odd-numbered years, so that in the absence of a presidential contest, the highlight in a midterm election is likely to be a contest for U.S. Senate or House of Representatives, and if the midterm features only U.S. House races, not all of those contests may be competitive.

A second factor that discourages participation is Louisiana's unique election law that formerly had all candidates, regardless of party, compete in the initial contest. Candidates who poll a majority in the first round are elected. Consequently, the general election includes only those offices for which no candidate polled a majority, forcing the top two vote-getters to appear in a runoff. Most congressional contests feature incumbents, and most incumbents attract majority support in the first round so that many Louisianans have no incentive to return to the polls at the time of the general election in nonpresidential years since nothing remains to be decided. Louisiana abandoned this mechanism in federal elections in 2008, instead returning to closed-party primaries with runoffs followed by a November general election.

When non-Hispanics are removed from the ranks of white voters, the percentages increase slightly. Even after removing non-Hispanics, black voters turned out at higher rates than did whites in 1998. For other years, the gap between black and non-Hispanic whites is approximately one percentage point wider than between blacks and whites when Hispanics have not been excluded.

Based on self-reported turnout rates from the census, Louisiana blacks always vote at higher rates than do African Americans in the North and West in presidential years. The greatest difference came in 1992 when 71.5 percent of Louisiana blacks but only 53.8 percent of African Americans in the non-South participated. In 2000, the difference was 10 percentage points. The smallest difference in a presidential year came in 1988 when 61.5 percent of Louisiana blacks, along with 55.6 percent of African Americans from outside the South, went to the polls.

In the three midterm elections when turnout among Louisiana blacks fell below 40 percent, African Americans outside the region voted at higher rates. The 1994 difference reached almost 10 percentage points, while in 1982 it exceeded 15 percentage points. In other midterm election years, the turnout rate for blacks in Louisiana exceeded that outside of the region. In 1998 and 2002, approximately 46 percent of the African Americans in the Bayou State reported voting compared with approximately 40 percent of blacks outside of the region.

The longitudinal figures from the Census Bureau do not show African American participation in Louisiana increasing over time. However, they do show that throughout the period, participation rates for the two races in Louisiana are quite comparable with a higher African American than white participation rate some years. Registration and turnout among Louisiana African Americans usually exceeds that for nonsouthern blacks.

Louisiana is one of the few states to maintain registration records by race, thus making it possible to examine actual registration figures in addition to the self-reported figures collected by the Census Bureau. These materials appear in table 4.2 and show that the number of black registrants has increased from 163,414 at the time that the Voting Rights Act was initially passed to more than 850,000 four decades later. This five-fold increase in black registration comes at a time when the total registration in the state increased by a little more than 140 percent.

With black registration increasing more rapidly than total registration in the state, African Americans now constitute a larger share of the total number of registrants. When the VRA was enacted, fewer than one in seven registrants was black. By the first renewal in 1970, a fifth of the registrants were African American. At the time of the 1982 renewal, blacks made up almost a quarter of the registered electorate. The figures for mid-2008 show 30 percent of the registrants to be African American. The increase for blacks has continued despite the massive exodus from Louisiana following Hurricane Katrina. The 2008 figure exceeds the black share of the citizen adult population estimated by the Census Bureau to be 29.3 percent in 2006. Table 4.2 provides further evidence that the barriers to African American registration that existed forty years ago have long since come down.

Unlike most of the South, Louisiana has partisan registration. The vast bulk of the state's black registrants enrolled with the Democratic Party. The presidential candidacy of Barack Obama spurred black Democratic registration, which grew by more than thirty thousand between the time of the state's presidential primary vote and the middle of 2008. New black registrants increased the black share of all Democratic registrants from 44.8 to 46.2 percent.

TABLE 4.2. Black voter registration and turnout in Louisiana, 1965–2008

	Total voter registration	Black registration (La. Board of Registration)	Black % of registered voters (La. Board of Registration)
1965	1,190,122	163,414	13.7
1970	1,438,727	298,054	20.7
1975	1,798,032	408,696	22.7
1980	2,015,402	465,005	23.0
1985	2,175,264	550,225	25.3
1990	2,121,302	561,379	26.5
1995	2,400,086	689,046	28.7
1998	2,678,337	771,506	28.9
1999	2,713,859	783,294	28.9
2000	2,771,477	802,069	28.9
2001	2,750,124	798,526	29.0
2002	2,797,471	817,527	29.2
2003	2,766,081	812,578	29.4
2004	2,875,232	852,675	29.7
2006	2,890,891	862,096	29.8
2008	2,887,345	877,052	30.4

Sources: Data for 1965 to 1975 were taken from James Bolner, ed., *Louisiana Politics: Festival in a Labyrinth* (Baton Rouge: Louisiana State University Press, 1982), 305. Data for 1980 to 1995 were provided by the Office of the Louisiana Commissioner of Elections, Baton Rouge. Figures from 1965 to 1995 appear in Wayne Parent and Huey Perry, "Louisiana: African-Americans, Republicans and Party Competition," in *The New Politics of the Old South*, 3rd ed., ed. Charles S. Bullock III and Mark Rozell (Latham, Md.: Rowman and Littlefield, 2007). Figures for 2000 and 2006 were taken from the Louisiana Secretary of State's Web site: www.sos.louisiana.gov/stats/Post_Election_Statistics/Statewide/.

Since 1998, Louisiana's secretary of state has released figures showing turnout by race. Across the last eight years, African Americans have cast between 22.6 and 30 percent of the votes in the often-determinative first round. African Americans constituted the largest share of the electorate in 1998 and have come close to matching the 29.9 percent of the registered voters. Black turnout came close to matching the black share of the registrants in two recent years when they accounted for more than 27 percent of the participants (1998, 2004). Black participation fell off in 2006 when it constituted less than a quarter of the participants. With no

U.S. Senate seat being contested, the congressional elections failed to inspire the African American electorate.

Barack Obama's candidacy mobilized Americans for the 2008 presidential primary. Black voters cast almost 40 percent of all ballots in the presidential primary and accounted for 55.7 percent of the votes in Louisiana's Democratic contest. Exit polls show Obama taking 82 percent of the black vote in the state on the way to a 57 to 36 percent triumph over Hillary Clinton. Obama's share of the total vote slightly exceeded the black percentage of the participants in the Democratic primary.[7]

A comparison of recent turnout rates with registration rates for the past decade indicates that in 1998, blacks turned out at higher rates than the rest of the electorate since they constituted a larger share of the electorate (29.9 percent) than of registrants (28.9 percent). From 1999 to 2007, African Americans voted at lower rates than other Louisianans, although in 2003 and 2004 the difference was small as the black share of registrants was less than 3 percentage points greater than the black share of the voters. In the 2008 presidential-preference primary, blacks made up 30.4 percent of registrants but accounted for 39.7 percent of turnout.[8]

The historic use of the open primary system leaves few opportunities in Louisiana to assess the importance of the black vote within the Democratic Party. The presidential preference primary provides a rare insight into the racial makeup of the Democratic electorate. In 2008, the Democratic presidential primary attracted almost 400,000 voters. Tabulations by the secretary of state indicate 55.7 percent of these were African Americans. The return of closed, party primaries with runoffs will likely increase the influence of African American voters on which Democratic candidates advance to the final general election for federal offices.

AFRICAN AMERICAN OFFICE HOLDING

In 1969, Louisiana had 65 African American officeholders, of whom 11 served at the parish (or county) level while 23 held municipal offices and 9 served on local school boards. Within three years, black officeholders in the state had grown to more than 100, and in another three years that figure had doubled to 237. Three more years pass and yet another hundred black officeholders had been elected, bringing the totals to 75 in

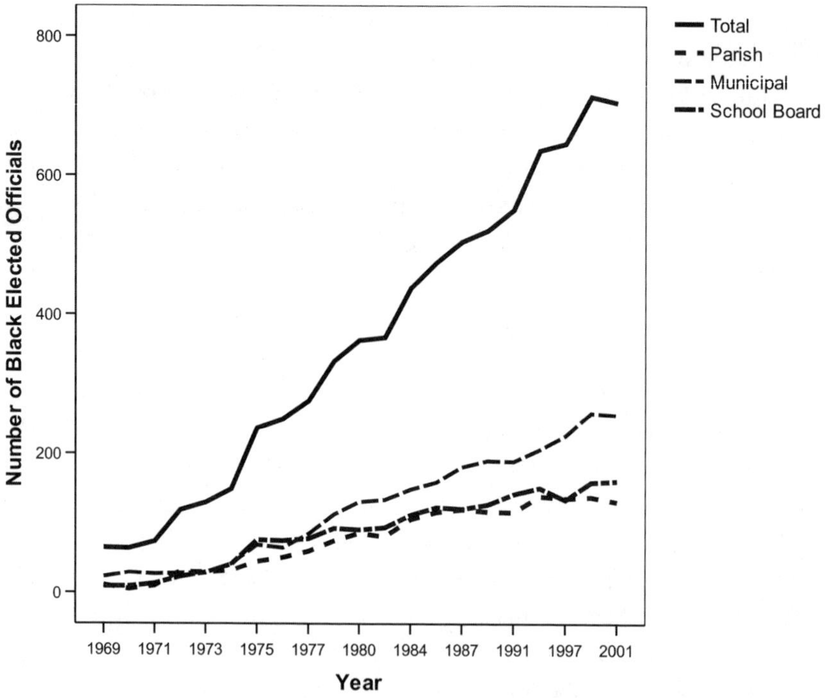

Figure 4.1. Black elected officials in Louisiana, 1969–2001. *Source:* Various volumes of the *National Roster of Black Elected Officials* (Washington, D.C.: Joint Center for Political and Economic Studies).

parish offices, 113 in city offices, and almost 100 in school board positions. Thereafter, growth slowed and black officials did not exceed 400 until the mid-1980s. By 1987, the state had more than 500 black officeholders as reported in figure 4.1. As of 2001, more than 700 African Americans had been elected in Louisiana. This included 131 parish officers, most of whom held the post of police juror (which corresponds with county commissioner elsewhere).

African Americans in Congress

Until upset in the 2008 general election, William Jefferson was among the most senior African American members of Congress, having first been elected in 1990. He took over the majority-black congressional district that had been represented by the Boggs family for forty-four years.[9] Majority leader Hale Boggs held the seat until his death in an Alaskan plane crash, upon which his widow, Lindy, succeeded him. During the course of the Boggs family's almost half century of representation, this New Orleans district became increasingly African American, reaching 59 percent black after the 1983 redistricting. During her last years in Congress, Lindy Boggs faced challenges from African Americans, but her attentiveness to the constituency enabled her to turn aside those opponents. Upon her retirement, a large field of competitors emerged, and Jefferson, a senior state senator, defeated Marc Morial, son of a New Orleans mayor and a future mayor himself, in a runoff election.

In Louisiana, like Georgia and North Carolina, satisfying the demands of the U.S. Department of Justice drove the redistricting politics of the early 1990s. Unlike in the other two states where DOJ rejected a congressional map for having an insufficient number of majority-black districts, in Louisiana the message was sent in another form. DOJ rejected the plan for the Board of Elementary and Secondary Education that had only a single majority-black district.[10] The legislature realized that a congressional plan that contained only one African American district would also face rejection and consequently drew a second district.[11]

The chair of the senate redistricting committee, Cleo Fields, who, at 23, had become the youngest senator ever elected in the state, designed a heavily black district to be used starting in 1992. His creation, which became known as the "Zorro" district because it somewhat resembled a capital *Z*, managed to string together the black-majority precincts in Shreveport, Monroe, Alexandria, Lafayette, and Baton Rouge. This ungainly district stretched more than six hundred miles across the state, running along the northern border with Arkansas almost to Texas and along the entire stretch of the state's Mississippi River boundary, and then extending an arm as far as Lafayette in Cajun Country. In its search for black voters, the Zorro district included parts of twenty-eight of Louisiana's sixty-four parishes. This district was so far flung that the authors of the *Almanac of American Politics* speculated that "a walk over the boundaries of this district might take as long as Lewis and Clark's journey through the Louisiana Purchase."[12] Fields, who had unsuccessfully challenged a Republican incumbent two years earlier, took a commanding lead in the eight-candidate field with 48 percent of the vote in the first round. He romped to victory in the runoff with almost three-fourths of the vote to arrive in Congress just after his thirtieth birthday.

A challenge to Fields' 67 percent black 4th District was awaiting trial when the Supreme Court ordered a hearing on North Carolina's 12th District in *Shaw v. Reno*.[13] Even before the North Carolina panel could respond to the *Shaw* opinion, a three-judge panel in Louisiana threw out the Zorro district.[14] The legislature came up with a new plan that continued to link the black populations from Lafayette to Baton Rouge and on up to Shreveport in the northwest corner but did so in a more direct fashion that produced a district 250 miles long. The new 4th District did not tiptoe along the state's eastern and northern borders but instead took a diagonal shot up from Baton Rouge to Shreveport. The same plaintiffs successfully challenged this district for being drawn primarily on the basis of race.[15] The Supreme Court declined to rule on this appeal because the Court determined that the appellants lacked standing.[16] Nonetheless, the state embraced a plan initially prepared by the trial court when it developed another map.[17] The third map eliminated Fields' 4th District while maintaining the two-thirds black New Orleans district. Rather than confront a white Republican incumbent in a more than 70 percent white district, Fields retired from Congress and made an unsuccessful bid to become governor (discussed later in this chapter).

The post-2000 census plan maintained the New Orleans district at 64 percent African American. No other Louisiana district currently has a black majority in its population. Through 2008, Jefferson successfully confronted challenges from other African American candidates. In 2006, however, his prospects dimmed amid allegations that he had taken a $100,000 bribe, an action caught on film in a sting operation. Federal authorities found $90,000 hidden away in the congressman's refrigerator and touched off a brief episode of bipartisan congressional outrage when, armed with a warrant, the FBI searched Jefferson's Capitol Hill office. Jefferson ultimately survived this embarrassing episode. After leading a field of thirteen candidates with 30 percent of the vote in the first round, Jefferson took 57 percent of the vote to defeat another African American, state representative Karen Carter, by a margin of 57 to 43 percent.

In 2008, in one of the nation's most surprising upsets, Jefferson lost to a Vietnamese-American Republican in a low-turnout contest. The new representative has the most heavily black district of any member of Congress. The election of immigrant lawyer Ahn "Joseph" Cao was a shock to many Louisiana political observers: Cao—a Republican, who came to the United States from Vietnam at the time of the fall of the Saigon government—prevailed by capitalizing on Jefferson's scandal and turning out his vote in a low-turnout election delayed by hurricanes. Cao's election completes an interesting evolution of the Louisiana 2nd District from representation by a white male Democrat, to a white female Democrat, to an African American male Democrat, to an Asian American Republican.

Other efforts by African Americans to win congressional seats have not met with success. Faye Williams lost runoffs to Republican Clyde Holloway for central Louisiana's 8th Congressional District in 1986 and 1988. Two years after Williams's second effort, Fields secured 84.7 percent of the black vote in another loss to Holloway.[18]

African Americans in the State Legislature

The first African American to be elected to the Louisiana legislature since Reconstruction won a seat in 1966. After the drawing of new districts in the early 1970s, black house members jumped to eight and then gradually increased during the course of that decade. By 1990, 14 percent of the 105-member lower chamber was African American. The redistricting done in 1991 created twenty-five districts in which most registered voters were black.[19] Later that year, blacks won twenty-three of these districts, which produced the more-than 50 percent increase in black house representation shown in table 4.3. Since 1993, the black proportion in the house has fluctuated but always remained above 20 percent.

The state senate has had black members since 1971. As in the house, the numbers initially grew slowly and did not reach 10 percent of the thirty-nine–member chamber until 1985. The race-based redistricting of the early 1990s demanded by the Department of Justice resulted in nine majority-black districts, eight of which elected an African American in 1991. At the beginning of the new century, African Americans held 23 percent of the senate seats.

TABLE 4.3. Racial makeup of the Louisiana legislature, 1965–2007

	Senate	% Black in Senate	House	% Black in House
1965	0	0.0	0	0.0
1967	0	0.0	1	1.0
1969	0	0.0	1	1.0
1971	1	2.6	1	1.0
1973	1	2.6	8	7.6
1975	1	2.6	8	7.6
1977	1	2.6	9	8.6
1979	1	2.6	9	8.6
1981	2	5.1	10	9.5
1983	2	5.1	11	10.5
1985	4	10.3	14	13.3
1987	5	12.8	14	13.3
1989	5	12.8	15	14.3
1991	4	10.3	15	14.3
1993	8	20.5	24	22.9
1995	8	20.5	22	21.0
1997	9	23.1	24	22.9
1999	9	23.1	22	21.0
2001	9	23.1	22	21.0
2003	9	23.1	23	21.9
2005	9	23.1	23	21.9
2007	9	23.1	23	21.9

Source: Data compiled by the authors.

PSC and BESE

In addition to the legislative chambers and the congressional delegation, African Americans have won seats on two other collegial bodies elected from single-member districts. The Public Service Commission (PSC) has five districts and the Board of Elementary and Secondary Education (BESE) elects eight members from single-member districts.[20]

In 1998, PSC District 3 elected Irma Dixon, a black female, in a runoff over incumbent white Democrat John Schwegmann. The district encompassed most of the majority-black congressional District 2 before continuing up the Mississippi River into the Holy Name parishes below Baton Rouge.

(Dixon would later wage an unsuccessful challenge to African American representative Bill Jefferson in Congressional District 2.) In 2004, Dixon was eliminated from a runoff by African American candidates Lambert Boissiere III and former congressman Cleo Fields. Boissiere subsequently bested Fields in the runoff.

The eight BESE districts have elected as many as two African Americans at a time. In 1999, the Orleans Parish-based BESE District 2 elected Keith Johnson. Johnson was defeated for reelection in a 2003 runoff by another African American candidate, Louella Givens. In the central-Louisiana BESE District 8, African American Linda Johnson bested two other black candidates without benefit of a runoff and was returned to the BESE in 2003.

Statewide Candidacies

In 1995, Cleo Fields joined the multicandidate gubernatorial field to succeed the tainted Edwin Edwards who had dominated Pelican State politics for a quarter of a century. Recall that under Louisiana's unique election law, all candidates compete in an initial heat regardless of party rather than running for a party nomination as in most other states. No candidate got a majority, and Fields made it into the runoff against conservative white Republican Mike Foster, the grandson of a former governor.[21] Democratic candidates had a combined majority of the vote in the initial balloting, but Fields could not unite the followers of his fellow partisans.[22] In the closing days of the dog-eat-dog campaign leading up to the initial vote, the two top Democrats, Fields and Mary Landrieu (the daughter of a New Orleans mayor and later elected to the U.S. Senate), sniped at one another as they sprinted toward the cutoff point for the runoff. Landrieu appealed for support by prophesying that Fields could not beat Foster. In the critical fight to advance to the runoff, Fields edged out Landrieu by nine thousand votes.

Jealousies among leading black politicians also hampered Fields. New Orleans mayor Marc Morial did not throw his full support behind Fields but rather endorsed both the former member of Congress as well as State Treasurer Landrieu.[23] After losing the runoff, Fields continued to harbor ill-feelings toward Landrieu. They almost sabotaged her 1996 Senate race, where she eked out a victory of less than six thousand votes in the runoff.

Fields polled 38 percent of the vote in the runoff against Foster. The Mason-Dixon exit poll indicated that Fields took just 16 percent of the white vote. Further, 45 percent of self-identified white liberals reported voting for Foster, who outspent Fields by more than eight to one in the runoff. Black voters did constitute 31 percent of the turnout in the runoff primary. According to the Baton Rouge *Advocate*'s Scott Dyer, "Regardless of whether anyone wants to admit it, the politics of race is the trump card in the 1995 governor's election. When one candidate is only polling 3 percent to 4 percent of Louisiana's black voters and the other candidate is only polling from 13 percent to 18 percent of the state's white voters, it's kind of silly for anyone to contend that racial politics are not a factor."[24] Four years later, in a multicandidate primary for governor, African American congressman Bill Jefferson polled 30 percent of the vote against Mike Foster, who was reelected, again with 62 percent of the vote. Polling data indicated a similar racial structure to the vote in 1999 as in 1995.

Cleo Fields and Bill Jefferson are the only serious black candidates to have run for governor in Louisiana. Still, the early 1990s witnessed two racially charged elections in the Pelican State. In both the 1990 Senate election and the 1991 gubernatorial election, the leading challenger was David Duke, a former leader of the Ku Klux Klan and a longtime outspoken opponent of civil rights for African Americans. Duke lost both of these efforts but managed 44 percent of the vote against longtime incumbent senator Bennett Johnston. The next year, Duke finished only 2 percentage points behind Edwin Edwards in the first round of the gubernatorial primary as both took about a third of the vote. In the runoff, with the Republican national establishment openly supporting the Democrat, Duke, who had served a term as Republican legislator, was held to 39 percent of the vote. While Duke lost both contests, he was the preference of most white voters in the state.[25]

Most recently, in 2004, Arthur Morrell sought the open U.S. Senate seat vacated by Democrat John Breaux. He pulled an estimated 5 percent of the African American vote, finishing well behind white Democrats Chris John and John Kennedy among black voters, and far behind primary winner John Vitter, who prevailed without a runoff.

RACIAL VOTING PATTERNS

Table 4.4 presents estimates of racial voting behavior in contested congressional elections since 1992. In elections from 1992 and 1994, African American candidates usually fared well among white voters although they had much less drawing power among white than black electors. For example, in the initial primary in the 2nd District in 1992, William Jefferson, led among both black and white voters. He attracted approximately 90 percent of the African American vote but just under half of the white vote. However, a second African American candidate drew another 25 percent of the white vote so the only white candidate in the contest polled barely a quarter of the white vote.

In the 1992 primary for the 4th District, Cleo Fields won the African American vote with approximately 60 percent support and finished a close second among white voters with 22.5 percent of the vote. That vote share was only six-tenths of a point less than the estimate for the leading candidate among white voters. In the runoff for that position between two African American candidates, Fields took commanding majorities among both black and white voters.

In the 1994 first primary, Jefferson took the vast majority of the black vote and ran a close second among white voters. In the 4th District in 1994, Fields faced a single opponent and while the incumbent attracted almost all the black vote, he failed to get even a third of the white vote.

Partisanship influences vote choices. For example, in the 5th District in 1992, the leading Republican candidate, Jim McCrery, who polled a majority of the white vote while Jerry Huckaby, the leading Democrat, took approximately 80 percent of the white vote. In the runoff in that district, polarization was even more pronounced with Huckaby winning approximately 90 percent of the black vote while McCrery took more than 70 percent of the white vote. Similarly, in 1992 in the 6th District, the two Republicans, Richard Baker and Clyde Holloway, combined for approximately 70 percent of the white vote. Ned Randolph, a Democrat, took the bulk of the African American vote.

Analysis of elections since 1998 shows that African American candidates won half of these twenty-two primaries and runoffs and in six contests a majority of the white and black voters supported the same candidates.[26] In

TABLE 4.4. OLS estimates of racial voting patterns in Louisiana congressional elections

	Candidate	Primary		Runoff	
		Whites	Blacks	Whites	Blacks
1992, District 2	**Irvin**	25.2	9.0		
	Jefferson	48.6	90.0		
	Johnson	26.2	1.1		
1992, District 4	**Fields**	22.5	60.8	64.7	79.1
	Hall	4.3	0.9		
	Jones	4.4	18.5	35.3	20.9
	Myers	23.1	0.0		
	Ross	3.1	1.7		
	Shyne	15.9	8.3		
	Ventre	18.6	1.1		
	Williams	8.1	8.8		
1992, District 5	Huckaby	20.0	80.8	27.2	92.2
	Knox	2.0	3.2		
	McCrery	51.4	2.1	72.8	7.8
	Milton	1.1	5.8		
	Thompson	25.4	8.1		
1992, District 6	Baker	37.3	–6.2	52.1	34.1
	Holloway	35.1	48.4	47.9	65.9
	Randolph	27.6	57.8		
1994, District 1	Livingston	83.6	48.0		
	McNeir	10.3	32.9		
	Simmons	6.1	19.1		
1994, District 2	**Jefferson**	42.2	96.9		
	Lawrence	7.7	1.0		
	Lehman	5.2	1.6		
1994, District 3	Accardo	25.3	15.1		
	Tauzin	74.7	84.9		
1994, District 4	**Fields**	31.4	98.8		
	Slocum	68.6	1.2		
1994, District 5	Kidd	7.9	56.6		
	McCrery	89.2	33.0		
	Simmons	2.8	10.4		
1994, District 6	Baker	84.5	50.9		
	Ward	15.5	49.1		
1994, District 7	Ceasar	5.9	19.3		
	Hayes	51.1	67.5		
	Holloway	43.0	13.2		
1998, District 6	Baker-R	65.9	1.8		
	McKeithen-D	34.1	98.2		

TABLE 4.4. OLS estimates of racial voting patterns in Louisiana congressional elections (*continued*)

	Candidate	Primary		Runoff	
		Whites	Blacks	Whites	Blacks
2000, District 1	Armato-D	10.1	88.1		
	Deaton-D	3.6	24.9		
	Rosenthal-I	1.3	4.7		
	Simanonok-I	1.1	5.2		
	Vitter-R	84.0	<0.0		
2000, District 3	Albares-I	20.2	59.7		
	Bourque-I	4.0	8.1		
	Rosenthal-I	3.0	9.1		
	Tauzin-R	58.2	23.1		
2000, District 4	Green-D	11.8	63.6		
	McCrery-R	83.4	29.7		
	Skains-I	2.4	2.9		
	Taylor-I	2.4	3.8		
2000, District 5	Beall-D	15.6	64.2		
	Cooksey-R	79.7	20.0		
	Dumas-I	2.4	5.7		
	Melton-I	2.4	10.0		
2000, District 6	Baker-R	80.7	24.3		
	Rogillio-I	17.0	73.7		
	Wolf-I	2.4	1.9		
2000, District 7	Harris-I	17.5	7.7		
	John-D	82.5	92.3		
2002, District 1	Hawxhurst-I	2.8	25.8		
	Monica-R	11.2	32.3		
	Namer-R	3.7	10.5		
	Vitter-R	82.4	31.5		
2002, District 2	Clement-I	5.6	2.6		
	Dixon-D	36.6	14.6		
	Hunt-D	6.7	1.4		
	Jefferson-D	9.8	78.5		
	Sullivan-R	41.5	2.9		
2002, District 3	Beier-I	6.8	17.9		
	Iwancio-I	4.1	10.6		
	Tauzin-R	89.1	71.4		
2002, District 4	Jacobs-I	2.1	2.0		
	McCrery-R	78.8	57.7		
	Milkovich-D	19.1	40.3		
2002, District 5	Alexander-D	14.7	77.7	40.2	98.3
	Barham-R	20.5	6.8	59.8	0.7
	Fletcher-R	30.0	1.2		
	Holloway-R	31.2	3.3		

TABLE 4.4. OLS estimates of racial voting patterns in Louisiana congressional elections (*continued*)

	Candidate	Primary Whites	Primary Blacks	Runoff Whites	Runoff Blacks
2002, District 5	Melton-R	1.0	8.6		
	Mouser-I	0.5	0.9		
	Wright-R	2.1	1.5		
2002, District 6	Baker-R	88.0	67.1		
	Moscatello-I	12.0	32.9		
2002, District 7	John-D	84.8	98.9		
	Valletta-I	15.2	1.1		
2004, District 1	Armstrong-D	5.1	35.8		
	Jindal-R*	81.8	5.1		
	Mendoza-D	3.7	18.8		
	Rogers-R	2.8	0.6		
	Watts-D	2.8	19.0		
	Zimmerman-D	3.7	15.1		
2004, District 2	**Jefferson-D**	51.1	99.6		
	Schwertz-R	48.9	0.4		
2004, District 3	Baldone-D	9.7	13.7		
	Caccioppi-D	0.6	10.8		
	Chiasson-R	0.3	6.9		
	Melancon-D	16.7	57.3	41.0	97.8
	Romero-R	26.2	6.7		
	Tauzin-R	37.8	4.7	59.0	2.2
2004, District 5	Alexander-R	74.7	20.7		
	Blakes-D	8.7	71.4		
	Scott-R	16.5	7.9		
2004, District 6	Baker-R	86.7	22.5		
	Craig-D	8.4	56.3		
	Galmon-D	4.9	21.2		
2004, District 7	Boustany-R	47.5	<0.0		
	Carriere-D	2.1	1.7		
	Cravins-D	12.3	81.1		
	Mount-D	26.1	14.4		
	Thibodaux-R	12.0	0.2		

Sources: Ronald E. Weber, "Turnout, Participation, and Competition in 1992 Louisiana Congressional Elections" (August 16, 1993) and Exhibit 4 for *Hays v. Louisiana*, n.d., for analysis through 1994; analysis from 1998 to 2004 by authors. Partisanship of candidates not indicated in Weber's analysis.

African American candidates in **boldface**.

*Jindal is Indian American.

Mendoza is Hispanic.

nine contests most black voters supported an unsuccessful candidate; in the two remaining elections, the African American vote split so that no candidate attracted as much as 40 percent of the black vote. In all nine elections in which most blacks supported a loser, the white vote coalesced behind a Republican. At the same time, in seven of these contests most blacks voted for a Democrat, and in two other cases most blacks backed an independent. In one contest in which the black vote split, the regression analysis estimates indicate that the winner, David Vitter, polled 31.5 percent of the black vote, not even a percentage point less than the estimated black support for the candidate who drew the most African American support.

Further support for the proposition that party is a major factor when African American and white voters differ in their preferences can be gleaned from table 4.4. In 2002, Rodney Alexander won as a Democrat in the 5th District where he polled almost all of the black vote in the runoff after getting three-fourths of the black vote in the primary. He won despite losing the white vote to his Republican opponent by a three-to-two margin. Alexander switched parties just before the filing period in August 2004. The rationale for the change was likely political—George Bush carried his district by 17 points in 2000—and the timing was such that it prevented Pelican State Democrats from recruiting a viable challenger to the fifty-seven-year-old incumbent. In his reelection bid, Republican Alexander managed barely a fifth of the African American vote while sweeping three-fourths of the white vote.

PSC and BESE

Louisiana elects two major boards via district elections. In addition to congressional and state legislative elections, districts elect the state Board of Elementary and Secondary Education (BESE, or the "Bessie Board") and the Public Service Commission (PSC). Analysis of racial voting patterns for the BESE and PSC appear in table 4.5.

In half of the twelve primary and runoff contests for the BESE, majorities of black and white voters preferred opposing candidates: the initial BESE primaries in Districts 3 and 7 in 1999; the BESE runoff in District 6 in 1999; and the 2003 runoffs in Districts 1, 2, and 6. In two of these six contests the candidate preferred by African American voters prevailed—in the

TABLE 4.5. Estimates of black and white voter preferences, Louisiana BESE and PSC elections, 1998–2004

Year, District	Candidate	Primary Whites	Primary Blacks	Runoff Whites	Runoff Blacks
BESE Elections					
1999, District 3	Buquet-D	60.8	36.2		
	Terrebonne-D	39.2	63.8		
1999, District 6	Blanchard-R	27.4	17.3		
	Dent-R	38.4	4.2	53.4	15.1
	Musemeche-D	34.2	78.5	46.6	84.9
1999, District 7	Bayard-D	59.9	46.1		
	MacKnight-D	40.1	53.9		
1999, District 8	**Hunter-D**	26.1	27.8		
	Johnson-D	48.8	57.2		
	Wise-I	25.1	2.0		
2003, District 1	Contois-R	29.9	<0.0		
	Dastugue-R	38.4	<0.0	61.7	16.4
	Ferguson-D	31.7	100.0	38.3	83.6
2003, District 2	C'bell-Rock-D	12.3	13.8		
	Givens-D	34.5	30.4	46.8	62.0
	Johnson-D	36.1	39.7	53.2	38.0
	Wilson-D	17.1	16.2		
2003, District 5	Herford-R	35.7	23.8		
	Stafford-D	64.3	76.2		
2003, District 6	Bel-D	23.8	79.6	29.7	100.0
	Broussard-R	48.3	2.7	70.3	<0.0
	Hammatt-R	27.8	17.6		
PSC Elections					
1998, District 3	**Charbonnet-D**	19.0	29.0		
	Dixon-D	30.2	38.0	40.6	87.6
	Schwegmann-D	50.8	11.4	59.4	12.4
1998, District 4	Muller-R	15.2	50.0		
	Sittig-D	84.8	50.0		
2000, District 2	Field-R	71.2	41.8		
	Warner-I	28.8	58.2		
2002, District 1	Blossman-R	71.1	36.7		
	Schwegmann-I	28.9	62.3		
2002, District 5	Campbell-D	40.5	48.2	49.0	90.9
	Crowley-I	11.4	2.0		
	Guy-R	9.3	8.5		
	Owen-D	38.8	41.3	51.0	9.1
2004, District 3	**Boissiere-D**	61.3	25.2	81.4	33.6
	Dixon-D	24.0	15.8		
	Fields-D	14.8	59.0	18.6	66.4

Source: Ordinary least squares (OLS) estimates.

African American candidates in **boldface**.

District 6 runoff in 1999 and in the District 2 runoff in 2003. None of the four cases in which the black-preferred candidate failed involved a black candidate, and none occurred in a majority-black constituency. Partisanship is less important in the BESE contests: most blacks rally to the Democrat while most whites support the Republican in only a third of the contests covered in the table. Three other primaries (District 6 in 1999 and 2003 and District 1 in 2003) saw most blacks back a Democrat who managed only about a third of the white vote as two Republicans split the bulk of the white support.

Nine Public Service Commission contests also appear in table 4.5. Black and white voters give majority support to opposing candidates in six of those contests: the District 3 runoff in 1998, the District 2 primary in 2000, the District 1 primary and the District 5 runoff in 2002, and the District 3 primary and runoff in 2004. In two cases the minority-preferred candidate prevails (District 3 in 1998 and District 5 in 2002), and in the 2004 District 3 primary the minority- and white-preferred candidates (both black) both advanced to a runoff where the white-preferred candidate prevailed in a majority-black district. In none of the PSC contests did whites support a Republican while blacks voted for a Democrat.

Statewide Constitutional Offices

There have been twenty-six statewide primaries and runoffs held in Louisiana from 1995 to 2003. The open primary system encourages fractionalization of the electorate, an effect readily visible in table 4.6. In only two of the nineteen contested first-round contests for statewide constitutional office in table 4.6 does a majority of black voters oppose a majority of white voters (2003 for attorney general and 1999 for governor). In eight contests one or both racial groups exhibited no majority preference. Of seven runoffs, two produced opposing racial majorities: the 1995 and 2003 gubernatorial runoffs. Of the total of twenty-six statewide primaries and runoffs since 1995, only four resulted in majority preferences for both racial groups in opposition, and in just two cases did the candidate preferred by the African American electorate fail (the 1995 gubernatorial runoff and the 1999 gubernatorial primary). However, these two cases are the two major instances of African American candidates running for—and losing—statewide office in Louisiana. (An African American competed in the six-candidate field for lieutenant governor in 2003 but managed less than five percent of the black vote, most of which lined up behind the successful candidate.)

Despite the losses of Cleo Fields and William Jefferson in the decisive gubernatorial contests of 1995 and 1999, in nineteen of the twenty-six contests, the candidate who drew majority support from black voters won, and in a twentieth case, the 1995 gubernatorial primary, the choice of most African Americans advanced to the runoff. In another four contests, African American voters were not cohesive.

White voters achieved cohesion less often than did African Americans. In sixteen contests most whites backed the winning candidate while in eight elections the white vote was not cohesive. In two contests (the 2003 gubernatorial runoff and the race for attorney general that year), the white preference lost. Thus the number of instances in which the white majority preference lost equals the number of contests in which the majority black preference lost.

Partisanship is less significant in these statewide contests than in the congressional elections presented in table 4.4. Fourteen of the statewide contests saw majorities of both African American and white voters rally behind one candidate so in most of these elections party did not separate voters by race. However, in all four statewide elections in which most blacks favored one candidate while most whites threw their support behind an alternative, most blacks preferred the Democrat while most whites backed a Republican. In the remaining eight contests, one or both racial groups did not display cohesion.

United States Senate Elections

Louisiana had six primaries or runoffs for the U.S. Senate between 1996 and 2006. In all four instances in table 4.6 in which African Americans cast a majority of their votes for a candidate, that individual succeeded. In the other two contests the African American vote was not cohesive: 42.4 percent of the African American vote went to Richard Ieyoub in the 1996 primary, while in 2004, the black vote divided almost evenly between two contenders, each of whom got almost 40 percent. The only African

TABLE 4.6. Estimates of white voter and black voter preferences in Louisiana statewide constitutional offices and U.S. Senate, 1995–2004

		Primary		Runoff	
Year, District	Candidate	Whites	Blacks	Whites	Blacks
1995, Governor	Foster-R	36.1	3.4	87.0	17.1
	Fields-D	0.8	64.7	13.0	82.9
	Landrieu-D	17.2	12.8		
	Roemer-R	18.1	7.9		
	Others (*n* = 12)	27.7	11.2		
1995, Lt. Governor	Blanco-D	39.1	43.3	60.2	79.1
	Kreiger-R	14.6	8.1	39.8	20.9
	John-D	16.0	23.8		
	Others (*n* = 8)	30.2	24.8		
1995, Att'y General	Deaton-R	8.8	9.6		
	Ieyoub-D	73.9	82.0		
	Tarpley-R	13.4	0.0		
	Wells-I	3.9	5.4		
1995, Sec'y of State	McKeithen-R	58.9	51.4		
	Schmidt-D	34.6	28.6		
	Winfield-D	6.5	20.0		
1995, Treasurer	Chehardy-R	29.2	6.7		
	Duncan-D	33.1	68.8	53.8	74.0
	Joseph-R	8.6	7.4		
	Theriot-D	29.1	17.1	46.2	26.0
1995, Insurance Comm.	Brown-D	63.0	67.4		
	Fletcher-I	8.5	5.0		
	Jones-D	4.1	10.4		
	Nungesser-R	28.1	16.2		
1995, Agriculture Comm.	Fresina-D	5.2	4.0		
	Johnson-R	21.1	13.5		
	Odom-I	73.7	82.5		
1995, Election Comm.	Anderson-R	27.0	8.3		
	Fowler-D	73.0	91.7		
1999, Governor	Foster-R	81.2	8.9		
	Jefferson-D	8.4	82.1		
	Others (*n* = 9)	10.4	8.9		
1999, Lt. Governor	Blanco-D	75.6	91.4		
	DuPlantis-R	12.2	2.4		
	Martin-R	10.6	2.6		
	Roberts-Joseph-I	1.5	2.9		
1999, Treasurer	Duncan-D	45.2	42.0		
	Kennedy-D	54.8	58.0		
1999, Insurance Comm.	Boudreaux-R	34.7	2.4	48.1	19.8
	Brown-D	41.9	72.6	51.9	80.2
	Riddick-D	23.4	15.0		

TABLE 4.6. Estimates of white voter and black voter preferences in Louisiana statewide constitutional offices and U.S. Senate, 1995–2004 (*continued*)

Year, District	Candidate	Primary Whites	Primary Blacks	Runoff Whites	Runoff Blacks
1999, Election Comm.	Jenkins-R	32.1	7.9	49.1	27.1
	Fowler-D	17.3	46.2		
	Terrell-R	16.3	16.0	50.9	72.9
	Others (*n* = 8)	34.3	29.8		
2003, Governor	Jindal-R*	31.7	7.9	52.3	14.9
	Blanco-D	21.8	7.3	47.7	85.1
	Ieyoub-D	10.9	34.5		
	Leach-D	9.3	27.0		
	Ewing-D	12.4	18.9		
	Downer-R	9.3	<0.0		
	Others (*n* = 10)	4.4	8.8		
2003, Lt. Governor	Ankeshein-R	1.4	0.3		
	Bennett-R	7.6	4.7		
	Holloway-R	28.9	13.6		
	Landrieu-D	41.6	79.9		
	Schorr-R	1.3	0.3		
	Schwegmann-R	19.2	0.9		
2003, Sec'y of State	McKeithen-R	74.1	68.5		
	Lewis-I	6.4	3.6		
	Donovan-D	19.5	27.9		
2003, Att'y General	Foti-D	45.0	74.9		
	Terrell-R	55.0	25.1		
2003, Insurance Comm.	Kyle-R	32.6	25.5	47.2	16.9
	Wooley-D	29.2	25.1	52.8	83.1
	Johnson-D	4.5	11.1		
	Fontenot-R	14.3	8.7		
	Fletcher-D	15.1	27.5		
	Bell-I	4.3	2.2		
2003, Agriculture Comm.	Johnson-R	38.5	10.4		
	Odom-D	61.5	89.6		
1996, U.S. Senate	Landrieu-D	19.5	21.0	37.1	78.6
	Jenkins-R	26.3	16.4	62.9	21.4
	Ieyoub-D	8.6	42.4		
	Duke-R	19.2	4.8		
	Others (*n* = 11)	26.3	15.3		
1998, U.S. Senate	Breaux-D	55.6	80.1		
	Donelon-R	41.1	7.8		
	Others (*n* = 6)	3.2	12.1		
2002, U.S. Senate	Landrieu-D	32.6	78.5	36.9	91.4
	Terrell-R	28.9	6.6	63.1	8.6
	Cooksey-R	23.3	6.4		
	Perkins-R	12.0	4.2		
	Others (*n* = 5)	3.4	8.1		

TABLE 4.6. Estimates of white voter and black voter preferences in Louisiana statewide constitutional offices and U.S. Senate, 1995–2004 (*continued*)

		Primary		Runoff	
Year, District	Candidate	Whites	Blacks	Whites	Blacks
2004, U.S. Senate	Vitter-R	64.2	11.8		
	John-D	26.3	39.6		
	Kennedy-D	6.7	38.7		
	Morrell-D	0.7	5.1		
	Three others	2.0	4.7		

Source: Ordinary least squares (OLS) estimates.

African American candidates in **boldface.**

*Jindal is an Indian American.

American candidate to seek the Senate polled just 5 percent of the black vote in 2004.

Cohesion eluded white voters in two contests. Of the four elections in which most whites settled on a candidate, their choice won only twice. In the 1996 and 2002 runoffs, most African Americans supported the winner while most whites preferred the loser.

The decisive 1996 and 2002 contests were the only ones in which most black voters opposed most whites, and in both instances the black preference won. In these two elections, most African Americans opted for the Democrat while the bulk of the white vote went to the Republican.

FEDERAL MONITORING

From 1995 through 2005, Louisiana had more election change proposals rejected by the Department of Justice than any other state (nineteen). Eight of these involved redistricting plans drawn to accommodate shifts in population identified by the 2000 census. Five other objections involved efforts by the city of Shreveport to annex adjoining land. These were all withdrawn in 1997 when the city agreed to change the format of its elections.

During the previous decade (1985–1994), Louisiana had the third-largest number of objections (sixty-two) following Texas and Mississippi. During that decade, easily the most common basis for DOJ objection was a redistricting plan. While an examination of each of these objections is far beyond the scope of this chapter, it is likely that DOJ's inclusion of Section 2 as a consideration when making a Section 5 review figured into a number of these. DOJ rejected the state's proposal for the BESE, as previously noted, for failure to increase the number of majority-black districts. Another objection ultimately reviewed by the U.S. Supreme Court involved the Bossier Parish School District. This objection also rested on the failure of the submitting jurisdiction to increase the number of districts likely to elect African Americans. It would not be surprising if a number of the other objections also stemmed not from a retrogressive plan but from a plan that did not attempt to maximize the number of black districts.

Fraga and Ocampo identified 17,765 submissions made by Louisiana jurisdictions to DOJ pursuant to the requirements of Section 5 between 1990 and 2005.[27] Across these sixteen years, DOJ objected to 158 submissions or 0.9 percent of the total. In addition to registering objections 158 times, DOJ asked the submitting authority to provide additional information on 983 of the submissions. The most frequent basis for these requests for additional information were precincts (355), annexations (186), polling places (185), and redistricting (147). Upon receiving additional information, an objection was levied eighty-one times while in another thirty-eight instances the submitting authority withdrew its request for approval. The relatively large number of requests for additional information on proposals for redistricting conforms with our suspicion that DOJ was often seeking to prompt a jurisdiction to create additional majority-black districts.

In the early 1990s the Department of Justice frequently requested that jurisdictions take steps to maximize black representation in the course of reviewing reapportionment plans. A Louisiana case put an end to those efforts. Prior to the 1990s the standard under which DOJ had reviewed reapportionment plans had been non-retrogression as established in the *Beer* case.[28] Under *Beer,* so long as a new plan did not reduce the number of majority-minority districts or substantially reduce minority concentrations in majority-minority districts, DOJ would approve the plan. During the early 1990s, however, DOJ incorporated Section 2 into its Section 5 reviews.[29] As a result of including Section 2 standards in Section 5 reviews, DOJ objected to plans that were not guilty of retrogression but where the department believed the submitting authority had failed to prove the absence of a discriminatory purpose in the plan it submitted. Thus, even a plan that increased the number of districts likely to elect African Americans would fail to secure preclearance if DOJ believed that still greater numbers of majority-minority districts could have been drawn and the jurisdiction failed to provide an acceptable explanation for why it did not adopt such a plan. Years after most of these redistricting plans had been reviewed by DOJ, the Supreme Court held that the only appropriate standard for Section 5 reviews was retrogression. Whether it would be possible to fashion additional majority-minority districts in a jurisdiction could not be considered during the course of a preclearance review.[30] Had this interpretation of the preclearance process been in effect in the early 1990s, the 4th Congressional District won by Cleo Fields would never have existed.

CONCLUSION

The initial goals of the Voting Rights Act have long since been achieved in Louisiana. African Americans register and vote in large numbers and have done so for years. The percentage of blacks among Louisiana registrants equals or exceeds the African American share of the state's voting-age population. The share of the voting electorate that is African American has at times exceeded its share of the registrants and in other years has been only slightly less than the black share of registrants.

Since Democrats continue to hold most statewide constitutional offices, blacks see their choices for important offices win more often than not. In several highly visible elections, the black preference bested the white choice, as in the gubernatorial elections of 1991 and 2003 and the U.S. Senate elections of 1990, 1996, and 2002.

On occasion black preferences defeat the white choice, but this pattern does not extend to contests in which the black preference is an African American. In the two statewide contests featuring a competitive black candidate, the decisive 1995 and 1999 gubernatorial elections, the African American came up short despite polling 82 percent of the black vote. For a statewide candidate attracting just over 80 percent of the Louisiana

African American vote to win, it would be necessary to get at least 37.1 percent of the white vote, assuming 30 percent of all turnout is African Americans. Fields managed only 13 percent of the white vote in 1995, and Jefferson, running against an incumbent, fared even worse with less than 10 percent of the white vote.

The Fields and Jefferson defeats fit a pattern in which the racial cleavage parallels a partisan divide. Especially in congressional elections, but also in some statewide contests, whites line up behind a Republican while blacks go with the Democrat. A Democratic candidate who is an African American may provide a catalyst to the growing trend of race and party moving along parallel lines. While blacks frequently give 80 percent or more of their votes to a Democratic candidate, a comparable level of white cohesion occurs only when an African American has made it to the runoff and the white vote goes to the African American's Republican opponent. Put simply, the presence of black candidates results in greater white cohesion for white Republicans in Louisiana.

Extensive African American political participation has come to provide critical support to Democratic candidates as growing numbers of whites vote for Republicans. While the white vote has been drifting toward the GOP, Louisiana whites are not as consistently Republican as in some other southern states, and several Democrats have attracted the support of most whites. Although it has not prevented movement toward the GOP, Edwin Edwards' distinctive electoral format adopted thirty years ago has achieved his goal of retarding the erosion of support for the Democratic Party.

CHAPTER 5

VIRGINIA

In Richmond, the Virginia Capitol also doubled as the capitol for the Confederacy. Many of the Civil War battles were fought on the state's soil, and the symbolic end to the insurrection came at Appomattox Court House when General Lee surrendered to General Grant. Decades later, Harry Byrd (D), the leader of Virginia's ruling faction and long-time senator, designed the strategy of massive resistance used by the South to delay efforts at school desegregation. In light of the state's prominent role in opposing the extension of civil rights, it is nothing short of remarkable that the first southern state to have an African American lieutenant governor and the nation's first state ever to elect an African American governor is Virginia. In 2007, the Virginia legislature unanimously passed a resolution in which the state went on record as apologizing for slavery. This set off a call for similar apologies in several other states.

Virginia adopted a poll tax early in the twentieth century and continued its usage until it was invalidated by national constitutional amendment and litigation in the mid-1960s.[1] Other disfranchising techniques adopted by Virginia included the literacy test with an understanding clause.[2] For eighteen years, the state also had a white primary, but after a federal court invalidated the practice in 1930, Virginia, unlike Texas, did not make alterations or otherwise seek to reinstate it.[3]

At the time of the 1964 presidential election, approximately 38.3 percent of Virginia's voting-age African Americans had registered to vote. This was the highest level of black registration among the states that were entirely covered by the initial version of the Voting Rights Act.[4] The overall registration for Virginia at the time of the 1964 election stood at 52.5 percent of the voting-age population (VAP). Thus the state met the threshold for registration to avoid coverage by Section 5. The state was brought under Section 5, however, because only 45 percent of its VAP voted that year. Low turnout was a carryover from the heyday of the Byrd machine that thrived on nonparticipation. As V. O. Key, Jr., reports, the Byrd machine needed to attract as little as 5 percent of the VAP in order to win statewide elections since turnout in gubernatorial primaries exceeded 10 percent of VAP only once from 1925 to 1945.[5]

As of 1964, fourteen Virginia counties had less than 25 percent of their black adults registered to vote and in two counties the figure fell below 10 percent.[6] In addition, Virginia is unique in having independent cities—municipalities that exist outside of counties and which can expand into counties and so shrink the county. Three of these independent cities also had black registration rates below 25 percent. A unique feature for Virginia is that in one county and three independent cities the ranks of African American registrants exceeded the nonwhite adult population as calculated in 1960. In the great bulk of the counties and municipalities, between 30 and 60 percent of the nonwhite VAP had signed up to vote as of 1964.

By the fall of 1967, estimates placed the black registration at 55.6 percent of the voting-age population. Had Virginia been required to meet the participation threshold incorporated in the 1970 version of the Voting Rights Act, which used the 1968 election as its benchmark, the Old Dominion would have surpassed the threshold for Section 5 coverage. In 1968, 58.9 percent of the VAP as calculated from the 1960 census cast ballots.

BLACK REGISTRATION AND TURNOUT

Virginia no longer maintains voter registration figures by race. Consequently, the most reliable figures for registration and turnout of African Americans in Virginia are the estimates developed after each election by the Census Bureau (appendix B). Between 1980 and 2006, Virginia's white population reported being registered at higher rates than did African Americans except in 1986. This is a greater consistency of higher white than black registration than is found in most southern states covered by Section 5. As is often found for southern states, the greatest disparity occurs in 1980, when 65.4 percent of white but only 49.7 percent of African American voting-age adults report being registered. By 1982, the difference had been reduced to just over 7 percentage points, and in 1984, only 1.6 percentage points. Then in 1986 the self-reported registration among African Americans is 3 points greater than for whites.

Unlike for most other southern states, more recent years also reveal much higher percentages of white than black Virginians reporting being registered. In the five most recent elections through 2006, the rate at which whites registered is roughly 10 percentage points or more above the black rate. The greatest gap in recent years opens up in 2002 when only 47.5 percent of African Americans versus 64.1 percent of the whites reported being registered to vote. Even the 2004 election that often saw black registration equal or exceed white registration did little to narrow the gap in Virginia: 57.4 percent of the black and 68.2 percent of the white adults reported having been registered. Excluding Hispanics from the number of registered whites boosts the white figure by 1.2 percentage points in 1998 and by 3.4 percentage points in 2004, and non-Hispanic white registration exceeds black registration by anywhere from 11 to almost 19 percentage points.

In several other southern states, black registration rates exceeded those for African Americans living in other parts of the country. That pattern occurs with less frequency in Virginia, where it appears only in 1986, 1992, and 1996. Nonsouthern blacks registered at slightly higher rates than Virginians in 1988, 1990, and 2006. However, in the most recent midterm election shown in the table, blacks outside the South registered at rates 1.6 percentage points greater than blacks in Virginia.

As with the pattern for in-state registration, the census survey reports in appendix B show Virginia whites voting at higher rates than blacks between 1980 and 2006. In only 1986 did a higher proportion of blacks than whites say they had voted. White turnout exceeded black turnout by relatively small margins in 1982 and 1984. More often election years saw relatively large differences as white turnout increased far more rapidly than did black turnout. Since Virginia does not elect its state legislators and constitutional officers in even-numbered years, off-year participation rates are frequently low. In 1998 and 2002, only about a quarter of Virginia's black adults and a third of the whites bothered to vote. In 2006, black participation rose to a third of the age eligible while among whites it came in a bit below half. Excluding Hispanics from the estimate of white turnout boosts the white participation rate. For 1998 and 2000, the increase is in the neighborhood of 1 percentage point, but in 2004 and 2006, excluding Hispanics increases white participation by 3 points.

Virginia blacks usually turn out at substantially lower rates than whites, but Old Dominion blacks occasionally approximate or even exceed African American turnout in the rest of the nation. In both presidential elections of the 1990s, higher percentages of Virginian than nonsouthern African Americans voted. In 2000, the turnout rate was almost identical for the two groups although slightly higher outside of the South. However, by 2004 non-South blacks voted at substantially higher rates than Virginia blacks.

In 1980, approximately 10 percentage points more of the nonsouthern than Virginian blacks turned out. That is the greatest disparity for a presidential year. In 1998 and 2002, nonsouthern African Americans turned out at rates at least 10 percentage points higher than did Virginia blacks. The difference was especially great in 1998 when 40.4 percent of the African Americans outside the South but only 23.8 percent of those in Virginia picked up a ballot. The 2006 elections saw the disparity shrink to 3.4 points. In most years, Virginia whites also vote at lower rates than whites outside the South, although that gap also shrank in 2006. The disparity is due to Virginia's practice of electing statewide elected officials and state legislators in odd-numbered years.

AFRICAN AMERICAN OFFICE HOLDING

When record keeping on the numbers of African Americans in public office began in the late 1960s, Virginia had only thirty. Of these, two-thirds served in municipal offices, with only two holding county positions. The growth in the number of black officials in the Old Dominion came more slowly than in other southern states. Not until the mid-1980s did Virginia have more than one hundred black officials. In that year,

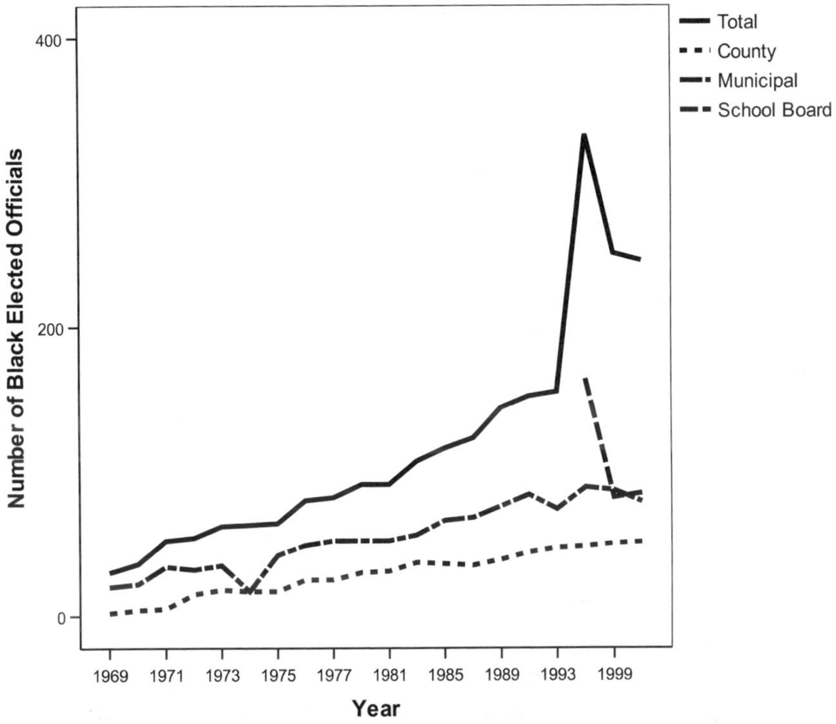

Figure 5.1. Black elected officials in Virginia, 1969–2001. *Source:* Various volumes of the *National Roster of Black Elected Officials* (Washington, D.C.: Joint Center for Political and Economic Studies).

just over half held municipal office while approximately a third served at the county level.

A glance at figure 5.1 indicates a major reason for the smaller number of black elected officials in Virginia than elsewhere in the South: the state's tradition of having appointed school boards until 1997. With the election of school board members, the number of black elected officials reported by the Joint Center for Political and Economic Studies doubles to 333, with almost exactly half of these serving on school boards. However, two years later, the number of school board members reported by the Joint Center is halved and the total number of black officials falls by eighty-two. The numbers drop again slightly in 2001 so that in the most recent enumeration, fewer than 250 blacks hold office in Virginia.

African Americans in Congress

Under the impetus of Section 2 of the Voting Rights Act, Virginia created a majority-black district in 1991. This new district sprawled throughout much of the Tidewater region, running from the mouth of the James River up to Richmond and over to Petersburg while including some rural counties north of the river. It had a 64 percent black population. In 1992, the new 3rd District sent to Congress Robert Scott, the second African American to serve in the state senate. Scott won a commanding two-thirds of the vote in the Democratic primary and romped to victory with almost 80 percent of the vote in the general election. Scott, unlike some of the other African Americans newly elected to Congress in 1992, ran well among both white and black voters.

The 3rd District was one of those successfully challenged in the wake of *Shaw v. Reno*.[7] The new, somewhat more compact district still extended along the James River from the Chesapeake Bay to Richmond, but it became whiter as the black percentage dropped by 10 points. Nonetheless, Scott continued to win more than three-fourths of the vote.

The 2000 census showed Scott's district to be almost 13 percent below the ideal population for a Virginia congressional district. Scott felt so safe in his seat that at the time of the 2001 redistricting, he urged the legislature to reduce the minority concentration in his district and to increase it in the neighboring, south-side 4th District. The legislature ignored Scott's generosity and maintained the black percentage in the 3rd District at 56 percent black—the same black concentration that the 2000 census had shown to be present. Rather than increase the black proportion in District 4, the legislature reduced it from 39 to 33 percent in the new plan.

The incumbent's neighborliness was at least in part motivated by the near miss of an African American candidate in a special election held in the 4th District in 2001, conducted to fill the vacancy caused by the death of Norman Sisisky (D-Va.). In that election, in a district that was an estimated 39 percent African American, black Democratic state senator Louise Lucas narrowly lost to white Republican state senator Randy Forbes by 52 to 48 percent, a margin of 5,800 ballots. African American political leaders believed that if the black percentage could be boosted just ever so slightly in the 4th District, then an African American would have a good chance of winning.

The black turnout rate had been 29.7 percent of the black voting-age population, while 30.1 percent of the white VAP went to the polls.[8] Some had thought that black turnout might have been higher in a general election, and therefore a black candidate would have fared better at that time than in the special election. The claim that a general election contest might heighten the prospect of electing a minority candidate of choice is dashed by an evaluation of the November 2001 statewide elections. When the turnout data for the state constitutional offices are reconstituted inside the boundaries of Congressional District 4, the estimated black voter turnout was 28.9 percent of black VAP. This is dwarfed by a 43.0 percent white VAP turnout rate within the district.[9]

The 2001 special election contest was racially polarized. Only 9.7 percent of whites voted for the black Democratic candidate, while nearly all the black vote went for Lucas. In three major statewide races reconstituted within the boundaries of District 4 in 2001, the Democratic share of the white vote ranged from an estimated 15.1 percent for black Democratic attorney general candidate and assembly delegate Don McEachin,[10] to 32.3 percent for the successful Democratic gubernatorial candidate, white suburbanite Mark Warner.[11]

African Americans in the State Legislature

African Americans have served in the Virginia lower chamber since 1967 when two blacks won elections. The growth in black representation in the lower chamber has come slowly as indicated in table 5.1. For the next decade, black membership was never more than two and only reached four in 1979. This pattern is unlike in most other southern states where new districting plans frequently produced a substantial increase in African American legislative presence. In the Virginia House of Delegates, the increase since 1979 has been consistent but gradual. Early in the new century, blacks held eleven of the one hundred seats in the lower chamber. This is substantially lower than the almost 20 percent of the state's voting-age population that is African American.

TABLE 5.1. Racial makeup of the Virginia General Assembly, 1965–2007

	Senate	% Black in Senate	House	% Black in House
1965	0	0.0	0	0.0
1967	0	0.0	2	2.0
1969	1	2.5	2	2.0
1971	1	2.5	2	2.0
1973	1	2.5	1	1.0
1975	1	2.5	1	1.0
1977	1	2.5	1	1.0
1979	1	2.5	4	4.0
1981	1	2.5	4	4.0
1983	2	5.0	4	4.0
1985	2	5.0	5	5.0
1987	2	5.0	7	7.0
1989	3	7.5	7	7.0
1991	3	7.5	7	7.0
1993	4	10.0	7	7.0
1995	5	12.5	8	8.0
1997	5	12.5	9	9.0
1999	5	12.5	10	10.0
2001	5	12.5	10	10.0
2003	5	12.5	11	11.0
2005	5	12.5	11	11.0
2007	5	12.5	11	11.0

Source: Data compiled by the authors.

As indicated in figure 5.2, Virginia ranks at the bottom of the nine Section 5 southern states in terms of black proportional representation in the state legislature relative to the black proportion of the citizen voting-age population. Only two southern Section 5 states exceed proportionality—Florida and Alabama—but four states approach or exceed 80 percent of proportionality, and every other state except Virginia exceeds two-thirds of proportionality (this topic is revisited in the concluding chapter). States with greater proportionality or extra-proportionality will tend toward the upper right-hand corner of the figure; those with poor proportionality will be toward the lower left corner. Virginia ranks below all other southern states in terms of black proportionality in the state legislature, but ranks ahead of Border South states such as Kentucky and Oklahoma, but behind

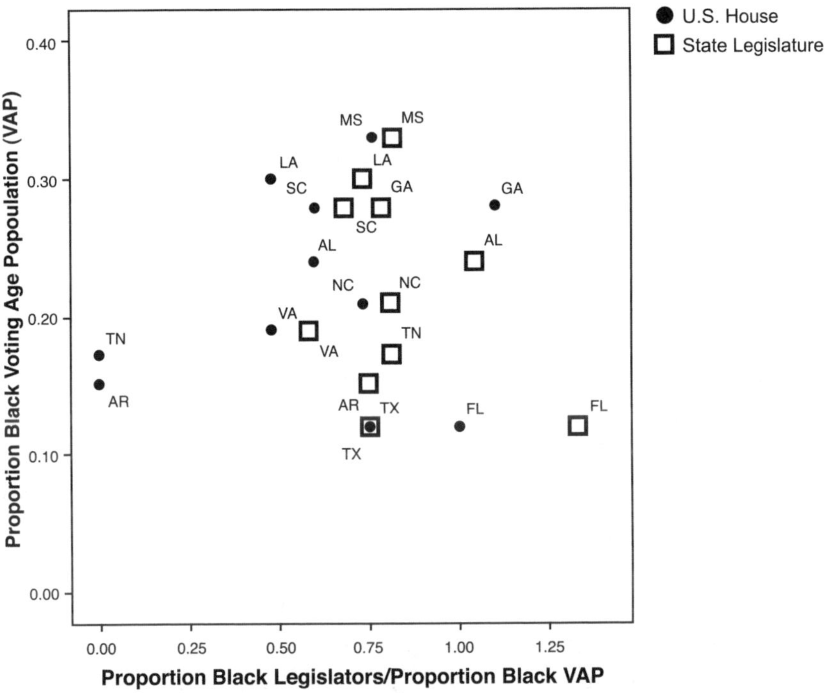

Figure 5.2. Proportionality in black legislative representation in the southern states, 2007. *Source*: Data compiled and computed by the authors.

non-Section 5 states Tennessee (proportionality score = .81) and Arkansas (proportionality score = .75). Figure 5.2 shows Virginia and Louisiana tied at the bottom in terms of black congressional proportionality.

The first black state senator, Douglas Wilder, won election in 1969. He continued his service in the senate until 1985 when he won election as lieutenant governor. During most of his tenure he was the only African American senator in the forty-member body. The pattern for change in black membership in the senate is much like that in the Virginia House of Delegates. The growth has been gradual, beginning in 1983, and is not tied to changes in district lines. By the early part of the twenty-first century, African Americans held five of forty seats. While their proportion of the senate is slightly larger than their percentage in the House of Delegates, it is substantially less than the black percentage among voting-age Virginians.

African Americans in Statewide Office

Virginia elects fewer statewide officials than any other southern state save for Tennessee. In the Old Dominion, only the governor, lieutenant governor, and attorney general run statewide.

As previously noted, in 1985 Douglas Wilder won election as lieutenant governor. He thus became the first African American to hold this position in the South. Since fewer than one in five registered voters in Virginia is black, Wilder's victory relied upon substantial support from white Democrats. Ecological regression analyses and ecological inference analysis indicate that Wilder received between 41 and 47 percent of the white vote in 1985.

Virginia is now the last state in the union to restrict its governor to a single term. Virginia's lieutenant governor is typically a serious candidate for the top position after the governor does his term. And so it was with Wilder. Virginia makes far less use of primaries than other southern states, so Wilder did not have to secure the nomination in a primary but rather was chosen at a state convention. Wilder ran well in preelection polls and seemed to be assured of a comfortable victory in the exit polls. However, when the votes were actually counted, his victory margin was razor thin, less than 6,800 out of almost two million votes cast, prompting a recount. Wilder attracted a share of the white vote, yet many whites who voted for his Republican opponent, Marshall Coleman, hesitated to acknowledge to pollsters that they were not going to support the black candidate, giving rise to the Wilder or Bradley effect much discussed in the run-up to the 2008 presidential election.

Exit polls conducted by CBS News show Wilder getting 92 percent of the black vote and 44 percent of the white vote, which would translate into a 53–47 victory, with a margin of error at 95 percent confidence of ±2.9 points, assuming African Americans constituted 18 percent of the voters who turned out. Wilder's victory fell just outside this range. His white vote share was lower than calculated from the exit poll sample since he did not win by 6 percentage points. To place the Wilder contest in perspective, he ran better among African American voters but worse among whites than others on the Democratic ticket. Donald Beyer, the Democratic nominee for lieutenant governor, ran just 4 points better than Wilder among whites but 12 points worse among African Americans in the exit poll. Mary Sue Terry (D), who won reelection as attorney general, ran 9 points better among whites and 12 points worse among African Americans than Wilder.[12] While Wilder's victory was far smaller than had been anticipated, it was a victory, and in that sense is an impressive display of biracial politics when compared to the other notable gubernatorial elections involving a black candidate. In California's 1982 and 1986 elections, Los Angeles mayor Tom Bradley (D) twice lost despite initial polling showing him competitive. In his second bid, Bradley managed only 37 percent of the vote against incumbent George Deukmejian (R).[13]

Wilder's victory, narrow as it was, marked the last Democratic victory in a Virginia gubernatorial election for a dozen years. Republicans George Allen and James Gilmore, III, won the governorship in 1993 and 1997. Thus Wilder did better at appealing to a wide range of Virginia voters than either of the two white Democrats who sought to succeed him.

The rising tide of Republicanism crested in 1993 and 1997 when the GOP won all three statewide offices, and subsequently took control of the legislature. Exit polling data from Edison Media Research for the 1997 Virginia gubernatorial election demonstrate a powerful racial dimension to the partisan preferences of gubernatorial voters. Gilmore, the prevailing Republican, pulled an estimated 61 percent of the white vote, compared to just 14 percent of the black vote. Gilmore's Democratic opponent attracted less of the white vote, according to exit polls, than did Wilder. The contests for attorney general and lieutenant governor saw voting patterns similar to the Gilmore-Beyer gubernatorial election as more than 80 percent of the electorate reported straight-ticket voting for the three major offices.[14]

Republicans held these posts until 2001, when Democrats recaptured two of the three statewide constitutional offices of the commonwealth. Democrats regained momentum behind the candidacy of the narrow loser of the 1996 U.S. Senate general election. Mark Warner, a northern Virginia entrepreneur, won the governorship with a comfortable five-point margin, while Tim Kaine carried the lieutenant governor's slot by a two-point margin as reported. The performance of Don McEachin, the African American Democratic nominee for attorney general, pales in comparison. McEachin ran more than 10 percentage points behind the top of the Democratic ticket.[15] Some of the difference in the support for McEachin compared with Warner is that the gubernatorial nominee had the experience of a previous statewide contest. Moreover, Warner—who made his fortune in what became Nextel—spent $5 million out of his own pocket in the contest, a sum that few candidates could muster.[16] McEachin's showing was also substantially worse than Democrats running for the three statewide offices in 2005. While Republicans narrowly captured the offices of lieutenant governor and attorney general, the two losing Democrats each got at least 49.3 percent of the vote and Kaine, who moved up from lieutenant governor to the top office, won with 51.7 percent. The Democratic candidate for attorney general lost by just 323 votes, improving over McEachin's margin by 370,000 votes. To some extent, McEachin's poor showing was probably due to his race.[17]

While McEachin fared poorly with the Virginia electorate, Barack Obama won the state in the 2008 Democratic presidential primary with one of his best showings as he took 64 percent of the vote. Exit polls estimate that not only did he win 90 percent of the black vote; he narrowly beat Hillary Clinton among white voters, taking 52 percent of their votes. Of course in November, Obama faced a whiter (30 percent of the Democratic primary voters were black) and more conservative electorate. Nonetheless, in recent years Democrats have done better in Virginia than in much of the South as indicated by winning the last two gubernatorial elections, sending Jim Webb to the Senate in 2006, and regaining a narrow majority in the state senate in 2007. These successes served as a prelude to Obama winning Virginia's electoral votes, the first Democratic presidential nominee since 1964 to do so.

RACIAL VOTING PATTERNS

While Doug Wilder failed to command the support of most white voters in his gubernatorial bid, U.S. Rep. Robert Scott, the first African American to represent a portion of Virginia in Congress in approximately a century, ran impressively among white voters.

The bulk of table 5.2 deals with Democratic congressional candidacies in the Tidewater region from 1986 through 1994. Most of the estimates presented here come from a report prepared by Ronald Weber as part of the *Moon v. Meadows* suit challenging Congressional District 3 as violative of the standards established in *Shaw v. Reno* and *Miller v. Johnson*. The estimates involving black Democratic candidates, except for Scott in 1986 and Lucas in 2001, come from the expert report prepared by Lisa Handley, another expert in that same *Moon v. Meadows* litigation.

Table 5.2 shows that nonincumbent Democrats tended to run poorly among white voters. For example, in the 1st District, held for many years by Republican Herb Bateman, no Democrat attracted as much as 40 percent of the white vote. Robert Scott's 1986 challenge to Bateman attracted less white support than did other Democrats according to the regression estimates but is the median case in terms of the white support in homogenously white precincts. Prior to the redrawing of District 3 to give it a black majority, white Democrats ran very poorly with white voters. In the 7th District in the early 1990s, the Democratic nominee attracted only about one-seventh of the white vote. In a similar fashion, when Owen Pickett ran for an open seat in the 2nd District in 1986, he got less than 30 percent of the white vote according to the OLS estimate, a performance in keeping with other 1st District Democrats.

Democratic incumbents generally did better, and Pickett attracted half of the white vote in his first reelection bid. After district reconfiguration in the early 1990s, Pickett continued to get a majority of the white vote. In the 4th District, incumbent Norman Sisisky received approximately half of the white vote in 1992 and 1994 and almost three-fourths of the white vote in his last contested election. In both the old and the new districts, Sisisky frequently had no Republican opposition. After his death, Louise Lucas, an African American, managed only approximately 10 percent of the white vote in the special election to fill the vacancy. Her performance is comparable to that of Bobby Scott in the 1st District fifteen years earlier.

Against this background, Scott's ability to attract half of the white vote in the open 3rd District in 1992 is a remarkably strong showing for a Democrat. A different kind of research, perhaps involving field interviews, would be necessary to determine why Scott did so much better in 1992 than he did six years earlier or than Lucas did nine years later.[18] Perhaps the quality of the campaign and the candidates or Scott's experience gained in the earlier congressional bid might account for his much stronger performance in 1992.

TABLE 5.2. OLS estimates of white support for Democratic candidates in Virginia, 1986–2001

	Democratic candidate	White % for Democrat
Congressional District 1		
1986	**Scott**	9.2
1988	Ellenson	11.5
1990	Fox	34.0
1992	Fox	31.5
1994	Sinclair	18.1
Congressional District 2		
1986	Pickett	29.0
1988	Pickett	50.5
1990	Pickett	73.1
1992	Pickett	51.7
1994	Pickett	54.4
Congressional District 3		
1986	Powell	17.0
1988	No Democratic nominee	
1990	Starke	27.0
1992	**Scott**	50.7
1994	**Scott**	46.5
Congressional District 4		
1986	Sisisky	No Republican nominee
1988	Sisisky	No Republican nominee
1990	Sisisky	68.7
1992	Sisisky	57.6
1994	Sisisky	49.1
1996	Sisisky	74.0
1998	Sisisky	No Republican nominee
2000	Sisisky	No Republican nominee
2001*	**Lucas**	9.7
Congressional District 7		
1992	Berg	14.9
1994	Berg	14.2
Statewide		
1985, Lt. Governor	**Wilder**	40.8
1989, Governor	**Wilder**	28.0

Sources: Lisa R. Handley, "Liability Issues in *Moon v. Meadows*" (September 4, 1996); Ronald E. Weber, "Final Report on Liability Issues for Hearing in *Moon v. Meadows*" (August 2, 1996); and Ronald Keith Gaddie, "An Evaluation of Voter Participation and Vote Choice in Virginia's 4th Congressional District," prepared for *Hall v. Commonwealth* (June 1, 2002).

*The 2001 special election was necessitated by Norman Sisisky's death. The estimate of white voting preferences were made using Gary King's ecological inference program.

African American candidates in **boldface**.

TABLE 5.3. Estimates of racial support for Democratic Party candidates in Virginia Congressional District 3, 1992–2004

		OLS Estimates		EI Estimates	
		Black	Nonblack	Black	Nonblack
1992	Scott	.966	.469	.953	.481
1994	Scott	1.000	.403	.988	.440
1996	Scott	.986	.553	.979	.575
1998	Scott	1.000	.518	.986	.557
2000	Scott	—No opponent—			
2002	Scott	—No opponent—			
2004	Scott	1.000	.484	.925	.515

Source: Ordinary least squares (OLS) and ecological regression (EI) estimates from 1992 through 1998 are from Ronald Keith Gaddie, "An Evaluation of Racial Polarization and the Election of Minority Legislative Candidates of Choice in the Vicinity of Virginia Congressional Districts 3 and 4." Prepared for *Hall v. Commonwealth,* June 2003. The authors computed estimates from 2004.

Note: Cell entries are estimated proportions of the vote for the candidates.

Table 5.3, excerpted from a previous analysis by Gaddie,[19] shows OLS and ecological inference estimates of support for Rep. Bobby Scott in his reelection bids through 2004.[20] Scott twice won reelection without opposition (2000 and 2002), and in 1996, 1998, and 2004, at least two estimates in each year show Scott commanding a majority of the white vote. The estimates of white support for Scott in 1992 and 1994 in table 5.3 are several percentage points lower than in table 5.2 and do not show Scott with a majority of the white vote in his initial election. A possible explanation for the inconsistency is different weightings being applied to the data by those making the estimates (the data analyzed in table 5.3 are not weighted).

The bottom of table 5.2 presents estimates of Douglas Wilder's performances in two statewide contests. These estimates from Lisa Handley's expert report show that when winning the office of lieutenant governor, Wilder attracted just over 40 percent of the white vote.[21] The 40 percent of the white vote in this open seat contest exceeds the figure managed by Pickett in 1986 although it fails to match Scott's 1992 showing in the 3rd District. Four years later, Handley estimates that Wilder won approximately a third of the white vote on his way to becoming governor, a performance similar to Pickett's in his initial congressional bid and substantially greater than Louise Lucas's showing in the 4th District special election. According to Handley, as a gubernatorial candidate, Wilder received a share of the white votes similar to that often obtained by Democratic challenges but substantially less than usually won by Democratic incumbents.

Ecological inference analysis and OLS estimates of county-level data presented in table 5.4 indicate that Wilder's share of the white vote in the gubernatorial bid was down by 5 to 6 points when compared to his earlier run for lieutenant governor. These estimates indicate that Wilder's 1989 performance among whites was roughly comparable to that of subsequent Democratic candidates for statewide office. The estimates based on county-level data for lieutenant governor in table 5.4 are quite similar to the Handley estimates based on precinct-level data. For the gubernatorial election, the county-level analysis shows Wilder attracting far more of the white vote than do the precinct-level estimates. The county-based estimates are in line with the exit poll results from 1989 and therefore overestimate Wilder's support among whites but may be closer to the actual vote share than the 28–35 percent reported by Handley.

Democrats rebounded in 2001, reclaiming two of three statewide offices behind Mark Warner and Tim Kaine. However, the failing statewide candidate, African American Don McEachin, ran less well with white voters. Analyses of white voter preferences in the Tidewater region show McEachin running 16 points behind the successful Democratic candidates for governor and lieutenant governor. Exit polling showed a similar disparity.[22] Attributing all of the difference to race is to load on a single-factor explanation that is not reflected in the public record. McEachin survived a difficult (and rare) statewide primary of four candidates and was more closely associated with liberal positions on gun control and crime. According to one pre-election assessment,

> McEachin, a personal-injury lawyer who is the first black to run for the Virginia office on a major party ticket, has been hampered by a bruising primary in June to win the nomination. No sooner had he won the four-way race, which drained his campaign war chest, than the party's gubernatorial candidate, Mark R. Warner, disassociated from his positions on capital punishment and gun safety. "He hasn't had a lot of support from the top of the ticket, and he utilized

TABLE 5.4. Estimates of white support for Democrats in statewide constitutional offices in Virginia, 1985–2005

Year/Office/Candidate		OLS	EI
1985	Governor (Baliles)	51.9	40.8
	Lt. Governor (**Wilder**)	47.3	46.2
1989	Governor (**Wilder**)	42.0	40.6
	Lt. Governor (Beyer)	46.5	41.3
1993	Governor (Terry)	32.2	42.9
	Lt. Governor (Beyer)	46.5	41.2
1997	Governor (Beyer)	36.6	38.6
	Lt. Governor (Payne)	40.8	41.3
	Att'y General (Dolan)	38.7	41.1
2001	Governor (Warner)	46.8	*
	Lt. Governor (Kaine)	43.7	*
	Att'y General (**McEachin**)	30.2	*
2005	Governor (Kaine)	42.5	*
	Lt. Governor (Byrne)	41.1	*
	Att'y General (Deeds)	45.5	*

Source: Computed by authors from data obtained from Virginia State Board of Elections and the Geospatial & Statistical Data Center at the University of Virginia.

*EI estimation would not converge to create unique solution.

African American candidates in **boldface**.

> resources in the primary that he has not been able to replenish. . . . His campaign has struggled. If he wins, he'll win on the coattails of the guy at the top. The sense is that if Earley is close, then Kilgore wins."[23]

McEachin was outspent by almost one-third, a disparity probably not fully reflective of the costly primary he survived.

Evidence from State Legislative Elections

In a 2003 report, Gaddie examined elections involving African American candidates in legislative districts in the parts of Virginia usually included in Congressional Districts 3 and 4.[24] He used the two accepted techniques for analyzing voter preferences introduced previously in our work: ecological regression and ecological inference (EI) analyses. Estimates of black voter and nonblack voter preferences for each contest appear in table 5.5.

Of thirty-three legislative general election contests examined in table 5.5, in fewer than half (fourteen) did both the EI and OLS estimates show pluralities of whites and blacks choosing different candidates.[25] In ten contests, both estimating techniques show pluralities of black and white voters agreeing on the same candidates with all but state house District 74 in 2001 actually reporting majorities of both races rallying to the same candidate. In the other nine contests, the ecological regression estimates and the ecological inference estimates disagree as to whether pluralities of whites and blacks opposed one another. Those districts are: in 1993, house Districts 61, 93, 95; in 1995, senate District 5 and house Districts 62 and 69; in 1997, house District 74; in 1999, senate District 2; in 2001, house District 92. The black candidate of choice prevailed in all nine of those cases.

The discrepancies between EI and ecological regression occur when the nonblack vote is closely divided. The critical .500 vote share value is typically within the predictive errors of the point estimates for EI and ecological regression in these cases. Gaddie notes that, "If we considered all of the mixed cases to be racially polarized, it would mean that polarized voting is occurring roughly two-thirds of the time in black-white legislative contests in this part of Virginia. . . . However, black candidates of choice won about 85% of all legislative contests examined, and won both polarized and other contests with similar frequency."[26]

So while blacks and whites often voted in opposition, the result did not rise to the level of legally significant, racially polarized bloc voting. Black candidates and black candidates of choice won far more often than they lost. Black candidates who were candidates of choice won in thirty of thirty-three instances.

Black candidates are winning in Virginia, but those victories are not equally large. Support for black candidate of choice varies, specifically among white voters, and this variation is related to the type of candidate confronted. Table 5.6 divides contests by candidate of choice and type of opponent—white independent, white Republican, black Republican—and averages the support overall and by racial group for each type of contest. Estimated black vote share for black candidates of choice is high across the board, but highest for those candidates who confront white, independent opponents, and lowest among those who confront Republicans. Black support for candidates of choice is lowest, on average, when the opponent is a black Republican.

Table 5.5. OLS and EI estimates of support for black candidates in Tidewater region state legislative general elections

			OLS		EI	
	Contest	Black candidate	Black	Nonblack	Black	Nonblack
1991	Assembly District 70	Ealey	1.000	.261	.923	.288
	Assembly District 77	Forehand	.124	.995	.222	.895
	Assembly District 89	Jones	.995	.565	.939	.588
	Assembly District 95	Crittenden	.991	.509	.961	.555
	State Senate District 5	Miller	1.000	.421	.992	.459
	State Senate District 16	Marsh	1.000	.222	.926	.330
	State Senate District 18	Lucas	.969	.080	.910	.142
1993	Assembly District 61	Green	.650	<0		
	Assembly District 70	Jones	1.000	.202	.933	.259
	Assembly District 71	Cunningham	.973	.806	.969	.816
	Assembly District 77	Spruill	.938	.562	.912	.545
	Assembly District 80	Melvin	.829	.721	.819	.731
	Assembly District 93	Sharpe	<0	.184	.988	.248
	Assembly District 95	Crittenden	.984	.467	.976	.524
1995	Assembly District 62	Brown	.570	.115	.482	.124
	Assembly District 69	Moore	.050	.511	.096	.403
	Assembly District 70	Jones	.949	.284	.932	.323
		Moore	.024	.023		
	Assembly District 74	McEachin	.917	.300	.830	.485
	Assembly District 77	Spruill	.999	.553	.960	.560
	Assembly District 80	Melvin	1.000	.171	.934	.286
	State Senate District 5	Miller	.697	.523	.994	.461
	State Senate District 18	Lucas	.947	.097	.893	.201
1997	Assembly District 71	Baskerville	.942	.792	.931	.792
	Assembly District 74	Meachin	981	.510	.992	.486
1999	Assembly District 90	Robinson	.965	.066	.904	.077
	Assembly District 92	Christian	.814	.640	.837	.581
	State Senate District 2	Maxwell	.922	.566	.890	.133
2001	Assembly District 63	Bland	.675	.359	.647	.394
		Dance	.325	.641	.353	.606
	Assembly District 71	Baskerville	.991	.563	.949	.606
	Assembly District 74	Miles	.714	.484	.712	.496
	Assembly District 90	Robinson	.896	.111	.794	.143
	Assembly District 92	Christian	.967	.370	.814	.544
	Assembly District 95	Crittenden	.963	.353	.953	.329

Source: Ronald Keith Gaddie, "An Evaluation of Racial Polarization and the Election of Minority Legislative Candidates of Choice in the Vicinity of Virginia Congressional Districts 3 and 4," prepared for *Hall v. Commonwealth,* June 2003.

TABLE 5.6. Support for black candidates of choice, controlling for opponents, in Virginia general elections

	Opponent is:		
Black candidate of choice's:	White, GOP	Black, GOP	White, Ind.
Total vote share	.573	.630	.744
Estimated black vote share (eco. reg.)	.860	.810	.930
Estimated black vote share (EI)	.848	.776	.904
Estimated nonblack vote share (eco. reg.)	.301	.424	.513
Estimated nonblack vote share (EI)	.368	.496	.504
N	15	2	15

Source: Derived from the data in table 5.5.

Most of the vote shift, however, is among white voters. When black candidates of choice confront white independents, they garner, on average, majority white voter support; however, when confronting Republicans, especially white Republicans, the black candidates of choice run an average of 14 to 21 percentage points lower. Black-versus-white contests result in stark black-versus-white choices when Republicans run rather than when the opponent is an independent, which indicates a strong partisan component to the vote choice in these biracial contests, or, as Gaddie observed, "This result indicates that polarization, by being more pronounced in the more-partisan context, reflects a function of party."[27]

FEDERAL MONITORING

Despite having relatively low rates of black registration and turnout, Virginia has drawn fewer objections from the Department of Justice (DOJ) than most of its southern neighbors. During the first decade of the Voting Rights Act, Virginia received only eight objections. The only southern state with fewer was North Carolina, and unlike the Tar Heel State, where Section 5 applied to only forty counties, all of Virginia was subject to the preclearance requirement. In each of the next two decades, Virginia had fewer objections than any other southern state that had been covered by Section 5 since its initial passage. From 1975 to 1984, DOJ objected to ten submissions from Virginia, and in the next decade the number of objections fell to seven. In the most recent decade, DOJ turned back six submissions from the Old Dominion. That number exceeds the figures for Alabama (two) and North Carolina (four). Of the six most recent objections, five came in response to redistricting plans drawn to accommodate the 2000 census, with three of these directed at Northampton County.

From 1990 through 2005, Virginia jurisdictions submitted a total of 16,697 proposed changes to DOJ for approval and experienced twelve objections.[28] On approximately 1 percent of these submissions (176), DOJ requested additional information. Approximately a quarter of these requests involved the location of polling places and a quarter dealt with precincts while almost a fifth involved redistricting. Upon receiving additional information, DOJ found nothing to object to in 146 of these instances. Only eight items in which more information was requested resulted in an objection.

As another indicator that parts of Virginia have scored well in terms of compliance with the Voting Rights Act, thirteen jurisdictions have bailed out, which means that they satisfied a court that they should no longer have to comply with Section 5. These thirteen Virginia jurisdictions have been the only ones to have emerged from Section 5 coverage in recent decades.[29] The jurisdictions involved include nine counties and four independent cities. The nine counties run along the western edge of the state, making an almost contiguous line from the Maryland border most of the way to the North Carolina border. Three of the cities are also in the western part of the state, with the fourth one, Fairfax, being in metropolitan Washington.

CONCLUSION

Black registration and turnout have increased but still lag white participation levels in the commonwealth. Black voter turnout in Virginia often lags behind the rest of the United States. The proportion of African American legislators compares less favorably with the black proportion in Virginia's adult population than is found in similar comparisons in other southern states subject to Section 5. However, black candidates in the southeastern part of the state often defeat white opponents to win seats in the assembly and senate and they not infrequently win a majority of the white vote.

Beginning in the 1980s, both black and white Democratic candidates for statewide constitutional office have struggled to secure a majority of the white vote. Of the eighteen statewide contests held between 1985 and 2005, Democrats have won ten, including two of three races featuring African American candidates. Of the nine contests for which estimates of racial preferences appear in table 5.4, the Democrat carried the bulk of the white vote in no more than one election. Even when confronted with a solidly Republican white vote, Democrats still managed to win half the statewide contests by relying on a coalition that combines overwhelming African American support with a sizable minority of the white vote. That coalition accomplished what no other state has achieved: the election of a black chief executive.

Most recently, in 2006, the black vote was critical in electing Democrat Jim Webb to the Senate, thereby ending the presidential hopes of GOP incumbent senator George Allen. In this increasingly competitive state, the black vote can be decisive. In 2005, it helped elect a Democratic governor with 51.7 percent of the vote and almost sufficed to sweep the three statewide offices for Democrats. A Republican lieutenant governor won with a margin of less than twenty-three thousand votes, while in the contest for attorney general, the Republican's margin of victory was a scant 323 votes out of almost two million cast. In the 2006 Senate race, Webb attracted 85 percent of the black vote in exit polls while the unsuccessful incumbent, Allen, carried the white vote with 58 percent. The 2008 election saw former Governor Mark Warner win the open Senate seat in a landslide with 64 percent of the vote which included an impressive 56 percent of the white vote.

Electoral patterns suggest that African American and white Democratic congressional candidates perform similarly after controlling for incumbency status. Nonincumbent Democrats, regardless of race, typically attract little white support. On the other hand, incumbent Democrats—both black and white—can usually get the bulk of the white vote. African

American member of Congress Robert Scott succeeded in attracting approximately half the white vote when seeking the open 3rd District and continues to run well with white voters, even winning without opposition in two of the three most recent elections through 2006.

CHAPTER 6

South Carolina

V.O. Key, Jr., writes of the "harshness and ceaselessness of race discussion in South Carolina."[1] After noting the size of the black population in the state, Key observes that "South Carolina's preoccupation with the Negro stifles political conflict."[2] Of all the former Confederate states, South Carolina had, proportionally, the largest slave population and the largest proportion of white households owning slaves. Historically, it was the most bellicose in defense of slavery from prior to the founding of the United States through the beginning of the Civil War, when the first shot was fired in Charleston harbor. The status and subjugation of blacks in South Carolina was a priority of white political leadership and a matter of public policy.

The behavior of whites in South Carolina at the end of the nineteenth century and on into the twentieth century illustrates Key's black-threat hypothesis.[3] The state's population was almost 60 percent black in 1900 and remained majority black through the 1920 census. For more than half a century after the Civil War, if African Americans had had access to the ballot, and had voted cohesively, they could have elected the statewide officials. Many counties would have been subject to black rule in a fair electoral environment, and the influence of black votes would have persisted well beyond 1920 in some counties. The racial environment was rent with white supremacist rhetoric as race baiters like "Pitchfork Ben" Tillman encouraged whites to keep blacks subordinated.

South Carolina whites headed off the possibility of black political dominance (or even influence) by instituting techniques designed to restrict black political participation. The state adopted a literacy test in 1895 and employed a white primary from 1896 until 1947. As part of its broad panoply of disfranchising techniques, South Carolina adopted a poll tax in 1895 and continued to require payment of this tax through the 1950 election cycle. The state also used a multiple-box law to maximize the potential ballot spoilage by inattentive or illiterate voters. The challenge facing voters was to separate their ballots and deposit the correct proportion in the correct box. For example, one box might be for gubernatorial ballots while another might contain the votes for attorney general. Failure to put the right ballot in the right box resulted in the ballot being excluded. This was a technique designed to make it difficult for illiterates to complete the voting process since they could not read the identifying labels for the boxes. To prevent a literate voter telling illiterate friends the location of the boxes, they were shifted periodically during the course of Election Day.

After the U.S. Supreme Court finally struck down use of the white primary in 1944,[4] South Carolina launched extraordinary efforts to maintain the white primary by repealing all state legislation relating to the conduct of primary elections.[5] The opposition to black participation proved so successful that estimates place the number of black registrants at three thousand in 1940.[6]

In 1948 South Carolina governor J. Strom Thurmond led the States' Rights Party in a presidential bid—a campaign that stressed traditional southern distrust of federal authority and the commitment to continued subjugation of African Americans' political and economic ambitions.[7] Creation of the States' Rights Party came in reaction to the early steps taken by the national Democratic Party toward promoting equality for blacks. President Truman had desegregated the nation's armed forces through executive order, and at the 1948 Democratic National Convention, liberals led by Senate nominee Hubert Humphrey (D-Minn.) had adopted planks promoting civil rights. Angry southerners had stormed out of the convention and later assembled in Birmingham, Alabama, where they staged their own convention. This meeting nominated Thurmond for president along with Mississippi Governor Fielding Wright for vice president.[8] Thurmond's candidacy succeeded in carrying his home state as well as Alabama, Mississippi, and Louisiana. The campaign failed to secure enough electoral votes to deny a majority of the Electoral College to the nominees of either major party, thereby throwing the election into the U.S. House of Representatives where southerners might have been able to extract concessions on issues dealing with race from the eventual winner.

BLACK REGISTRATION AND TURNOUT

Despite the state's eagerness to secede, its actions encouraging civil war, and a long history of race-baiting oratory, by 1964 South Carolina had a higher share of its African American voting-age population registered to vote than any other Deep South state.[9] At the time of the 1964 presidential election, 37.3 percent of the state's black population along with 75.7 percent of the white population had signed up to vote.[10] While South Carolina whites registered at higher rates than blacks, the state's black registration rate was roughly twice that of Alabama and more than five times the percentage in Mississippi.

Not only did blacks register at relatively high rates in South Carolina, very few counties achieved the almost total exclusion of black voters that was found in other Deep South states. Prior to the Voting Rights Act, only two of the forty-six counties in the Palmetto State had less than 10 percent of their black adults registered to vote.[11] In contrast, seventeen Alabama counties and thirty Georgia counties had less than 10 percent of their adult African Americans registered to vote when the Voting Rights Act was adopted.[12]

Within two years after the signing of the initial Voting Rights Act, a majority (51.2 percent) of South Carolina's adult black population along with 81.7 percent of the white population had signed up to vote. By 1967, after federal examiners had registered 3,403 blacks in Clarendon County, 69.4 percent of the county's black population was on the registration rolls—a tenfold increase from 1964. In McCormick County, which was not immediately visited by federal examiners to sign up voters, black registration had risen from 9.3 percent of the age eligible in 1964 to

43.5 percent by the middle of 1967. The proportion of the black population registered to vote in South Carolina had been 9.5 percentage points below that of its northern neighbor before the Voting Rights Act. By 1967 North and South Carolina had almost identical shares of their black voting-age populations registered.[13]

Census Bureau estimates of registration by race in South Carolina from 1980 through the 2006 presidential election appear in appendix B. During the 1980s, registration rates differed little by race in the Palmetto State. In three of the five elections in the 1980s, higher proportions of African Americans than whites reported being on the voter rolls. The greatest disparities come in 1984 and 1988. In the latter year, 61.8 percent of whites compared with 56.7 percent of blacks had registered. This reversed the 1984 pattern when 62.2 percent of the African Americans and 57.3 percent of the white South Carolinians had registered to vote. During the 1990s, white registration rates generally exceeded those for blacks, although in 1990, black registration exceeded the white figure by 5.7 points. From 1998 through 2004, the two races reported registering at comparable rates, but in 2006 the black rate exceeded whites' by 7.6 points—the largest difference in the entire time period. In 2004, each race reached record high levels of registration with the white figure 3 points above that for African Americans. The sharp decline for whites in 2006, which puts white registration at the lowest level since 1990, raises suspicions about the reliability of the sample.

Self-reported black registration has increased over time. For three of the elections in the 1980s, fewer than 60 percent of the adult blacks reported being registered. Thereafter, the figure dips below 60 percent only in 1994 when it falls to 59 percent. Approximately 68 percent of blacks had registered in the three elections of 1998 through 2002 while the figure increases to a record 71.1 percent in 2004. The 71.1 percent of blacks who reported being registered in 2004 exceeds the white registration rate for any year other than 2004 when the white figure is 74.4 percent.

Beginning with 1998, the Census Bureau has provided estimates of white registration exclusive of Hispanics. Excluding Latinos has essentially no impact on the white registration figure for 1998. In other years, excluding Hispanics raises the white estimate by at least one percentage point, with the largest effect coming in 2006 when the non-Hispanic white figure is 3.3 points higher than the figure that includes Latinos. Black registration continues to equal or exceed that for non-Hispanic whites in the three midterm elections. The non-Hispanic white registration figure in 2000 exceeds the black estimate by just over a percentage point and by 4.4 points in 2004. Overall, eliminating Hispanics has a modest impact on the white registration estimate.

In the earlier elections, especially 1982 through 1988, blacks living outside the South registered at higher rates than those in the Palmetto State. Beginning with 1990, a larger proportion of black South Carolinians than nonsoutherners registered, except for in 1992. While differences between South Carolina and the non-South were modest through 1996, a substantial gap opens up beginning in 1998 when 68 percent of the blacks in South Carolina but only 58.5 percent of the nonsouthern blacks registered. In recent years the disparity has been around 10 points.

Appendix B also contains Census Bureau postelection turnout estimates. In half the elections, South Carolina blacks report voting at higher rates than whites although the differences were modest in 1980 and 1986. The largest difference in favor of African Americans comes in 2006 when 48.9 percent of the blacks but only 41.2 percent of whites reported voting. Previously, the greatest difference occurred in 1984 with 51.4 percent black and 47.9 percent white turnout. In some years when whites voted at higher rates than blacks differences are substantial. For example, in 1988, 11.6 percentage points more whites than blacks voted, and in 1992, 61.6 percent of whites compared to 48.8 of blacks voted. Blacks and whites cast ballots at similar rates from 2000 to 2004; then blacks achieved a 7.7 percentage point advantage in 2006.

For most elections, 40 to 50 percent of black adults voted with the outliers being 1982 and 1994, when approximately 39 percent of blacks turned out, and in 2000 and 2004, when approximately 60 percent of the African Americans went to the polls. In midterm elections, black participation rates are closer to 40 percent. The high point came in 2002 when almost 49 percent of blacks reported voting.

Elimination of non-Hispanic whites has no impact in terms of whether blacks or whites vote at higher rates. While excluding Latinos boosts the white turnout rate, it continued to be less than the black voting rate in

2000, 2002, and 2006. In the other two years removing Latinos increases the participation rate for whites by less than a percentage point, thus slightly widening the gap between white and black voting rates.

Comparing turnout rates for South Carolina blacks with blacks outside the region shows that in the 1980s the nonsoutherners voted at higher rates than in South Carolina. In 1990, 44.6 percent of South Carolina blacks participated in the election compared with 38.4 percent of the non-South blacks. In 1994 and 1996, differences between South Carolina and non-South blacks are small although figures for South Carolina trail those for the non-South. In the five most recent elections, black participation in South Carolina outpaces the non-South. These differences increase from a South Carolina advantage of 2.4 percentage points in 1998 to 7.6 percentage points in 2000 to 9.4 percentage points in 2002. They drop to 2.8 points in 2004, then rebound to 10.9 points in 2006.

Whether compared to the self-reported participation rates of whites in state or blacks outside of the state, South Carolina black participation compares favorably. These comparative rates of participation suggest that obstacles to African-American registration and voting have been eliminated in the Palmetto State.

South Carolina was one of the first states to report actual registration and turnout figures by race. Table 6.1 shows black and white registration and turnout in general elections beginning with 1972. Since these are actual counts, they are not subject to overreporting that can result in overestimation of registration and turnout in the Census Bureau reports. The turnout percentages in table 6.1 use the registration figures as the denominator unlike the Census Bureau figures in appendix B where the denominator is the adult population.

Registration has increased dramatically for both races. The number of African American registrants tripled over the thirty-four–year period. In 1972 fewer than a quarter of a million African Americans had signed up to vote, but in 2006 the figure had reached 702,181 and exceeded the number of white registrants in 1972 by 35,000. During this same period, the number of white registrants grew by more than a million to 1.75 million. In 1972, blacks made up roughly one-fourth of the state's registrants; thirty-six years later, at the time of the 2008 presidential primary, blacks

TABLE 6.1. Registration and turnout by race in South Carolina, 1972–2006

	Registration		Turnout				
	Black	White	Black	White	Turnout Black %	Turnout White %	% Black of Turnout
1972	224,854	666,510	152,546	533,812	67.8	80.1	22.2
1974	261,110	736,302	120,799	416,126	46.3	56.5	22.5
1976	284,926	827,810	192,170	620,878	67.4	75.0	23.6
1978	291,486	804,742	157,567	485,761	54.1	60.4	24.5
1980	319,826	914,363	222,580	696,901	69.6	76.2	24.2
1982	341,709	886,963	189,908	497,990	55.6	56.1	27.6
1984	388,948	1,005,186	262,476	754,155	67.5	75.0	25.8
1986	368,954	928,767	197,746	572,810	53.6	61.7	25.7
1988	388,255	1,047,722	245,304	796,542	63.2	76.0	23.5
1990	358,469	995,933	184,743	608,871	51.5	61.1	23.3
1992	387,624	1,149,516	286,911	950,556	74.0	82.7	23.2
1994	376,981	1,122,608	203,243	749,877	53.9	66.8	21.3
1996	489,850	1,324,927	294,983	908,503	60.2	68.6	24.5
1998	552,066	1,469,697	281,289	817,195	51.0	55.6	25.6
2000	622,244	1,643,955	350,749	1,082,784	56.4	65.9	24.5
2002	557,342	1,490,026	284,354	832,582	51.0	55.9	25.5
2004	659,366	1,655,816	433,732	1,197,416	65.8	72.3	26.6
2006	702,181	1,750,533	260,902	843,230	37.1	48.1	23.6

Sources: Biennial reports of the South Carolina Board of Elections and www.state.sc.us/scsec/election.html.

comprised 28.6 percent of the registrants. This exceeds the black share of South Carolina's citizen adult population, which the Census Bureau estimated to be 27.2 percent as of 2006.

Black turnout in presidential years has almost tripled during the period covered in table 6.1, growing from 155,000 to 433,000. Every presidential election except for 1988 drew more blacks to the polls than had the previous presidential contest. In 1976 and 1984, black participation rose by 40,000 over the election four years earlier. Black turnout jumped 56,000 from 1996 to 2000 and then shot up by another 83,000 in 2004. Increased turnout among African Americans has roughly kept pace with growing registration rates so that approximately two-thirds of the black registrants have cast ballots in presidential elections throughout the period. One exception comes in 2000 when black voting fell to only 56.4 percent before rebounding to 65.8 percent in 2004. The rate for 2004 actually fell below that for black participation in most presidential years going all the way back to 1972 when 67.8 percent of the much smaller number of black registrants voted. Part of the reason for the 2000 and 2004 turnout rates being somewhat lower than in many of the presidential elections is the record number of black registrants.

In 2004, African Americans cast 26.5 percent of the votes in South Carolina, an increase of 4.4 percentage points over the 22.2 percent of the vote casts by blacks in 1972. After black turnout bottoms out in 1994 at 21.3 percent, it bounced up 3 percentage points in the next election. The figure in 2004 (26.5 percent) is the second highest in the time period examined, exceeded only by 1982 when blacks accounted for 27.6 percent of all ballots cast in South Carolina. The share of the votes cast by African Americans in 2004 is less than 2 percentage points below the black share of the voting-age population in South Carolina as estimated by the Census Bureau in 2004. When the much smaller denominator of registration is used rather than the age-eligible population used in appendix B, participation rates for both blacks and whites are higher. Among whites, the 80.1 percent turnout rate in 1972 was exceeded only in 1992. Until 1996, at least three-fourths of the white registrants participated in presidential years. In 1996 and 2000, white turnout sagged to two-thirds of the registrants but rose to 72.3 percent in 2004.

As usually occurs, midterm turnout runs substantially lower than that of presidential years. In 1974, only 46 percent of the black registrants turned out. In subsequent midterm elections, most black registrants cast ballots with the high point (55.6 percent) coming in 1982. Even with midterm black registration setting records in 1998 and 2002, black turnout hovered above 50 percent before plummeting in 2006 when the black participation rate fell to its lowest point in more than three decades. Black abstinence in part reflects the lack of interest generated by contests that year since white turnout also hit bottom. However, the absence among blacks was more pronounced than among whites as African Americans accounted for fewer than a quarter of the ballots, their lowest share since 1994.

While the rate at which black registrants go to the polls is typically a few percentage points lower than the rate for whites, the data in table 6.1 and appendix B indicate that whatever barriers to black participation may have existed forty years ago have been largely, if not totally, overcome. Black registration and turnout have increased dramatically.

The actual figures on turnout rates indicate that African Americans have not voted at higher rates than whites in South Carolina in contrast with the self-reports of participation for some recent years. While the figures in table 6.1 are more reliable than those in appendix B, comparisons with most other states are not possible using the table 6.1 data since most states do not maintain registration data by race or report turnout data by race.

AFRICAN AMERICAN OFFICE HOLDING

When record keeping began in 1969 on the numbers of African American elected officials, South Carolina had twenty-eight. Almost two-thirds of these held municipal offices while only four held county positions and two served on school boards. By 1974, the number of black officeholders in South Carolina had risen to 116. As of 1980, the number exceeded 200, and five years later it broke 300. The most recent figures (see figure 6.1) for 2001 show a total of 534 black officeholders. Among this number are 252 serving in cities and 83 holding county office. Another 157 serve on school boards. The 2001 figures show a slight dip from those at the end of the 1990s.

Early efforts to elect blacks in South Carolina met with opposition from whites who controlled the Democratic Party. Consequently, in South Carolina, as in Alabama and Mississippi, a separate black political party, the United Citizens Party, sprang up. The UCP slated candidates for the legislature, some local offices, and at least one congressional seat in the early 1970s.[14] According to Leggette, the UCP managed to elect only three local officials and soon disappeared after endorsing three of its leaders who ran successfully for the state house in 1970. Recognizing that a separate black party would siphon votes from the Democratic Party, South Carolina Democrats quickly moved to make peace with the new party and in 1970 appointed an African American as an assistant director for the state party.

African Americans in Congress

The South Carolina congressional districting plan for the 1990s created a majority-black district. The 6th District, which included parts of Charleston, Columbia, and all of Florence, was drawn to be 62 percent black. With

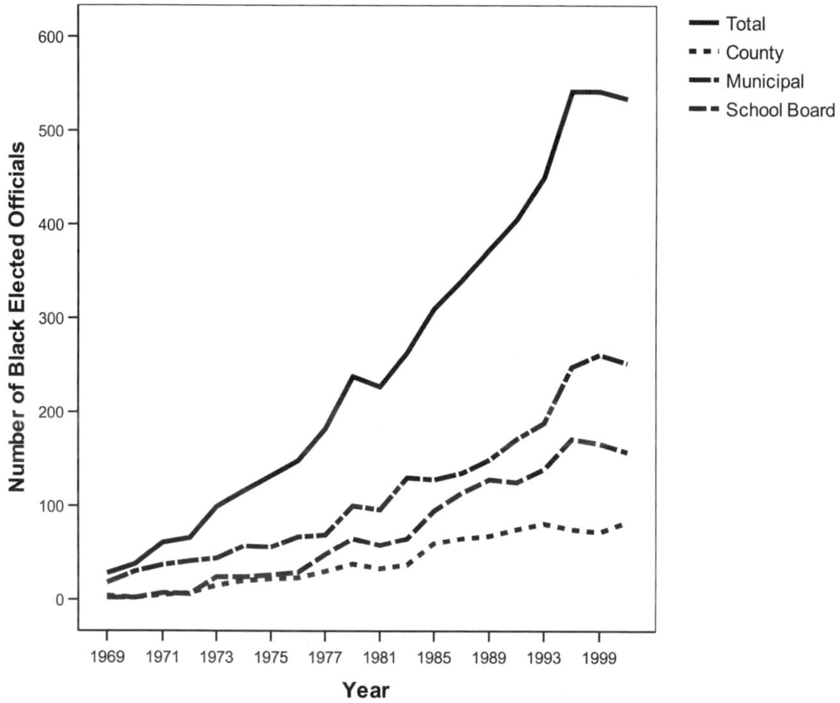

Figure 6.1. Black elected officials in South Carolina, 1969–2001. *Source:* Various volumes of the *National Roster of Black Elected Officials* (Washington, D.C.: Joint Center for Political and Economic Studies).

this heavy concentration of African Americans, the white incumbent, Robin Tallon, who had a reputation for being responsive to black concerns,[15] opted not to seek reelection.[16] James Clyburn, who had spent the previous eighteen years as the commissioner for Human Affairs and who had twice lost bids to become secretary of state, easily defeated a distinguished field of fellow African Americans. While Clyburn had not held elected office, he defeated three state legislators, taking 56 percent of the vote in the initial primary. Clyburn continues to represent the 6th District and appears to be invulnerable even though the district's black population dropped below 57 percent in 2002. When Democrats regained control of the U.S. House in the 2006 election, they chose Clyburn as the majority whip, the third-highest position in that institution's Democratic

Party hierarchy. He is also seen as a power in the state, and prior to the 2008 presidential primary, candidates sought his endorsement.

Republicans' first major success in the Deep South came in South Carolina. This early success stemmed from the decision of Sen. Strom Thurmond to switch to the Republican Party in 1964. Thurmond, a former governor and 1948 States' Rights Party nominee for president, gave the GOP credibility at a time when Republicans in other parts of the Deep South struggled to achieve any success below the level of the presidential elections. Thurmond's credibility helped lead conservatives into the South Carolina GOP and contributed to the Republican capture of the governorship in 1974. By the 1990s, the Republican Party dominated South Carolina politics. Republicans won three consecutive gubernatorial elections between 1986 and 1994, and after 1994 held four of the six congressional seats. For more than a decade, Democrats have held only two South Carolina congressional districts, with one of these being Clyburn's seat.

African Americans currently hold half of the Democratic congressional seats, after more than two decades of earlier black candidacies coming up short. The first African American to win a Democratic nomination, Matthew Perry (later a federal judge), polled 44 percent of the vote against Floyd Spence (R) in the district that contained Columbia in 1974. During the 1980s, Spence again confronted African American challengers in his 64 percent white district. In 1982, the black challenger, Ken Moseley, won 41 percent of the vote. It is highly unlikely that blacks will win a second congressional seat in the Palmetto State.

African Americans in the State Legislature

The South Carolina house of representatives holds the distinction as the only American state legislative chamber to have ever had an African American majority. Briefly in the immediate aftermath of the Civil War, blacks held most seats in the lower chamber.[17] The success enjoyed by African Americans in winning seats in the South Carolina house was short lived, as elsewhere in the South, as white males who had served the Confederacy regained the franchise and began imposing obstacles that reduced black participation.

The first three blacks chosen for the 124-member state house in modern times won election in 1970. As table 6.2 shows, the black share of the membership in the South Carolina house tripled in 1975, reaching 10 percent. This dramatic growth in the number of African Americans in the house came as a result of a court order requiring that only single-member districts be used for the lower chamber, and the new plan created twenty-four black-majority districts.[18] Modest growth in the black proportion occurred over the next two decades. Increasing the number of majority-black districts in the house to twenty-seven in the early 1980s resulted in no additional blacks being elected immediately although a sixteenth African American joined the chamber in 1985. Then, in 1995, the black percentage rose to almost 20 percent. Since the mid 1990s, the black seat share in the house has fluctuated around 20 percent, reaching its highest point, 21.77 percent, in 2007.

In 1998, Democrats chose an African American to be their leader in the house. Earlier in the decade, when Democrats still had a majority in the house, a black lawmaker had failed in his bid to become Speaker Pro Tempore. Members of the Black Caucus have occasionally chaired committees in the house, and even after Republicans seized control of the chamber, some committees had black Democratic leadership.[19]

Traditionally the South Carolina senate dominated the politics of the state. Senators elect judges, and in the past, some held important administrative posts while sitting in the upper chamber.[20] Until the implementation of the one-person, one-vote judicial mandate, each South Carolina county had its own state senator. Each of these forty-six senators was a major, if not the dominant, force in the county. The senator controlled the finances of the county through the supply bill, which had to be enacted by the state legislature and provided funding for county functions. The practice of giving each county its own senator did not survive the 1960s, but the state sought to maintain the sanctity of county boundaries when required to equalize population among senate districts by combining counties into multimember districts when necessary. As a result of the relatively large electoral districts represented by South Carolina senators, all had white majorities. The first African American did not reach the upper chamber until 1983 when DeQuincey Newman won a special election to one of the five seats allocated to Richland County (Columbia).[21]

TABLE 6.2. Racial makeup of the South Carolina legislature, 1965–2007

	Senate	% Black in Senate	House	% Black in House
1965	0	0.0	0	0.0
1967	0	0.0	0	0.0
1969	0	0.0	0	0.0
1971	0	0.0	3	2.42
1973	0	0.0	4	3.23
1975	0	0.0	13	10.48
1977	0	0.0	13	10.48
1979	0	0.0	13	10.48
1981	0	0.0	15	12.10
1983	1	2.17	15	12.10
1985	4	8.70	16	12.90
1987	4	8.70	16	12.90
1989	5	10.87	16	12.90
1991	6	13.04	17	13.71
1993	7	15.22	18	14.52
1995	6	13.04	24	19.35
1997	8	17.39	26	20.97
1999	7	15.22	26	20.97
2001	7	15.22	24	19.35
2003	7	15.22	25	20.16
2005	8	17.39	25	20.16
2007	8	17.39	27	21.77

Source: Data compiled by the authors.

The redistricting plan implemented in 1984 eliminated multimember senate districts. In the new single-member district plan, ten districts had black population majorities and African Americans won four of these. Table 6.2 shows that the number of black seats in the forty-six–member senate has fluctuated between six and eight since 1991 and was eight in 2008. The plan adopted by the legislature in 2003 has nine districts in which most adults are African American.

A study of the activities of African Americans in the legislature during the 1970s and 1980s concluded that they had little influence.[22] Blacks introduced relatively few pieces of legislation and had little success in acquiring leadership positions. Only one black member served on an exclusive committee.

Republicans took control of the state house in 1995 and a decade later held 60 percent of the seats. They won a majority in the senate in 2001 and by 2005 held 59 percent of the seats. As Democrats have become the minority party, blacks have come to constitute larger shares of the shrunken party. Of the fifty-one house Democrats in 2007, twenty-seven were African Americans. In the upper chamber, eight of twenty Democrats were black. With loss of control by Democrats, African American legislators have little prospect of playing significant roles in the South Carolina legislature, though black clout in the Democratic caucus is enhanced.

Statewide Candidacies

No African American has won a statewide office in South Carolina in modern times. Theo Mitchell, a black state senator, did win the Democratic nomination for governor in 1990. This nomination, however, was widely seen as having little value because of the popularity of the incumbent Republican Carroll Campbell. Mitchell was further weakened by federal indictments and managed only 27 percent of the vote. He had difficulty mobilizing even the black community. Exit poll data for South Carolina in 1990 show Campbell with 24 percent of the African American vote.[23]

The growing significance of the black vote within the Democratic Party came after Republicans emerged as the majority party in the state based on its ability to appeal to most white voters. As a consequence, Democrats have struggled to win any offices. By 2005, only two of the nine constitutional offices in the Palmetto State—commissioner of education and state treasurer—had a Democratic incumbent. Democrats allowed the position of adjutant general to go to a Republican by default since no Democrat came forward to contest the position. Republicans dominated the 2006 elections, winning all but one statewide office.

African Americans competed for two statewide posts in 2002. Steve Benjamin was the Democratic nominee for attorney general while Rick Wade represented the Democratic Party in the contest for secretary of state. The seven Democrats who lost in 2002 took an average of 45.8 percent of the vote.[24] The two African American candidates received the smallest vote shares among the losing Democrats; their percentages were no more than 2.7 percentage points below the average. In losing his bid for attorney general, Wade came within a third of a percentage point of the vote share for then-incumbent Democratic governor Jim Hodges. These results suggest that race has little direct impact on the voting behavior of South Carolina voters, per se. Instead, with Republicans winning all but two of the statewide offices being contested, party seems to be a better predictor, though the party environment is racially constructed. The tide toward the Republican Party was so strong in 2002 that two Democratic incumbents, Governor Hodges and Comptroller General Jim Lander, both fell to Republican challengers.

Further evidence of the degree to which partisanship may be more significant than race is offered in table 6.3. This table shows the racial makeup of individuals who participated in the Democratic primaries from 1984 through 2006. In the 1980s, whites constituted almost two-thirds of the Democratic primary voters. The number of Democratic primary participants and the share of the Democratic primary vote cast by whites decline over time. In 1996, for the first time, more African Americans than whites voted in the Democratic primary. In the next two primaries, slightly more white than black voters asked for Democratic ballots. But in the 2002 Democratic primary, which had a record low number of participants at just over 114,000, 61 percent of those relatively few voters were African Americans. This is the primary that chose the nominees who fared so poorly in the general election for constitutional offices. In the 2004 primary, far more African Americans than whites again participated, with blacks making up 58 percent of the Democratic primary electorate. In 2006, almost 60 percent of the Democratic primary participants were black. African Americans also dominated the 2008 presidential primary, casting 56.4 percent of the vote and giving Obama his first primary win. Over time, as the role of the Democratic primary in choosing those who will lead South Carolina has declined, so has the interest of white voters who increasingly leave the choices of Democratic candidates to African Americans.

The overall Democratic primary vote has decreased substantially over time. In 1986, a midterm election to choose nominees for state constitutional officers, almost 360,000 voters helped select those Democratic nominees. In the two most recent midterm elections, fewer than 150,000 voters participated in the Democratic primary. (Since South Carolina

TABLE 6.3. Turnout in South Carolina primaries, 1984–2008

	Democratic participation			
	Total turnout	Nonwhite	% Nonwhite	GOP turnout
1984	373,258	130,998	35.1	48,494
1986	359,577	135,018	37.5	59,027
1988	334,615	116,056	34.7	76,739
1990	219,755	95,028	43.2	103,540
1992	274,032	112,169	40.9	182,557
1994	314,341	136,342	43.4	302,909
1996	206,354	107,130	51.9	230,414
1998	149,257	73,715	49.4	176,406
2000	194,796	93,558	48.0	197,923
2002	114,346	70,003	61.2	384,944
2004	184,288	106,917	58.0	357,831
2006	146,062	87,120	59.6	277,003
2008 Presidential	516,853	291,317	56.4	438,697

Source: South Carolina Secretary of State at www.state.sc.us/scsec/election.html.

does not register voters by party, individuals have the option of choosing to participate in either party's primary when they go to the polls.) As voters, and especially whites, have fled the Democratic primary, interest in the Republican primary has surged with GOP primary voters increasing from 48,494 in 1984 to 384,944 in 2002. Republican primary participation exceeded that on the Democratic side for the first time in 1996. Every year since then, more voters have asked for Democratic than Republican ballots with the greatest difference coming in 2002 when the Republican primary drew more than three-fourths of all primary participants.

As the numbers of participants in the Democratic primary have declined, so have the numbers of African Americans who have participated in that selection process, even as they have come to dominate it. From 1984 through 1996, in all but one year, at least 107,000 nonwhites voted in the Democratic primary. In the five most recent Democratic primaries, more than 100,000 nonwhites participated only in 2004. The drop-off in the number of nonwhite Democratic participants cannot be explained by substantial increases in nonwhite participation in the Republican primary. Only in 2002 and 2004 had as many as 10,000 nonwhites taken Republican primary ballots.

Democrats designated South Carolina as the first southern state to vote on primary delegates for presidential candidates in 2008, an honor bestowed on the state in light of its sizable black electorate. With blacks casting most of the votes, and with Barack Obama beating Hillary Clinton by a margin of 78 to 19 percent among black voters, he beat her 55 to 26 percent in the overall vote.

Problems confronted by African Americans seeking major offices in South Carolina may be as much a result of their partisanship as their race. Most whites support Republicans in the general election and by substantial margins vote in the Republican primary while the bulk of the vote in the Democratic primary is cast by African Americans.[25] With Republicans dominating the congressional delegation, both chambers of the legislature, and the state's constitutional officers, it is not surprising that African Americans have not won high-profile posts.

RACIAL VOTING PATTERNS

James W. Loewen, a University of Vermont sociologist, conducted an extensive study of racial voting patterns in South Carolina for the period 1972 through 1985. His analysis of 130 elections, most of which were local, used data provided by the U.S. Department of Justice from the State Election Commission files. Loewen examined only contests for single-member districts and ones in which there was at least one serious black candidate and one serious white candidate.[26] Loewen found that, on average, 90.2 percent of the whites voted for white candidates while, on average, 85 percent of blacks voted for a black candidate. He observed that "[b]lack voting behavior began somewhat less polarized than white but soon increased to nearly the white level." Loewen divided the elections into two-year segments. Only in the 1978–79 periods were blacks more cohesive (an average of 91.8 percent of blacks voted for a black candidate) than whites (an average of 87.5 percent of whites voted for a white candidate). Loewen noted that "[w]hites bloc voted even more than blacks, making it difficult for black candidates to win."[27] For three congressional contests Loewen found that blacks averaged giving 74.8 percent of their voters to a black candidate while 78.8 percent of the white candidates backed a white candidate.[28] From his examination of racial voting, Loewen concluded that "white and black candidates had a

50/50 chance when 51.3 percent of the valid ballots for the office were cast by black voters."[29]

Loewen testified before the House Judiciary Subcommittee holding hearings on the extension of the Voting Rights Act in 1981, that, "Bloc voting is not diminishing, or if it is, only at a glacial rate. By State, that includes a division of the pre-1975 elections versus post-1975 elections across the South, I found that that the proportion of whites voting white decreased from 94 to 92 percent, hardly much movement."[30] Loewen then further opined that in black-white contests, "Characteristics of the candidate seem to make little difference to white voters. . . . Among whites then, race typically determines election outcome, nothing but race."[31] Later in his testimony, Loewen elaborated,

> I think what is happening is that the blacks are going by qualifications, incumbency, well-knownness on the part of both the black and white candidates. That indicates that a substantial part of the black population is not routinely bloc voting. And, of course, I argued perversely that the white population, which does not usually show this kind of variation, thereby does show that race is the only factor that makes a difference to them.[32]

Loewen was not entirely pessimistic: "By 1991 I hope that white bloc voting is decreased, so that blacks are not shut out by such policies, and so that we can infer that whites no longer oppose a possibility of black political power with such unanimity. I think there is potential for such a finding at that time, but the factual situation today is quite different."[33]

A more recent study provides evidence on racial voting patterns in a set of four black-versus-white South Carolina congressional contests. These four contests involve the initial election of James Clyburn, the first African American member of Congress from South Carolina in the twentieth century, and his next three reelections. The recent data show a great deal of change from what Loewen observed. Unlike in the 1970s and 1980s when whites were more cohesive than blacks, today black voters are far more cohesive than white voters. Relying on OLS regression and EI estimates of cohesion (refer to appendix A) for both black and white voters, the range of black-voter cohesion is between 95 percent and 100 percent, while white voters cast between 22.7 percent and 37.1 percent of their votes for Clyburn, depending on the year and estimation technique.[34]

The lowest level of cohesion reported for black voters indicates at least 95 percent support for the black candidate. This is more than 20 percentage points greater black cohesion that Loewen observed in the three congressional contests that he studied between 1980 and 1984. White cohesion in the more recent congressional contests, especially after the initial Clyburn election in 1992, is not only much less than the black cohesion but is also lower than Loewen's white figures for the early 1980s. Along with at least 95 percent of the black vote, Clyburn got 30 percent or more of the white vote in 1996 and 1998. All but two of twelve estimates show him with more than 25 percent white support. Whites have become more willing to vote for a black candidate while blacks have become far less willing to support a white candidate.

One of the explanations for the change is that the contests observed by Loewen were either Democratic primaries or runoffs while the Clyburn races from the 1990s were general elections. Thus, in the more recent elections, voters had a partisan cue available that they did not have in the Democratic contests studied by Loewen. In the Clyburn contests, partisan differences parallel racial differences.

Table 6.4 presents comparative data on white support for white Democratic congressional candidates in South Carolina. Only in 1992 did a white Democrat, John Spratt, attract the bulk of the white vote. In the next three elections Spratt polled 40 to 49 percent of the white vote. For 1996 and 1998, we have estimates for nonincumbent Democratic nominees. These candidates receive between one-sixth and one-third of the white vote, which is in line with the white support for Clyburn, South Carolina's African American member of Congress. With the exception of Darrell Curry, the Democratic nominee in 1996 in the 4th District, nonincumbent white Democrats achieved roughly the same share of the white vote as Clyburn managed once he established himself as an incumbent. Curry ran more poorly among whites than Clyburn did in his first bid for Congress. On the other hand, Clyburn, even with his seniority, has never attracted as large a share of the white vote as has gone to the other Democratic incumbent, John Spratt. Of course, a fact that may explain the difference is that Spratt has staked out more conservative positions than Clyburn.

Although not shown here, Democratic candidates whether black or white achieved overwhelming black support. In 1998, the two white

TABLE 6.4. Estimates of white support for white Democratic U.S. House candidates in South Carolina, 1992–1998

	District	Candidate	OLS	EI
1992	Congressional 5	Spratt*	52.1	52.0
1994	Congressional 5	Spratt*	42.1	43.6
1996	Congressional 3	Dorn	29.4	29.3
	Congressional 4	Curry	16.7	17.9
	Congressional 5	Spratt*	42.4	42.3
1998	Congressional 2	Frederick	27.1	29.6
	Congressional 4	Reese**	31.4	32.8
	Congressional 5	Spratt*	45.1	48.6

Source: Charles S. Bullock III and Richard E. Dunn, "The Demise of Racial Districting and the Future of Black Representation," *Emory Law Journal* 48 (Fall 1999), 1209–1253.

OLS = ecological regression; EI = ecological inference.

*Democrat is incumbent.

**Open seat.

Democratic challengers ran as well among black voters as did longtime incumbent Spratt. Indeed, the two white challengers did as well among black voters as James Clyburn.[35]

Estimates of white support for Democratic congressional candidates since 2000 appear in table 6.5. In five contested congressional districts in 2000, the Democratic nominee received between 18.5 percent (District 3) and 47.1 percent (incumbent Spratt's District 5) of the estimated white vote. Black incumbent Clyburn had the second-best showing among whites, earning 37.4 percent of their votes in District 6. By comparison, the Gore-Lieberman ticket garnered an estimated 25 percent of the white vote statewide.

Three congressional seats were contested by both major parties in 2002. The white vote was heavily Republican, with Democrats pulling just 16.8 percent in District 4 and 18.4 percent of the white vote in District 3, while Clyburn captured an estimated 31.1 percent of the white vote. In 2004, Democrats contested four congressional districts. Democratic challengers managed just 13.5 percent of the estimated white vote in District 4 and 19.7 percent in District 2. The two Democratic incumbents Spratt (District 5) and Clyburn (District 6) competed more successfully for white votes than did the Democratic nominees for president (22.4 percent) and

TABLE 6.5. Estimates of white voter support (%) for Democratic candidates in South Carolina, 1998–2006

	1998	2000	2002	2004	2006
Congressional District 1	26.9*	*†	*†	25.8*	
Congressional District 2	28.5*	*†	19.7*	22.0*	
Congressional District 3	18.5*	18.4	*†	25.5*	
Congressional District 4	*†	16.8*	13.5	14.6*	
Congressional District 5	47.1+	+†	49.4+	42.8+	
Congressional District 6	**37.4+**	**31.1+**	**30.6+**	**19.9+**	
Adjutant General	29.6*		—*		27.5*
Agriculture Comm.	—+		33.8		25.1
Att'y General	33.6*		**27.9***		—*
Comptroller	39.4		31.2+		34.2*
Governor	40.7*		33.5+		32.6*
Lt. Governor	30.1*		28.3		36.5*
Sec'y of State	28.9*		**26.1***		23.7*
Supt. of Education	46.9		47.0+		35.3
Treasurer	36.8*		37.8+		34.1
President (statewide)		25.0		22.4*	
U.S. Senate (statewide)				26.9	

Source: Ecological regression estimates computed by authors from data obtained from South Carolina Secretary of State elections Web site (www.state.sc.us/scsec/stats.html).

African American candidates in **boldface**.

+Incumbent Democrat.

*Incumbent Republican.

†No Democratic candidate.

the U.S. Senate (26.9 percent). However, in 2006 stark differences emerge in patterns for Clyburn and Spratt. Spratt continues to pull a sizeable share of the white vote, while Clyburn's estimated 19.9 percent share ranks below that of the white Democratic challengers in three of the other four congressional districts. Only Spratt breaks 26 percent of the estimated white vote share.

As previously shown, Republicans are experiencing greater success in winning congressional seats and in the state legislature where they are now dominant. The increases in Republican dominance are also visible in the statewide positions and, as with other offices, result from declining shares of the white vote going to Democratic candidates.

Results of statewide elections for 1998, 2002, and 2006 also appear in table 6.5. The estimated Democratic share of the white vote in 1998 ranged from a low of 28.9 percent in the secretary of state contest to a high of 46.9 percent in the superintendent of education contest. The Democrat who ran second best among whites, Jim Hodges, upset incumbent Republican governor David Beasley, taking an estimated 40.7 percent of the white vote. (Exit polls showed Hodges with 38 percent of the white vote, along with 90 percent of the black.)[36] In the race for lieutenant governor, incumbent Republican Bob Peeler defeated challenger and former lieutenant governor Nick Theodore, who garnered 30.1 percent of the white vote. In open-seat contests for superintendent of education and comptroller, Democrats polled 46.9 percent and 39.4 percent of the white vote respectively. In the treasurer contest, the Republican incumbent was bested by the Democrat he ousted in 1994, who attracted 36.8 percent of the white vote. In the remaining contests involving Republican incumbents, unsuccessful Democrats attracted 28 to 34 percent of the white vote.

The 2002 election results reveal further decay in white support for Democrats. Of the eight contested statewide offices, Democratic incumbents held four while Republicans had vacated the other four to seek the nomination to run against Governor Jim Hodges (D). Two of the four Democratic incumbents—Governor Hodges and Comptroller Jim Lander—lost. Hodges pulled an estimated 33.5 percent of the white vote, 7.2 points less than in 1998, while Lander got 31.2 percent of the white vote, down 8.2 points. The successful Democratic candidates for superintendent of education and treasurer drew 47 percent and 37.8 percent of the white vote respectively, which is about the same as in 1998.

In the open seats, two of the four Democratic candidates were African American—Steve Benjamin for attorney general, and Rick Wade for secretary of state. Benjamin and Wade had the weakest showing among white voters in taking 27.9 and 26.1 percent of the vote, respectively. Their performances, however, were only slightly weaker than that of the white nominee for lieutenant governor who got 28.3 percent of the white vote and the losing Democratic nominee for agriculture commissioner who received just over a third of the white vote. The losing Democratic incumbents for governor and comptroller also had performances among white voters very much in line with the losing Democratic challengers.

The 2006 election results are reflective of the voting in 2002. With no Democratic incumbents running and six of nine constitutional offices having Republican incumbents, no Democrat received more than 37 percent of the estimated white vote. All of the Republican incumbents prevailed, and both the open position previously held by Democrats—superintendent of education—and the sole position held by a Democratic incumbent—treasurer—went Republican. Grady Patterson, in being evicted from the treasurer's office, only had a falloff in estimated white support of 3.7 points from his previous election in 2002.

Analysis of the black vote (not shown here) reveals consistent support well in excess of 90 percent for Democratic candidates. The white vote in recent elections varies depending on incumbency status, with some, but—as 2002 shows—not all incumbent Democrats pulling more of the white vote than open-seat Democrats or challengers. Since 2000, the vote among whites for black Democratic candidates has been only slightly lower than for white candidates of the same incumbency status, while the black vote is largely fixed regardless of the race of the candidate or incumbency status. With united black support, for Democrats to carry statewide elections in South Carolina they now need to attract at least 35 percent of the white vote. As the results in table 6.5 indicate, even that modest share often proves elusive. Since Democrats' only success was the election of the superintendent of education by a margin of less than five hundred votes, we can assume that Democrats in the most recent election had little appeal for white voters.

Results since Loewen's analysis suggest a need to modify his conclusion. A restatement now might be that for black voters, the only thing that is important is party. Blacks vote overwhelmingly for the Democratic nominee regardless of that person's race or qualifications and will not vote for a Republican, regardless of the Republican's qualifications or status as an incumbent, a challenger, or a contestant for an open seat. While party also seems to be important as a correlate of white voting behavior, there are more whites willing to vote for a black Democrat than there are blacks willing to vote for a white Republican.

The analysis included in this chapter suggests that while black candidates in South Carolina are no longer as disadvantaged as they were a generation ago at the time of Loewen's analysis, they run slightly worse than do comparable white candidates, and this seems to be because the African Americans attract a bit less of the white vote than do white Democrats. Scholars have factored in these considerations in analyzing the levels of black concentration needed for African Americans to elect the candidates they prefer.

David Epstein and Sharyn O'Halloran take into consideration the greater cohesion of black than white voters in South Carolina. Their analysis of South Carolina state senate elections from 1988 through 1994 concludes that the black community has an equal opportunity of electing its preferred candidate in districts once blacks constitute 46.7 percent of the voting-age population.[37] While higher concentrations of African Americans increase the likelihood that their preferred candidate will prevail, the rates at which blacks register and vote, combined with the cohesiveness of the black and white electorate, now enables African Americans to determine an electoral outcome even when they constitute less than half of the voting-age electorate.

John Ruoff has also examined the question of how heavily black a district must be for African American candidate preferences to succeed. Based on elections held between 1980 and 1992, Ruoff estimated that blacks had an 85 percent chance of electing their preference once the black population of a district reached 57 to 58 percent.[38] Thus his data base differs from the more recent set of elections considered by Epstein and O'Halloran. In addition, Ruoff focuses on the black percentage in the total population while Epstein and O'Halloran consider voting-age population. Finally, Ruoff sets an 85 percent threshold for success while Epstein and O'Halloran use a 50 percent probability for success. Ruoff might agree that blacks now have at least an equal chance of electing their preferred candidates even in districts in which whites constitute a slight majority of the voting-age population.

FEDERAL MONITORING

In the forty years following passage of the Voting Rights Act, 120 proposed changes in election laws from South Carolina drew objections from the

Department of Justice (DOJ). Eighty-six of these occurred between 1975 and 1994. In the most recent decade DOJ issued only fourteen objections to South Carolina jurisdictions. Half of these most recent objections involved redistricting plans. Two of the others involved annexations. All were local proposals except for an objection to the 1997 redistricting of the state senate. From 1990 through 2005, South Carolina submitted 15,358 proposed changes to DOJ and DOJ objected to 66.[39] In addition to the objections, there were 579 instances in which DOJ asked the submitting authority for more information. In the vast share of these instances (432), once more information was received, DOJ approved the proposed change.

CONCLUSION

South Carolina had relatively high levels of black registration even before the Voting Rights Act. Over the last decade, black registration rates have increased and in some recent years equaled those of whites. Black registration in South Carolina now exceeds that outside the South. Recent presidential elections have seen record highs in black turnout in South Carolina. Again in some recent years Census Bureau estimates place black turnout higher than white turnout. However, the official records maintained by the South Carolina Board of Elections show whites turning out at higher rates than African Americans. The nonwhite share of all registrants has increased so that at the time of the 2008 presidential primary (the most recent figures available as this is written), it stood at 28 percent, a bit lower than the black proportion of the state's adult population. The nonwhite registration figure as of the 2008 general election stood at 30.4 percent.

Black office holding has grown tremendously since the late 1960s. In the latest statewide tabulation, more than five hundred African Americans—including one member of Congress and thirty-five state legislators—held office in the Palmetto State. Black representation in the legislature continues to lag the black proportion of the population.

One obstacle to the election of African Americans is their partisanship. The state has become strongly Republican as the white electorate increasingly gives its support to the GOP. Black Democrats do almost as well as white Democrats. Democrats of both races command overwhelming majorities of the black vote but rarely secure a majority of the white vote. Indeed, Democrats increasingly struggle to get much more than a third of the white vote. While black candidates run slightly worse than white Democrats, the race of the candidates seemingly plays a much smaller role than partisanship in explaining outcomes.

CHAPTER 7

NORTH CAROLINA

North Carolina adopted disfranchising techniques in 1900, when amendments to the state constitution imposed a literacy test and a poll tax. Only twenty years later, however, North Carolina became the first southern state to eliminate the poll tax as a condition for voting.[1] The literacy test remained in place until struck down by the Voting Rights Act. Unlike most other southern states, North Carolina did not make use of a white primary as a technique for limiting African American participation.[2]

Not all of North Carolina is subject to the trigger mechanism of the Voting Rights Act, and therefore only certain counties are required to have their election ordinances precleared by the Department of Justice. The trigger mechanism written into the 1965 statute hinges on the presence of tests or devices that prospective voters must satisfy. That provision, coupled with a turnout rate in the 1964 presidential election or a registration rate at the time of that election of less than 50 percent of the age-eligible electorate, subjected thirty-nine of North Carolina's counties to preclearance. The 1975 amendments to the Voting Rights Act, which dealt with language minorities, brought a fortieth North Carolina county under the preclearance requirement. Statewide legislation affecting elections, such as redistricting plans, and all changes in the forty counties must go through the preclearance review before being implemented.[3]

That the original Voting Rights Act applied to fewer than half of North Carolina's counties while being applied statewide in six other states is in keeping with a popular notion that North Carolina is more progressive than many of its southern neighbors. V. O. Key, Jr., contributed to this idea with a subtitle for his North Carolina chapter, "Progressive Plutocracy." Key elaborates concerning North Carolinians:

> The citizens are determined and confident; they are on the move. The mood is at odds with much of the rest of the South—a tenor of attitude and of action that has set the state apart from its neighbors. Many see in North Carolina a closer approximation to national norms, or national expectations of performance, than they find elsewhere in the South. In any competition for national judgment they deem the state far more "presentable" than its southern neighbors. It enjoys a reputation for progressive outlook and action in many phases of life, especially industrial development, education, and race relations.[4]

Others have noted a disjuncture between the image of North Carolina, especially that held by its own citizens, and reality. Bass and de Vries subtitle their chapter on the state "The Progressive Myth." They note that "although North Carolina has changed with the times, it is perhaps the least changed of the old Confederate states."[5] According to Bass and de Vries, race became a significant element in North Carolina politics immediately after Key published his book. In the hotly contested 1950 Senate election, Willis Smith, who polled 40.5 percent of the vote, trailed University of North Carolina president Frank Graham, who got 49.1 percent in the Democratic primary. Smith played the race card and was rewarded with a 51.8 percent victory in the runoff. A key staffer who helped mold the Smith racial appeal was Jesse Helms, who would be elected to the Senate himself a generation later. Despite the Smith victory, three North Carolina members of the House broke with other southeastern Democrats and refused to sign the Southern Manifesto (condemning the *Brown v. Board of Education* decision). Voters again exacted a price for this and defeated two of the three in the next Democratic primary.

Paul Luebke has more recently and more thoroughly explored the inconsistencies in North Carolina politics.[6] The University of North Carolina (Greensboro) sociologist and state legislator traces the competition between modernizers and traditionalists for control of the North Carolina body politic. At times both forces have not only coexisted but enjoyed success. During much of Helms's four Senate terms, progressive Democrat Jim Hunt served as the state's governor. However, in the 1984 Senate election, the one contest where they faced off against each other, the conservative Republican won a third term.[7]

BLACK REGISTRATION AND TURNOUT

The U.S. Civil Rights Commission estimated that when the Voting Rights Act was originally passed, just over a quarter of a million nonwhites and 1.9 million whites had registered to vote in North Carolina. These figures translated into 46.8 percent of the nonwhites—distinguishing North Carolina from other states brought under Section 5—and 96.8 percent of the whites of voting age.[8] A year and a half after passage of the Voting Rights Act, figures reported by the North Carolina State Board of Elections for all but three medium-size counties showed 277,404 nonwhites and 1,602,980 whites registered to vote. African American registration had increased from 46.8 to 51.3 percent of the age eligible, while among whites, 83 percent of the age eligible appeared on the purged registration roles.

The share of the nonwhite voting-age population that had registered by 1967 in the counties subject to Section 5 was substantially lower than the state as a whole. In these counties, just over 40 percent of the nonwhite voting-age population had registered. In only five of the thirty-nine counties had a majority of the voting-age population (VAP) registered as of 1967. Thus the rate of registration among nonwhites in the Section 5 counties continued to lag that for the remainder of the state. The counties covered by Section 5 included all of those in which most adults as of 1960 were nonwhite. These counties tended to have small to moderate populations, with only one of the state's major counties (Guilford, which contains the city of Greensboro) subject to Section 5.

Although minority registration remained lower in Section 5 counties than statewide, the basis for activating the trigger mechanism is not that a majority of the nonwhite population be registered but rather that less than half of the total population was registered as of 1964. By 1967, 62.2 percent of the total VAP based on the 1960 census had registered in the Section 5 counties.

Appendix B provides figures on black and white registration from 1980 through 2006 as compiled from surveys done by the U.S. Bureau of the Census after each general election. In 1980, just under half of the age-eligible blacks in North Carolina reported being registered to vote, while 63.7 percent of the adult whites claimed to be registered. The black registration percentage in 1980 approximated that of thirteen years earlier, whereas the white registration rate had dropped 20 points from 1967. The disparity in reported racial registration rates widened in 1982 to almost 19 percentage points. Thereafter the disparities have been smaller, shrinking to 7.5 points in 1984 and remaining at roughly that size through the rest of the 1980s. Beginning with 1984, black registration rates have exceeded those for 1967. White registration has yet to achieve the levels of 1967.

The disparity in self-reported registration shrinks to 3.5 percentage points in 1990. It then expands to more than 8 percentage points in the next two midterm elections before shrinking back to approximately 5 points in 2002. In the presidential elections of 1992, 1996, and 2000, approximately 5 percentage points more of the white than the African American VAP had registered. In 2004, for the first and only time, black registration exceeded that for whites, with 70.4 percent of African Americans and 69.4 percent of the whites indicating that they registered, a pattern that did not persist into 2006.

Since 1998 the Census Bureau has estimated white participation exclusive of Hispanics. This modification boosts the white registration figure by approximately 4 percentage points beginning in 2000, with the largest difference, 5.2 points, occurring in 2006. After making this adjustment, the non-Hispanic white registration rate exceeds that for blacks by 2.8 points in 2004 but by 10 points in 2006—the largest disparity since comparisons between African Americans and non-Hispanic whites have been possible.

During the 1980s, African Americans living outside of the South always reported higher registration rates than did North Carolina's black population. The greatest disparity occurred in 1982, when 61.7 percent of the nonsouthern African Americans registered compared with 43.6 percent of the black VAP in North Carolina. During the remainder of the decade, the disparity was approximately 7 percentage points. Beginning with 1990, the reported registration rate among North Carolina blacks usually slightly exceeded that of African Americans living outside the region. In 1990 North Carolina blacks were 1.7 percentage points more likely to be registered than were nonsouthern blacks. The largest advantage for North Carolina blacks comes in the two most recent elections with Tar Heel African Americans registering at rates more than 7 percentage points higher than nonsouthern blacks.

One of the two elections since 1990 in which black registration in North Carolina did not exceed that of the non-South comes in 1994 when 58.3 percent of the nonsouthern blacks but only 53.1 percent of North Carolina's blacks had registered. In 1998, the other year inconsistent with the post-1990 pattern, 58.5 percent of nonsouthern blacks and 57.4 percent of North Carolina blacks reported registering.

The disparity in black and white registration rates persists in North Carolina, but the racial disparity has reversed when comparing African Americans in North Carolina and those outside of the South. In each of the four most recent elections, a higher proportion of North Carolina African Americans than nonsouthern blacks registered.

Appendix B also contains Census Bureau estimates of turnout by race in North Carolina from 1980 through 2006. During the 1980s, whites reported voting at rates at least 8 percentage points greater than did blacks, and in the first three elections, differences exceeded 10 percentage points. Since 1996 the disparities have been less than 9 percentage points. In 1990, 1998, and 2002, the differences are modest, with the smallest difference coming in 2002, when 42.2 percent of blacks and 43.5 percent of whites reported going to the polls in the general election.

Only in 2004 do Census Bureau estimates show blacks voting at higher rates than whites. Among blacks, 63.1 percent said they participated in the 2004 election, compared with 58.1 percent of the whites. The reported black participation in 2004 exceeds any figure for whites in the entire time series and is 9 points higher than the second-highest figure for African Americans. This higher reported participation among blacks is also a break with the previous pattern in which whites' participation rates exceeded those for blacks by the largest margins in presidential years. The anomalous figures for 2004 do not persist, and in 2006 white turnout runs 8 points higher than black.

Even the elimination of Hispanics from the turnout figure for whites does not reverse the pattern for 2004. While the share of white non-Hispanics who turned out rises to 61.5 percent, that remains 1.6 points lower than the African American turnout rate. For the other years for which a non-Hispanic white figure is available, it widens the disparity between white and black participation as white turnout increases by 1 to 3 points.

During the 1980s, self-reported black participation in North Carolina was substantially below that in the non-South. In each of those five election years except for 1986, black turnout in North Carolina was at least 9 percentage points lower than in the non-South. Beginning with 1990, black turnout rates in North Carolina exceed those for the non-South in three of the seven election years, including a difference of almost 3 percentage points in 2002. The greatest disparity in favor of North Carolina blacks came in 1990, when the difference was almost 10 percentage points. On the other hand, the greatest overall disparity since 1990 came in 1994, when 40.2 percent of African Americans outside the South said they voted compared with only 28.3 percent participation in North Carolina. In 1992, 1996, and 1998, the figures for North Carolina and the non-South were quite similar, with differences of less than 3 percentage points. As with the comparison with Tar Heel whites, North Carolina blacks participated at higher rates than nonsouthern blacks in 2004, but two years later the pattern reversed, with blacks outside the region voting at a rate almost 6 points higher than in North Carolina.

The patterns reported in the second part of appendix B indicate that black participation rates in North Carolina are increasingly approximating and sometimes exceeding those outside the South. There has also been a pattern of North Carolina self-reported black participation becoming increasingly like that of Tar Heel whites, although whites continue to report voting at higher rates than do blacks except in 2004.

North Carolina is one of the five southern states that maintains registration data by race. Racial registration figures from the State Board of Election are available beginning with 1990. The official figures show that in 1990, 635,000 blacks and 2.68 million whites had registered. Black registration in North Carolina increases by more than 482,000 from 1990 to 2006. After 150,000 additional blacks signed up by October 2008, black registration had doubled to 1.27 million. White registration had increased by two-thirds after September 2008, climbing from 2.68 to 4.49 million. In 1990, African Americans constituted 19 percent of the state's registered voters. By 2008, the proportion had increased to 21.1 percent, which approximates 20.5 percent of the state's VAP estimated to be black in 2006 by the Census Bureau. Actual black registration figures far exceeded those estimated by the Census Bureau, which reported 785,000 black registrants in 2006 compared with the state's count of 1.1 million.

North Carolina does not consistently report official figures on turnout by race. Among those who had registered as of October 2002 and therefore were eligible to vote in that year's elections, 41 percent of African Americans cast ballots as did 60 percent of whites. It should be noted here that the denominator in calculating turnout is registrants, while in appendix B, the Census Bureau uses the voting-age population as the denominator. The participation rates for the two races converge substantially in the 2004 presidential election. That year, the state reports that 59 percent of its black registrants and 66 percent of its white registrants went to the polls, which is similar to the Census Bureau estimates.

The statistics maintained by the North Carolina Board of Elections show that since the beginning of their data presentation in 1972, most North Carolinians have registered to vote. The figures range from a low of just under 60 percent in 1978 to a high of more than 85 percent in 2004; the figure in 2006 was just over 83 percent. In every presidential year, a majority of the registrants went to the polls, reaching the highest point, 69.9 percent, in 2008. In most midterm elections, less than a majority of registrants turned out. The exceptions came in 1986 and 1990. In the most recent midterm election (2006), just 37 percent of the registered voters cast ballots. When participation is calculated as a share of the voting-age population, only infrequently did most North Carolinians cast ballots. Only in 1992 and 2004 did most of the age eligible go to the polls, with almost 55 percent of the adult population voting in 2004. Participation rates in midterm elections are lower than in presidential elections, and in three midterm elections, fewer than 30 percent of the adults participated.[9]

The turnout figures show a general increase over time in the share of the voting-age population casting ballots once type of election is controlled. Through 1996, Census Bureau estimates of voter participation in North Carolina are often 10 percentage points higher than those calculated using the official turnout figures. Since 1998, Census Bureau turnout estimates and state turnout figures based on voting-age population always differ by less than 5 percentage points.

In the North Carolina counties subject to Section 5, the number of African Americans registered to vote is now more than four times as high as the nonwhite registrants in 1967. In 2006, 528,848 African Americans had registered in these counties, up from just under 121,000 nonwhites in 1967. This compares with 1,223,692 whites on the voting rolls in 2006, an increase from 523,669 in 1967. As of 2006, African Americans constituted 28.8 percent of the registered voters in the Section 5 counties, compared to 18.8 percent of the registrants in 1967 who were not white.

AFRICAN AMERICAN OFFICE HOLDING

At the outset of record keeping on the numbers of African American elected officials, North Carolina had 40 in 1969, with almost two-thirds of these serving in cities. Within three years, the total had reached 103, of whom two-thirds served at the municipal level with very few county officials. The number of black county officials did not exceed 10 until 1975, at which point there were still ten times as many municipal as county black officials. By 1976, the number of black officials reached 218 and increased to 353 in 1987. During the four years between 1985 and 1989, figure 7.1 shows a dramatic increase of more than 50 percent in black elected officials.

This dramatic increase is attributable to the implementation of Section 2.[10] The initial interpretation of that section modified in the Voting Rights Act in 1982 came in a North Carolina case (described in the introduction).[11] With the Supreme Court's blessing for efforts to force multimember and at-large plans to be converted into single-member districts, large numbers of new African Americans won local offices. In North Carolina much of the increase in black elected officials came at the municipal level where numbers rose from 162 in 1985 to 279 four years later.

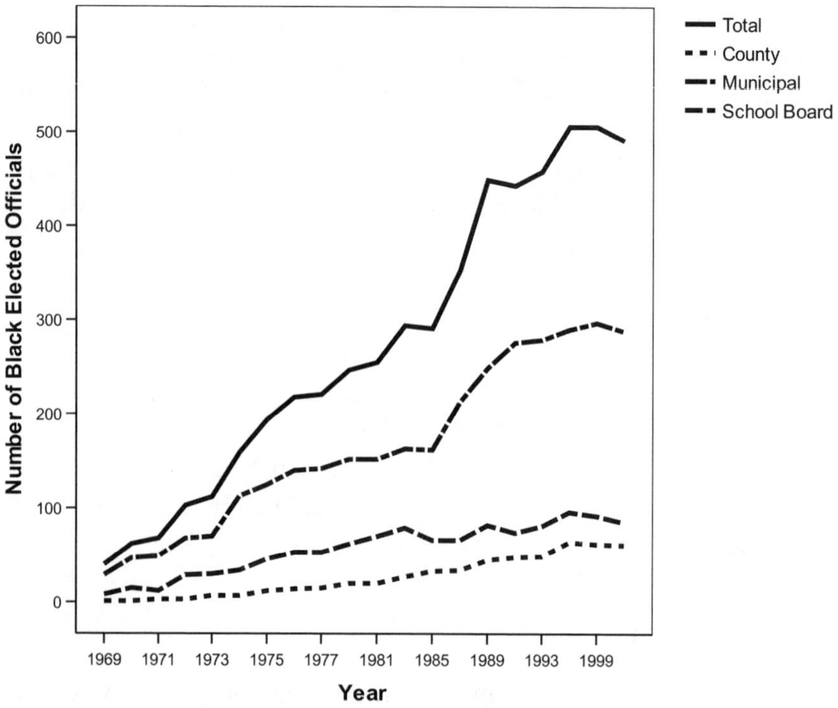

Figure 7.1. Black elected officials in North Carolina, 1969–2001. *Source:* Various volumes of the *National Roster of Black Elected Officials* (Washington, D.C.: Joint Center for Political and Economic Studies).

As the twentieth century came to a close, North Carolina had approximately five hundred African Americans in public office. Just under 60 percent of the public officials held municipal office. The state still had fewer than one hundred black school board members, and the one hundred counties in the state had elected fewer than sixty-five black officials.

African Americans in Congress

African Americans have held two of North Carolina's seats in Congress since implementation of the 1992 districting map. The initial map drawn by the state had one majority-black district located in the eastern part of the state. The U.S. Department of Justice (DOJ), which has authority to review the North Carolina's districting plan since almost half of the state is subject to Section 5, rejected that map. In rejecting North Carolina's first effort, DOJ essentially instructed the state that to secure approval it would need to create a second majority-black district. It had been many years since North Carolina had even one majority-black congressional district, so creation of such a district was more than required under the non-retrogression rule that had been the standard in Section 5 reviews.[12] In denying preclearance, DOJ turned to Section 2 and measured North Carolina's effort against a "max-black" standard. Since the state could have created a second majority-black district, DOJ required it.

In response to this directive, the Republican minority in the legislature pushed for a second majority-black district in the southern part of the state extending from Charlotte eastward. Democrats, however, opted for an alternative configuration that had been originally drawn by a Republican legislator. This alternative, which became known as the I-95 district because it tracked closely with the interstate highway, linked blacks in a series of urban areas in the Piedmont. The district ran from Gastonia in the west to Charlotte, then northward as far as Winston-Salem before picking up High Point, Greensboro, and extending on eastward before ending in Durham. This 160-mile-long district united urban black populations but carefully avoided nearby concentrations of whites so as not to violate equal population standards. In some places the district was no wider than two lanes of I-95 as it knifed through concentrations of whites on its way to black urban centers. At times the district crossed over from the northbound lanes to the southbound lanes so that it was contiguous only at a touch point.

The configuration of this district outraged Duke University Law School Professor Robinson Everett. Everett, who had once served as the chief judge of the Court of Military Appeals, filed suit on behalf of voters who objected to the plan. The three-judge federal court that convened in North Carolina thwarted Everett when it found the issue he raised to be nonjusticiable. Everett appealed to the Supreme Court and succeeded in convincing a five-person majority that he had a claim. Writing for the majority, Justice Sandra Day O'Connor noted: "Put differently, we believe that reapportionment is one area in which appearances *do* matter. A reapportionment plan that includes in one district individuals who belong to the same race, but who are otherwise widely separated by geographical and political boundaries, and who may have little in common with one another but the color of their skin, bears an uncomfortable resemblance to political apartheid."[13]

Following a hearing on the merits, the three-judge panel rejected Everett's claims. After a second appeal to the Supreme Court, however, Everett finally prevailed and the Court struck down the 12th District for violating the Equal Protection Clause because it had been drawn predominately on the basis of race.[14] Of course, drawing a district by focusing on race was precisely what DOJ had demanded of the North Carolina legislature. DOJ and a majority of the Supreme Court were at odds and the Court held the upper hand since it gets to interpret the Constitution.

The state legislature produced a new plan that shortened the distance spanned by the 12th District so that it extended only from Charlotte to Winston-Salem and Greensboro. Everett, however, continued to believe that race had been the predominate consideration in drawing this map in which the 12th District was 46.7 percent African American and filed another challenge. The trial court granted plaintiff's motion for summary judgment forcing the legislature to draw a third map.[15] In the third map, which was used in the 1998 election, the black percentage in the district dropped to 35.6 and the district extended only from Charlotte to Winston-Salem.

The state appealed the summary judgment, asserting that the legislature relied on partisan and not racial data in drawing the second map. Since the state's claims meant that the case involved a controversy, the Supreme Court overturned the trial court decision and ordered a full hearing on the merits.[16] In the subsequent hearing, the three-judge trial panel found again for the plaintiffs. The plaintiffs introduced into evidence an e-mail from the staff person primarily responsible for redistricting to the senator who led the redistricting effort. The staffer asked the chair of the Senate committee for guidance: "I have moved Greensboro Black community in to the 12th and now need to take 'bout [*sic*] 60,000 out of the 12th. I await your direction on this."[17] The trial court agreed with the plaintiffs that this e-mail indicated that race and not partisan considerations had been the predominant motivation in shaping the 12th District.

The state appealed again, and in *Easley v. Cromartie*—the Supreme Court's fourth ruling on North Carolina redistricting efforts during the

TABLE 7.1. Change in two North Carolina congressional districts' racial makeup

District	% black in population			
	1993–1998	1999–2000	2001–2002	Since 2003
1	57.3	50.3	50.3	50.5
12	56.6	35.6	46.7	44.6

Source: Data obtained by the authors from North Carolina State Board of Elections.

1990s—the state finally won.[18] Justice O'Connor, who had supported the first two challenges to North Carolina's plan, switched sides and now joined the more liberal wing of the court in a 5–4 opinion. In *Easley,* the Supreme Court accepted the state's contention that it had relied predominately upon partisan data from elections held almost a decade earlier and had considered race as nothing more than a secondary factor if that.

Table 7.1 shows the changes in the racial makeup of the two districts that have elected African Americans since 1992. The 12th District, represented by Melvin Watt since 1993, lost its black majority with the first remapping pursuant to *Shaw* in 1998. Despite a dramatic drop in the black population from 56.6 percent to 35.6 percent, Watt won handily, taking 56 percent of the vote. The next redistricting, the one used for the 2000 election, increased the black percentage in the 12th District to 46.7 percent of the population, and again, Watt won easily with 65 percent of the vote. With the redrawing following the 2000 census, the black percentage dropped to 44.6 percent, but Watt continues to win reelection with around two-thirds of the vote.

The 1st District in the eastern part of the state was represented by Eva Clayton from 1993 until 2003. Frank Ballance succeeded Clayton but resigned in 2004 shortly before pleading guilty to federal fraud charges. G. K. Butterfield, the third African American since 1993, currently holds the seat. The district has had a black majority in its population since 1993 although the voting-age population and the registered electorate have been majority white since the redistricting of 1998.

Melvin Watt has successfully fashioned a biracial coalition and defended his seat even as his district has undergone three reconfigurations and had its black population substantially reduced. In the more rural 1st District, the black percentage has remained higher than in the 12th; nonetheless, Eva Clayton and her successors have also fashioned biracial coalitions. The elections of African Americans Ballance and Butterfield following Clayton's retirement in 2002 indicate that it was not just incumbent Clayton who could win in this district in which most voters were white. In the critical 2002 Democratic primary, Ballance took 47 percent of the vote and thereby avoided a runoff. The only white candidate in the four-person field finished second with 26 percent of the vote. Now that many whites choose to participate in the Republican primary, it is not necessary that districts be majority minority in order to nominate African Americans.[19]

The success of African Americans in winning and holding two congressional seats in North Carolina since 1993 contrasts with earlier unsuccessful efforts. Immediately after the 1982 redistricting, Mickey Michaux, a black legislator, ran for the open 2nd District that included Durham and portions of northeast North Carolina. In the initial primary, Michaux captured 44 percent of the vote while Tim Valentine, a white former legislator, took 33 percent. The remainder of the vote went to a second white candidate. In the early 1980s, North Carolina still required a majority vote for nomination, a threshold later lowered to 40 percent. In the runoff, Valentine leapfrogged past Michaux and won the Democratic nomination with 54 percent. The district in which Valentine defeated Michaux was 40 percent black by total population. In 1984, a second black legislator, Kenneth Spaulding, challenged Valentine in the primary. Valentine once again survived but with only 52 percent of the vote.

Michaux's runoff defeat after having led in the primary prompted the Reverend Jesse Jackson to make the runoff requirement (used by a number of southern states in their primaries) a major issue in his 1984 campaign for the Democratic presidential nomination. Jackson contrasted Michaux's fate with the experience of Harold Washington who won the Democratic nomination to become mayor of Chicago with a plurality vote against multiple white candidates.

As far back as 1972, Chapel Hill mayor Howard Lee competed for the open 2nd District congressional seat. In this 40 percent black district, Lee, one of the first African Americans to be elected mayor of a predominately white city in the South, lost the Democratic nomination. Paul Luebke, a Democratic legislator and sociologist, speculates that Lee probably did not help himself in this conservative district by running as an economic populist.[20]

African Americans in the State Legislature

The first African American elected to the North Carolina legislature in modern times won a state house seat in 1968. Little increase in the black presence in the house occurred until after the 1982 redistricting when blacks won 11 of the 120 seats. During the 1980s, black representation in the house hovered around 10 percent. After the next redistricting in the early 1990s, black representation increased so that during the 1990s African Americans filled approximately 15 percent of the house seats as shown in table 7.2. Redistricting at the beginning of the new century had no immediate impact on the number of African Americans serving in the house. The 2006 election, however, saw two additional African Americans elected, which brings the total to twenty-one—the largest number of African Americans to serve in that chamber.

The substantial increase in the black membership of the house came following the redistricting of the early 1980s when North Carolina continued to make extensive use of multi-seat districts. This practice provided the impetus for the first Supreme Court decision interpreting Section 2 of the Voting Rights Act as amended in 1982. That provision allowed for plaintiffs to succeed when challenging existing election laws upon proof that the status quo gave minorities less opportunity than whites to "elect representatives of their choice." Plaintiffs challenged two senate and five house districts. At the time of the filings, four of the house districts were represented by a total of five African Americans. These five black legislators were part of the twenty-two representatives elected from these four districts. A four-seat senate district had no black member but had elected an African American for three terms during the 1970s. The Supreme Court upheld the lower court decision for six of the seven districts at issue. In house District 23, in which one of its three seats had been filled by a black legislator consistently since 1972, the high court found no violation of Section 2.[21] But in the other districts, the Supreme Court found that the use of multimember districts reduced the ability of blacks to elect their candidates of choice.

TABLE 7.2. Racial makeup of the North Carolina General Assembly, 1965–2007

	Senate	% Black in Senate	House	% Black in House
1965	0	0.0	0	0.0
1967	0	0.0	0	0.0
1969	0	0.0	1	0.8
1971	0	0.0	2	1.7
1973	0	0.0	3	2.5
1975	2	4.0	4	3.3
1977	2	4.0	4	3.3
1979	1	2.0	4	3.3
1981	1	2.0	3	2.5
1983	1	2.0	11	9.2
1985	3	6.0	13	10.8
1987	2	4.0	13	10.8
1989	5	10.0	14	11.7
1991	5	10.0	14	11.7
1993	7	14.0	18	15.0
1995	7	14.0	17	14.2
1997	7	14.0	17	14.2
1999	7	14.0	17	14.2
2001	7	14.0	18	15.0
2003	6	12.0	18	15.0
2005	7	14.0	19	15.8
2007	7	14.0	21	17.5

Source: Data compiled by the authors.

In finding for the plaintiffs, the Supreme Court established a three-part test to be used in lawsuits involving Section 2. The plaintiffs must prevail on all three items in order to win. The first question to be explored by a court is whether the minority group is sufficiently large and geographically compact that it could constitute a majority of a proposed single-member district. Second, the minority group must demonstrate that it is politically cohesive. Third, the minority group must show that although it is politically cohesive, its choices are usually defeated by the bloc vote of the majority.

For the Court to move on to a fuller consideration of all the circumstances outlined in the U.S. Senate Report that accompanied the 1982 Voting Rights Act, plaintiffs must prevail on all three elements. Elements set forth in the Senate Report include whether blacks have ever won the office at issue, whether past discrimination continues to have a political consequence, and whether a slating arrangement from which minority input is excluded determines officeholders (see box 7.1). If plaintiffs succeed on the first two portions of the *Gingles* test but the evidence shows that the candidates preferred by minorities usually win elections, then even though racially polarized voting may characterize the politics of the community, plaintiffs would not be entitled to relief since their choices succeed in the at-large context.

Box 7.1. The Senate Factors

In order to give context to assessing a discriminatory effect discovered under Section 2, Congress left guidance in the legislative record regarding what might constitute a "totality of circumstances." These factors, derived from the factors advanced in *White v. Regester* and *Zimmer v. McKeithen*, articulated nine circumstances that might be present in whole or in part to demonstrate the discriminatory environment in which the effect occurred. The nine factors that form the basis of the analysis preferred by Congress, derived from *White* and *Zimmer*, are

1. the extent of any history of official discrimination in the state or political subdivision that touched the right of the members of the minority group to register, to vote, or otherwise to participate in the democratic process;

2. the extent to which voting in the elections of the state or political subdivision is racially polarized;

3. the extent to which the state or political subdivision has used unusually large election districts, majority vote requirements, anti–single-shot provisions, or other voting practices or procedures that may enhance the opportunity for discrimination against the minority group;

4. whether the members of the minority group have been denied access to the candidate-slating process, if there is such a process;

5. the extent to which members of the minority group in the state or political subdivision bear the effects of discrimination in

such areas as education, employment, and health, which hinder their ability to participate effectively in the political process;

6. whether political campaigns have been characterized by overt or subtle racial appeals;

7. the extent to which members of the minority group have been elected to public office in the jurisdiction;

8. whether there is a significant lack of responsiveness on the part of elected officials to the particularized needs of the members of the minority group;

9. whether the policy underlying the state or political subdivision's use of such voting qualification; prerequisite to voting; or standard, practice, or procedure is tenuous.

Source: Justin J. Wert, Ronald Keith Gaddie, and Charles S. Bullock III, "The Future of the 1965 Voting Rights Act: Judicial Decision-Making in Congress and the Presidency," presented at the annual meeting of the Southern Political Science Association, New Orleans, La., 2009.

Note: The factors demonstrated in *White v. Regester* (412 U.S. 755, 1973) were (1) a history of official discrimination against minorities, (2) the existence of a white slating group and racial campaign tactics, (3) cultural and language barriers and depressed voter registration, (4) a lack of responsiveness by elected officials to the needs of the minority community, and (5) use of numbered post and majority vote requirements. *Zimmer v. McKeithen* (485 F.2d 1297, 5th Cir. 1973) expanded on the factors from *White*, to include enhancing factors such as (1) the existence of large districts, (2) majority vote requirements, (3) anti–single-shot voting provisions, and (4) the lack of provisions for at-large candidates running from particular geographical subdistricts.

The *Gingles* decision opened the way for literally hundreds of challenges to at-large local elections and multimember legislative systems. This litigation, which generally succeeded, substantially increased the numbers of minority elected officials on collegial bodies. Interestingly, winning the lawsuit had no substantial increase in the numbers of blacks serving in the North Carolina house. It was not until the redistricting carried out in the early 1990s that the number of black representatives showed a substantial increase.

In finding that the multimember districts diluted black political influence, the Court relied heavily upon the evidence presented by the plaintiffs to demonstrate the presence of racial bloc voting. The Court put its stamp of approval on two techniques for measuring racial voting patterns. One of these is the homogenous precinct approach that calculates the share of the vote in heavily black precincts going to each candidate and the share of the vote in heavily white precincts going to these candidates. The second approach used by the plaintiffs' expert, political science professor Bernard Grofman of the University of California at Irvine, was ecological regression, and it is this approach that Grofman put more confidence in. The Court accepted Grofman's definition that racial bloc voting occurs when white and black voters prefer different candidates. Thus if the candidate preferred by black voters loses despite receiving the bulk of the black vote, this would be evidence of racial bloc voting.

In the state senate, no black won a seat until 1974, when two members entered the upper chamber. During the next fourteen years blacks held no more than three of the fifty seats in the senate. In 1989, following the *Gingles* decision, the number of black senators rose to five, and after a new redistricting in the early 1990s, it went to seven, which remained the number in 2008. The 2004 Census Bureau estimates show African Americans comprising 20.5 percent of North Carolina's voting-age population. Blacks held 16.5 percent of the seats in the legislature in 2008.

African American legislators have succeeded in achieving powerful positions within the institution. Dan Blue chaired the Democratic House Caucus before becoming the first black to be chosen Speaker of a southern legislature, a position he held for four years prior to the Republican takeover of the chamber in 1995. In the two years before the GOP takeover, Milton Fitch, another African American, served as the majority leader. In 2003, blacks held two of four Democratic whip positions and served as the co-majority whip in the senate.[22] A second black senator held the post of deputy president pro tempore. Of the numerous committee chairs, African Americans held twelve of forty-nine in the house and three of twenty-three in the senate in 2000. Among the most powerful positions held were senate chairs of Ways and Means and Appropriations, and, in the house, of Appropriations. In the 2005 session, Jeanne Hopkins Lucas served as majority whip in the senate and one of her colleagues was the deputy president pro tempore. African Americans chaired two committees including the Appropriations committee on General Government and Information Technology. In the house, African Americans chaired the Finance Committee along with twelve others. One member of the Black Caucus was the Democratic whip in the house.

African Americans in Statewide Office

A high-profile African American candidate has twice won the Democratic nomination for the U.S. Senate from North Carolina. In 1990, Harvey Gantt, who had been the first African American student at Clemson University and later won election as mayor of Charlotte, sought the Democratic nomination for the U.S. Senate. To win the Democratic nomination, Gantt defeated Michael Easley (later to become North Carolina's governor) with 57 percent of the primary vote.

The general election pitted Gantt against Jesse Helms, the Republican incumbent seeking his fourth term in the Senate. Despite being outspent by Helms by a margin of more than two to one, most polls showed Gantt leading until the closing days of the campaign. Helms pulled out a 53 percent victory after airing what has become a classic racial-appeal advertisement. What has become known as the "white hands" ad showed a pair of white hands crumpling an envelope. The voice-over commiserated:

> You needed that job, and you were the best qualified. But they had to give it to a minority because of a racial quota. Is that really fair? Harvey Gantt says it is. Harvey Gantt supports Ted Kennedy's racial quota law that makes the color of your skin more important than your qualifications. You'll vote on this issue next Tuesday. For racial quotas: Harvey Gantt. Against racial quotas: Jesse Helms.[23]

This racial appeal helped mobilize conservative white Democrats in the eastern part of the state. Known as Jessecrats, they were willing to forsake their Democratic moorings in order to support Helms.

In 1996, Gantt again opposed Helms as the conservative Republican mounted his last Senate election bid. The results were very similar to those six years earlier as Helms won again with 53 percent of the vote. Even though Gantt failed in his two bids for the Senate, his performance was on par with that of the white Democrats who opposed Helms.

In 1984, Helms had beaten Jim Hunt who had just completed two successful terms as governor. Helms devastated the popular governor with a series of ads showing conflicting statements made by the governor on key issues that then asked, "Jim, where do you stand?" Helms took that election with 52 percent of the vote. Six years earlier, he had defeated state Insurance Commissioner John Ingram with 55 percent of the vote. While this was Helms's largest margin, it came against a Democrat who ran little more than a shadow campaign as Helms outspent Ingram by a margin of $7.5 million to $264,088.[24] In his initial election, Helms had won the seat being vacated by B. Everett Jordan with 54 percent of the vote against U.S. Rep. Nick Galifianakis. Thus, the 53 percent of the vote that Helms took in his two victories over Gantt was right in line with his vote share against white Democratic opponents.

Between the two Gantt defeats came a statewide victory for an African American. In 1992, Ralph Campbell, the brother of Atlanta mayor Bill Campbell, won the Democratic nomination for state auditor and then went on to win in the general election. Four years later, Campbell won a second term in this constitutional office and did so when on the same ballot with Harvey Gantt. As Gantt was losing, Campbell ran 4 percentage points ahead of the Democratic Senate candidate. Campbell won a third term in 2000 but failed in his bid for a fourth term.

The 2004 elections proved more difficult for Democrats than previous ones as the Democratic nominees lost the presidency, a Senate seat, the commissioner of agriculture and commissioner of labor posts, as well as the auditor position. Although unsuccessful, Campbell polled 49.6 percent of the vote and took approximately one thousand more votes than did the Senate nominee, Erskine Bowles. Since more votes were cast in the Senate than the auditor's contest, Campbell ran 2.6 points ahead of Bowles. Campbell got almost 6 percentage points more of the vote than did the Democratic presidential ticket that included North Carolina's retiring senator John Edwards.

In a much earlier statewide contest in 1976, Howard Lee, who seven years earlier had been elected mayor of the majority-white university town of Chapel Hill, made it into the runoff for the Democratic nomination for lieutenant governor. Lee's white opponent, conservative Democrat Jimmy Green, turned to a racial appeal by running newspaper ads that contained pictures of the two candidates.[25]

The North Carolina Supreme Court currently has one black member—its first African American woman. She is, however, not the court's first black member. The representative from the 1st Congressional District, G. K. Butterfield, served briefly on the Supreme Court but was one of the victims of rising Republicanism. As far back as 1986, Henry Frye, who ultimately became chief justice, won a seat on the Supreme Court. Recently, black Democratic justices like white Democrats have fallen to Republicans in their election bids. Currently the Supreme Court has only two Democrats, one of whom, Justice Patricia Timmons-Goodson, was appointed to fill a vacancy by Democratic governor Mike Easley in early 2006. Although judicial elections became nonpartisan with the 2004 election, five Supreme Court justices are Republicans, several of whom very narrowly defeated Democrats.

North Carolina's second-highest court is the fifteen-member Court of Appeals. This body, which uses three-member panels to hear appeals on a wide range of issues, has had several African American members. At times there have been as many as three. As of 2008, two blacks served on this court. Both the Court of Appeals and the Supreme Court are elected statewide.

RACIAL VOTING PATTERNS

Estimates of racial voting behavior prepared by Richard Engstrom provide an indication of how North Carolina blacks and whites voted in the early 1980s. The Engstrom estimates indicate that Mickey Michaux and Kenneth Spaulding lost in Congressional District 2 despite winning approximately 90 percent of the black vote because they failed to attract as much as 15 percent of the white vote in this 40 percent black district.[26] As table 7.3 shows, Howard Lee running in the Democratic primary in District 4 in 1984 attracted a larger share of the white vote (24.3 percent) than did Michaux or Spaulding, but was substantially weaker among black voters and failed to win the Democratic nomination.

In the 1992 District 1 primary, the black vote was splintered among four African American candidates. However, they shared approximately 90 percent of that vote. In the runoff, general, and special 1992 contests in District 1, Eva Clayton took more than 90 percent of the black vote. In the general and special elections, the white vote is far less cohesive than

TABLE 7.3. Estimates of support by race for African American candidates in North Carolina congressional and statewide contests, 1982–1998

		Voter support for African American candidates					
		Primary		Runoff		General Election	
Contest	Candidate(s)	White	Black	White	Black	White+	Black+
1982 Congressional 2	Michaux	13.88	88.55	13.12	91.48		
1984 Congressional 2	Spaulding	14.10	89.70				
1984 Congressional 4	Lee	24.32	68.57				
	Winters	9.17	13.86				
1992 Congressional 1	Clayton	1.38	51.88	0.00	93.26	33.93	95.22
	Riddick	3.00	15.07				
	Hardaway	0.10	11.08				
	Powell	0.53	11.02				
1992 Congressional 1†	Clayton					41.15	98.46
1990 U.S. Senate	Gantt	22.61	70.67	38.25	86.29	36.73	98.14
	Hannon	1.20	1.01				
1990 Court of Appeals	Johnston					43.08	100
1992 Auditor	Campbell	31.14	65.01			43.16	100
1994 Congressional 12	Watt*					32.2 (36.4)	100 (98.7)
1996 Congressional 1	Clayton*					27.9 (34.3)	100 (99.0)
1996 Congressional 12	Watt*					35.3 (41.8)	100 (99.3)
1998 Congressional 1	Clayton*					27.9 (33.0)	100 (98.2)
1998 Congressional 12	Watt*					32.8 (38.3)	100 (98.7)

Sources: Richard Engstrom, "Racial Differences in Candidate Preferences in North Carolina Elections," report in *Shaw v. Reno;* Charles S. Bullock III and Richard E. Dunn, "The Demise of Racial Districting and the Future of Black Representation," *Emory Law Journal* 48 (Fall 1999): 1209–1253.

Note: All candidates are Democrats unless otherwise indicated.

*Incumbent.

†Special election to fill the remainder of the term of late incumbent Walter Jones, Sr.

+Figures in parentheses are EI estimates.

the black vote with Clayton getting a third of the white vote in the general election and two-fifths of the white vote in the special election.

The results for the six statewide contests in table 7.3 also show black voters to be generally more cohesive than white voters. In three of the contests, the black candidates get virtually all of the African American vote, and in the 1990 Senate runoff, Gantt takes 86 percent of the black vote. In those four contests, 36 percent or more of the white votes are also cast for the black candidate. In the other two contests, the white vote is somewhat more cohesive than the black vote. In the 1990 Senate primary, Gantt takes 70.67 percent of the black vote while more than 76 percent of the white vote goes for Mike Easley, the unsuccessful white candidate. In the 1992 Democratic primary for auditor, Campbell gets 65 percent of the black vote while 69 percent of the white vote is cast against him.

Table 7.3 also provides more recent regression and EI estimates of racial voting behavior in Districts 1 and 12. These show that in 1994, 1996, and 1998, the black vote continued to be substantially more cohesive than the white vote. The African American candidates consistently got more than 95 percent of the black vote in general elections. They usually attracted more than 30 percent of the white vote with Watt able to get slightly larger shares of the white vote than did Clayton.

Table 7.4 presents estimates of white support for white Democratic candidates running in North Carolina congressional districts between 1994 and 1998. Like in table 7.3, this table presents two sets of estimates of white support for the Democratic nominees. No Democratic candidate consistently attracts a majority of the white vote. Indeed, it is rare for a white candidate to be the candidate of choice among white North Carolinians. To put the performance of the two African American members of Congress from North Carolina in perspective, their failure to attract most white voters is in line with the difficulties encountered by their white Democratic colleagues. By the mid-1990s, white North Carolinians had become predominately Republican in their congressional voting preferences. However, the share of the white vote going to the two African American incumbents, Eva Clayton in the 1st District and Melvin Watt in the 12th District, is somewhat lower than the share of the white vote going to white Democratic incumbents. The African American incumbents, however, do frequently attract more white support than do white Democratic challengers.

This same point is reinforced by the analysis of the more recent congressional contests. Table 7.5 presents OLS estimates of white voter preferences in congressional elections in 2000 and 2002. All but two of these contests involved incumbents. The three white incumbents each attracted a majority of the white vote in 2000. While both black incumbents won reelection, they did less well, winning 40 and 46 percent of the white vote. The performance

TABLE 7.4. White support (%) for white North Carolina Democratic U.S. House candidates, 1994–1998

	White candidate	OLS	EI
1994			
Congressional 2	Moore	33.4	36.0
Congressional 3	Lancaster*	40.3	39.8
Congressional 4	Price*	46.3	44.0
Congressional 5	Sands	35.7	38.5
Congressional 7	Rose*	46.5	47.1
Congressional 8	Hefner*	44.0	47.0
Congressional 9	Blake	30.4	34.4
Congressional 10	Avery**	25.8	27.1
Congressional 11	Lauterer**	38.1	38.5
1996			
Congressional 2	Etheridge**	42.4	45.8
Congressional 3	Parrott**	26.4	27.1
Congressional 4	Price**	48.6	48.9
Congressional 5	Cashion**	28.8	28.4
Congressional 6	Costley**	19.6	22.9
Congressional 7	McIntyre	48.1	48.4
Congressional 8	Hefner*	44.9	48.0
Congressional 9	Daisley**	28.6	32.3
Congressional 10	Neill**	26.0	26.5
Congressional 11	Ferguson**	37.5	37.8
1998			
Congressional 2	Etheridge*	44.3	50.3
Congressional 3	Williams**	29.6	30.5
Congressional 4	Price*	49.9	51.5
Congressional 5	Robinson**	23.3	25.5
Congressional 8	Taylor	32.6	37.6
Congressional 9	Blake**	22.3	25.5
Congressional 11	Young**	39.8	41.5

Source: Charles S. Bullock III and Richard E. Dunn, "The Demise of Racial Districting and the Future of Black Representation," *Emory Law Journal* 48 (Fall 1999): 1209–1253.

Note: OLS = ecological regression; EI = ecological inference.

*Incumbent.

**Challenger.

of the black incumbents exceeded that of white challengers who attracted between 20.5 and 39.2 percent of the white vote. In 2002, as two years earlier, white incumbents had the greatest appeal among white voters, and each of these three attracted majorities among whites. The black incumbent, Melvin Watt in the 12th District, polled 41.8 percent of the white vote. Four of the white challengers attracted less than a third of the white vote while in District 11; the white Democrat got 38.1 percent of the white vote. Two districts had open seats. In the newly created 13th District, the white nominee did better than Representative Watt as he managed to take 43.7 percent of the white vote. In the 1st District where ten-year veteran Eva Clayton retired, Frank Ballance managed less than 16 percent of the white vote.

The analysis of a decade's worth of white voting in North Carolina congressional elections shows white incumbents are the most successful Democratic candidates among white voters. They are followed by black incumbents, who run 10 percentage points or more behind white incumbents among white voters. White challengers hold the weakest appeal for white voters as they tend to run at least 5 percentage points poorer than black incumbents among white voters. The single black candidate for an open seat received an especially poor response from whites.

An examination of recent statewide election voting patterns (table 7.6) shows no Democratic candidates for statewide office able to carry the white vote. In 1996, 2000, and 2004, Democrats won thirteen of thirteen, thirteen of sixteen, and nine of twelve statewide partisan offices that were contested. In 1996, when the Democrats last swept all of the state offices, African American candidate Ralph Campbell commanded the lowest share of the white vote, 40.8 percent, in barely winning the election. In 2000 he garnered the second-lowest share of the white vote (39.7 percent) in his narrow reelection victory. Campbell went down to defeat in 2004, though he bested two other losing Democrats in terms of white vote share. Overall, when Democrats won statewide, they ran as incumbents and garnered at least 40 percent of the white vote statewide. Campbell's weaker showing among white voters when compared with other Democratic nominees fits the pattern for Democratic congressional contests. The black incumbent running statewide fared poorer among white voters than did white incumbents. Indeed Campbell, as an incumbent, frequently got smaller shares of the white vote than did white Democratic challengers.

TABLE 7.5. Congressional election results for Democratic candidates in North Carolina, 2000–2002

Year/District	Candidate	Democrat's vote share	Democrat's white vote share+
2000			
1	**Clayton** *	**66.0**	**46.0**
2	Etheridge *	58.0	51.6
3	McNairy **	37.0	36.3
4	Price *	62.0	55.9
5	— †	—	—
6	— †	—	—
7	McIntyre *	70.0	66.4
8	Taylor **	44.0	36.6
9	McGuire **	30.0	20.5
10	Parker **	29.0	25.7
11	Neill **	42.0	39.2
12	**Watt** *	**65.0**	**40.0**
2002			
1	**Ballance**	**63.8**	**15.7**
2	Etheridge *	65.4	53.3
3	—	—	—
4	Price *	61.1	55.4
5	Crawford *	29.8	27.9
6	— †	—	—
7	McIntyre *	71.1	67.3
8	Kouri **	44.6	28.8
9	McGuire **	25.8	22.1
10	Daugherty **	37.8	32.0
11	Neill **	42.8	38.1
12	**Watt** *	**65.2**	**41.8**
13	Miller	54.7	43.7

Source: Data obtained from North Carolina State Board of Elections.

African American candidates indicated in **boldface**.

+Ecological regression estimates.

*Incumbent.

**Challenger.

†No Democratic candidate.

TABLE 7.6. EI statewide election results in North Carolina, 1996–2004

	1996		2000		2004	
	Democratic % of total vote	Democratic % of white vote+	Democratic % of total vote	Democratic % of white vote+	Democratic % of total vote	Democratic % of white vote+
Att'y General	59.1	48.3	51.2	39.4	55.6	44.6
Auditor	**49.9++**	40.8	**50.5**	39.7	**49.6**	38.6
Agriculture Comm.	57.8	46.7	50.6	40.2	49.96	38.1
Insurance Comm.	56.7	46.3	57.0	45.4	57.6	46.9
Labor Comm.	51.0	40.9	50.0	39.0	47.9	37.5
Lt. Governor	55.0	44.8	52.0	41.5	55.6	
Governor	55.9		52.0	42.1	55.6	46.2
Sec'y of State	53.5	42.4	54.0	43.3	57.3	46.4
Supt. of Public Instruct.	52.0	42.4	53.0	42.5	50.1	39.4
Treasurer	50.6	41.8	55.0	43.9	54.5	42.6
U.S. Senator	**46.6**					
President	44.3		43.1		43.6	
Court of Appeals, post 1	52.0	43.1	49.9	39.2	55.1	49.6
Court of Appeals, post 2	49.9	39.6			54.5	50.4
Court of Appeals, post 3	51.5	40.8			57.8	51.8
Court of Appeals, post 4	50.6	39.9				
Court of Appeals, post 5	51.5	40.5				
Supreme Court, post 1	55.7	46.1	48.0	38.0		
Supreme Court, post 2	51.3	41.4				

Source: Data computed by the authors.

+Ecological regression estimates.

++Plurality winner.

African American Democratic candidates indicated in **boldface**.

FEDERAL MONITORING

Of the southern states identified by Section 4 of the 1965 Voting Rights Act, North Carolina had the fewest objections to its proposed changes in election law. Only five of its proposals in the first decade drew objections. This low incidence of problems may reflect the fact that less than half of the state was covered by Section 5. During the next decade, the Department of Justice (DOJ) rejected twenty-three proposed changes, which was lower than any of the other covered southern states except for Virginia, which had only ten rejections. During the decade of 1985 to 1994, again, North Carolina had received fewer objections from DOJ, of the states originally covered except for Virginia. In the most recent decade, North Carolina had fewer objections than Virginia with only four, although Alabama did even better with only two objections. DOJ registered only two since 1997, and both of these involved redistricting plans from Harnett County.

A recent study of DOJ preclearance activity from 1990 through 2005 identifies 8,229 preclearance admissions from North Carolina jurisdictions. Of these, 99.6 percent got precleared.[27] DOJ's initial response to 232 of the 8,229 submissions was to request additional information. Approximately half of these involve a change in the method of election. Another 30 dealt with annexations and 28 of these submissions involved redistricting plans. Upon getting further information, DOJ approved 169 of the 232 submissions about which it had raised question. The submitting authority withdrew 21 of the questioned submissions. Five of these withdrawals have come since 2000. Three of the submissions withdrawn during the current decade involved redistricting plans.

CONCLUSION

Substantial progress has been observed in North Carolina voting rights, although the state still exhibits a racially charged political atmosphere. This division has largely insinuated itself into the party electoral process, where black and white voters are able to coalesce to elect candidates statewide, including occasional black candidates, and contribute to the election of descriptive representatives from the minority community.

Minority representation has not achieved full proportionality. Referring back to figure 5.2 in the Virginia chapter (chapter 5), we can observe how North Carolina ranked when compared to the other eight southern Section 5 states in terms of attaining black proportionality in the legislature and the congressional delegation. The Tar Heel State ranks fourth in terms of congressional delegation proportionality and fifth of nine on state-legislative proportionality.

Black voters are more likely to vote in North Carolina than in the nonsouthern states, but North Carolina black voters register and turn out at lower rates that North Carolina whites. The disparity between black and white voter participation has declined dramatically over the past two decades as the two races are now less than 4 points apart on rates of participation, according to Census Bureau estimates.

Black voters have been able to elect candidates of choice to the legislature and the U.S. House, and have continued to do so with the departure of incumbents from districts with lower black voter percentages than in the early 1990s. The success of Frank Ballance and G. K. Butterfield in succeeding Representative Clayton from the low-country 1st Congressional District is indicative of this ability.

While African Americans have been successful occasionally in statewide contests and more frequently in congressional and state legislative districts where blacks constitute a large plurality if not a majority of voters, the evidence indicates that race still plays a role in white voter decisions. Black Democrats attract smaller shares of the white vote than do white Democrats. This is true even for incumbents who have often broadened their base of support. While African American incumbents usually run better with white voters than do nonincumbent white Democrats, the black incumbents are less successful in appealing to white voters than are incumbent white Democrats.

Statewide, the ability to elect candidates preferred by blacks will rest on the ability to create coalition with white voters. For the past decade, Democrats have generally succeeded in creating such coalitions. The lack of success of African American candidates in 2004 indicates that the very fine line of white minority support required to elect Democrats could be crossed in the near future.

PART II

The 1975 Amendment States

CHAPTER 8

Texas

In August 2005, Texas joined California, Hawaii, and New Mexico as the fourth state in which most residents were not Anglo whites. According to Census Bureau estimates, 50.2 percent of the Texas population now belonged to a racial or ethnic minority group.

Despite having a substantial minority population, being part of the Confederacy, and anchoring the western end of the Black Belt, when the initial Voting Rights Act was crafted under the watchful eyes of President Lyndon Johnson, Texas was one of four southern states not caught by the trigger mechanism in Section 4. Texas escaped because it did not have one of the banned tests as a prerequisite for voting. Although Texas collected a poll tax, the legislation did not identify that impediment as a test or device. While it is hardly surprising that the Texan president would set a threshold that would not make his home state subject to the most demanding features of the legislation, the history of the Lone Star State is not free of racial disfranchisement. University of Houston professor and Texas politics maven Richard Murray points out:

> In the immediate aftermath of the Civil War, blacks became a political force in Texas in counties that had high percentages of slaves. The Twelfth Legislature, elected under a new constitution pushed through by Radical Republicans, included two black senators and

nine black representatives. Within a few years, however, white conservative Democrats regained control of Texas politics and began the systematic disenfranchisement of the African American population, which was completed with the approval of a state poll tax in 1901 and the establishment of a white primary system. By 1906 there were only about 5,000 black voters on the rolls.[1]

Efforts to eliminate black participation from the primary began with the Democratic Executive Committee, which in 1904 required prospective voters to swear that: "I am a white person and a Democrat."[2] Later, allowing only whites to participate in the Democratic primary became a part of state law, and the state maintained the white primary until 1944. The Texas white primary faced continuous attacks in the courts that produced a 1927 Supreme Court decision.[3] In two suits filed by an El Paso physician, the Supreme Court found that the implementation of the white primary violated the Equal Protection Clause of the Fourteenth Amendment because of involvement of the state.[4] In the mid-1930s, the Texas government completely disassociated itself from requirements concerning who could participate in the Democratic primary, but the party itself barred the participation of African Americans. This approach found favor with the Supreme Court, which concluded that a private association had the authority to restrict membership.[5] In 1944, however, the Supreme Court finally invalidated the white Democratic primary because of the integral part played by the primary in determining who would hold public office in Texas.[6] Since Democrats dominated Texas politics, the winner of the Democratic primary invariably won the general election. Consequently, allowing African Americans to vote in the general election simply gave them the opportunity to participate in a meaningless plebiscite where the winner of the Democratic primary received confirmation. The final nail in the white primary coffin came in a 1953 Texas case out of Fort Bend County. The all-white Jaybird Party held a primary prior to the Democratic primary. Invariably, the winners of the Jaybird primary won the Democratic nomination and ultimately went on to hold public office. The Jaybird primary thus played the integral role in selecting public officeholders in the Houston-area county.[7]

The poll tax remained a prerequisite for participation in state elections until 1966. Although political scientist V. O. Key, Jr., dismissed the poll tax as a significant source of black disenfranchisement at the time of its adoption, later scholars assert that it and the white primary excluded Latinos as well as blacks.[8] Texas, unlike most of its southern neighbors, never required a literacy test as a prerequisite for registration.[9]

Had the 1965 legislation considered the poll tax to be a discriminatory prerequisite to voting, Texas would have been brought under Section 5 since less than half of its voting-age population cast ballots in 1964. Turnout in the presidential election that saw native son Lyndon Johnson win a full term reached only 47.46 percent. Four years later, the Lone Star State had a 55.6 percent turnout rate and therefore would have avoided the 1970 update of the Voting Rights Act.

The notable successes achieved by African Americans in Section 5 states made Texas Latinos eager for a similar legislative assist in promoting political activities among their population. A major impetus for the extension of the legislation in 1975 that included language minorities came from the Texas Latino community.[10]

The 1975 reauthorization extended the provisions of the Act to address voting discrimination against linguistic minorities, defined as "American Indian, Asian American, Alaskan Natives" or people "of Spanish heritage." The reauthorization also recalibrated the presence of tests or devices and levels of electoral participation to November 1972. For linguistic minorities, the new legislation recast "test or device" to encompass the provision of minority-language electoral information in political subdivisions and states where a linguistic minority constituted more than 5 percent of the citizen voting-age population (VAP). More precisely, the minority-language provision trigger covers any jurisdiction or political subdivision where on November 1, 1972: More than 5 percent of the voting-age citizens were members of a single-language minority group; registration and election materials were provided only in English; and fewer than 50 percent of the voting-age citizens registered to vote or voted in the 1972 presidential election. The minority-language provision covered all of Alaska, Arizona, and Texas, and parts of California, Florida, Michigan, New York, North Carolina, and South Dakota.

MINORITY REGISTRATION AND TURNOUT

While Section 5 did not impact Texas in either the initial Voting Rights Act or its 1970 amendments, the Commission on Civil Rights treated Texas like other southern states and reported its incidence of black registration in the wake of the 1965 legislation. By 1967, the Voter Education Project (VEP) estimated that a higher proportion of the nonwhite than white population had registered to vote in Texas. The VEP estimates reported by the Commission on Civil Rights indicated that 61.6 percent of nonwhites compared with 53.3 percent of whites had signed up to vote, making Texas the only southern states in which nonwhite registration rates exceeded the white figure.[11] The explanation for this unusual pattern may well reflect low levels of participation of white Hispanics. The Civil Rights Commission report provides no separate figures for Spanish-surnamed voters so that surmise cannot be fully explored.

The Voter Education Project, a nongovernment organization that awarded small grants to local groups engaged in getting African Americans registered to vote, estimates that in 1964, 375,000 blacks had registered to vote in Texas.[12] This would mean that blacks constituted 12.4 percent of the Texas registrants. By 1968, VEP estimates that Texas had 540,000 black registrations, which would be 13.2 percent of the state's voters. That figure equals the Texas nonwhite population in 1960.

For more recent estimates of registration by race, we turn to figures from the Bureau of the Census (appendix B). The figures for Latino registration show little variation over the generation included in the table. The lowest percentage of Latinos who report having registered is 39.1 percent in 2002. That figure, however, differs little from figures reported in 1980, 1990, 1994, 1998, and 2006. On the high side, 45.5 percent of the adult Latinos registered in 1988.

The impact of a substantial noncitizen population is readily apparent. Beginning with 1998, the Census Bureau has developed estimates from which can be computed participation rates among Hispanic voting-age citizens. In each year most Hispanic citizens had registered. There is little variation in the registration rates for Latino citizens with 56 to 60 percent of the eligible adults signed up to vote.

The registration rates for whites are also relatively constant over time, ranging from a low of 57.7 percent in 2002 to a high of 66.5 percent in 1988. In 1980, the difference between white and Latino registration was 22.1 percentage points; a quarter century later, the difference was 20 percentage points. The 2000 and 2002 figures present two of the smallest differences in recent years with white registration being approximately 18 percentage points higher than Latino registration. These are not the smallest differences since the two midterm elections of the 1980s had differences of 15.1 and 16.2 percentage points.

White figures are impacted by the way the group is defined. In the earlier years, Hispanic "whites" were not excluded from the calculation of Anglos. In order to maintain comparability throughout the time period, white figures are presented in appendix B that include white Hispanics. Separate breakouts for non-Hispanic whites have been available only since 1998. In that election, 69.4 percent of the voting-age Anglo non-Hispanics reported registering. In 2004, the non-Hispanic white registration figure had increased to 73.6 percent. When white non-Hispanics and Latino citizens are compared, the differences range from 12 to 15 percentage points. In 2000 when 60 percent of the Latino citizens registered, the figures for Anglos stood at 71.8 percent. The greatest difference appears in 2004 when 58.8 percent of Latino citizens registered compared with 73.6 percent of the non-Hispanic whites.

The gap between Latino and black registration has grown over time. In 1980, the difference was approximately 17 percentage points, while in 2004 it reached almost 27 percentage points, the largest in the time period covered. As with comparisons made with whites, comparing Latino citizens with African Americans narrows the differences. For three elections, the Census Bureau broke out estimates for black non-Hispanics. Differences in registration rates between Latino citizens and black non-Hispanics range from 8.2 points in 1998 to 10 points four years later. In 2006, the gap between Latino citizens and all blacks stood at 4.3 points.

From 1980 through 1994, whites usually registered at higher rates than African Americans. In the fourteen-year period, only in 1986 did the black registration rate exceed that of whites. While whites registered at higher rates than blacks in the other years in this period, only in 1980 was the difference more than 3 percentage points. Beginning with 1996, the registration figure for blacks exceeds that for whites, with a 7 percentage point difference from 2000 to 2004. The higher black than white registration in recent years results from many Latinos being included in the white population for computational purposes. If Hispanics are excluded, then the registration figures for non-Hispanic whites increase by 10 percentage points in 1998 and 2000 and by a dozen points in the next three elections. For three elections, non-Hispanic whites can be compared with non-Hispanic blacks. When that is done, the white turnout rate exceeds the black figure by 2.4 to 5 percentage points.

In the years for which the most-detailed figures are available, non-Hispanic whites register at the highest rates (appendix B). African Americans register at rates slightly lower than white non-Hispanics. Latinos register at lower rates than either other group, but among those who are citizens, Latino registration runs about 10 percentage points lower than for African Americans.

The bottom of the first table in appendix B provides registration figures for the non-South as a baseline for comparison. Throughout the time period, registration rates for Texas Latinos exceeded that for those outside the South. In most years, the difference has been roughly 10 percentage points. The registration rates were most similar in 1980 when 39.3 percent of the Texas Latinos compared with 35.5 percent of those outside the region reported being registered. The largest difference occurred in 1988 when 45.4 percent of Texas Latinos but only 32.4 percent of nonsouthern Latinos registered.

Estimated registration rates of Latino citizens in the non-South are not available; however, a comparison can be made with nationwide estimates. When noncitizens are excluded, Latino registration rates in Texas still exceed those for the entire nation, although the disparities are smaller than when figures for all Latino adults are used. In part this is because the Texas data are incorporated into, and raise, the national figures. If the Texas data were excluded from the national figures, then the difference between Texas and the rest of the nation would appear greater.

Since 1990, Texas African Americans have registered at higher rates than blacks outside the South. In the early part of this period the difference was often less than 2 percentage points. But by 2000 and 2002, the gap had grown to 8 points. Prior to 1990, the black registration rate in the non-South outpaced that in Texas except for 1986.

The second table in appendix B provides the Census Bureau estimates for turnout by ethnic group. For each of the three groups the usual sawtooth pattern is visible. In presidential elections, Latino turnout ranges from 27.9 percent in 1996 to a high of 33.2 percent in 1988. The first presidential election (1980) had almost an identical rate of Latino turnout as the most recent two through 2004, with participation rates all between 29 and 30 percent. The share of the Latino voting-age population that has turned out in midterm elections ranges from a low of 15.3 percent in 1998 to a high of 26.8 percent in 1982. In presidential elections, Hispanic turnout is approximately 60 percent of the Anglo turnout. For the first two midterm elections in the series, Latino participation ran a bit above 60 percent of Anglo participation. Since then, Latinos have participated at about half the rate of Anglos in midterm elections.

Beginning in 1998 the Census Bureau has provided estimates that can be used to calculate turnout among Latino citizens. For the two most recent presidential elections through 2004, just over 40 percent of the Hispanic citizens voted. That percentage is more than 10 points higher than when all adult Hispanics is used as the denominator. In the midterm elections approximately a quarter of the Latino citizens went to the polls. Prior to 1996, whites had the highest voting rates. In the six most recent elections, however, African Americans turned out to vote at higher rates than whites. Latinos were a distant third in turnout rates.

The Census Bureau has provided turnout estimates for non-Hispanic whites since 1998, and from 1998 to 2002 it estimated turnout among non-Hispanic blacks. Excluding Latinos results in higher participation rates among the remaining Anglos and African Americans. When non-Hispanics are compared, the turnout rate among whites exceeds the black figure by less than a percentage point in 2000 and 2002. In 1998, non-Hispanic white turnout was 5.7 points higher than for blacks. More recently, the Census Bureau has not provided an estimate for non-Hispanic blacks. However, based on the modest increase in black turnout that results from the exclusion of Hispanics in the three previous elections, it is unlikely that non-Hispanic blacks voted at a higher rate than the non-Hispanic whites in 2004 or 2006.

The longitudinal trend for African Americans shows a rise in participation. Black turnout rates in the two most recent presidential elections are the highest recorded in the quarter century covered in appendix B. Turnout in 2002 exceeded any previous midterm participation rate by at least 4.5 percentage points. African American turnout in presidential elections peaked two years earlier.

The bottom of the second table in appendix B provides data for the non-South as a point of comparison. In most years, Texas Latino participation rates track closely with those for Latinos outside of the South before falling behind in 2006. In eight election years, participation rates were higher among Latinos in Texas than outside the South, but differences were usually small. The greatest disparity came in 1988 when Latino participation in Texas was 6.4 percentage points higher than in the non-South. Only in 1998 was the turnout rate among nonsouthern Latinos substantially greater than for those in Texas.

In appendix B, we also incorporate estimates for national turnout among Latino citizens (the Census Bureau does not report estimates for the non-South for this component of the electorate). For each of the five elections for which the comparison is feasible, the turnout rate among Latinos nationwide runs higher than in Texas. Unlike with the registration figures, where higher rates in Texas pulled up the national figures, the lower turnout of Texas Hispanics pulls down the national figure so that if non-Texas figures were available, the disparity with Texas would expand.

Black turnout is usually higher in the non-South than in Texas, although the differences have declined over time. In the first two elections, differences exceeded 10 points but thereafter declined. In 2000 and 2002 Texas African Americans voted at rates 4 percentage points above those outside the South. The two most recent elections saw a swing back to the older pattern with black turnout in the non-South slightly above the Texas rate.

Since 1992, Texas has reported the numbers of registrants with Spanish surnames. This provides another indicator of the rates at which Latinos are registering to vote. The problem with using surnames is that some Latinos have Anglo names. This may be particularly true of Latinas who have Anglo husbands and take their names, or the offspring of such unions who nonetheless consider themselves Latino, much like New Mexico governor Bill Richardson. Of course, the reverse pattern also occurs with Anglo

TABLE 8.1. Spanish surname voter registration in Texas, 1992–2006

	Total registration	Spanish registration	Surname % registered
1992	8,444,786	1,216,514	14.41
1994	8,639,197	1,315,422	15.23
1996	9,538,779	1,559,789	16.35
1998	9,587,025	1,790,764	18.68
2000	10,267,241	2,002,942	19.51
2002	10,333,415	2,111,446	20.43
2004	10,958,702	2,274,125	20.75
2006	10,960,696	2,356,638	21.61

Source: Texas Secretary of State's office.

women and their children often assuming the surnames of their Latino husbands. Another potential problem is that some names that are widespread among Hispanics may also be used by people with other heritage, such as Italian. Thus, the measure is not perfect, but it does provide an additional indicator of Hispanic participation in Texas.

Table 8.1 reports the number of registrants as well as the proportion of registrants who have Spanish surnames. In 1992, Spanish-surnamed registrants made up approximately one-seventh of the Texas electorate. The numbers and share of all registrants with Spanish-surnames has grown so that by 2004, slightly more than one in five registrants had a Spanish-surname. The 20.75 percent of the registrants who have Spanish surnames is less than the 28.6 percent of the 2000 voting-age population who were Latinos. However, the presence of Latinos among registrants is approaching the 22.3 percent of the citizen voting-age population that was Hispanic in 2000.

MINORITY OFFICE HOLDING

At the time of the passage of the initial Voting Rights Act there were fewer than seven African Americans holding public office in Texas.[13] Four years later, the number had only grown to twenty. Indeed, it was not until the mid-1970s that Texas, the largest state in the South and the one with far more governmental units than any other southern state, had as many as one hundred black officeholders. Another decade passed

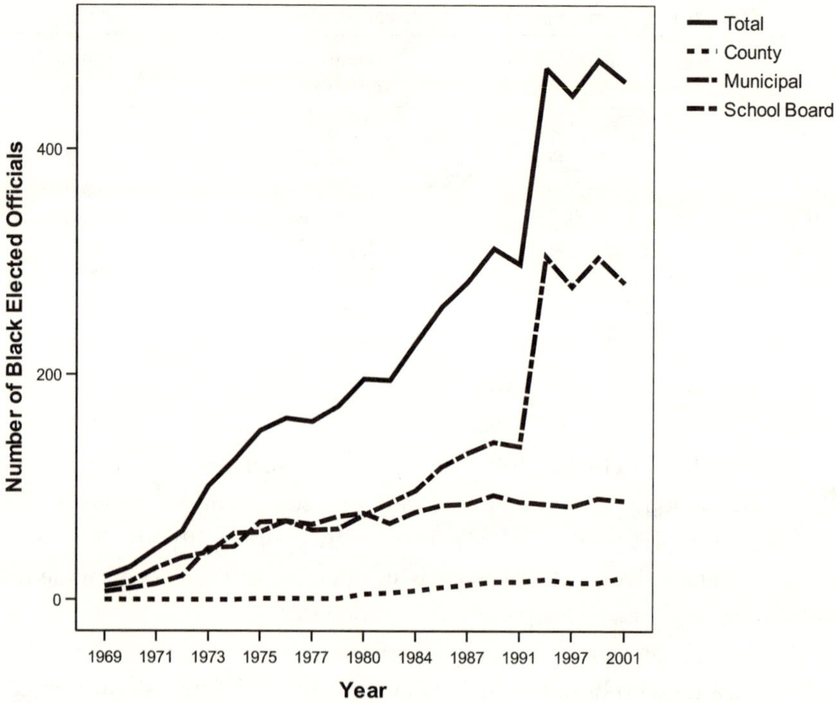

Figure 8.1. Black elected officials in Texas, 1969–2001. *Source:* Various volumes of the *National Roster of Black Elected Officials* (Washington, D.C.: Joint Center for Political and Economic Studies).

before Texas had more than two hundred blacks holding public office. Very quickly, by the late 1980s, the numbers rose to three hundred as the impact of *Thornburg v. Gingles,* which opened the way for challenges to at-large electoral systems, rippled across the country. The largest growth came between 1991 and 1993 when black officeholders increased from 298 to 472. The most recent survey, conducted in 2001 by the Joint Center for Political and Economic Studies, found Texas with 460 African Americans holding public office. The numbers of blacks holding county office has remained small, with only twenty holding offices across the Lone Star State's 254 counties. The bulk of the black officials have served in municipal offices throughout much of the period covered in figure 8.1. At the onset of the new century, more than 60 percent of the black officeholders served in cities. School boards now account for almost one hundred black elected officials, a number that has largely been stable since the late 1980s.

Texas has led all states in the number of Latino officeholders. After the 1972 election, the one used to bring Texas under Section 5 of the Voting Rights Act, the state had 565 Hispanics holding public office. Over the next eleven years, the number of Latino officeholders more than doubled to 1,427.[14] In 1996, Texas boasted almost 1,700 Latinos in public office, and by 2003 that number had swelled to almost 2,000, one of whom held a statewide post. By 2005 Texas had 2,137 Hispanic public officials.[15] California, the state with the second largest number of Latino officeholders, had roughly half the number found in Texas while New Mexico, the state that ranked third in the number of Latino officeholders, had fewer than one-third as many as Texas. Indeed, more than 40 percent of all Hispanics holding elected office in the nation served in the Lone Star State. The great bulk of the Texas Latino officeholders are Democrats, although until recently the state's Republican congressional delegation had one Hispanic and a few continue to serve in the state legislature.

Minority Members of Congress

Henry Gonzales became the first Latino member in Congress from Texas when he won a special election in January of 1962. A second Hispanic, Kika de la Garza, won in the state's southernmost district—a district that included Brownsville, Harlingen, and McAllen—in 1964. The 1982 reapportionment, which brought Texas three new seats, coincided with the creation of a third heavily Hispanic district in south Texas that elected Solomon Ortiz. A fourth Latino joined the Texas delegation in 1984 when Albert Bustamante triumphed in a district that extended from the San Antonio suburbs to the border.

Democrats intended the redistricting of 1992 to increase the number of Latino members in the U.S. House to six. One new district extended north out of the Rio Grande Valley, while a second district, strangely shaped and predominately Hispanic, was drawn in Houston. The Valley district performed and elected Frank Tejeda, but in Houston, even though 54 percent of the VAP was of Hispanic origin, the leading Latino candidate, Ben

Reyes, ultimately lost by 1,200 votes to an Anglo Democrat after a contested runoff. Reyes had led in the initial primary and then finished 180 votes behind Gene Green in the runoff. Reyes challenged the runoff results claiming that Republicans had participated. Although he prevailed in his litigation, he lost in the second runoff.[16]

The 1992 elections also saw the first Republican Latino elected as Henry Bonilla defeated Albert Bustamante (D) after press reports surfaced that the incumbent was under investigation by the FBI for racketeering.[17] This geographically expansive district—which extended along much of the Texas-Mexico border, then north to San Antonio—was home to a large number of Latino noncitizens, thus heightening the influence of the Anglo vote, which tends to be Republican. A sixth Latino won a seat in 1996 when Silvestre Reyes (D) triumphed in the El Paso open seat long held by Anglo Democrats.

After taking control of both chambers of the Texas legislature in 2003, Republican lawmakers carried out a controversial mid-decade redistricting in which they created an additional 68.6 percent Hispanic seat anchored in the South Valley as shown in table 8.2. As in 1992, Latino hopes for an additional member of Congress were dashed when an Anglo Democrat won the new district in 2004. Liberal Lloyd Doggett, whose Austin district had been splintered in the Republican gerrymander, ran for reelection in the new district that extended from the Valley to the Austin suburbs. Doggett easily defeated a Latina in the Democratic primary. Consequently, the number of Texas Latinos in Congress has not increased as Anglos held two districts that have large Latino concentrations since Gene Green continues to turn back challenges in the Houston district.

One issue in the litigation involving the Republican plan of 2003 focused on the one Texas Republican Latino in Congress. Most experts who testified in the trial challenging the new plan did not consider Henry Bonilla to be Latinos' candidate of choice since most of those voters had backed his Democratic challengers. Allan Lichtman's regression (OLS) and homogenous precinct (HP) estimates, reported in table 8.3, are that in contested general elections from 1992 through 2002, Bonilla captured between 8 and 30 percent of the Hispanic vote along with 83 to 88 percent of the Anglo vote.[18] The 2003 map reduced the likelihood that a Democrat could defeat Bonilla by swapping out Latinos for Anglo voters. The analysis

TABLE 8.2. Latino-majority congressional districts in Texas, 2002 and 2004

District	Citizen VAP*	SSVR**	Expected % Democrat+	Observed % Democrat†
		A. 2002 Districts (Balderas map)		
15	69.3	67.0	64.2	100.0
16	69.9	67.5	61.6	100.0
20	61.6	61.5	62.5	100.0
23	57.4	55.3	57.2	47.2
27	63.5	61.6	59.1	61.1
28	61.4	59.6	66.1	71.1
29	42.8	42.5	67.5	95.2
		B. 2004 Districts (HB-3 map)		
15	58.5	56.7	60.7	57.8
16	69.9	67.5	61.6	67.5
20	60.8	59.9	63.1	65.5
23	45.8	44.0	48.7	29.4
25	55.0	55.6	72.5	67.6
27	60.4	58.0	58.7	63.1
28	56.2	54.3	61.7	59.0
29	46.7	45.9	64.5	94.1

Sources: Ronald Keith Gaddie, "Expert Report of Ronald Keith Gaddie, Ph.D. in *Sessions v. Perry*" (2:03-CV-354, United States Federal Court for the Eastern District of Texas, 2003), prepared for the State of Texas, November 21, 2003; and Texas Secretary of State.

*Voting-age population (VAP) and citizen VAP figures are from the 2000 census.

**SSVR: Spanish surname voter registration (from the 2002 election cycle).

+"Expected" vote is % Democratic vote in 2002 lieutenant governor's race in Texas.

†Observed vote is actual % Democratic vote for candidate in respective election.

performed by veteran expert witness Professor Richard Engstrom (then of the University of New Orleans) for the G.I. Forum (a Mexican American civil rights organization started after World War II by Dr. Hector Garcia of Corpus Christi) revealed that in three of six Hispanic-majority Valley districts, the vote share for Hispanic-preferred candidates fell when compared to the map used in 2002. However, only in one district—Bonilla's District 23—did the share of votes for Hispanic-preferred candidates fall below a majority.[19]

Democrats and Hispanic groups challenged the 2003 Republican redistricting plan. In 2006, the Supreme Court upheld the power of the legislature to carry out a mid-decade redistricting but struck down the

TABLE 8.3. Estimates of Hispanic and Anglo voter preferences for Henry Bonilla in Texas Congressional District 23, 1992–2002

	OLS % Hispanic	EI % Hispanic	OLS % Anglo	EI % Anglo
1992	23	30.5	87	85.4
1994	29	43.3	83	78.0
1996	30	37.7	83	88.5
1998	26	40.0	85	83.9
2000	20	34.6	83	78.4
2002	8	—	88	—

Sources: Allan J. Lichtman, "Report of Allan J. Lichtman on Voting Rights Issues in Texas Congressional Redistricting," submitted in *Sessions v. Perry,* 2003; Allan J. Lichtman, "Report on Congressional Districts in Texas," submitted in *Del Rio v. Perry,* 2001. EI estimates are from Jonathan N. Katz, "Report on Texas Congressional Redistricting: Minority Opportunities and Partisan Fairness," submitted in *Del Rio v. Perry,* 2001.

Bonilla district. The court concluded that it violated the Voting Rights Act because it reduced the opportunity for Latinos to elect their candidate of choice in that district. The legislature had sought to get around that problem by creating a new majority-Hispanic district (the one won by Lloyd Doggett), which they argued took the place of the now more Anglo Bonilla district. To correct the problem identified by the Supreme Court, the Texas legislature reconfigured the Bonilla district to increase its Hispanic population to 65 percent of the voters.[20]

In the subsequent election, which was staged as a special election since the legislature did not draw the new district until after the regular Texas primary, Bonilla faced a pool of seven challengers. In the initial round held at the time of the November general election, he led the field by a substantial margin but failed to secure the majority needed for election. He took 49 percent of the vote well ahead of his nearest challenger, former representative Ciro Rodriguez, who managed only 20 percent. In the runoff held in early December, Bonilla suffered the fate that often overtakes incumbents who are forced into a runoff.[21] Rodriguez, who had been unseated in the Democratic primary by a fellow Hispanic after the 2003 redistricting, now regained a seat in Congress representing a different district. He defeated Bonilla by a margin of 54 to 46. One redistricting removed Rodriguez from Congress. A second one returned him to Washington.

Texas currently has seven majority-Latino congressional districts; six elect Hispanics, while one elects an Anglo Democrat who is the Hispanic electorate's candidate of choice in general elections. Overall, 21.8 percent of Texas congressional districts are Latino majority districts that elect a candidate of choice in the general election, a figure roughly comparable to the state's Latino citizen VAP in the most recent census. Texas briefly enjoyed an eighth majority-Latino district, the 25th, which was tossed by the U.S. Supreme Court in the LULAC case. This district reconstituted as a 42 percent Latino district that continued to elect its Anglo Democratic incumbent, and will likely trend toward having a majority Latino population in the future.

Although Texas was not brought under Section 5 as a result of discrimination against African Americans, the Department of Justice has been concerned about black congressional representation. In the 1960s, congressional mapmakers deliberately split the black electorate in Harris County to reduce its political influence. Electing an African American would wait until the 1971 redistricting paved the way for state senator Barbara Jordan (D) to win the newly drawn district in central city Houston.[22]

When Jordan arrived in Congress in 1972, she joined Georgia's Andrew Young as the South's first two African American representatives elected in the twentieth century. The seat that Jordan won has remained in the hands of an African American ever since and is now filled by her third successor, Sheila Jackson Lee (D). During much of the time that the district has sent African Americans to Congress, it has had only a black plurality, not a black majority. The successful African Americans have fashioned multiracial coalitions in which they attract substantial support from Latinos along with some of the Anglo vote.

A second black female senator, Eddie Bernice Johnson, used her position on the Reapportionment Committee to create a majority-black district in Dallas in 1992. Johnson easily won that district and continues to represent it. She has testified that but for the personal ambition of fellow Democrat Martin Frost (D), a black district could have been created in the metroplex a decade earlier.[23]

The mid-decade redistricting carried out by Republicans in 2003 resulted in a third African American going to Congress. Al Green won District 9, a district located in southwest Harris County drawn to be 37 percent black

TABLE 8.4. Black-access districts, Balderas (2002) and HB-3 (2004), in Texas

District	% Black VAP	% Latino VAP	% SSVR	Expected* % Democrat	Observed** % Democrat
A. 2002 Districts (Balderas map)					
18	42.1	29.1	14.2	76.4	76.9
30	40.3	27.7	11.4	74.2	74.3
B. 2004 Districts (HB-3 map)					
9	36.5	30.3	13.7	71.0	72.2
18	40.3	32.2	16.0	75.0	88.9
30	41.0	30.7	12.5	78.5	93.0

Sources: Ronald Keith Gaddie, "Expert Report of Ronald Keith Gaddie, Ph.D. in *Sessions v. Perry*" (2:03-CV-354, United States Federal Court for the Eastern District of Texas, 2003), prepared for the State of Texas, November 21, 2003; and Texas Secretary of State.

*"Expected" vote is % Democratic vote in 2002 lieutenant governor's race in Texas.

**Observed vote is actual % Democratic vote for candidate in respective election.

and only 17.4 percent Anglo. Green bested freshman Anglo Democrat Chris Bell, who had represented portions of the new district, in the Democratic primary by an almost two-to-one margin. Green dominated the black vote in the March 2004 primary, and easily won the November general election by a 72 percent to 26 percent margin. Bell had won the old 25th District in 2002, although he was not the candidate of choice of blacks in this district that was 22 percent black and 31 percent Hispanic.

Changes to the majority-black congressional districts in Dallas and Houston did not imperil the ability of African American voters to elect their candidate of choice in 2004 as reported in table 8.4. African American incumbents were reelected in 2004 with 89 percent and 93 percent respectively in Districts 18 and 30 as neither faced major-party opposition. Richard Murray, who provided evidence on behalf of the two black incumbents in the 2003 trial, indicated that changes to the Dallas district had "minimal" impact on the African American population, though the newly added Latino wards might portend increased "black-brown" competition in the future.[24] In Houston, Murray warned that the growing Latino presence might ultimately threaten blacks' ability to elect their candidate of choice in District 18.[25]

With three African Americans in the thirty-two–member Texas congressional delegation, blacks now hold 9.4 percent of the seats. That is slightly less than the black share of the Texas citizen VAP, which the Census Bureau estimated to be 11.6 percent in 2004.

Minority State Legislators

Latinos have a long history of serving in the Texas house of representatives. Data compiled by the Mexican American Legislative Caucus shows a Latino in the state house as far back as 1947. For the period recorded in table 8.5, which begins with 1965, there have always been at least nine Latinos in the house. The number of Latino representatives almost doubled between 1973 and 1977, increasing from ten to eighteen. The numbers hovered around twenty until implementation of a new districting plan in 1993, when the number of Latino representatives rose to twenty-six. Around the turn of the century, the number of Latinos in the Texas house reached 30 members, or 20 percent of the chamber, before slipping to twenty-nine in 2008.

Although Latinos had served in the state senate previously, none were members in 1965. Henry Gonzalez, who had been the only Hispanic senator, left the chamber in 1962, when he won a special election to Congress. Since a Latino senator won in 1966, the numbers have slowly increased, reaching seven in 1997. At that point, Latinos held 22.6 percent of the senate and 18.7 percent of the house seats. The number of Hispanic senators has remained relatively constant since 1987 and has never exceeded seven in the thirty-one–member chamber. In 2007, Latinos held just over 19 percent of the seats in both Texas chambers. This figure equals about three-fourths of the Hispanic citizen VAP as estimated by the Census Bureau in 2004.

Table 8.5 also shows the numbers and percentage of African American legislators. The first African American legislator to be elected to the senate, Barbara Jordan, triumphed in a Houston district in 1966. She held that seat for three terms before giving it up for a successful run for Congress. After a decade without an African American state senator, Houston sent another black senator in 1982, and then four years later, Eddie Bernice Johnson, also destined to become a congresswoman, became the first black senator from Dallas. African Americans continue to hold a pair of senate seats so that their representation in the senate is roughly half their percentage of the 2004 VAP.

TABLE 8.5. Latino and African American Texas state legislators, 1965–2007

	Latino Senate	Latino House	% Latino Senate	% Latino House	Black Senate	Black House	% Black Senate	% Black House
1965	0	9	0.0	6.0	0	0	0.0	0.0
1967	1	10	3.23	6.7	1	2	3.23	1.33
1969	1	11	3.23	7.3	1	2	3.23	1.33
1971	1	9	3.23	6.0	1	2	3.23	1.33
1973	2	10	6.45	6.7	0	8	0.00	5.33
1975	2	14	6.45	9.3	0	9	0.00	6.00
1977	3	18	9.68	12.0	0	13	0.00	8.67
1979	4	17	12.90	11.3	0	13	0.00	8.67
1981	3	17	9.68	11.3	0	13	0.00	8.67
1983	3	21	9.68	14.0	1	13	3.23	8.67
1985	4	19	12.90	12.7	1	13	3.23	8.67
1987	6	19	19.35	12.7	2	13	6.45	8.67
1989	6	19	19.35	12.7	2	13	6.45	8.67
1991	5	22	16.13	14.7	2	13	6.45	8.67
1993	6	26	19.35	17.3	2	14	6.45	9.33
1995	6	27	19.35	18.0	2	13	6.45	8.67
1997	7	28	22.58	18.7	2	14	6.45	9.33
1999	7	30	22.58	20.0	2	14	6.45	9.33
2001	7	30	22.58	20.0	2	14	6.45	9.33
2003	6	27	19.35	18.0	2	14	6.45	9.33
2005	6	27	19.35	18.0	2	14	6.45	9.33
2007	6	29	19.35	19.3	2	14	6.45	9.33

Source: Data compiled by the authors.

African Americans have been present in the house since 1967 without interruption. They experienced a substantial increase from two to eight after the 1971–72 redistricting. Their number increased again in 1977 to thirteen. In the next three decades, the number of black representatives has fluctuated between thirteen and fourteen as new districting plans have had no impact.

An extensive analysis of African American activities in the Texas legislature concluded that on relevant issues, the Black Caucus enjoyed success when it was united.[26] Black Democrats became chairs of some committees in both chambers, including, on occasion, some important committees. For example, Rodney Ellis chaired the Senate Finance Committee when Democrats had a majority in the upper chamber.

The senate has a tradition of naming chairs from both parties and this has allowed some minorities to continue to serve as chairs even after Republicans took control of that body. For example, as of 2007, Ellis chaired the Government Organization Committee while the other African American senator, Royce West, chaired the Intergovernmental Relations Committee. Two Hispanic Democrats served as senate committee chairs in 2007. Eduardo Lucio chaired the International Relations and Trade Committee while Leticia Van de Putte chaired the Veterans Affairs and Military Instillations Committee. Judith Zaffirini, the most senior Latino in the senate, served as co-chair of the Higher Education Subcommittee. She had previously chaired the Health and Human Services Committee and for many years served on the powerful Appropriations Conference Committee. In the 2007 session, minorities chaired four of the fourteen senate committees. However, with Republicans now in control of the senate, the influence of the body's minority members has declined, as it has also declined in the Texas house.

Statewide Minority Candidates

A number of minority candidates have sought statewide office in Texas. The state maintains a database showing candidate race for all levels of offices, for primaries and general elections. Of the 140 major-party nominees for statewide office from 1992 to 2004, six were African American and thirteen were Hispanic; six of the minority candidates were Republicans while thirteen were Democrats.

Democratic minority candidates have met with limited success statewide. In 1992, an African American, Morris Overstreet, won reelection to the Criminal Court of Appeals, and in 1994, Dan Morales won another term as attorney general (see table 8.6). Both left office after losing primary bids for higher posts (Overstreet for attorney general, Morales for governor). Raul A. Gonzalez, now a lawyer in private practice, received 81 percent of the vote in his reelection to the state Supreme Court in 1994. Since 1996, no minority Democrat has won statewide office in Texas; indeed, no Democrat of any race has won statewide office. As indicated in table 8.6, the high-water mark for any Democrat since 1996 is 46.53 percent of the vote, which was won by Charlie Holcomb in a bid for the Criminal Appeals court.

The decline of the Democratic vote in general elections is independent of the race or ethnicity of the Democratic candidates. From 1992 to 1994, votes shifted away from Democratic candidates although the range in vote share for Democrats is substantial and a number of Democrats attracted a majority of the vote. Starting in 1996, no Democrat commands a plurality of the vote. From 2000 to 2004, all Democratic candidates perform poorly, regardless of race, and the percentage of votes for most are tightly clustered in the low 40s. Nearly all of the loss of support by Democrats comes among Anglo voters. In 1992 and 1994, seven Democrats running statewide received majority Anglo support, including all three of the successful minority candidates running for office. Since 1996, no Democrat has approached majority support among Anglo voters, and after 2000 no Democrat commands more than 35 percent of the Anglo vote statewide. In 2006, of eight Democrats who sought partisan statewide office in Texas, only two—the candidates for railroad commissioner and supreme court justice—broke 30 percent of the Anglo white vote, and the Anglo white Democrat running for governor garnered just 18 percent of the white vote, 5 points behind the Latino Democratic nominee for lieutenant governor, Maria Luis Alvaredo (see table 8.6).

Candidate race is not a factor in the decline of support for Democratic candidates in the sixty-six statewide contests from 1992 to 2004. Tests of the difference of mean vote by race of candidate—for the overall vote and the Anglo vote share—shows that differences in the vote shares for Anglo, African American, and Hispanic candidates are insignificant ($F = .285$ and .940, respectively).[27] When one subjects the percentage of the Anglo vote captured by Democrats to a multivariate test, controlling for the race or ethnicity of the Democratic candidate and a temporal counter set to 0 in 1992 and increasing by a value of +1 for each passing year, the decline of the Anglo vote for Democrats is not significantly related to a candidate's ethnicity. African American and Hispanic candidates fare no worse than Anglo Democrats. Indeed, the coefficients for black and Hispanic candidates are actually positive, meaning that minority Democrats run stronger than Anglo Democrats.[28] On the other hand, the negative coefficient reported in the endnote shows that the Democratic vote share drops by just more than 2 percentage points each election.

TABLE 8.6. Candidate race and ethnicity, minority preferences, and statewide election outcomes in Texas, 1992–2006

	Office	Candidate	% Vote	% Anglo vote†
1992	Railroad Commissioner	*Lena Guerrero**	39.26	32.5
1992	Justice, Supreme Court, Place 1	Oscar H. Mauzy*	43.10	37.7
1992	Judge, Court of Criminal Appeals	*Pete Benavides**	49.49	40.4
1992	Judge, Court of Criminal Appeals	**Morris L. Overstreet***	51.04	53.3
1992	Justice, Supreme Court, Place 2	Rose Spector	52.22	46.8
1992	Judge, Court of Criminal Appeals	Charles F. (Charlie) Bai	52.80	50.9
1992	Justice, Supreme Court, Place 3	Jack Hightower*	56.79	55.6
1994	Commissioner of Agriculture	Marvin Gregory	35.98	24.0
1994	U.S. Senator	Richard Fisher	38.30	27.3
1994	Justice, Supreme Court, Place 3	Jimmy Carroll	43.24	40.2
1994	Justice, Supreme Court, Place 2	Alice Oliver Parrott	43.81	37.3
1994	Railroad Commissioner (unexpired)	Mary Scott Nabers*	44.86	43.5
1994	Judge, Court of Criminal Appeals	Betty Marshall	45.53	40.5
1994	Governor	Ann W. Richards*	45.87	36.0
1994	Judge, Court of Criminal Appeals	Charles Campbell*	46.04	41.9
1994	Railroad Commissioner	James E. Nugent*	48.14	48.6
1994	Commissioner, General Land Office	Garry Mauro*	50.19	48.6
1994	State Treasurer	Martha Whitehead*	50.29	46.4
1994	Attorney General	*Dan Morales**	53.70	55.1
1994	Comptroller of Public Accounts	John Sharp*	55.48	57.4
1994	Lieutenant Governor	Bob Bullock*	61.48	63.7
1994	Justice, Supreme Court, Place 1	*Raul A. Gonzalez**	81.31	80.6
1996	Justice, Supreme Court, Place 3	John B. Hawley	15.89	10.2
1996	Railroad Commissioner	*Hector Uribe*	39.01	23.6
1996	Chief Justice, Supreme Court	Andrew Jackson Kupper	40.57	29.2
1996	Justice, Supreme Court, Place 2	Gene Kelly	42.66	32.7
1996	U.S. Senator	*Victor M. Morales*	43.94	28.9
1996	Judge, Court of Criminal Appeals	Bob Perkins	44.53	36.8
1996	Justice, Supreme Court, Place 1	Patrice Barron	45.51	34.1
1996	Judge, Court of Criminal Appeals	Frank Maloney*	46.20	35.7
1996	Judge, Court of Criminal Appeals	Charles Holcomb	46.53	38.7
1998	Governor	Garry Mauro	31.18	18.4
1998	Commissioner, General Land Office	*Richard Raymond*	39.85	28.4
1998	Justice, Supreme Court, Place 3	David Van Os	39.89	28.0
1998	Railroad Commissioner	Joe B. Henderson	40.63	33.3
1998	Justice, Supreme Court, Place 1	Mike Westergren	41.81	30.6
1998	Commissioner of Agriculture	L. P. (Pete) Patterson	42.08	31.7
1998	Judge, Court of Criminal Appeals	Winston Cochran	42.21	32.3
1998	Justice, Supreme Court, Place 4	Jerry Scarbrough	43.09	33.7
1998	Attorney General	Jim Mattox	44.18	36.6
1998	Judge, Court of Criminal Appeals	Charles F. Baird	46.03	36.1
1998	Justice, Supreme Court, Place 2	Rose Spector*	46.47	36.3

TABLE 8.6. Candidate race and ethnicity, minority preferences, and statewide election outcomes in Texas, 1992–2006 (*continued*)

	Office	Candidate	% Vote	% Anglo vote†
1998	Lieutenant Governor	John Sharp	48.19	37.9
1998	Comptroller of Public Accounts	Paul Hobby	48.99	39.7
2000	U.S. Senator	Gene Kelly	32.34	17.7
2000	Judge, Court of Criminal Appeals	William R. Barr	43.08	29.7
2000	Presiding Judge, Criminal Appeals	Bill Vance	43.89	30.3
2002	Comptroller of Public Accounts	Marty Akins	32.92	18.3
2002	Commissioner of Agriculture	Tom Ramsay	37.81	21.7
2002	Judge, Court of Criminal Appeals	John W. Bull	39.14	24.4
2002	Governor	*Tony Sanchez*	39.96	21.5
2002	Judge, Court of Criminal Appeals	*J. R. Molina*	40.00	22.8
2002	Chief Justice, Supreme Court	Richard G. Baker	40.50	25.2
2002	Attorney General	Kirk Watson	41.08	24.4
2002	Commissioner, General Land Office	David Bernsen	41.48	28.0
2002	Railroad Commissioner	Sherry Boyles	41.48	29.3
2002	Justice, Supreme Court, Place 1	*Linda Yanez*	41.54	23.8
2002	Justice, Supreme Court, Place 2	Jim Parsons	41.88	27.0
2002	Judge, Court of Criminal Appeals	Pat Montgomery	42.60	26.8
2002	Justice, Supreme Court, Place 3	William E. Moody	43.23	28.7
2002	U.S. Senator	**Ron Kirk**	43.32	27.2
2002	Justice, Supreme Court, Place 4	*Margaret Mirabal*	45.90	29.4
2002	Lieutenant Governor	John Sharp	46.03	34.0
2004	Justice, Supreme Court, Place 9	David Van Os	40.76	24.4
2004	Railroad Commissioner	Bob Scarborough	40.94	28.5
2004	Judge, Court of Criminal Appeals	J. R. Molina	42.14	25.3
2006	Comptroller of Public Accounts	Fred Head	37.01	23.74
2006	Commissioner of Agriculture	Hank Gilbert	41.78	29.18
2006	Governor	Chris Bell	29.78	18.02
2006	Attorney General	David Van Os	37.23	24.85
2006	Commissioner, General Land Office	Valinda Hathcox	40.96	28.03
2006	Railroad Commissioner	Dale Henry	41.73	30.29
2006	Justice, Supreme Court, Place 2	Bill Moody	44.88	31.84
2006	Presiding Judge, Court of Criminal Appeals	J. R. Molina	43.35	27.26
2006	U.S. Senator	Barbara Ann Radnofsky	36.04	22.47
2006	Lieutenant Governor	*Maria Luis Alvaredo*	37.44	23.37

Source: Data computed by authors and from Texas Secretary of State's office.

†OLS estimates.

*Incumbent.

African American candidates in **boldface**.

Latino candidates in *italics*.

Democrats hoped to reverse their series of losses in 2002 when they fielded what became known as the "Dream Ticket" because of its ethnic diversity. African American Dallas mayor Ron Kirk won the U.S. Senate nomination by defeating 1996 Senate nominee Victor Morales and Anglo representative Kent Bentsen. For governor, Hispanic businessman Tony Sanchez prevailed, while for the powerful post of lieutenant governor, Democrats chose an Anglo, former comptroller John Sharp. The primary victories of Kirk and Sanchez (and Morales's attaining a runoff slot against Kirk for the Senate) affirmed the observation of Texas politics expert Richard Murray: "Black and Hispanic candidates have real opportunities to secure the Democratic nomination both at the state level and in many districts where minority voters are a majority of the primary electorate . . . as the Democratic primary electorate has shrunk, it has become much more heavily black and Hispanic in composition."[29]

The Dream Ticket designed to appeal to all ethnic and racial groups turned out to be nothing more than a pipe dream, as Kirk ran little better than other Democrats among Anglo voters, Sanchez ran worse, and Sharp, the top Democratic vote-getter, only managed a paltry 34 percent of the Anglo vote. Richard Murray notes that "general election voting in Texas very much follows class and racial/ethnic lines," and, it is evident that race and party are structured together in vote choice, but race of the candidate is not the issue. Democratic candidates, regardless of their ethnicity, fail with Anglo voters.[30]

Failure to attract Anglos was not the sole explanation for the collapse of the Dream Ticket. Sanchez's candidacy for governor failed to spark a dramatic increase in Hispanic participation according to the Census Bureau estimates. Fewer than 20 percent of the Latino adults and just 27.4 percent of Latino citizens voted. Hispanic turnout in 2002 was higher than 1998, the year with the lowest Hispanic participation in the last quarter century. But Sanchez's presence on the ballot failed to boost Latino participation anywhere near to what occurred in recent presidential elections. In contrast, the Kirk candidacy coincided with the highest black participation rate in any midterm election at least since 1982, and thus his presence on the ballot may have encouraged black turnout.

Texas political scientist Jerry Polinard observes that "the continuing impact of race on elections can be seen by studying recent statewide results. While Hispanic candidates are able to win elections in local areas and in districts that are drawn specifically for them or that are heavily Hispanic, Hispanics hold statewide offices in percentages far less that their percentage of the population as a whole."[31] Hispanics constitute over a third of all adult Texans and 22.3 percent of the voting-age population in the most recent census, but they held no more than two of the twenty-seven statewide constitutional offices in Texas in the 1990s.

While minorities have suffered the same fate as Anglos when running on the Democratic ticket, minorities who have campaigned as Republicans have tasted success. Since 1994, two Hispanics and four African Americans identified in the Texas state candidate database have been nominated for statewide offices as Republicans. Of these six, all but one—Teresa Doggett in 1994—prevailed in the general election. All of the winners pulled 63 to 85 percent of the Anglo vote, showings consistent with the performance of Anglo Republicans. Currently two Republican African Americans and a Hispanic serve as justices on the Texas Supreme Court.

RACIAL VOTING PATTERNS

Each of the three major ethnic groups in Texas frequently votes cohesively. Analyses of Democratic congressional primaries in Texas reveal various coalitions emerging among the three sets of players. Sometimes Anglos, African Americans, and Latinos vote together, but in other contests, Hispanics coalesce with Anglos against the preference of black voters. A third arrangement is for black voters to align with Anglos against the preferences of Latinos. A fourth pattern is for blacks and Latinos to share a candidate preference that is rejected by Anglos. In general elections, partisanship trumps ethnicity as a voter cue.

Primary Elections

Table 8.7 presents estimates of Anglo, African American, and Hispanic voter support for candidates in select 1992 Democratic congressional primaries and runoffs. In four of the nine primaries analyzed, most Anglo, African American, and Latino voters shared a candidate preference. Included in this group was the majority-Hispanic District 16, which renominated the Anglo

TABLE 8.7. Ecological regression (EI) estimates of racial voting patterns in select Texas congressional primary elections, 1992

	Candidate name	White	Black	Hispanic
1992 Democratic primary				
District 2	Groce	14.3	5.0	14.9
	Williamson	17.4	1.9	12.5
	Wilson*	68.3	93.1	72.7
District 4	Hall*	64.2	93.0	40.2
	Sanders*	35.8	7.0	59.8
District 16	Artalejo	1.2	11.0	6.1
	Coleman*	52.9	60.4	69.4
	Jones	13.3	–4.9	2.0
	Ponzio	31.5	33.5	22.4
District 18	**Leland**	–125.0	87.1	25.0
	Spates	225.0	12.9	75.0
District 23	*Bustamante*	21.1	71.2	83.6
	Mulvaney	78.9	28.8	16.4
District 25	Andrews*	82.1	85.2	92.7
	Whipple	17.9	14.8	7.3
District 29	**Burks**	5.5	15.4	–1.1
	Garcia	34.2	–6.2	17.9
	Green*	80.8	35.4	1.1
	Luna	0.0	–16.9	27.4
	Reyes	–20.5	72.3	54.7
District 30	**Hanutz**	–70.0	6.1	0.6
	Johnson	170.0	93.9	93.4
1992 Democratic runoff				
District 29	Green*	151.6	40.6	14.4
	Reyes	–51.6	59.4	85.6

Source: Ronald E. Weber, "Preliminary Report of Ronald E. Weber," in *Vera vs. Richards*.

African American candidates indicated with **boldface**.

Hispanic candidates indicated with *italics*.

*Anglo candidates indicated with an asterisk.

incumbent. Despite facing a Latino challenger, incumbent Ron Coleman got his strongest support from Hispanic voters. Eddie Bernice Johnson also drew majority support for all ethnic groups in winning the nomination in the newly created District 30.

In Houston's District 18, blacks overrode the preference of Anglo and Hispanic voters to renominate the African American incumbent Mickey

Leland. In two other districts, minorities backed a Hispanic candidate while Anglos favored an Anglo. In District 29, black and Hispanic voters coalesced behind a Latino, Ben Reyes, who lost to an Anglo, Gene Green, in the runoff.[32] The black and Hispanic preference in District 23, Albert Bustamante, was renominated over Anglo opposition.

The presence of substantial black and Latino communities in Houston and Dallas–Fort Worth has raised questions about the cohesion of those groups in party primaries. African American and Hispanic voters coalesce in general elections but they do not necessarily unite behind a brown or black candidate when there is also an Anglo in the primary field.[33] Homogenous precinct analysis and ecological regression estimates of minority and Anglo voter cohesion in select Democratic primaries in Dallas, Tarrant, and Harris counties featuring minority-versus-Anglo candidates in Democratic primaries supports this conclusion. In each county, Morris Overstreet, the black candidate for attorney general, got the bulk of the African American vote but was rejected overwhelmingly by other voters. In Tarrant and Dallas counties, black and Anglo voters united against De Leon, the Latino candidate for agriculture commissioner who ran very well with Latino voters. In primaries that pit an Anglo against a Latino, blacks and Anglos coalesce in support of the Anglo candidate. When an Anglo faced an African American, Latinos and Anglos united behind the Anglo.[34] A similar pattern was observed in Austin municipal elections in the 1970s.[35]

General Elections

African American and Hispanic candidates can win Democratic nominations although these successes may not be based on the support from a coalition of the minorities. In statewide general elections, Anglo voter support for Democrats is declining. In congressional elections, Anglo support for Democratic candidates varies greatly, both in the majority-minority districts and in predominantly Anglo districts that have more minority residents than average.

Table 8.8 presents Jonathan Katz's ecological inference (EI) estimates of Anglo and minority voter support in Texas congressional districts from 1992 through 2000.[36] The first part of the table shows the Hispanic versus non-Hispanic voter preferences for contested elections in seven Hispanic-majority districts. In twenty-two of the twenty-seven contests, Hispanic and Anglo preferences differed in the general election. The exceptions—District 29 (1994, 1996, and 2000), District 20 (1998), and District 28 (1994)—all involved incumbents, although many of the contests in which the groups disagree also had incumbents. Eight uncontested general elections account for the balance of cases. Anglo preferences for Republicans are most pronounced in congressional District 23, though this district also shows the strongest Hispanic support for a Republican, incumbent Henry Bonilla. The Hispanic preference prevailed in every contest except those involving Representative Bonilla, indicating that while Anglo and Hispanic preferences were opposed, the racial polarization is not legally significant.

During the 1990s African Americans and other voters usually opposed each others' preferences in general elections in the two districts with black members of Congress. Ecological inference (EI) estimates for these contests appear in table 8.8. In the Dallas-based District 30, the nonblack electorate never cast a majority of its votes for the Democratic candidate, Eddie Bernice Johnson. In contrast, in the 1996 and 2000 elections in Houston's District 18, majorities of black and nonblack voters lined up behind the Democrat. Despite disagreements in candidate choice between black and other voters in six of eight contested elections, the African American choice won.

In sum, the black electorate is more uniformly Democratic than are Hispanic voters. Only congressional District 27 has Latino cohesion (more than 91 percent in each election) comparable to that exhibited among African Americans in Districts 18 and 30.

The last part of table 8.8 presents results for eight districts with a greater-than-average black population in the 1990s. Black cohesion in these predominantly Anglo districts is usually comparable to that found in the districts that elected African Americans. With one exception, African Americans preferred the Democratic candidate, and in all but seven elections, black cohesion exceeded 80 percent. Anglos gave more than 60 percent support to Democrats only twice, while their support slips below 40 percent eight times. In sixteen of the thirty-two cases for which Katz provides estimates, all of which involve only white candidates,

TABLE 8.8. Ecological interference (EI) estimates of the predominant minority voting behavior in Texas congressional districts

	Hispanic	Anglo	Hispanic	Anglo	Hispanic	Anglo	Hispanic	Anglo
A. Hispanic-Majority Districts*								
	District 15		District 27		District 16		District 28	
1992	.748	.341	.912	.242	.746	.202	—	—
1994	.851	.381	.933	.350	.769	.351	.888	.508
1996	.896	.260	.946	.409	.921	.391	.946	.465
1998	.882	.387	.948	.489	—	—	—	—
2000	—	—	.910	.431	.929	.294	—	—
	District 20		District 29		District 23			
1992	—	—	.643	.430	.695	.146		
1994	.758	.49	.857	.502	.567	.220		
1996	.892	.339	.745	.566	.623	.115		
1998	.747	.509	—	—	.600	.161		
2000	—	—	.891	.552	.654	.216		

	Black	Anglo	Black	Anglo	Black	Anglo	Black	Anglo
B. African American Access Districts*								
	District 18		District 30					
1992	.947	.332	.945	.382				
1994	.965	.470	.926	.377				
1996	.945	.620	.958	.363				
1998	—	—	.931	.446				
2000	.941	.549	—	—				

	Black	Anglo	Black	Anglo	Black	Anglo	Black	Anglo
C. Anglo Districts with African American VAP over 15%								
	District 1	(16.10%)+	District 2	(15.00%)	District 5	(16.30%)	District 9	(20.60%)
1992	—	—	.569	.560	.974	.528	.904	.464
1994	—	—	.718	.542	.863	.438	.861	.384
1996	.883	.463	.613	.518	.700	.902	.942	.435
1998	.930	.541	.608	.588	.902	.363	—	.518
2000	.980	.505	—	—	.853	.371	—	.488
	District 11	(15.60%)	District 22	(14.30%)	District 24	(20.50%)	District 25	(23.00%)
1992	.853	.651	—	—	.853	.504	.936	.412
1994	.847	.570	—	—	.746	.435	.921	.379
1996	.892	.520	.210	.312	.919	.453	.928	.389
1998	—	—	.503	.294	.773	.466	.860	.508
2000	.848	.514	.596	.292	.795	.521	.954	.471

Source: Jonathan N. Katz, "Report on Texas Congressional Redistricting: Minority Opportunities and Partisan Fairness," submitted in *Del Rio v. Perry*, 2001.

*Districts identified as part of the minority baseline by the court in *Balderas v. Perry*.

+Percent African American voting-age population (VAP) in district.

black and nonblack majorities supported the same candidate, a higher incidence of agreement than found when the Democratic candidates were usually minorities.[37]

District 24 presented an intriguing twist on the issue of minority access, cohesion, and performance. This district had a 20.5 percent African American voting-age population and a 30.7 percent Hispanic voting-age population (14.3 percent Spanish surname voter registration) at the time of the 2002 redistricting. The representative elected, Anglo Democrat Martin Frost, had not confronted a minority opponent but was regularly supported by minority voters. Separate EI estimates of Hispanic, African American, and Anglo white voting indicate the greatest cohesion for Frost among Hispanics, next among African Americans, and a split Anglo white electorate.[38]

There is a racial structure to the partisan preferences of Texas voters. The white vote is now solidly Republican in statewide elections and in the congressional elections when the Democratic nominee is a minority. When the Democratic candidate is an Anglo, Anglo voters offer less support than do minority voters, although white Democratic incumbents are more likely to carry the bulk of the Anglo vote than are even minority incumbents. However, while Anglo Democrats do better among Anglo voters than minority candidates, the ranks of Anglo Democrats serving in Congress from Texas dropped sharply following the 2003 redistricting. Despite infrequently attracting majorities among Anglos, the minority-preferred candidate has consistently won in predominantly minority districts, except District 23 when represented by Republican Henry Bonilla from 1993 to 2007.

In the 109th Congress (2005–2006), only one Anglo Democrat represented a non majority-Hispanic district. Following the 2006 election, Chet Edwards was joined by former representative Nick Lampson as the latter won the seat vacated by former House majority leader Tom DeLay (R). However, the Lampson victory resulted from a unique circumstance—because of the timing of the indicted DeLay's retirement, no Republican candidate appeared on the ballot and voters wanting to vote for the GOP had to write in the name of Shelly Sekula Gibbs.[39] In 2008 Lampson lost when confronted by a Republican challenger.

FEDERAL MONITORING

Since Texas was brought under Section 5 by the 1975 Voting Rights Act, the Department of Justice has rejected 203 proposed changes of law in the state. Approximately half of these objections (107) came following the 1982 extension of the VRA statute. Only Mississippi has encountered a larger number of objections than Texas, but Texas has far more counties, cities, and school districts than any other southern state. The submitting authority withdrew another 388 proposed changes after the Department of Justice sought additional information.[40] Most of the objections over the last quarter century (sixty-one) have involved redistricting plans. At least some of the objections came because the Department of Justice was requiring jurisdictions to devise plans that also pass muster under Section 2. In the late 1990s, the Supreme Court ruled those requirements to be inappropriate.[41]

From 1990 through 2005, Texas jurisdictions submitted 112,261 proposed changes to the Department of Justice for preclearance.[42] Ultimately, 120 of these—or one-tenth of 1 percent of the proposed changes—failed to receive preclearance from DOJ. For slightly more than 1 percent of the proposed changes, DOJ requested further information before passing upon the proposed changed. The most frequent of these requests involved changes in polling places (394) and methods of election (381). Another 174 involved redistricting, while in 105 a municipality sought to annex property. Upon receiving further information, DOJ approved 897 of the 1,512 proposals for which it sought additional information. Another 140 proposals were withdrawn by the submitting authority, while in forty-three cases the submitting authority never responded to the request for additional information.

The federal government has infrequently exercised its option of sending observers to the Lone Star State to monitor its elections. From 1988 through 2004, observers monitored only ten elections.[43]

CONCLUSION

Over time, Texas has witnessed growing minority voter mobilization, an increase in minority candidacies, the election of minority representatives, and, more recently, the emergence of a partisan environment that militates against the election of minority-preferred Democrats to statewide posts.

Census Bureau estimates show Latino voter registration and participation holding stable over the past two decades. While registration among Latino citizens in Texas outpaces that nationwide, Hispanic citizens in Texas vote at lower rates than Latino citizens nationwide. In contrast to the Census Bureau estimates that show little longitudinal change, Spanish surname registration data maintained by Texas indicate an increase in Hispanic voter registration. From 1992 to 2004, the share of the Texas registrants who have Spanish surnames increased by more than 40 percent so that one in five Texas registrants has a Spanish surname.

African American registration and turnout has increased in recent years to attain record highs. Among citizens, black participation rates still lag those for Anglos, although in some recent years the differences have been all but eliminated.

The numbers of Latinos and African Americans serving in Congress and the state legislature have grown since Texas was brought under Section 5 of the Voting Rights Act in 1975. Following the 2003 congressional redistricting, African Americans constitute almost a tenth of the delegation, and a quarter of the districts have Hispanic majorities although one of these lacked a Hispanic majority among voting-age citizens. Following the 2006 election, all eight general-election winners in heavily Hispanic districts were the candidates of choice of most Hispanics.

While the ranks of minorities have increased in the congressional delegation and the state legislature, white Democrats have become more scarce. After the 2004 election, only three Anglos served in the eleven-member Democratic congressional delegation. The Texas house of representatives had fewer Anglo than Latino Democrats. In the state senate, minority Democrats outnumbered Anglo Democrats. The evidence from these legislative delegations dovetails with the patterns derived from statewide elections to underscore that Democrats win in districts having heavy concentrations of minority voters. When the electorate is overwhelmingly Anglo, Republicans usually win, although some Democratic incumbents can hang on thanks to their name recognition or their reputation for serving their constituents.

Few Hispanics or blacks currently hold statewide offices, and no Hispanic-preferred candidate has prevailed statewide in more than a decade. This outcome is a result of the heavy investment of the Hispanic vote and Hispanic politicians in the Democratic Party. No Democrat has prevailed in a statewide contest since 1996, and the decline of voter support in general—and Anglo voter support in particular—is consistent for all Democrats seeking state offices in Texas, regardless of the race of the candidate. African Americans who have run as Republicans have succeeded and two serve on the state Supreme Court.

The results of congressional elections suggest that minority Democratic candidates attract smaller shares of the Anglo vote than do Anglo Democrats, but it is currently all but impossible for Democrats to win statewide in the Lone Star State. The fate of the 2002 Dream Ticket underscores the unacceptability of Democratic nominees regardless of their ethnicity. The black candidate for the U.S. Senate, the Latino nominee for governor, and the Anglo candidate for lieutenant governor all went down to defeat despite being well funded and getting extensive media coverage.

Long-term trends suggest that minority influence will grow in Texas. As noted at the outset of this chapter, Texas no longer has a majority population. All projections show Latinos composing a larger share of the state's population. If Republicans do not develop an appeal that wins over increasing shares of the growing Latino vote, Democrats seem destined to win more offices and become competitive again in statewide contests. The 2006 and 2008 elections have seen the GOP margins reduced in the state house. As of 2009, Republicans' hold on the house has slipped to a single seat. While some of the GOP losses may be a reaction to the behavior of the Speaker, others may be a harbinger of the impact of the demographic changes under way.

CHAPTER 9

FLORIDA

Prior to the widespread availability of air conditioning, many people found Florida too hot, too mosquito ridden, and too undeveloped for civilized habitation. As recently as the end of World War II, Florida had the smallest population of any southern state. Its traditions were similar to those of the other ten states that had seceded. Although Florida's population was small, at the turn of the twentieth century almost half of its residents were African American, and they, like the white population, lived in the northern portion of the state.

Southern traditions designed to minimize black political participation were also practiced in Florida. In 1889, Florida adopted a poll tax. It also followed the practice adopted in South Carolina seven years earlier and made use of multiple ballot boxes, whereby voters had to separate their ballots and deposit the correct proportion in the correct box, and failure to put the right ballot in the right box spoiled the ballot. While the short-lived multiple-box provision was a *de facto* literacy test, Florida did not adopt a formal literacy test.[1] When the Voting Rights Act was initially passed in 1965, Florida was one of four southern states not subject to Section 5. The Sunshine State did not meet either criterion for inclusion.

It had no test or device as defined by Section 4 of the legislation, and the official statistics kept by Florida's secretary of state showed 51.2 percent of the adult black population to be registered at the time of the 1964 presidential election. Moreover, the state's 3,087,699 voting-age citizens (1960 census) cast 1,854,481 votes, easily exceeding the 50 percent threshold for turnout and registration.

The majority of African Americans had registered even though a few Panhandle counties had African American registration rates similar to those found north of the Florida border in south Alabama and Georgia. For example, in two counties (Lafayette and Liberty), each with fewer than 250 adult African Americans, none had registered to vote.[2] In a few other north Florida counties, black registration rates were low. They stood at 11.6 percent of the age-eligible blacks in Gadsden, the state's only majority-black county.

By the fall of 1966, the figures maintained by Florida's secretary of state showed black registration rising to 63.6 percent of the age eligible. In Lafayette County, black registration had risen from 0 to 67.1 percent, while in Liberty it had gone from 0 to 73.8 percent. In Gadsden County, black registration remained low although it had tripled in the course of two years to 37.7 percent. By 1966, only ten counties had less than half of the adult blacks registered, and in only one county were fewer than a third of the adult blacks registered. The one county that continued to show little progress was Union, where black registration increased from 11.8 to only 16.2 percent. The report prepared by the U.S. Commission on Civil Rights shows that of the eleven states of the old Confederacy, a higher proportion of Florida's adult blacks registered to vote in the aftermath of the Voting Rights Act than in any other state except Tennessee.[3]

The relatively open access African Americans had to the ballot box in Florida resulted in the state not being made subject to Section 5 of the Voting Rights Act when the Act was extended in 1970. The subsequent, new trigger mechanism adopted in 1975 brought five of Florida's sixty-seven counties under Section 5 and the preclearance requirement. Section 5 of the Voting Rights Act as amended in 1975 became applicable to Collier, Hardee, Hendree, Hillsborough, and Monroe counties because they had concentrations of Spanish speakers. The five counties are in the southern half of the state. Hillsborough, which contains Tampa, is the most heavily urban county. Collier contains Naples, the southernmost city on Florida's west coast. The other three counties—Hardee, Hendry and Monroe—are much more rural although Monroe does contain the Florida Keys and the city of Key West.

Latinos have supplanted African Americans as the state's largest minority group as thousands of immigrants from Latin America and Puerto Rico have settled in South Florida, where most of Florida's Hispanic population lives. Of the state's 2.7 million Hispanics in 2000, more than 48 percent lived in Dade County, and over 62 percent (1,674,581) lived in Dade, Broward, Collier, and Monroe. Florida's five Section 5 counties, however, do not contain the bulk of the language minorities in the state. The covered county with the largest linguistic-minority population (Hillsborough) has a Hispanic population so dispersed that the crafting of minority-majority districts for the population in the county is impossible at present.

What Moreno and Hill describe as the "South Florida Economic Enclave"—the combination of Latino-targeted businesses and services for a growing, vibrant Latino working and middle class—is expanding out of Dade County and into Collier County.[4] According to Moreno and Hill, the western part of Collier County is an effective extension of Dade County; a similar phenomenon is at work in the upper Keys, where most of the population of Monroe County is located. Since the 1980s, this economic enclave has also been a source of Latino political mobilization, in no small part due to the ABC ("anybody but a Cuban") movement among Miami whites in the 1970s and 1980s. Dade County Latinos have been highly mobilized ever since.

Florida's 2000 census indicates a state population that is 14.4 percent black and 16.8 percent Hispanic. Of the voting-age population of 12,336,038, 12.7 percent were black and 16.1 percent were Hispanic. In 2000, Latinos accounted for 11 percent of the registered voters in Florida. Approximately 802,000 of the state's 1,265,000 voting-age Latino citizens had registered to vote. Among registered Latinos, approximately 678,000 turned out in 2000 (84.5 percent).

MINORITY REGISTRATION AND TURNOUT

Census Bureau estimates for registration in Florida from 1980 through 2006 for Latinos, blacks, and whites appear in the first table of appendix B. Latinos sign up to vote at a substantially lower rate than do Anglos or blacks. The range in Latino self-reported registration is from a low of 22.7 percent in 1994 to a high of 39.1 percent in 2002. After bottoming out in 1994, Latino registration exceeded 35 percent in the next five elections before receding to less than one-third in 2006. Nonetheless, even at the highest level of registration (2002), the rate at which Latinos signed up to vote is almost 9 percentage points below that for blacks and more than 25 points lower than that for Anglos. Despite the persisting disparities, the differences across ethnic groups have narrowed, although the 2006 data show a widening gap reminiscent of much earlier years.

With the single exception of 1986, whites have always registered at higher rates than blacks in Florida. Frequently the racial differences have been in the neighborhood of 10 percentage points. As far back as 1982 but as recently as four of the last five elections in the time series, white registration ran at least 10 points above that for blacks. At times the gap has narrowed with the most dramatic example coming in 1986 when the black registration rate (61.3 percent) exceeded that for whites (59.9 percent). Rates converged again in 1996 when white registration was only 3 percentage points higher than the black rate.

When non-Hispanic whites are eliminated, the figure for the remaining whites increases by several percentage points. At least two-thirds of Florida's non-Hispanic white adults have signed up to vote. That figure exceeds the registration rate for blacks by approximately 17 to 20 points and exceeds the figure for Latinos in recent years by more than 30 percentage points.

When Florida Latinos are compared with those outside of the region, appendix B shows that prior to 1986, the figures outside the South exceeded those in Florida. The largest difference came in 1982 when just over a third of the nonsouthern Hispanics but barely a quarter of the Florida Hispanics reported registering. Beginning with 1986, Florida Latinos have registered at higher rates than their peers outside the region with the single exception of 1994, a year in which the Florida registration rate (22.7) is so far out of line with other figures that one wonders about its accuracy. The 22.7 percent Latino registration is more than a dozen points below the figure for adjacent years and 6.4 percentage points below that for the non-South. In most of the other elections over the last twenty years, the Florida figures have been slightly above those for the non-South, with a negligible difference in 2006. The greatest difference comes in 2002 when 39.1 percent of the Florida Latinos compared with 30.6 percent of those outside the South had registered to vote.

In the thirty years since passage of the 1975 Voting Rights Act, the rate of Hispanic registration has increased slightly in Florida. Also over that time period, Florida Latinos have become more likely to register than have their peers outside the region. When black registration rates in Florida are compared with those in the non-South, the non-South figures are higher in every year except for 1996. In that single year, Florida's black registration is 2.6 percentage points higher than that for the non-South. In most years, the non-South figure exceeds that in Florida by 10 percentage points.

Census Bureau estimates of turnout from 1980 to 2006 indicate that Hispanic turnout is consistently lower than that for either Anglos or blacks. The proportion of the adult Florida Latino population that has gone to the polls ranges from a low of 18 percent in 2006 to a high of 34.1 percent in 1988 and 34 percent in 2004. Like for the other ethnic groups in the state, Latino participation follows a seesaw pattern—rising in presidential years then dropping in midterm elections. The range in Latino turnout in presidential years is narrow; it extends from 29 percent in 1996 to a high of 34.1 percent in 1988. The range of participation in midterm elections is greater with a low of 18 percent in 2006 and a high of 28 percent in 1986. The greatest participation of Latinos in midterm elections does not quite equal their lowest rate of participation in presidential elections.

The biggest disparity between Latino and African American turnout comes in 1980 when just over half of Florida's black voting-age population (VAP) voted compared with 29.3 percent of the Latino VAP. Twenty-four years later, the disparity had shrunk to just over 10 percentage points. In the first three midterm elections in appendix B, blacks voted at rates at least 11 percentage points higher than Latinos. The most recent midterm election had a 15.5 percentage point gap.

In the 1980s, Anglo turnout often exceeded Latino turnout by 25 percentage points. Roughly this disparity showed up again in 2004. The smallest difference in Latino and Anglo turnout rates came in 2002 when the white turnout rate exceeded that for Latinos by 17.4 percentage points.

While black turnout exceeds that for Latinos, it always trails the white figure. The smallest difference came in 1986 when 47.5 percent of whites and 42.4 percent of blacks turned out. In most years, the disparity is 10 points or greater and hit 16 points in 1988 and almost 14 points in 2004. When non-Hispanics are removed from the white figure, the white figure increases by 4 to 7 percentage points, thereby expanding the difference between whites and minorities.

Comparison of Hispanic participation in Florida and the non-South reveals that, for the first three elections, Latinos outside the South voted at higher rates than in Florida with the greatest difference coming in 1982 when 25.8 percent of the nonsouthern Latinos compared with 18.6 percent in Florida voted. Beginning with 1986, Latino turnout in Florida has exceeded that in the non-South in every year except 1994, when the nonsouthern figure marginally exceeds that for Florida with both being just above 20 percent. In some years, the Florida figure was only marginally higher than that for the non-South (1990 and 1998). In the two most recent midterm elections, Florida Hispanics voted at much higher rates than Hispanics outside of the South, and in 2006, 34 percent turned out in Florida compared with 21.3 participation outside the region.

Black turnout in Florida always lags that outside of the region. Differences were smallest—less than 3 percentage points—relatively early in the quarter century covered (1980, 1986, and 1990). In four of the seven most recent elections, nonsouthern African Americans have turned out at rates at least 10 percentage points higher than in Florida. In the two most recent midterm election years, the differences were approximately 7 percentage points. The smaller recent differences have come in midterm elections. The time series in appendix B provides no evidence that Florida blacks have increased their participation rates in comparison with other groups.

Florida's secretary of state, the official responsible for maintaining registration records, reports on the numbers of voters registered by race. However, prior to 2006 the secretary did not provide a separate enumeration for self-identified Latinos or those who have Spanish surnames.

TABLE 9.1. Racial and ethnic voter registration in Florida, 1994–2008

	White, non-Hispanic		Black, non-Hispanic		Other		Unknown/ not given		
	No.	%	No.	%	No.	%	No.	%	Total
1994	5,845,494	89.1	614,384	9.4	99,720	1.5	0	0.0	6,559,598
1996	6,565,941	81.3	845,179	10.5	583,862	7.2	82,895	1.0	8,077,877
1998	6,586,453	80.1	865,974	10.5	655,259	8.0	112,580	1.4	8,220,266
2000	6,804,182	77.7	934,261	10.7	796,249	9.1	218,025	2.5	8,752,717
2002	7,044,287	75.6	1,027,817	11.0	924,825	9.9	305,431	3.3	9,302,360
2004	7,478,490	72.6	1,223,875	11.9	1,192,082	11.6	406,843	3.9	10,301,290
					Hispanic		Not given/ other		
2006	7,508,682	72.0	1,248,459	12.0	1,113,883	10.7	414,098	4.0	10,433,849
2008	7,773,419	69.1	1,468,682	13.1	1,355,270	12.0	650,263	5.8	11,247,634

Source: Florida Department of State, Division of Elections.

However, the slight decline from the number of voters in the "other" category in 2004 to the "Hispanic" category in 2006 suggests that most of the voters classified as "other" prior to 2006 were Hispanic. Table 9.1 presents the tabulations for the period 1994 through 2008.

From 1996 to 2004, the number of "other" registrants doubled from about 580,000 to almost 1.2 million while white Anglo registrants increased from 6.57 to 7.48 million. Black registration increased by 45 percent from 845,000 in 1996 to more than 1.2 million by 2004. Black voters still outnumbered the "other" category despite there being fewer African Americans in Florida's adult population than Hispanics. The burst of enthusiasm surrounding the Obama candidacy coupled with Democrats' efforts to boost registration pushed the African American share of registrants to 13.1 percent of the registered electorate in 2008, which approximates the state's black voting-age population. The "other" category increased from 1.5 to 11.6 percent of Florida's registrants in 2004. This figure is well below the 16.1 percent of the Florida population identified as Hispanic in 2000. It is likely that some share of those voters whose race or ethnicity is unknown are also Latinos. It is also likely that at least some Latinos may have checked the "white" box when registering to vote. The number of registrants opting not to indicate their race or ethnicity doubled between 2000 and 2004 to 3.9 percent. With all of the other components of the registrants increasing, the white share has dropped substantially. It fell from 89.1 percent in 1994 to 72.6 percent a decade later.

A separate breakout is now available for Hispanics (see table 9.1). In 2006, 10.7 percent of Florida's registrants were Hispanics, a figure that rose to 12 percent when registration books for the 2008 general election closed. The 1.36 million Hispanic registrants remain 100,000 less than the 1.47 million blacks who were registered, although the gap between the two groups continues to narrow. Although record numbers of whites appeared on the registration rolls in 2008, their share of the electorate continues to fall so that they constituted less than 70 percent of all registrants by 2008, a drop of 20 percentage points since 1994.

MINORITY OFFICE HOLDING

The first available figures on the numbers of Latino elected officials in Florida come from the mid-1980s when fewer than fifty served. Over the next two decades, the numbers of Latinos holding office doubled. As reported in figure 9.1, most Latinos served in municipal offices, with relatively few holding county or school board positions. Until 2000, the National Association of Latino Elected Officials provided separate breakouts for different kinds of local offices, but after 2000, the bureau began reporting all local offices in a combined figure, which is reflected in the continuation of the "municipal" line. In the most recent years, no separate breakout is available, but it seems reasonable to assume that municipalities continue to be the locale from which most Latinos are elected.[5]

The period for which the numbers of African American officeholders in Florida exist is much longer; it extends back to 1969. As figure 9.2 shows, in 1969 the state had only twenty-four African Americans holding office. By 1980, the number exceeded one hundred, and since 1993 there have been more than two hundred black officeholders. In the early years, more than 80 percent of the African American officials served in cities. While municipalities continue to be the level of government most likely to elect blacks, now only little more than half of the black officials serve in cities. The number of African Americans holding county office has grown from one in 1967 to twenty-nine in 2001, while the number serving

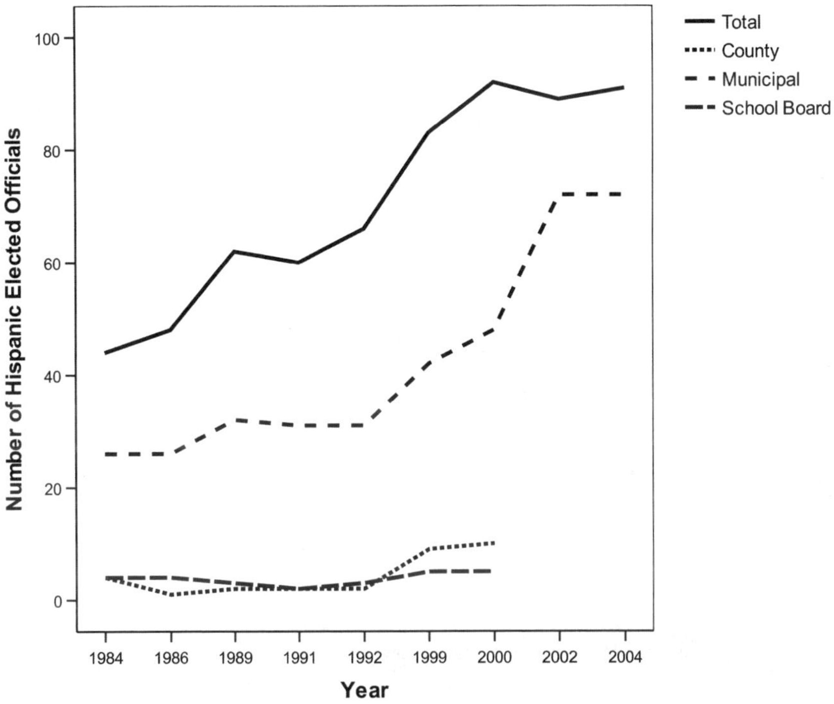

Figure 9.1. Hispanic elected officials in Florida, 1984–2004. *Source:* Various volumes of the *National Roster of Hispanic Elected Officials* (Washington, D.C.: National Association of Latino Elected and Appointed Officials Education Fund).

on school boards has grown from zero in 1969 to fifteen or sixteen, a number that has fluctuated over the last twenty years.

Minority Members of Congress

In a special election held in August 1989 to fill the vacancy created by the death of the ancient New Deal Democratic representative Claude Pepper, Ileana Ros-Lehtinen (R) became the first Cuban American elected to Congress. She is also the first Hispanic woman to be elected to Congress from any state. This continued Ros-Lehtinen's string of firsts. In 1982, she had become the first Latina elected to the Florida legislature. The congressional

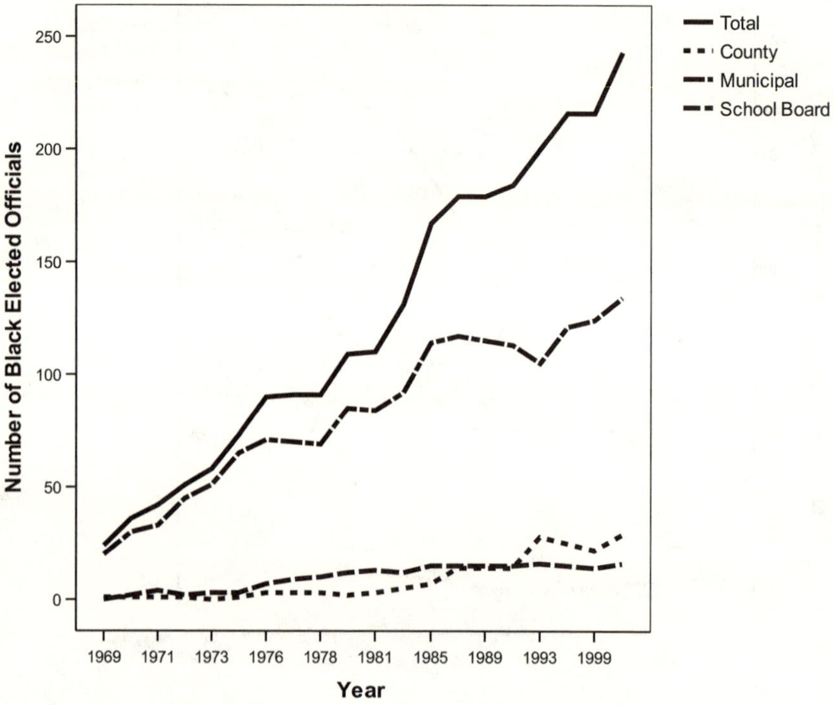

Figure 9.2. Black elected officials in Florida, 1969–2001. *Source:* Various volumes of the *National Roster of Black Elected Officials* (Washington, D.C.: Joint Center for Political and Economic Studies).

district that elected her was 51 percent Spanish origin as of 1980. When she was elected, it was estimated to be 37 percent Cuban American.[6]

Three years after her initial election, a second Cuban American, also from Miami, joined Ros-Lehtinen. Her new neighbor, Lincoln Diaz-Balart (R), won his seat as a result of a districting plan that created a second heavily Hispanic district. Diaz-Balart, who had been in the Florida legislature for the previous six years, attracted no opposition in either the primary or the general election as he won this more than 70 percent Hispanic district.

Following the 2001 redistricting, South Florida got a third predominately Hispanic district. The new district elected Mario Diaz-Balart (R), the younger brother of Lincoln who had followed his older sibling into the Florida senate.[7]

Since 2003, Florida has had three Cuban American representatives along with three African Americans. Three black legislators entered Congress in 1992 as a result of a racially gerrymandered map drawn by a Tulane law professor working for a three-judge federal panel. The map created a compact majority-black district in Miami and two others that were among the many strange shapes fashioned to satisfy U.S. Department of Justice demands in the early 1990s. Arguably the stranger of the two, Corrine Brown's 3rd Congressional District became known as the "bugsplat" or "fishhook" district. It extended just inside the Atlantic coast from Jacksonville all the way down to Orlando. The western arm of the district reached from Jacksonville as far south as the university city of Gainesville.

After this district was successfully challenged following *Shaw v. Reno*,[8] its black concentration dropped from 55 to 47 percent.[9] In the wake of the reduced black concentration, Brown attracted relatively serious Republican challengers and has exceeded 60 percent of the vote only twice. Following the post-2000 redistricting, Brown's district was 49.3 percent black.

Another majority-black district, the northern portion of which formed a rough rectangle, contained portions of St. Lucie, Martin, and Palm Beach counties. However, the district also had a long tail that ran south along the Florida East Coast Railroad to pick up Fort Lauderdale's black population, and it finally gathered up a few more African Americans in northern Dade County.[10] The initial election drew five Democrats. A white state legislator, Lois Frankel, led the field with 35 percent of the vote while Alcee Hastings, a former federal judge, narrowly edged out another African American with 28 percent of the vote. The bitter runoff saw Hastings attack his opponent, saying of her, "The bitch is a racist."[11] Hastings more than doubled his vote total in the runoff while Frankel increased hers by less than a third, allowing the former federal judge to win with 58 percent of the vote. In the 1992 general election, Hastings, despite having been impeached and removed from the bench, took 59 percent of the vote. In his subsequent reelection bids, he has always gotten at least 73 percent. The district as configured following the 2000 census was 51.2 percent African American.

The compact African American district in Miami elected Carrie Meek, a twenty-four–year veteran of the Florida legislature. She retired after a decade and her son Kendrick now holds the seat which was 55.2 percent black in 2002.

Table 9.2 indicates the racial and ethnic composition of Florida's twenty-five current congressional districts. The three districts electing African American representatives—Districts 3, 17, and 23—constitute almost half of all the districts that cast a majority of their votes for Al Gore for president in 2000. The three Hispanic-majority congressional districts (18, 21, and 25) all elect Republican Latino representatives, and these districts have been solidly Republican although the 2008 elections saw a serious Democratic challenge to Mario Diaz-Balart. Of the twenty-five congressional districts, eight include portions of at least one of the five counties subject to Section 5. Two of the Hispanic-majority congressional districts and one of the districts with a performing majority for blacks are subject to preclearance review.

With three Hispanic and three black members of Congress, each minority group holds 12 percent of Florida's twenty-five congressional seats. The proportion of the seats held by each of the two minority groups roughly approximates the groups' share of the Florida voting-age citizen population, which is 13.3 percent African American and 14.9 percent Hispanic.

Minority State Legislators

Table 9.3 reports the numbers and percentages of the Florida legislators who are Latino and African American. The first Hispanic in modern times to serve was Roberto Casas, a Democratic state house member (and later state senator) from Hialeah in Dade County, who won a special election in January 1982.[12] In 1985, six years after the beginning of the Cuban American mobilization in response to the English-only movement in Miami, four Hispanics served in the state house, but none in the senate.[13] Two years later, Hispanic representation in the house doubled, and after the implementation of the new districting plan, it reached ten. The redistricting following the 2000 census brought the number of Latino house members to thirteen.

The first Latino senator arrived in 1987 and each of the next elections saw another Latino senator added. Since 1991, however, the number of Latino senators has remained frozen at three. In neither chamber have

TABLE 9.2. Florida congressional districts, black and Latino population, and Section 5 coverage

District	2000 presidential vote: Bush %	Gore %	% Black origin	% Latino origin	Section 5 county
1	68.90	31.10	14.00	3.00	
2	52.70	47.30	22.10	3.30	
3	34.90	65.10	49.30	8.00	
4	65.80	34.20	13.50	4.20	
5	54.10	45.90	4.50	5.60	
6	58.20	41.80	11.90	5.20	
7	53.90	46.10	8.80	6.90	
8	53.70	46.30	7.20	17.60	
9	54.20	45.80	3.50	7.90	Hillsborough
10	49.20	50.80	3.60	4.40	
11	39.00	61.00	27.40	20.00	Hillsborough
12	54.80	45.20	13.00	12.00	Hillsborough
13	54.50	45.50	4.40	7.70	Hardee
14	61.40	38.60	5.10	9.00	Hendry
15	53.70	46.30	7.30	11.30	
16	53.10	46.90	5.80	10.10	
17	15.20	84.80	55.20	21.20	
18	56.80	43.20	5.70	62.70	Monroe
19	27.20	72.80	6.10	12.70	
20	31.00	69.00	7.90	20.60	
21	57.90	42.10	6.50	69.70	
22	47.60	52.40	3.80	10.70	
23	20.20	79.80	51.20	13.70	
24	53.40	46.60	6.30	9.80	
25	55.10	44.90	10.00	62.40	Collier, Monroe

Source: Florida House Redistricting Committee, at www.floridaredistricting.org/.

Hispanics come to hold a share of seats commiserate with their share of the state's voting-age citizenry. The share of the legislative seats held by Hispanics remains lower than the proportion of "others" currently among Florida registrants. Most, but not all, of the Latino legislators have come from South Florida.

The first African American to enter the Florida house did so in 1969 when Joe Lange Kershaw won a Dade County seat.[14] The next elections sent the first African American woman, Gwen Cherry, to the house. As

TABLE 9.3. Latino and African American state legislators in Florida, 1967–2007

	Black legislators				Latino legislators			
	Senate	Senate %	House	House %	Senate	Senate %	House	House %
1967	0	0.0	0	0.0	0	0.0	0	0.0
1969	0	0.0	1	0.8	0	0.0	0	0.0
1971	0	0.0	2	1.7	0	0.0	0	0.0
1973	0	0.0	3	2.5	0	0.0	0	0.0
1975	0	0.0	3	2.5	0	0.0	0	0.0
1977	0	0.0	3	2.5	0	0.0	0	0.0
1979	0	0.0	4	3.3	0	0.0	0	0.0
1981	0	0.0	4	3.3	0	0.0	0	0.0
1983	2	5.0	11	9.2	0	0.0	2	1.7
1985	2	5.0	11	9.2	0	0.0	4	3.3
1987	2	5.0	11	9.2	1	2.5	8	6.7
1989	2	5.0	12	10.0	2	5.0	8	6.7
1991	2	5.0	14	11.7	3	7.5	8	6.7
1993	5	12.5	14	11.7	3	7.5	10	8.3
1995	5	12.5	12	10.0	3	7.5	10	8.3
1997	5	12.5	14	11.7	3	7.5	10	8.3
1999	5	12.5	15	12.5	3	7.5	11	9.2
2001	6	15.0	16	13.3	3	7.5	11	9.2
2003	7	17.5	18	15.0	3	7.5	13	10.8
2005	7	17.5	18	15.0	3	7.5	13	10.8
2007	7	17.5	19	15.8	3	7.5	12	10.0

Source: Data compiled by the authors.

reported in table 9.3, the number of blacks grew only slightly until the 1982 redistricting, after which the black representatives increased from four to eleven. In the succeeding twenty-four years, the African American presence in the house has grown slowly, but after the 2001 redistricting, it stood at 15 percent of the 120-member chamber before rising to 15.8 percent in 2007. The share of house seats held by African Americans exceeds the black percentage in Florida's voting-age population (13.3).

The first black senators, Miami's Carrie Meek and Arnette Girardeau from Jacksonville, won seats following the same early 1980s redistricting that almost trebled house African Americans. Throughout the life of that districting plan, the senate had two black senators. With the 1992 redistricting, black senators increased to five members, and since 2003, their numbers have stood at seven so that they hold 17.5 percent of the chamber's seats.

Minorities in Statewide Office

In 1986 Bob Martinez became the Sunshine State's only governor of Spanish heritage. This Republican, who had previously served as mayor of Tampa, was not part of the wave of Cubans who came to South Florida in the wake of Fidel Castro's takeover of their island. Martinez was a former union organizer and had once been a Democrat.

Martinez had several major stumbles during his term. Almost immediately after winning election, he proposed to levy a sales tax on services. This proposal angered two significant players in Florida politics since it would have required the collection of sales taxes from professionals, such as lawyers, and advertising, such as appears in newspapers. Since this misstep came early in his tenure, Martinez had time to make amends and perhaps secure a second term. The second miscue came toward the end of his term and sealed his fate. Immediately after the Supreme Court opened the way for states to impose some limits on access to an abortion, Martinez called a special session of the legislature. However, with Democrats controlling both chambers and eager to embarrass the Republican governor, his proposals were not enacted, thus suggesting a lack of both political muscle and political acuity. In his 1990 bid for reelection, Martinez fell to former U.S. senator Lawton Chiles (D-Fla.).

In 2004, Mel Martinez became the first Cuban American to win a U.S. Senate seat. He also became one of only two Latinos to serve in the 109th Senate as he joined fellow freshman Ken Salazar from Colorado. Martinez is the only Republican Latino senator, though he subsequently announced he will not seek a second term in 2010.

In 1976, Joseph Hatchett won a seat on the Florida Supreme Court. At that time, membership on the state's highest tribunal was selected through contested elections. Subsequently, the process changed. Incumbents now run on their records and simply seek a confirmation vote, a format known as the Missouri Plan. Upon Hatchett's election to the Supreme Court, he became the first African American not only to serve on that body but also the first to win a statewide election in the South.[15]

The first African American to serve in a statewide Florida constitutional office was House Education Committee chair Douglas Jamerson, who was appointed by Governor Lawton Chiles to fill the vacant commissioner of education post. Jamerson, who had served in the Florida house since 1982, failed in his bid for a full term as education commissioner. In an election that saw the two parties split the eight statewide contests on the ballot, Jamerson polled 46.6 percent of the vote. This was the weakest showing for any Democrat seeking a constitutional office but was substantially stronger than the 29.5 percent of the vote polled by the Democratic Senate nominee who was crushed by Sen. Connie Mack, the Republican returned to the U.S. Senate.

Minorities have rarely been candidates for statewide posts in Florida. The first African American to make such a bid, Alcee Hastings, unsuccessfully competed in the Democratic primary for secretary of state in 1990. Although defeated in that effort, he has served in the U.S. House since 1993.

REPRESENTATION AND THE SECTION 5–COVERED COUNTIES

Only five counties in Florida are subject to Section 5 of the VRA. It is possible that Section 5 coverage has resulted in greater success of minorities candidates in these five counties. Mitigating against that possible success, however, is the relatively small population of some of these counties. Moreover, in none of these counties do Hispanics, the group whose presence resulted in Section 5 coverage, constitute a majority. In this section we review the presence or absence of minority officeholders at the congressional, state legislative, and local level in Florida's Section 5 counties.

The Hispanic population in the Section 5 counties as of 2000 totaled slightly fewer than three hundred thousand. As table 9.4 shows, this population is disproportionately located in Hillsborough County, which accounts for two-thirds of the total for the five counties. In three of the counties, less than 20 percent of the population is Hispanic. In Hardee and Hendry where Hispanics constitute more than a third of the population, their numbers are still small. Since the average population for a Florida house district was 133,186 at the time of the most recent redistricting, only Hillsborough had a Hispanic concentration large enough to constitute the majority of a state house district. Even if all Collier Hispanics had lived in the same house district, they would not equal half the district population. In any of the five Section 5 counties except Hillsborough, if Hispanics are to

TABLE 9.4. Hispanic population in Section 5 counties in Florida

	Hispanic population	Hispanic % of county	% of all Florida Hispanics in county
Hillsborough	198,227	18.0	6.8
Hardee	9,991	35.7	0.3
Hendry	15,112	39.6	0.5
Collier	58,149	19.6	2.0
Monroe	12,369	15.8	0.4
All Section 5 counties	293,848		10.1
Dade County	1,354,343	57.3	46.3
State	2,922,723		16.8

Source: U.S. Census Bureau data.

live in a predominantly Latino house district, they will have to be combined with Hispanic concentrations in neighboring counties.

The heaviest concentration of Hispanics in Florida lives in the five southernmost congressional districts, but these are dominated by Dade County, and that county is not subject to Section 5. Hispanics constitute 51.5 percent of the voting-age population in these congressional districts. In both of the southernmost counties covered by Section 5—Monroe and Collier—the bulk of the Latino population lives in congressional districts that currently elect Latino candidates of choice from majority-Latino districts anchored in Miami-Dade.

Hillsborough County

Hillsborough County is 15 percent black and 18 percent Hispanic. The Hispanic population is widely dispersed across Hillsborough County. None of the dozen state house districts entering Hillsborough are majority Hispanic by voting-age population (VAP); indeed, the most heavily Latino district, 58, features only a 38.4 percent Latino VAP.[16] This is also the most heavily Latino district in the state house to be represented by Democrat Bob "Coach" Henriquez, a Latino. Of the twelve legislators in Hillsborough County's state house delegation, two are black (16.7 percent of all representatives), reflecting a proportional level of representation for the black community from Hillsborough County, while a third legislator is Latino. Three are Democrats, and they represent the three most heavily minority districts in the county and each belongs to a minority group.

Hillsborough County has two majority-black state house districts. House District 55, which stretches as a narrow urban ribbon from Saint Petersburg through Bradenton and south to Sarasota, has a 50.1 percent black VAP and is a safely Democratic with a 64 percent Democratic registration. Its residents voted almost 76 percent for Al Gore. The incumbent representative, Frank Peterman, is an African American. The other district, state house District 59, which runs from the university district into Tampa and then through Palm River to Progress Village, has a 52.6 percent black VAP and an additional 13.6 percent Hispanic VAP. The district is also safely Democratic (it voted over 75 percent for Al Gore in 2000) and is currently represented by African American representative Arthenia Joyner.

State Senate District 18, largely located in Hillsborough County but also taking in portions of Pinellas and Manatee counties, covers much of the same geography as state house Districts 55 and 59. The district is only 42 percent black and 18.9 percent Hispanic by population, with just 37.4 percent black VAP and 17.2 percent Hispanic VAP. The district is solidly Democratic, and currently elects African American senator Les Miller. Miller is one of four senators representing all or part of Hillsborough County. Initially elected in 2000, he is currently the senate minority whip.

The three members of Congress representing parts of Hillsborough County as of 2009 are all Anglos. Two are Republicans while Kathy Castor is a Democrat. Hispanics also hold two judgeships and one school board slot in Hillsborough. In addition, Tampa's mayor and three council members have Spanish surnames.

Collier County

The only majority-Latino state house district in the covered counties is house District 112, which encompasses southern Collier County from east of Naples and Marco Island, and then continues into northeastern Dade County and also picks up a small portion of Broward County (Miramar and Pembroke Pines). This district was drawn in response to an objection by the Justice Department to the initial plan for the continuation of the majority-Hispanic district in Collier County. Under the initial plan, house District 101 was to be a successor to a majority-Hispanic house district (102) that entered Collier County. Florida lawmakers contended that the creation of additional Hispanic representation opportunities elsewhere in the state compensated for the district eliminated in Collier. The DOJ rejected this proposition by noting that such an approach "would require a Section 5 review and assessment of all districts within a state, even where the statutory formula only identified individual counties for coverage. This is contrary to the plain meaning of Congress' coverage determinations and is an approach we therefore reject."[17]

The state argued against including part of Collier in a district with Dade County because to do so would mitigate against creating an eleventh majority-Hispanic district in Dade. Alternative proposals demonstrated how to create a majority-Latino district in Collier while maintaining eleven Hispanic majority districts in Dade County.

The Justice Department cited "clear evidence" of the need to maintain a Hispanic-majority district in Collier County based on the willingness of Latinos and the unwillingness of Anglos to vote for Hispanics in Collier County. The old majority-Hispanic district afforded an opportunity for Hispanic voters to elect a representative of choice. The state responded to the objection by extending a 66.7 percent Hispanic VAP district—District 112—into Collier. David Rivera, a Hispanic Republican from Miami, represents the 112th District.

District 101 retains a substantial Hispanic VAP minority (30.7 percent). Given demographic trends in western Broward County and Collier County, it is possible that this district might have a Hispanic majority in the coming decade.

The 25th Congressional District with its 62.4 percent Hispanic majority contains most of the land area of Collier, Monroe, and Dade. It is represented by Mario Diaz-Balart, a Republican Latino.[18]

Monroe County

Monroe County is contained within state house District 120 and senate District 39, which also encompasses parts of Collier County and Hendry County. House District 120 elects an Anglo Republican; Monroe County last sent a Latino to the state legislature in the nineteenth century. Senate District 39 is 32 percent black and 30.6 percent Hispanic by voting-age population, and encompasses most of the Latino population of Collier County. The senator from the district, Larcenia Bullard, is an African American Democrat who was initially elected to the house in 1992 and to the senate in 2002. This election of a black Democrat from a combined majority-minority district was forecast by Moreno and Hill, who observed in May 2002 that "whereas [elsewhere] one might combine black and Hispanics into a 'majority-minority' district in [*sic*] and have the district perform for Hispanic candidates, here [in South Florida] such a district would almost assuredly elect a black, not a Hispanic, candidate of choice" due to the generally Democratic voting habits of Anglo whites in South Florida.[19]

The bulk of Monroe County is in Congressional District 25, although the Keys are in District 18. Consequently, all of the residents of the county are currently represented by a Republican Latino legislator. Mario Diaz-Balart represents the 25th while Ileana Ros-Lehtinen represents the 18th. Although we lack estimates of Latino voting behavior in Monroe for these members of Congress, table 9.6 suggests that Monroe Hispanics may have preferred the unsuccessful Democratic challengers.

Hardee County

Hardee County has a population of 27,987 and is 35.7 percent Hispanic. The county is wholly contained in house District 66 and senate District 17. Latinos make up 11.3 percent of the population in the state senate district and 15.2 percent of the house district population. Hardee County residents account for approximately one-third of Hispanics in the senate district and two-thirds of residents in the house district. The house seat is held by an Anglo Republican. Hardee does not appear to have any Hispanics in elective office.

Hendry County

Hendry County has a population of 36,210 and is 39.6 percent Hispanic. Like Hardee, the Hispanic population is insufficient to constitute a viable core of a performing minority district, and, unlike Collier and Monroe counties, Hendry is too distant to be joined with the larger, politically active Latino population in Dade County in creating minority representation opportunities. The state representative for Hendry is a white Republican from Highlands County. Hendry does not appear to have any Hispanic elected officials.

RACIAL VOTING PATTERNS

Florida's two major minority groups have affiliated with opposing parties, although—as will be described shortly—the partisan preferences of Latinos are becoming less cohesive. African Americans in the Sunshine State, like elsewhere, constitute the core constituency for the Democratic Party, regularly voting for its nominees in overwhelming numbers. In contrast, Cuban Americans, who have been the most politically active Latinos in the state, have been staunchly Republican, attracted to the GOP by its outspoken opposition to the regime of Fidel Castro. Because of their differing loyalties, African Americans have generally seen their preferred candidates elected when Democrats have triumphed, while Latinos have seen their preferences put in office when Republicans have succeeded.

The political loyalties of Florida Latinos are becoming less monolithic. While the Cuban American population continues to be solidly Republican, some evidence suggests that younger members of that community are less committed to the GOP. Latinos who originate from some place other than Cuba are much less supportive of Republicans and, for the most part, back Democratic candidates. Alvaro Fernandez, the Florida director for the Southwest Voter Registration and Education Project, notes that "70 percent of Hispanics in Florida aren't Cuban" as evidence of the need to organize and register those Latinos as a potential bloc of voters for the Democratic Party.[20] Growing numbers of Puerto Ricans have moved into Florida in recent years. Unlike those who come from Latin America, Puerto Ricans can register and vote since they are U.S. citizens. Moreover, they tend to be staunch Democrats.

One distinguishing feature of the Dade County Hispanic community is that it is more heavily Cuban than the surrounding communities. Outside Dade County, in Monroe, Collier, and Broward, Cubans are less numerous among the Hispanic population. These Hispanic populations are also less concentrated than in Dade County. The distinction between Cubans and non-Cubans may be important from the perspective of cultural anthropologists. In the realm of politics, Latinos in Florida—regardless of the land of their ancestor—are united by anticommunist sentiments, opposition to English-only laws, and support for a variety of urban issues.[21] The trial court in *Martinez v. Bush* recognized the lack of political distinction within these communities and, like the Justice Department, considers Latinos in Florida to be a cohesive voting bloc regardless of national origin.[22]

What is especially instructive about the Latino vote in Florida is that it is so strongly defined by the Republican Party. Moreno and Hill's analysis of eight contests ranging from the statewide level down to local judicial races revealed a powerful relationship in South Florida between the Hispanic population and vote choice. In partisan races, these preferences always broke to the advantage of Republican candidates, even when the contest was between two Hispanics. Running a Latino as a Democrat did not reduce Hispanic Republicanism.[23]

While various groups can claim credit when their preference wins an election, the Latino vote has been critical in electing Republicans in several close contests. Exit polls indicate that George Bush won 54.5 percent of Florida's Hispanic vote in 2000 on his way to carrying the state by fewer than six hundred votes and thus winning the presidency. In 2004, Mel Martinez would have lost his bid for the U.S. Senate but for the support of 53.1 percent of the Latinos who went to the polls. While the Latino vote tipped the scales in favor of Republicans in these two high-profile contests, the divisions within the Latino community point up how inaccurate the stereotype of a unified, pro-GOP Latino vote has become.

Exit poll results in table 9.5 provide further evidence that the legacy of South Florida Cubans as a consistent, 80 percent Republican vote misstates Hispanic preferences statewide. Democrats have made recent inroads among other Hispanic voters, increasing their share from one-in-three or one-in-four Hispanic voters in 1994 to being highly competitive and nearing parity by 1998. In 2006, Democratic senator Bill Nelson won a majority of the Latino vote while Jim Davis, the Democratic nominee for governor, split the Latino vote with ultimate winner Republican Charlie Crist.

TABLE 9.5. Statewide Democratic candidate support by voter race or ethnicity, Florida, 1992–2006

	Black	Latino	Anglo
1992 President	89.0	38.1	37.2
1992 U.S. Senate	95.0	67.2	64.1
1992 U.S. House	83.8	50.0	50.8
1994 U.S. Senate	81.7	31.1	22.6
1994 Governor	94.6	33.3	44.9
1994 U.S. House	98.4	24.1	36.4
1996 President	90.4	51.3	46.3
1998 U.S. Senator	82.5	52.8	52.0
1998 Governor	78.9	40.0	38.6
1998 U.S. House	85.7	50.0	33.1
2000 President	93.2	48.4	39.8
2004 President	91.0	45.5	46.3
2004 U.S. Senate	84.1	46.1	47.7
2004 U.S. House	87.4	52.0	41.6
2006 U.S. Senate	92.0	57.0	56.0
2006 Governor	81.0	50.0	38.0

Sources: For 1992–2000, various Voter News Service exit polls; for 2004, Election Day surveys; for 2006, www.cnn.com/ELECTION/2006/pages/results/states/FL/S/01 and www.cnn.com/ELECTION/2006/page/results/states/FL/G/00.

The exit polls for 2006 provide separate breakouts for Cuban Americans and other Latino voters. The exit poll estimates are that slightly fewer Cuban Americans than other Latinos went to the polls, with the former group constituting 5 percent of total turnout while the latter group comprised 6 percent. The exit polls also confirm the partisan differences between the two groups. The Cuban Americans remained overwhelmingly Republican, casting 62 percent of their votes for U.S. Senate nominee Katherine Harris and 69 percent of their votes for Governor Crist. In contrast, two-thirds of the other Latinos supported the Davis gubernatorial candidacy and 74 percent signed on to the reelection of Senator Nelson.

Evidence of the degree of Democratic support registered by some non-Cuban Latinos comes from Osceola County, which is experiencing a rapid in-migration of Hispanics, many of whom have Puerto Rican backgrounds. In local elections in that county, which borders Orlando on the south, Democrats have consistently been the candidates of choice of Latino voters.[24]

Additional evidence of differences with regard to Hispanic participation and preferences emerges when comparing Collier and Monroe Counties to the more urban Dade County. Moreno and Hill provide estimates of Hispanic, black, and Anglo voter turnout for elections in 1998 and 2000 for four South Florida counties. In 2000, Moreno and Hill find comparable rates of Hispanic and Anglo participation in Dade County, and Hispanic turnout was between black and Anglo turnout rates in the previous midterm election in 1998.[25] Hispanic turnout is a third less in Monroe and 50 percent less in Collier than in Dade in 2000. In 1998 Collier and Monroe showed less Hispanic participation than Dade, especially in Collier where Hispanic turnout was less than a quarter of the rate observed in Dade. The rate of black participation in 2000 is about the same in all four counties.

Collier and Monroe differ from Dade on dimensions other than turnout. Estimates of Republican support in the counties in four statewide contests in 1998 and 2000 show different party preferences for Dade County Hispanics (who are primarily Cuban) compared with non-Cuban Hispanics elsewhere in South Florida. The estimated support for Republican candidates among Dade County Hispanics, as reported in table 9.6, was 83 to 97 percent. Collier Hispanics gave 7 to 31 percent of their votes to Republican candidates. The estimates for the small Monroe Hispanic population show Republican candidates getting 0 to 89 percent of the votes.

An examination of six statewide and legislative contests in Collier County in 2002 shows Latinos in that county to be far less supportive of Republicans than Cuban Americans in Miami-Dade have been. In six contests examined in table 9.7—governor, attorney general, agriculture commissioner, Congressional District 25 (a Hispanic-majority district), state senate District 39 (a combined black-and-Hispanic–majority district), and state house District 112 (a majority-Hispanic district)—only one Republican candidate commanded majority Hispanic support. Of three Hispanic Republicans running in the majority-minority districts,

TABLE 9.6. Estimated Republican candidate support by race and ethnicity in select Florida counties, 1998 and 2000

	Hispanic	Black	Anglo
President 2000			
Broward	54	0	35
Collier	31	0	63
Dade	83	0	27
Monroe	0	0	57
Governor 1998			
Broward	31	1	39
Collier	7	0	66
Dade	97	0	32
Monroe	89	1	50
Senator 2000			
Broward	56	0	36
Collier	29	0	63
Dade	83	0	29
Monroe	0	0	57
Educ. Comm. 1998			
Broward	21	3	45
Collier	*	*	*
Dade	*	*	67
Monroe	0	0	74

Source: Dario V. Moreno and Kevin A. Hill, "Expert Report on South Florida's Congressional Districts 17, 18, 21, and 25," submitted in *Martinez v. Bush*, 234 F. Supp. 2d 1275 (S.D. Fla. 2002), 1.

*Reliable estimate could not be derived.

only Rivera, in state house District 112, won the Hispanic vote in Collier, and his advantage over the Democrat, Gonzalez, is estimated to be less than 4 points.

The other Section 5 county for which we have data with which to analyze racial voting preferences is Hillsborough (Tampa). Table 9.8 contains precinct-level estimates of the Anglo, black, and Hispanic vote for statewide, congressional, and state legislative contests in Hillsborough in 2002 and 2004. The analysis indicates that the Anglo vote in Hillsborough is generally reliably Republican up and down the ticket, and the black vote is regularly Democratic. Latinos usually vote Democratically, though Republican congressional incumbents and members of the Bush family are able to pull majority Hispanic support in Hillsborough. The most

TABLE 9.7. Estimates of racial and ethnic preferences, statewide and legislative general elections, Collier County, Florida, 2002

	Candidate/Party	Anglo	Black	Hispanic
Congress, District 25	*Diaz-Balart*-R	58.7	<0	<0
	Betancourt-R	41.3	>100	>100
Governor	Bush-R	78.2	52.0	24.5
	McBride-D	21.3	47.3	70.4
	Kunst	0.5	0.7	5.1
Attorney General	Crist-R	68.7	44.2	34.1
	Dyer-D	31.3	55.8	65.9
Agriculture Comm.	Bronson-R	80.3	57.5	25.4
	Nelson-D	19.7	42.5	74.6
State Senate 39	*Marino*-R	39.8	11.4	32.1
	Bullard-D	60.2	88.6	67.9
State House 112	*Gonzalez*-D	34.5	34.4	48.4
	Rivera-R	65.5	65.6	51.6

Source: Ordinary least squares (OLS) estimates. Data compiled by authors.

African American candidate indicated in **boldface**.

Hispanic candidates indicated in *italics*.

heavily Hispanic state legislative district twice elected a Democratic Hispanic over a Republican Hispanic opponent, with overwhelming Hispanic support for the Democrat.

FEDERAL MONITORING

Federal monitors have not been sent into any of Florida's five Section 5 counties to watch election practices.[26] Nor has the power of objection been widely used in Florida. Of the five objections registered by the Department of Justice, four involved actions of the state legislature. The 1992 senate redistricting plan drew an objection as did the state house redistricting plan a decade later. The two other objections emerging from Section 5 coverage and directed at legislative action involved absentee voting. The only objection specifically directed at a county covered by Section 5 involved Hillsborough County and was issued in 1984. It was subsequently withdrawn.

TABLE 9.8. Estimates of racial and ethnic preferences, statewide and legislative general elections, Hillsborough County, 2002

	Candidate	Anglo	Black	Hispanic
Agriculture Comm.	Bronson-R	68.6	20.9	46.3
	Nelson-D	31.2	79.1	53.7
Attorney General	Crist-R	60.6	4.1	36.3
	Dyer-D	39.4	95.9	63.7
Governor	Bush-R	63.9	22.4	55.6
	McBride-D	36.1	77.6	44.4
Congress, Dist. 9	Bilirakis-R	77.3	<0	<0
	Kalogianis-D	22.7	>100	>100
State Senate 16	Sebest-R	76.9	>100	78.0
	McGinnis-Gimber-D	24.1	<0	22.0
State House 47	Ambler-R	44.5		17.8
	Steinberg-D	50.0		76.6
	Schwartzberg	5.5		5.6
State House 56	Murman-R	75.2	32.0	56.1
	Howard-D	24.8	68.0	43.9
State House 57	Culp-R	58.8		<0
	Farrell-D	39.1		<0
	Richmond	2.0		>100
State House 58	*Vila*-R	33.7	<0	<0
	Henriquez-D	66.3	>100	>100
State House 60	Homan-R	64.9		
	Romeo-D	32.3		
	Conley	2.8		
State House 63	Ross-R	80.9	99.0	21.5
	Downs-D	19.1	1.0	78.5
State House 67	Reagan-R	77.9	<0	57.6
	Stringfield-D	22.1	>100	42.4
President	Bush-R	66.6	6.6	30.8
	Kerry-D	32.8	92.4	68.7
	Other	0.6	0.8	0.5
Congress, Dist. 11	Davis-R	82.8	96.7	87.8
	Johnson-D	17.2	3.3	12.2
Congress, Dist. 12	Putnam-R	72.2	27.8	67.1
	Hagenmaier-D	27.8	71.2	32.9
State House 47	Ambler-R	64.6		50.6
	Snow-D	35.4		49.4
State House 57	Culp-R	83.6		<0
	Cope-D	16.4		>100
State House 58	Riis-R	56.4	<0	<0
	Henriquez-D	43.6	>100	>100
State House 60	Homan-R	76.6		39.0
	Perez-D	23.4		61.0

Source: Ordinary least squares (OLS) estimates. Data compiled by authors.

Hispanic candidates indicated in *italics*.

From 1990 through 2005, Florida submitted 2,409 proposed changes to DOJ for preclearance. DOJ objected to only seven of the proposed changes, which includes five separate elements in a 1998 objection. In addition to the handful of objections, DOJ requested more information on 176 of the proposed changes and ultimately approved 170 of these. Three of the items on which more information was requested were withdrawn while in three instances DOJ did register an objection.[27] The great bulk of the requests for more information, 100 of the 176, involved proposed changes in methods of election.

CONCLUSION

Census Bureau estimates indicate that the rate at which Latinos have registered to vote in Florida has increased slightly over the last quarter century. While the increase has been slight, the percent of Latinos registered in Florida has exceeded that for Hispanics outside the South since 1986 with the exception of 1994. Official information on registrants provided by the Florida secretary of state does not give a separate breakout for Hispanics although we suspect that they constitute much of the "other" category. From 1996 through 2004, the proportion of the registrants in the "other" category grew from 7.2 to 11.6 percent of all registrants in the state.

The Census Bureau estimates for turnout indicate no consistent change in the share of the Latinos of voting age who have cast ballots in Florida. However, the figures do not show an increase in the rates of Latino participation in Florida, but the figures do indicate higher rates of Latino voting in Florida than in the non-South since 1986 except for 1994. While the rate of Latino participation may not be increasing, if the number of Latino registrants has grown, then Latinos may be casting a larger share of the ballots in Florida. Evidence to support that proposition comes from the exit polls. In 1994, Latinos cast 8 percent of the ballots in the gubernatorial election. Twelve years later, the share of ballots in the gubernatorial election as reported in the exit polls stood at 11 percent, which slightly exceeds the Hispanic share of Florida registrants in 2006.

Census Bureau figures on black registration do not show a consistent increase in the share of the African American voting-age population (VAP) that has registered in Florida. Moreover, the rate at which Florida

African Americans registered to vote continues to be lower than in the rest of the nation. However, data from the Florida secretary of state show the numbers of blacks registered to vote increasing by about 50 percent from 1996 to 2006 so that the share of all registrants who are African American has grown from 10.5 to 12 percent, a figure very close to the percent black in Florida's VAP.

Census Bureau turnout estimates continue to show African Americans voting at much lower rates than Anglos. From 1980 until 2004, there is no evidence that the disparity between the two races is closing. Moreover, African Americans report voting at lower rates in Florida than in the non-South. Counter evidence comes from the 2006 exit polls, which show African Americans accounting for 14 percent of Florida's voters that year. If that sample accurately reflects the behavior of Florida African Americans, then they voted at a rate greater than their share of the registrants.

The rates of Latino and black turnout reported by the exit polls in 2006 may reflect a reaction to the U.S. Senate candidacy of Katherine Harris. Much of the Republican leadership in Florida had opposed the Harris candidacy, fearing that her prominent role in the 2006 election contest would spur turnout among staunchly Democratic voters still unhappy about her role in 2000, when as secretary of state she certified George W. Bush's victory in Florida.[28]

While turnout rates for Latinos and African Americans often lag those for Anglos, minorities have made significant gains in terms of descriptive representation in Congress. Since 1993, the Florida congressional delegation has contained three African Americans, and after the 2001 redistricting, the delegation's number of Latinos grew from two to three. The 12 percent of the congressional seats filled by each minority group roughly approximates each group's share of the voting-age population in the state.

Florida's African Americans have even larger shares of the seats in the state legislature. In both the Florida senate and house, African Americans hold a larger percentage of the seats than their share of the voting-age population.

In contrast, Latinos hold smaller shares of the seats in the Florida legislature than in the congressional delegation. Just over 10 percent of the house membership is Latino, while in the senate Latinos constitute 7.5

percent of the membership. Both of these figures are less than the share of Florida's population that is Latino.

Both ethnic groups have made gains in the numbers of elected officials in the state. The most recent figure for Latino elected officials is little more than one-third that for African Americans holding office in Florida. For both ethnic groups, the bulk of the officeholders serve at the municipal level.

It appears that part of the explanation for the greater success of African Americans than Latinos in winning office is that in districts that contain substantial numbers of both ethnic groups, African Americans are more likely to be elected. This is in part due to higher rates of registration and turnout among blacks than Latinos.

In the five counties covered by Section 5, the Latino population is either too small or too scattered to facilitate election of Hispanics. These two factors usually make it impossible to draw a state legislative district, much less a congressional district in these counties in which the bulk of the population is Latino. The one exception comes in Collier County, where many of the Latinos can be combined with an even larger Latino population in neighboring Dade County.

Estimates of voting preferences of Latinos in South Florida raise questions about the desirability of combining Miami-Dade Latinos with Collier or Monroe Latinos. The Latino population in Dade is heavily Cuban and provides strong support for Republicans. In Collier and other South Florida counties, the Latino electorate is more inclined to support Democrats. Thus, while a district that straddles the Collier-Dade boundary is likely to elect a Latino and thus provide descriptive representation for that ethnic group, the winner may well not be the candidate of choice of the Latinos in Collier, the county that is covered by Section 5 of the Voting Rights Act.

The potential impact of Section 5 on Florida, even if abuses directed at Hispanics were widespread, would probably not be addressed effectively. The counties with the largest Hispanic concentrations are not ones subject to Section 5. Thus to the extent that challenges are brought, they must come under Section 2.

PART III

Southern States Not Covered by Section 5

CHAPTER 10

TENNESSEE

Tennessee is one of only two former Confederate states never subjected to Section 5 of the Voting Rights Act. While the state did secede and some of its southwestern counties were part of the Black Belt, Tennessee has a different political history than its southern neighbors. In 1920, it became the first southern state to cast its Electoral College votes for a Republican in the twentieth century. Eight years later, Tennessee joined Texas, Virginia, Florida, and North Carolina in voting for Herbert Hoover. Tennessee's Republicanism, rooted at the base of the Smoky Mountains in the eastern part of the state, provided the basis for a viable Republican Party long after the GOP had died out in most of the rest of the South. Republicans won the Tennessee governorship in 1894, 1910, and 1920, an era when Democrats dominated the chief executive's office in other southern states. Indeed, when Tennessee was occasionally electing Republican governors in the first two decades of the twentieth century, Republicans had ceased to even offer candidates for their state's top office in much of the South.

Despite these differences, at the turn of the twentieth century, Tennessee joined the rest of the South in limiting black voting when it imposed a poll tax and banned helping illiterate voters.[1] The state adopted this obstacle to participation in 1890 but did not enact other requirements such as a literacy test, good character test, or understanding requirement—all items popular with a number of other southern states.[2] Kousser reports, however, that some towns did implement a literacy test.[3] The absence of the interlocking panoply of obstacles to black participation resulted in African Americans in Tennessee being more likely to vote earlier than in other southern states. V. O. Key, Jr., reports that African Americans provided some of the votes for the Crump machine that ruled Memphis and had great impact on state politics for many years.[4]

Tennessee avoided coverage by Section 5 of the Voting Rights Act because it activated neither component of the trigger mechanism included in Section 4 of that legislation. The trigger mechanism was set to identify states that had tests or devices as prerequisites to voting and in which less than half of the voting-age population had registered or voted in the 1964 presidential election. Figures compiled by the U.S. Commission on Civil Rights estimate that 72 percent of Tennessee's 1960 voting-age population (VAP) had registered to vote by 1964.[5] In the presidential election, the turnout rate equaled 54.7 percent of the 1960 voting-age population. Tennessee did not employ any of the tests or devices earmarked by the 1965 legislation. The state collected a poll tax, but as noted in the Texas chapter, the federal legislation did not identify the poll tax as a test or device prerequisite to registration.[6]

Not only did a majority of the Tennessee voting-age population register to vote, but the Commission on Civil Rights figures indicate that prior to the passage of the 1965 legislation, most nonwhites had registered—69.9 percent of nonwhites compared with 72.9 percent of whites. The share of the nonwhite adult population estimated to have registered in Tennessee was 18 percentage points higher than in any other southern state.

Although Tennessee was not subject to Section 5, registration increased in the state following enactment of the VRA. Within a couple of years, 71.7 percent of the nonwhite and 80.6 percent of the white VAP had registered to vote in the Volunteer State.

While Tennessee did not set off the triggers of the Voting Rights Act, two southwestern counties, Fayette and Haywood, had recently engaged in behavior that drew the attention of the Department of Justice. At the 1959 Democratic primary to select nominees for county officials in Fayette

County, poll workers turned away newly registered black voters with the statement that only whites could vote in the primary. It was probably the last instance of an all-white primary, coming fifteen years after *Smith v. Allright* had banned the practice.

In response to a voter registration drive in these heavily black counties, whites turned to economic intimidation. Once the cotton had been picked, white landowners ordered sharecroppers who had sought to register off the land. These expulsions removed some families who had farmed the land for decades. Other large landowners refused to contract with the now homeless farmworkers. With winter coming on, a black farmer allowed the homeless sharecroppers to camp on his land and a tent city sprang up. Whole families wintered in small tents with dirt, or often mud, floors and scant heat put out by primitive stoves. Not only did those seeking to become voters lose their jobs, but local merchants refused to sell them groceries or allow them to buy gas for their cars. Black landowners active in the voter registration effort could not get their cotton ginned. DOJ sued to halt economic intimidation in Fayette and Haywood, and in 1962 it secured a consent decree that ended the practice. Four years later the first African Americans won local offices in Fayette County.

BLACK REGISTRATION AND TURNOUT

Tennessee does not maintain registration or turnout records by race, but Census Bureau estimates exist for registration between 1980 and 2006 (see appendix B). Since most Tennesseans were registered to vote in the early 1960s, it is not surprising that the bulk of the voting-age population continues to be on the registration lists. Since 1980, the lowest incidence of registration among blacks came in 2006 when 53.5 percent reported being registered. The 2002 and 2006 figures are approximately 10 percentage points lower than in any other year, which prompts questions about the reliability of the samples. It seems improbable that black registration would drop from 64.9 percent in 2000 to 54.1 in 2002, rebound to 63.9 in 2004, then plummet to 53.5 percent in 2004. Except in 2002 and 2006, black registration has always been at least 63.9 percent and has gone as high 78.5 percent. Among whites, the nadir in registration comes in 2000 when 61.9 percent claimed to have registered to vote. That figure is in line with white registration that, since 1990, has been outside the 61.9 to 63.9 percent range only once.

In contrast with the figures from the 1960s reported by the Commission on Civil Rights that showed higher proportions of white than black adults registering to vote, black registration rates since 1980 often exceed those for whites. The greatest differences come in 1992 when 77.4 percent of African Americans compared with 63.4 percent of whites claimed to have registered. During the latter part of the 1980s, black registration rates ran at least 8 points higher than those for whites. Beginning with 1996, the registration rates for the two racial groups have been more alike. In three of the five most recent elections, blacks report registering at slightly higher rates than whites. The largest disparities, however, came in 2002 and 2006 when suspiciously low black registration rates result in a white advantage exceeding 8 percentage points.

Beginning in 1998, Census Bureau estimates provide additional breakouts for registration rates. Among the new estimates is one for non-Hispanic whites. Once Hispanics have been eliminated and the remaining white registration figures compared with those of blacks, they boost the white registration rate beginning in 2000. However, even following the exclusion of Latinos, black registration continues to outpace that for whites in 1998 and 2000. Even in 2004 when eliminating Hispanics increases the white registration figure by 1.5 percentage points, it barely eclipses the registration rate among blacks. In the two most recent midterm elections, non-Hispanic whites registered at rates more than 10 points above the questionable figures reported for blacks.

Black registration in Tennessee exceeds that in the non-South for every year except the atypical 2002 and 2006. Through 1994, the registration rate for Tennessee African Americans is often 10 points above that for blacks outside of the South with the greatest difference coming in 1992 when 77.4 percent of Tennessee's blacks compared with 63 percent of blacks in the rest of the nation reported being registered. More recently, the rates for Tennessee and non-South black registrants have converged.

What happens if we contrast the registration rates for Tennessee with those for Mississippi in appendix B? Prior to the passage of the 1965 Voting Rights Act, Tennessee and Mississippi were polar opposites in terms of the nonwhite registration rate. As noted above, 69.5 percent of Tennessee's adult blacks had registered before passage of the Voting Rights Act, compared with only 6.7 percent of Mississippi's black adults. In the immediate aftermath of the voting-rights legislation, black registration in Tennessee continued to be approximately a dozen percentage points higher than in Mississippi.[7] By 1980, Tennessee had lost its advantage. Black registration in Mississippi exceeds that in Tennessee in every year except 1994 when the Tennessee advantage is an insignificant 0.1 percentage points. In 1982 and 1984, the black registration rate in Mississippi was approximately 7 percentage points higher than in Tennessee. The disparity narrows during the late 1980s and through much of the 1990s before widening again. In 1998, African Americans were 6.5 percentage points more likely to register in Mississippi than Tennessee. That disparity expands until 2004, when it reaches approximately 12 percentage points to Mississippi's advantage. A difference of almost 20 points exists in 2006, but recall concerns about the reliability of the Tennessee estimate that year.

Near the bottom of the first table in appendix B are figures showing black and white registration rates for the median state among the seven states that were initially made subject to Section 5 by the 1965 Voting Rights Act.[8] Through 1996, the share of the adult black population in Tennessee that had registered to vote exceeded the median for the seven states. For the first eight elections, differences frequently exceeded 10 percentage points and reached more than 16 points in 1984 when 78.5 percent of the black adults in Tennessee compared with 62.2 percent in the median state had registered. For the last decade, however, the registration rates tend to have been greater for the median state than for Tennessee. After reaching parity in 1996, when just less than two-thirds of the adult African Americans both in Tennessee and the median state had registered, the figure for the median state moved ahead of Tennessee. In 2004, the median black registration figure for the seven states is 71.1 percent compared with 63.9 percent in Tennessee.

Census Bureau estimates for turnout appear in appendix B, as well. In all but four election years between 1980 and 2006, including the three most recent ones, African American turnout in Tennessee exceeds that for whites. In some years the difference is trivial as in 1980 and 2000, but in other years it is substantial. In 1984, 1988, and 1992, black adults voted at rates 7 to 8 percentage points greater than whites. In the new century, however, the advantage has gone to whites. The change results primarily from increased white participation in midterm elections.

Eliminating Hispanics from the calculation of turnout among whites raises the white participation figure. The increase, however, is insufficient to overcome the higher turnout reported for blacks in 1998. In 2000, the non-Hispanic white estimate is slightly above the black estimate, while before the exclusion of Latinos, the black figure had slightly exceeded the white figure. For the three most recent years, excluding Latinos increases the gap between white and black turnout so that it reaches almost 10 points in the two most recent midterm elections.[9]

Turnout rates for both races generally show a seesaw pattern with larger shares of the voting-age population going to the polls in presidential than in midterm elections. For both races, turnout rates exceed 50 percent in presidential years, yet only in 1982 did either racial group (in this case, blacks) achieve majority turnout in a midterm election.

Comparable turnout figures for the non-South at the bottom of the table show that the turnout rate among adult African Americans is higher in Tennessee than in the non-South, especially in presidential years. The greatest difference occurs in 1992 when turnout among black Tennesseans ran 9 points higher than for African Americans outside the South. In two other years, black voters in Tennessee turn out at rates at least 5 percentage points above those for the non-South. While non-South blacks report voting at higher rates than do black Tennesseans in four election years, the largest difference, 3.1 percentage points, comes in 1990. Recent midterm elections show African Americans voting at about the same rates in Tennessee and the non-South.

When we contrast turnout in Tennessee to turnout in Mississippi, we see that Mississippi African Americans voted at higher rates than Tennesseans in five of seven presidential years. The two exceptions come in 1992 when the turnout rate for Tennessee blacks is one point higher than in Mississippi and in 1996 when the Tennessee rate is 7.2 points higher. Otherwise, presidential elections bring blacks to the polls at higher rates in Mississippi than Tennessee, with the largest difference occurring in the most recent presidential election included in the table when two-thirds of Mississippi's African Americans but barely a majority of Tennessee's blacks cast ballots.

In three midyear elections Tennessee has higher black turnout than does Mississippi. In 1982 the two states' African Americans voted at identical rates. In 1994 and 1998 blacks went to the polls more frequently in Mississippi than Tennessee. The explanation for more African Americans often voting in Tennessee than Mississippi in midterm elections is that Mississippi chooses its constitutional officers and state legislators in odd-numbered years. Tennessee, like most southern states, elects its governor in the presidential midterm and its legislators in even-numbered years, although that clearly cannot account for the 12-point Mississippi advantage in 2006.

Comparison of Tennessee to the median among the seven southern states made subject to Section 5 in 1965 shows that, until recently, black turnout tended to be higher in Tennessee than the median state. Prior to 1998, the only year in which black turnout was greater in the median state than Tennessee came in 1990. For three of the elections in the 1980s, African American turnout ran approximately 10 percentage points higher in Tennessee than in the median state. For four of the five most recent election years, however, black turnout has been higher in the median state than in Tennessee, although in 2006 they were essentially the same. The largest difference occurs in 2004 when 62.1 percent of the African Americans in the median state voted compared with 51.3 percent in Tennessee.

The trend for the comparison between the median Section 5 state and Tennessee blacks is for Tennessee African Americans to vote at higher rates in the earlier period but for that advantage to decline beginning in the 1990s. Then, at the turn of the century, the relationship reverses and black participation in the median state outpaces that in Tennessee.

AFRICAN AMERICAN OFFICE HOLDING

When record keeping on the numbers of African American officeholders began in 1969, Tennessee had thirty-one as reported in figure 10.1. Seven years later, the number had grown to more than one hundred. The next twenty-five years saw a gradual increase from 106 to 180. At the beginning of the twenty-first century, Tennessee had fewer African American officeholders than any other southern state.

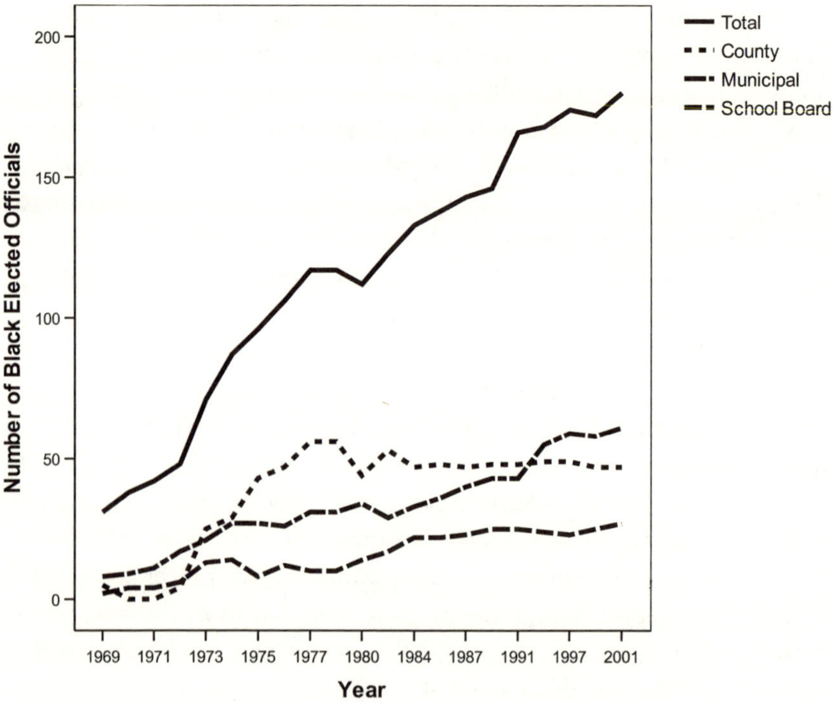

Figure 10.1. Black elected officials in Tennessee, 1969–2001. *Source:* Various volumes of the *National Roster of Black Elected Officials* (Washington, D.C.: Joint Center for Political and Economic Studies).

In the late 1970s, almost half of the black officeholders in Tennessee served at the county level. Over the next twenty-five years, the number of black county officials declined from fifty-six to forty-seven. The number of black school board members gradually increased, and, in 2001, twenty-seven served in that capacity. Only at the municipal level has there been a fairly constant growth in the number of black officeholders, and by 2001, a third of all Tennessee's African American officials were elected to city offices.

African Americans in Congress

In 1974, Tennessee became the third southern state to send an African American to Congress in the twentieth century. In that year, Harold Ford defeated Republican incumbent Dan Kuykendall by a razor-thin majority of 744 votes. The authoritative *Almanac of American Politics 1978* speculates that but for the reaction against Republicans spawned by the Watergate scandal, Kuykendall might have survived.[10] A redistricting carried out during his first term strengthened Ford's position by making the 9th District slightly more Democratic.

Harold Ford was part of a political family dynasty and won office before his thirtieth birthday. His Memphis district was just 47 percent black in total population, so like Georgia's Andrew Young and Texan Barbara Jordan, both of whom had initially been elected in 1972, he first won in a district that wasn't predominantly black. He remained in Congress until 1996, and his victory margins held comfortably above 60 percent until the 1990s. When he stepped aside after eleven terms, he did so in favor of his son and namesake, Harold E. Ford, Jr. The son, like the father, came to Congress when very young (age twenty-six).

The younger Ford proved to be more charismatic than his father and quickly established himself in the district. However, unlike his father, he had higher ambitions. After contemplating a run for the Senate and then drawing back, in 2006 he leapt at the chance to take the seat being vacated by Senate Majority Leader Bill Frist (R). Ford's departure from the House opened a free for all with fifteen candidates entering the Democratic primary. In this district that cast 70 percent of its votes for John Kerry in 2004, the winner of the Democratic nomination would almost certainly become the next member of Congress. The field of candidates included thirteen African Americans along with a seasoned white senator, Steve Cohen, who had lost badly in the Democratic primary that initially sent the younger Ford to Congress. Among the black candidates was Joe Ford, who was a cousin of the retiring incumbent and son of a Shelby County commissioner. The large field and especially the great number of black candidates resulted in the African American vote being fractured. Cohen led the pack with 31 percent of the vote, 6 percentage points ahead of the leading African American—an airlines labor lawyer who was the biggest fund-raiser. Harold Ford's cousin paced third with 12 percent of the vote. Cohen's victory came with 3 percentage points less of the vote than he had managed in his unsuccessful bid a decade earlier.

TABLE 10.1. Racial makeup of the Tennessee General Assembly, 1965–2007

	Senate	% Black in Senate	House	% Black in House
1965	0	0.00	0	0.00
1967	0	0.00	6	6.06
1969	2	6.06	6	6.06
1971	2	6.06	6	6.06
1973	2	6.06	7	7.07
1975	2	6.06	9	9.09
1977	2	6.06	9	9.09
1979	2	6.06	9	9.09
1981	2	6.06	9	9.09
1983	3	9.09	10	10.10
1985	3	9.09	10	10.10
1987	3	9.09	10	10.10
1989	3	9.09	10	10.10
1991	3	9.09	10	10.10
1993	3	9.09	12	12.12
1995	3	9.09	13	13.13
1997	3	9.09	13	13.13
1999	3	9.09	13	13.13
2001	3	9.09	14	14.14
2003	3	9.09	15	15.15
2005	3	9.09	15	15.15
2007	3	9.09	16	16.16

Source: Data compiled by the authors.

In any other southern state except for Florida and Virginia, Cohen would have had to consolidate his position in a runoff. But under Tennessee's plurality rule, this 59.5 percent black district had nominated a white Democrat for the first time in more than three decades. One of Ford's brothers, Jake, passed up the crowded Democratic primary and entered the general election contest as an independent. The pull of party, however, proved too great and Cohen easily won the seat, taking 59 percent of the vote. Jake Ford edged out the Republican nominee and placed second with 22 percent of the vote. Cohen quickly consolidated support and took three-fourths of the vote in the 2008 Democratic primary, holding his leading opponent, an African American businesswoman, Nikki Tinker, to less than 20 percent.

African Americans in the State Legislature

The first African American to enter the Tennessee house arrived in 1964, and two African American senators joined him in 1967. The first black legislator in Tennessee in modern times, like most African Americans who have served in the General Assembly over the last four decades, came from Memphis. The ranks of black senators have increased only to three, a number achieved with the implementation of a new redistricting plan in the 1982 election. That number, which constitutes 9 percent of the thirty-three–member senate, has held constant now for a generation.

The number of black representatives has grown (see table 10.1). The new redistricting plan of 1972 enabled a seventh African American to win a seat in the house. At the beginning of the next decade, the number of African Americans rose to ten. After the redistricting in the early 1990s, the number of black representatives increased to a dozen in the ninety-nine–member chamber. The post-2000 census adjustment created enough districts to increase the number of black representatives to fifteen following the 2002 election. African Americans now hold 16.2 percent of the house seats, which is proportional to their share of the total population (16.3 percent in the 2000 census).

African Americans have achieved positions of leadership in the Tennessee house. Lois DeBerry won election as the majority whip and then moved up to become the Speaker Pro Tempore. In 2003, blacks held three of the eight leadership positions within the Democratic Party in the house.[11] Blacks have also had some success in achieving committee chairs and passing legislation.[12]

After an extensive analysis of the activities of the Tennessee Black Caucus, Sharon Wright concludes that although this group is smaller than many of the black caucuses in southern states, it has enjoyed a degree of political success.[13] In some years in the late 1980s, African Americans had a higher success rate at passing legislation than did white legislators.

African Americans in Statewide Office

Unlike a number of southern states that elect their judges and multiple constitutional officers statewide, the only officials elected statewide in

Tennessee are the governor and senators. Even the presiding officer of the senate is not a lieutenant governor but rather chosen by the membership. John Wilder served as senate Speaker and lieutenant governor from 1971 until 2007. His bipartisan approach allowed him to survive changes in party control of that chamber until Republicans finally united in opposition and selected one of their own to be lieutenant governor, two years after the Republicans had finally consolidated control of the chamber with a stable majority.

While no African American has won statewide elective office, the state's Supreme Court does have a black justice. Justices on the Tennessee high court are appointed by the governor and, under a Missouri plan, serve eight years and then face the electorate with an up or down vote.

In 2006 Harold Ford, Jr., mounted a serious challenge for a U.S. Senate seat. In preparation for his Senate bid, Ford began moving toward the ideological middle on a number of policy issues. By 2005, he had compiled a moderate voting record. He was more liberal than 58.3 percent of the U.S. House members but more conservative than 41.7 percent of the membership.[14] Only twenty House Democrats had more conservative records than Ford, which meant that he was among the most conservative 10 percent of House Democrats. He edged out Georgia's Sanford Bishop as the most conservative member of the Congressional Black Caucus. Earlier in his career Ford had been more liberal, although he was never on the far left of his party.

Although five candidates entered the Democratic primary to pursue the Senate nomination, Ford quickly established himself as the dominant force. He secured the nomination with more than three-fourths of the ballots cast.

With the nomination in hand, Ford proved to be a formidable candidate in this "red" state. Throughout the campaign season, his efforts made this contest one of the most competitive races in the nation. He and the seat he sought were regularly viewed as having the potential to determine partisan control of the Senate. Several months before the election, polls showed Ford leading the Republican nominee, former Chattanooga mayor Bob Corker. However, as Election Day drew closer, the Republican first pulled even, then nosed ahead. The outcome seems not to have been influenced by race, and Ford did not attribute his loss to being black. The closest thing to a racial appeal in the campaign came in an ad sponsored by the Republican Party and not the Republican nominee. It sought to capitalize on Ford's reputation as a *bon vivant*. The television ad featured an attractive blonde alluringly asking Ford to give her a call.

Ultimately, Corker won the Senate seat by a margin of fifty thousand votes, which gave him a 51–48 advantage. Although some polls, particularly in October, had shown Ford narrowly ahead, the final polls before the election generally showed Corker with half the vote and Ford in the mid-40s. Interestingly, Ford actually secured a slightly larger percentage of the vote than the polls had anticipated. This is in sharp distinction from the experience of Douglas Wilder and his campaign for governor of Virginia. The Wilder experience—as well as that of Thomas Bradley, an unsuccessful African American candidate for governor of California—had shown black candidates doing better in preelection polls than on Election Day. Thus in Tennessee in 2006, there was not a tendency for white voters to give "politically correct" responses to pollsters and falsely indicate that they planned to vote for the African American and then turn around and support the white candidate.

Exit polls showed Ford taking 95 percent of the black vote while Corker won 59 percent of the white vote.[15] Among white voters there was a 5 percentage point gender gap: men gave 61 percent of their votes to Corker while women were less enthusiastic, providing the Republican with 56 percent of their vote. Overall, Ford narrowly won the female vote 51 to 48 percent, while among all males, Corker secured a 54 to 45 percent advantage. Each candidate took the overwhelming share of his fellow partisans and the two split the independent vote right down the middle. However, with Republican loyalists accounting for 38 percent of the turnout compared with 34 percent who identified themselves as Democrats, this provided the margin of victory for Corker. Ford actually carried 63 percent of the white voters who were not evangelical or born-again Christians. However, Corker took 65 percent of white religious conservatives, and they constituted a majority of the white electorate in Tennessee.

Tennessee joined Arkansas and Texas as the only southern states in which Hillary Clinton beat Barack Obama in the 2008 presidential primary. Clinton had a 14-point advantage as she took two-thirds of the white vote, doing better than Coker had two years earlier. Obama managed a quarter of the white vote along with 77 percent of the black vote, according to the exit polls.

RACIAL VOTING PATTERNS

Memphis is Tennessee's most populous city and one of the largest cities in the South. Like many other major cities in the region, it has an African American mayor. The city has had a black majority since 1986, and in 1991 the first African American mayor, W. W. Herenton, defeated incumbent Richard Hackett by 172 votes. In this hotly contested election, the vote was racially polarized with Herenton getting 95.2 percent of the black vote while Hackett got a comparable share of the white vote.[16]

The polarization evident in the 1991 election was nothing new in Memphis. Sharon Wright's analysis of racial voting patterns in the city shows white and black voters supporting opposing candidates as far back as 1975, when all of the serious competitors were white. Herenton failed to attract the bulk of the white vote in his first reelection bid. In 1995, he received 97 percent of the black vote, but almost 60 percent of the white vote went to his challenger.

The near unanimity in black support registered for Herenton replicated the experience of Harold Ford, Sr. In his eleven congressional campaigns, he never got less than 92.5 percent of the black vote in the primary, and in general elections, he always attracted at least 93 percent of the African American vote.[17] This pattern continued with his son, who in his 2002 reelection bid garnered nearly all of the black vote, according to ecological regression (OLS) estimates of precinct data in Shelby County. The younger Ford showed greater crossover appeal than his controversial father, and garnered an estimated 61.8 percent of the white vote in 2002. That estimate is some 30 points ahead of what Tennessee native Al Gore could attract from Shelby County whites; the OLS estimate of white support for Gore was 30.8 percent.

Table 10.2 provides regression estimates of white statewide voter support for president, governor, and U.S. Senate in elections since 2000. In contests for the U.S. House in 2000, incumbency clearly played a role, as Democratic incumbents dominated the white vote in the four districts

TABLE 10.2. Estimated white voter support for Democrats for president, U.S. Senate, and governor, 2000–2006, and U.S. House, 2000, in Tennessee

	Contest	White %	Dem. win?
2000	Congressional 1*	—	No
	Congressional 2*	—	No
	Congressional 3*	33.5	No
	Congressional 4*	32.0	No
	Congressional 5+	70.9	Yes
	Congressional 6+	70.4	Yes
	Congressional 7*	29.5	No
	Congressional 8+	73.9	Yes
	Congressional 9+	—	Yes
2000	President	43.6	No
2002	Governor	51.6	Yes
2002	U.S. Senate	46.2	No
2004	President*	39.2	No
2006	Governor+	64.9	Yes
2006	**U.S. Senate***	44.9	No

Source: Data computed by the authors.

African American candidates in **boldface**.

+Incumbent Democrat.

*Incumbent Republican.

where they won, while no Democrat broke 33.5 percent of the white vote when challenging a Republican incumbent.

In 2000, Democrats ran better statewide than in Shelby County, with Gore garnering an estimated 43.6 percent of the white vote. In 2002, Phil Bredesen took a majority of the white vote in his successful bid for the open gubernatorial seat. Of the six statewide contests in Tennessee since 2000, only Bredesen's gubernatorial candidacy has commanded majority white support, which he received in both 2002 and 2006. Estimated support by whites for Harold Ford, Jr., in 2006 is slightly behind the estimated white support for Democrat Bob Clement for the open U.S. Senate seat in 2002, and just ahead of the estimated white support for Gore and Kerry for president.

In 2006, Tennesseans had two statewide contests on the ballot. In the election for the Senate, as previously discussed, African American Democrat

Harold Ford attracted 40 percent of the white vote along with 95 percent of the black vote. In the gubernatorial contest, the incumbent Democrat, Phil Bredesen, equaled Ford's showing among African American voters. However, in winning a landslide victory, Bredesen did substantially better than Ford among white voters. Running against a weak opponent, Bredesen took two-thirds of the white vote. The 26 percentage point difference in the Bredesen and Ford showings with the white electorate cannot be attributed exclusively to the race of the candidates. Incumbency is usually a valuable asset, and Bredesen had it while Ford did not. Ford faced a well-financed opponent who had previous electoral experience, and Corker acquired name recognition statewide as he defeated two former Republican members of Congress on his way to getting the Republican nomination. In contrast, the underfunded Republican challenger for the governorship was a state senator who began with relatively little statewide name recognition.

Exit poll data from Tennessee since 1992 show only one election in which white and black voter preferences coincide: Democrat Phil Bredesen's reelection as governor in 2006 (see table 10.3). Had reliable exit poll data been available for 2002, they would probably indicate that Bredesen was favored by a majority of white and black voters. Of twelve statewide elections for presidential electors, governor, and U.S. Senate, in six instances less than 40 percent of surveyed white voters reported voting for the Democrat, and in two instances those percentages are in the 20s. Harold Ford, Jr., as the only black candidate on the ballot for statewide office in this time period, garnered 40 percent of the white vote to rank above the Democratic median for the twelve contests. In six of twelve elections black voters reported more than 90 percent support for Democratic candidates, and in only one instance (the 2004 presidential election) did the black Democratic vote share dip below two-thirds.

A final consideration is the problems faced by some of Ford's relatives. His uncle John had been forced from the state senate as part of a wide-ranging bribery investigation and was awaiting trial at the time of the election. In this FBI sting operation, Senator Ford allegedly took a bribe of more than $50,000. The state senate also voted expel John Ford's sister (Harold Ford's aunt), who had narrowly won the election to replace the indicted Ford. The senate concluded that the legality of her

TABLE 10.3. Racial preferences for Democratic candidates in Tennessee, select races, 1992–2006

	Office	Black votes (%)	White votes (%)
1992	President**	96.0	42.0
1994	U.S. Senate "A"*	88.0	36.0
1994	U.S. Senate "B"	83.0	32.0
1994	Governor	90.0	41.0
1996	U.S. Senate**	77.0	31.0
1996	President*	90.0	42.0
1998	Governor**	74.6	24.0
2000	U.S. Senate**	77.3	22.4
2000	President	92.0	36.4
2004	President**	65.0	34.0
2006	Governor*	92.0	62.0
2006	**U.S. Senate**	95.0	40.0

Source: Voter News Service (VNS) exit poll data.

Note: Tennessee had two U.S. Senate seats up for election in 1994. Sen. Jim Sasser (D) was up for reelection and lost to Dr. Bill Frist (R), while a special election to fill the balance of the term for Sen. Al Gore's seat was won by Fred Thompson (R).

African American Democratic candidate indicated in **boldface**.

*Democratic incumbent candidate.

**Republican incumbent candidate.

election was marred by irregularities including votes cast by several individuals who were dead or felons and therefore ineligible to vote.[18] In November 2006, Ophelia Ford returned to the senate with an overwhelming victory.

How much play is there in the rural white vote? The case of Tennessee's only remaining black majority county, Haywood, is informative. Ecological regression estimates indicate that in 2000 Haywood County whites cast just 30.4 percent of their ballots for Al Gore for president, yet they gave moderate incumbent Democratic U.S. representative John Tanner 69.6 percent of their votes. In 2002, Phil Bredesen, running for the open gubernatorial seat, garnered just 38 percent of the white vote in Haywood County (compared to an estimated majority in the rest of the state), while Tanner took nearly three-quarters of white ballots. Incumbent Democratic legislators representative Jimmy Naifeh and senator John Wilder (presiding officers of the respective chambers at that time) attracted majority support from whites in Haywood County.[19]

In the absence of a Democratic incumbent with local ties, the white vote appears to melt away from Democrats.[20] Democrats from other parts of the state have less appeal for west Tennessee whites (Gore claimed Carthage in middle Tennessee as home, while Bredesen, a former Nashville mayor, moved to the state from Massachusetts after graduating from Harvard). However, in congressional contests, race of incumbent does not seem to structure congressional voting preferences. The willingness to support Democratic incumbents down the ticket is evident in Tennessee.

CONCLUSION

Tennessee has, in many ways, advanced less in terms of voting-rights progress than other southern states—to some extent because it had less distance to travel on the way toward equality. The state had a high degree of black voter participation prior to 1964, but the distinctiveness of having high rates of black participation prior to the Voting Right Act and on into the 1970s and 1980s has been lost. Tennessee currently ranks behind Mississippi and the median for the original Section 5 states in the South in terms of black voter participation. The number of black elected officials has grown, but the state has fewer black officeholders than other southern states. Tennessee has a relatively long history of black legislators, but the state senate lags the state house in approaching proportionality for black representation. Most gains in black office holding since the 1980s have come at the municipal level. In 2007 for the first time in more than thirty years, no African American served in Tennessee's congressional delegation.

Race structures vote choice, but whites continue to vote heavily for incumbent Democrats. In the absence of a Democratic incumbent, the white vote is likely to go to the Republican. That pattern showed up in the 2006 U.S. Senate election between Harold Ford and Bob Corker. In losing that race, Ford managed 40 percent of the white vote, which was a stronger showing than made by Democratic challengers in 2000 congressional races.

Ford also ran substantially ahead of John Kerry, who managed only 34 percent of the Tennessee white vote in 2004. Ford's performance, however, did not equal that of fellow Tennessean Al Gore, who got 43.6 percent of the white vote in his 2000 presidential bid. However, in both the most-heavily black urban county and the most heavily black rural county, white voter preferences for Republicans up the ticket is more pronounced.

CHAPTER 11

Arkansas

Arkansas and Tennessee are the two southern states never to have been required to request preclearance for election law changes pursuant to Section 5 of the Voting Rights Acts. Arkansas is also distinctive in that it is the least populous southern state and is the smallest state west of the Mississippi River. The Mississippi River forms Arkansas's eastern boundary, and the plantation culture flourished in the rich river bottom. The African American population is concentrated in the counties along the river, the southern counties along the border with Louisiana, and as far north as the capital of Little Rock. A number of the counties along the eastern and southern borders of the state are part of the traditional Black Belt, and historically some of these were majority black in population.

Over the last half century the share of Arkansas's population that is African American has declined by almost one-third. The 1960 census showed Arkansas to be 22 percent African American. Each of the last two censuses has found the black population to be just under 16 percent.

Despite its small size and relatively small black population (15.6 percent in 2000), Arkansas at one time took center stage in the civil rights struggle. The first massive unrest surrounding school desegregation erupted in Little Rock at Central High School. When Governor Orval

Faubus failed to oversee implementation of the court order requiring desegregation, President Dwight Eisenhower sent in federal troops to restore order. Those troops had to remain on duty for an entire school year to protect the handful of black students both in the halls of the school and from mobs that gathered outside of the facility.

Governor Faubus, who wanted to break with tradition and serve more than two consecutive two-year terms as governor, did nothing to prevent violent white opposition. Siding with the forces of segregation paid off for Faubus as he won four more terms. In 1958, in the first election held after the Little Rock school riots, Faubus captured his largest vote share, 82.5 percent. The protests at Central High stoked racial passions to such a fevered pitch that in 1958 the incumbent member of Congress who represented Little Rock lost reelection to a political novice who mounted a write-in campaign. The incumbent lost reelection—not because he had advocated desegregation, but simply because he had urged his constituents to comply with federal law.

Following Faubus's six terms, a series of progressive governors led Arkansas. The first of these, Winthrop Rockefeller, was elected in 1966. He and Florida's Claude Kirk became the first Republicans to be elected governors in the South since 1920. Dale Bumpers, David Pryor, and Bill Clinton succeeded Rockefeller, with the future president tying the Faubus record by serving a dozen years as chief executive.[1]

Although Arkansas has not had to comply with the requirements of Section 5, the state's history includes use of techniques designed to restrict black political participation. The state adopted a poll tax in 1892 and for many years limited participation in the decisive Democratic primary to whites. It did not, however, implement a literacy test or an understanding test.[2] When ordered to eliminate the white primary, Arkansas established a complicated quadruple primary system. The quadruple primary separated the nomination of federal and state offices and for each of these offices had a preprimary something akin to the Jaybird primary used in Texas's Fort Bend County.[3] Under this stratagem, only whites would vote in the election that determined the identity of the ultimate officeholder. Thus only whites could vote in the preprimary for both federal and state offices where the field of candidates would be narrowed. Then in the regular Democratic primary, where blacks could participate, the electorate would confront only one candidate per office. V. O. Key, Jr., reports that except for the heavily black counties along the Mississippi River, African Americans could generally participate during this last-gasp effort to maintain an exclusively white primary selection process.[4] The complicated four-primary arrangement, an approach almost guaranteed to wear out the voters and thereby reduce participation, lapsed after being used only in 1946.

By 1965 when the Voting Rights Act was first passed, Arkansas did not have a test or device as identified by Section 4 of that legislation. Furthermore, the state easily surpassed the requirement that most of its voting-age population be registered since the number of registrants prior to the Act exceeded 60 percent of the voting-age population identified by the 1960 census. This included 65.5 percent of the white adults and 40.4 percent of nonwhite adults.[5] The number of votes cast in the 1964 presidential election equaled almost 54 percent of the state's adult population as of the 1960 census and thus exceeded the threshold for coverage under Section 5 of the Voting Rights Act.

Although not subject to Section 5, Arkansas has displayed some distinctly southern characteristics. It was the only Rim South state to vote for George Wallace in 1968.[6] In a closely divided contest, Wallace won the six electoral votes with 39 percent of the vote while Richard Nixon edged out Hubert Humphrey for second place by 2,531 votes. Unlike all of the other Rim South states, Arkansas did not vote for Dwight Eisenhower in either of his successful bids for the presidency. Indeed, Arkansas was the last southern state to vote for a Republican presidential nominee in the twentieth century, finally breaking its Democratic tradition in 1972. Arkansas was also the last state to break the color line in its legislature, known as the General Assembly. No African Americans served in the one hundred–member lower chamber until 1973. This came two years after the first blacks got elected in Alabama and South Carolina.

BLACK REGISTRATION AND TURNOUT

Since Arkansas is not subject to Section 5, federal registrars have not been sent to increase African American registration, and federal authorities do not carefully monitor the state's electoral practices. Nonetheless,

Arkansas experienced a substantial increase in black registration immediately after passage of the Voting Rights Act. The U.S. Commission on Civil Rights estimates that Arkansas saw an increase of more than thirty-three thousand African American registrants from 1963 to 1967. This boosted its share of the nonwhite adult population registered to vote to 62.8 percent, the third-highest black registration rate in the South, exceeded by Tennessee and Florida.[7] While Arkansas had the third-highest rate of black registrants, its white registration rate was the third lowest, exceeding only Texas and Virginia. In Arkansas it was estimated that 72.4 percent of the white adults had signed up to vote in the immediate aftermath of the Voting Rights Act.

At the time that the U.S. Civil Rights Commission compiled *Political Participation*, actual current figures for registration from Arkansas were unavailable. Post-VRA figures are estimates from the Voter Education Project, a private organization active in promoting registration drives among African Americans. Pre-VRA figures were compiled from the poll tax receipts that included a racial identifier.

Arkansas's pre-VRA nonwhite registration rate of 40 percent made it the fourth highest in the South. Nonetheless, the state had some problem areas. The 1960 census identified five counties in eastern Arkansas in which a majority of the adult population was nonwhite, though none of the counties even approached having a majority nonwhite registration. In each of the majority-black counties, most registered voters were white with a median of 69.1 percent. The median share of the adult nonwhite population registered to vote in these counties was 32.5 percent with a range from 13.8 percent in Crittenden to 52.6 percent in Chicot. In four of the counties—Crittenden, Lee, Phillips, and St. Francis—most adults had not registered prior to passage of the legislation. Therefore, had these counties used tests or devices as prerequisites to registration, they would have come under Section 5.

Arkansas once maintained its poll tax records by race, but it does not currently collect registration or turnout data by race. The 1980–2006 estimates developed by the Bureau of the Census provide the best figures on contemporary levels of participation (appendix B reports estimates of black and white adult registration and turnout rates). In most years the reported registration of blacks and whites has been quite similar. In all but four years the two figures have been within 5 percentage points. In 1984, 1986, 1988, 2000, and 2002, the difference in racial registration rates did not exceed 1 percentage point. The largest differences came in two midterm election years. In 1990, white registration was 11.8 percentage points above that for blacks, and in 1998 white registration exceeded black registration by 14.1 percentage points.[8] In 1984, 1988, 1996, and 2000, African American registration slightly exceeded white registration. Throughout the quarter century covered by the data, overall registration rates in Arkansas exceed the 50 percent threshold that triggered coverage by Section 5 in three different versions of the Voting Rights Act.

Beginning with 1998, the Census Bureau has provided estimates of white participation that exclude Hispanics. After making that adjustment, white non-Hispanics registered at a rate slightly higher than did blacks in 2000. For the other four years the exclusion of Hispanics results in an increased disparity between white and black registration with the difference reaching 10.9 points in 2006.

In eight years, black registration in Arkansas exceeded that in the non-South although typically the differences were not large. The greatest advantage for Arkansas African Americans comes in 2002 when 62 percent of black Arkansans were registered compared with 57 percent in the non-South. On the other hand, the greatest disparity in favor of the non-southern African Americans occurs in 1990 when 58.4 percent of blacks outside the South reported registering compared with the questionable estimate of 50.8 percent in Arkansas.

The bottom of the registration table presents median figures for the seven southern states initially covered by the 1965 Voting Rights Act.[9] Initially, African Americans in Arkansas registered to vote at rates higher than the median figure for the covered jurisdictions. In 1982 and 1984, the black registration rate in Arkansas ran almost 10 percentage points higher than the median state rate. Even in 1988, the Arkansas figure was 4.2 points higher. Beginning with 1990, the median figure exceeds that in Arkansas except in 1996, when the Arkansas registration rate is less than 1 percentage point above that of the median state. The figure for the median state substantially exceeds that for Arkansas in the two years when the Arkansas estimate is suspect. In 1990, the median figure is 11 points above the Arkansas registration rate, and in 1998 the median figure is more than 16 points higher than in Arkansas. In each of the two most recent presidential years included in the table, the median figure for the covered jurisdictions is approximately 8 percentage points above that for Arkansas, and in 2006 Arkansas is almost 10 points below the median. Thus, while the African American registration rates in Arkansas are fairly close to those for whites in the state and to those for blacks living in the non-South, the median rate of registration for African Americans in southern states initially made subject to Section 5 regularly outpaces the Arkansas figures over the last decade and a half.

Census Bureau estimates for turnout indicate that in every year except 2000, African American turnout in Arkansas is less than that of the state's white voters. The largest disparities come in 1990, 1992, and 1998, when the turnout for whites is approximately 14 percentage points higher than for blacks. The participation rates converge in 1996, 2000, and 2002, when differences are less than 3.5 percentage points. However, in 2004 just under half of the African American adults voted compared with almost 59 percent of the whites, and in 2006 a 12-point difference exists. In 2000, the one year when black turnout exceeded white turnout, blacks still voted at higher rates than whites when Hispanics are removed from the estimates for whites. For the other four years, the disparity between white and black participation increases once Hispanics are excluded. In 2004, the difference reaches 11.4 percentage points, then grows to almost 15 points in 2006.

The familiar seesaw pattern with higher participation rates in presidential than midterm years prevails for both races. Although the rate at which African Americans turn out sometimes slips below 50 percent in presidential years, the overall turnout rate for the state in presidential elections always exceeds the 50 percent threshold that was the cut point for coverage by the 1965, 1970, and 1975 Voting Rights Acts.

When African American turnout in Arkansas is compared with that of the non-South, blacks outside the South always report voting at higher rates than those in Arkansas except in 2002. Frequently the differences are small and in four years are less than 1 percentage point. The most pronounced difference comes in 1998; 40.4 percent of nonsouthern blacks compared with 31.1 percent of black Arkansans voted. In 2002, the one year in which higher proportions of blacks in Arkansas than in the non-South went to the polls, the difference is almost 5 percentage points.

A final comparison possible using figures presented in appendix B is between Arkansas and the median state among the seven covered by the preclearance provision included in the 1965 Voting Rights Act. In four of the seven midterm elections, the black turnout rate in Arkansas is greater than the median for the seven states. In three of those years differences were small, but in 1982, Arkansas blacks voted at a rate almost 9 percentage points higher than the median figure. On the other hand, in two of the three midterm elections in which black turnout was greater in the median state than in Arkansas, differences were sizable. In 1990, the difference was 10 percentage points, and in 1998, it exceeded 9 percentage points.

Arkansas African Americans also turned out at higher rates than the median state figure in the presidential elections of the 1980s. However, in the four most recent presidential elections through 2006, the median state figure exceeds that for Arkansas except in 1996 when the two are very similar. The greatest differences came in 1992 and 2004, when blacks turned out in the median state at rates approximately 12 percentage points higher than in Arkansas. The recent trend, particularly in presidential elections, is for black turnout to be greater in the median state than in Arkansas. The tendency for the participation rate in the median state to exceed that in Arkansas also extends to the white electorate, where the turnout figure for the median state has been higher than in Arkansas in every presidential election beginning with 1988. In contrast, in midterm elections, the white vote in Arkansas has exceeded the median figure in every year accept 1994.

AFRICAN AMERICAN OFFICE HOLDING

At the time of the first survey of black elected officials in 1969, Arkansas had fifty-five. Two-thirds of these served on school boards and most of the remainder held municipal offices. None served as a county official. Across the next thirty-two years, the number of African Americans holding office in Arkansas increased more than ninefold and exceeded five hundred by the beginning of the twenty-first century (see figure 11.1). This is the most dramatic gain in minority office holding in the Rim South. Most officeholders since the mid-1980s have served in cities. The large number of black municipal officials in Arkansas is attributable to the numerous

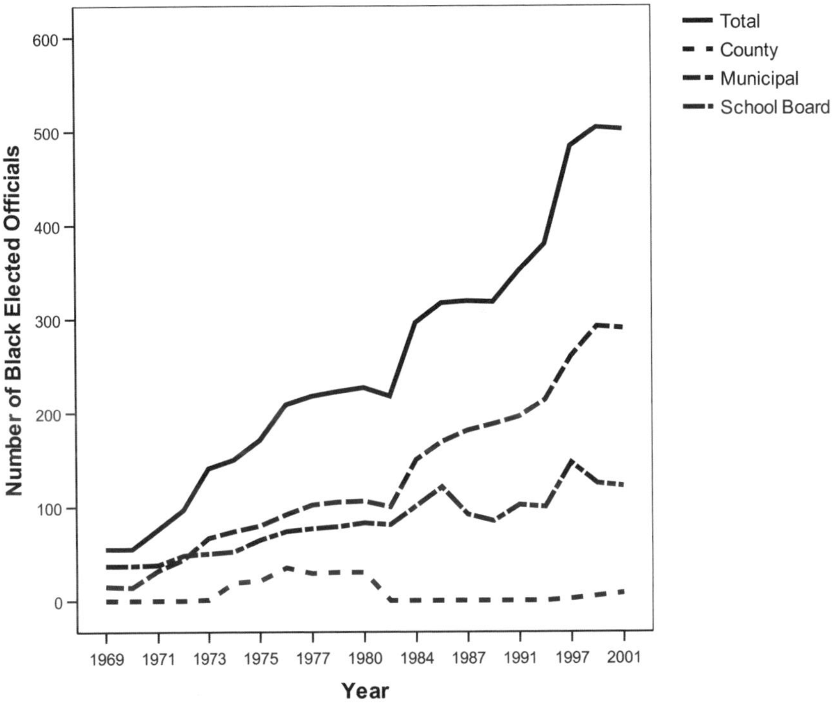

Figure 11.1. Black elected officials in Arkansas, 1969–2001. *Source:* Various volumes of the *National Roster of Black Elected Officials* (Washington, D.C.: Joint Center for Political and Economic Studies).

small towns that dot the state. In the most recent enumeration, approximately one-fourth of the black officeholders in Arkansas sat on school boards. Figure 11.1 shows approximately two dozen blacks in county offices during the latter part of the 1970s and then the number drops abruptly to zero.

African Americans in Congress

Arkansas is the only southern state not to have sent an African American to Congress since the onset of the Civil Rights Movement. With a black population of less than 20 percent and only four congressional districts, it would be difficult to create a majority-black district. In the early 1990s when the Department of Justice was pushing Section 5 jurisdictions to maximize the number of majority-minority districts, a black Arkansas legislator sought to fashion a black-influence congressional district (i.e., a district in which the black vote is less than the majority but could be determinative of outcomes). Rep. Ben McGee devised a version of the 4th District in which blacks constituted 42 percent of the population.[10] To achieve this concentration, the McGee plan included 87 percent of all Arkansas African Americans. The plan drew support from Republicans but was rejected by white Democrats who feared that concentrating blacks in a single congressional district would make two other districts more likely to elect Republicans.

Having a majority African American population is no longer a requirement for electing blacks to public office in much of the South. In a district in which blacks constituted more than 40 percent of the voting-age population (VAP), a cohesive black electorate is potentially positioned to determine the Democratic nominee. However, neither the Department of Justice in Section 5 states nor the courts have mandated the creation of black-influence districts. Republicans, who have held Arkansas's 3rd District in the northwest corner of the state for four decades, supported the effort to concentrate blacks in a single congressional district with the hope that by removing those loyal Democrats from neighboring districts, the GOP might be better positioned to win one or two of the remaining districts.

The 4th District, which spreads across the southern half of the state, has the greatest black concentration. Figures from the 2000 census show the district to be just under one-quarter African American. It currently is represented by a Democrat who defeated the incumbent Republican in 2000. In 1998, an African American, Judy Smith, ran in the 4th District, which at that time was 26.6 percent black. Smith managed 42 percent of the vote, a stronger showing than the Democratic nominee of 1996 but weaker than the 1994 challenger to the Republican incumbent. Smith gave up a seat in the legislature to make the run.

African Americans in the State Legislature

The first African Americans in modern times to enter the Arkansas General Assembly did so following the redistricting necessitated by the 1970s

Table 11.1. Racial makeup of the Arkansas General Assembly, 1965–2007

	Senate	% Black in Senate	House	% Black in House
1965	0	0.0	0	0.0
1967	0	0.0	0	0.0
1969	0	0.0	0	0.0
1971	0	0.0	0	0.0
1973	1	2.9	3	3.0
1975	1	2.9	3	3.0
1977	1	2.9	3	3.0
1979	1	2.9	3	3.0
1981	1	2.9	4	4.0
1983	1	2.9	4	4.0
1985	1	2.9	4	4.0
1987	1	2.9	4	4.0
1989	1	2.9	5	5.0
1991	3	8.6	9	9.0
1993	3	8.6	10	10.0
1995	3	8.6	10	10.0
1997	3	8.6	10	10.0
1999	3	8.6	12	12.0
2001	3	8.6	13	13.0
2003	3	8.6	13	13.0
2005	3	8.6	13	13.0
2007	4	11.4	11	11.0

Source: Data compiled by the authors.

census. In 1973, blacks held one of thirty-five senate seats and three seats in the one hundred–member house as Arkansas became the last southern state to desegregate its legislature. Since Arkansas is not subject to Section 5, the federal government was not in a position to require that it redraw its districts in order to enhance the likelihood of electing minority legislators. The senate did not gain an additional African American senator until a redistricting prior to the 1990 election prompted by a voting-rights suit brought under Section 2. This redistricting carried out at the very end of the 1980s, which relied upon census data almost ten years old, resulted in blacks winning three senate districts. As table 11.1 shows, as of 2006 Arkansas continued to have three African American senators.

In the house, the number of African American members grew slightly until the 1989 court-ordered redistricting that drew three majority-black senate districts and thirteen in the house. With the new districts of that plan, the number of black representatives jumped from five to nine. A tenth black representative won with another new plan, this one based upon the 1990 census. Over the last dozen years, the number of African American house members has increased gradually and currently stands at eleven. With 11 percent of the house membership, Arkansas blacks hold about four fewer seats than their share of the citizen voting-age population, which the Census Bureau estimated to be 14.8 percent African American in 2006.

Only slowly have African Americans gained influence in the Arkansas legislature. One handicap has been their small numbers. The other obstacle until recently was the low level of turnover. A small clique of senior white males controlled much of the decision making within the legislature in this state where turnover was the fourth lowest in the nation.[11] After two decades in the senate, its first black member, Jerry Jewell, achieved the symbolic position of president pro tempore. Through the end of the twentieth century, blacks never held more than one committee chair in either chamber.[12]

The small numbers of African Americans and the low turnover has also conspired to mean that the votes of the Black Caucus members have rarely been decisive. Parry and Miller suggest that African Americans can sometimes block or slow down legislation even if they can rarely shape it to meet their preferences.[13] Another obstacle for African Americans has been the lack of success of Republicans winning legislative seats. Republicans have never held more than thirty of the one hundred house seats or more than eight of the thirty-five senate seats. In a legislature that remains so overwhelmingly Democratic, opportunities for the Black Caucus to act as the balance of power have been rare.

While blacks have not often been in a position to determine the outcome of legislation in the Arkansas General Assembly, they have concentrated their numbers on committees especially relevant to African Americans. Research conducted by Kerry Haynie shows that in both 1979 and 1989, black legislators held seats on committees where the subject matter had great significance for African Americans and black legislators tended to be overrepresented on these committees.[14]

Haynie draws on the concept of incorporation to assess the potential influence that black legislators can wield in a legislative chamber.[15] Since Democrats retain control of the Arkansas legislature, its black members have the opportunity to be part of the governing coalition. As their numbers, seniority, and the prestige of their committee assignments have increased, so has their level of political incorporation or influence. Haynie calculates that black political incorporation, or influence, in the state house almost doubled between 1979 and 1989.[16]

Almost a generation has passed since Haynie's most recent observation in 1989. In 2006, all three black senators chaired a committee, although these were not committees that were particularly prestigious or that held especially great promise for black constituents. In the house, five members chaired committees, and two of these, education and public health, were ones that Haynie identified as being especially important for African Americans. Another member chaired a task force on the study of the homeless. Although none of Arkansas's black legislators chaired a prestige committee, it appears likely that had Haynie recalculated his incorporation score for the mid-2000s, he would have found substantial increase over his 1989 calculation.

Arkansas is one of the few southern states to impose term limits.[17] Restricting the tenure of legislators has already flushed from the system the old white men who dominated it for so long. Eliminating the extraordinary influence that some senior white members had accrued has the potential to boost Haynie's political incorporation score since blacks represent safe Democratic districts where they can expect to advance quickly in seniority in a system that now truncates seniority.[18]

Following the 2000 census, then-governor Mike Huckabee (R) proposed a redistricting plan to increase the number of majority-black districts to fifteen in the house and five in the senate.[19] Leading Democrats opposed this Republican plan, which might well have also increased the number of Republican legislators by making districts adjoining the new majority-black ones whiter and thus more likely to vote for the GOP. With Democrats dominating the legislature and the acquiescence of the Black Caucus, redistricting took a more modest approach and maintained the number of majority-black house districts at thirteen while adding a fourth majority-black senate district. The decision by the Arkansas Black

Caucus not to push for more seats likely to elect African Americans and instead to concentrate on promoting the fortunes of the Democratic Party parallels what was happening in some other southern states at the time, as described in the Georgia chapter (chapter 3).

African Americans in Statewide Office

Arkansas has not elected an African American to a statewide constitutional office. African American justices have served on its supreme court, chosen through nonpartisan elections. All of the African American justices were initially appointed; no black justice has been initially elected to the court without the advantage of already holding the seat. No African American justices were serving on the supreme court as of 2008.

In 2002, an African American ignored the odds and challenged Lieutenant Governor Winthrop Rockefeller. While Democrats did reasonably well that year, taking the U.S. Senate seat away from one-termer Tim Hutchinson and holding on to the slate of constitutional officers, both the Republican governor and lieutenant governor proved invulnerable against Democratic challengers.

Table 11.2 reports the results of statewide contests in Arkansas for 2002 and 2006. The only Republicans to win were the incumbent governor and lieutenant governor in 2002. The performance turned in by the one African American statewide candidate—Ron Sheffield, who sought to become lieutenant governor—was the weakest of the seven Democrats competing. Sheffield managed only 40 percent of the vote, 7 points behind the unsuccessful Democratic nominee for governor. Sheffield's poor showing is not necessarily a commentary on race relations in Arkansas. Four of the Democratic nominees had previously held statewide office, and one of these, Mark Pryor, is the son of a popular former senator and governor. Thus Sheffield had less name recognition going in to the contest than most of the others on the Democratic ticket. That combined with running against a popular incumbent contributed to Sheffield's poor performance. Democrats subsequently ran the table of statewide offices in 2006.

Not surprisingly, Barack Obama had one of his weakest performances in the 2008 Democratic presidential sweepstakes in the home of his chief rival. Hillary Clinton made her strongest showing in the state in which

TABLE 11.2. Democratic vote share in Arkansas statewide elections, 2002 and 2006

	2002			2006		
	Candidate	Vote	%	Candidate	Vote	%
Senator	Pryor	433,306	53.9			
Governor	Fisher	378,250	47.0	Beebe	430,765	55.6
Lt. Governor	Sheffield	318,592	40.0	Halter	437,490	57.4
Sec'y of State	Daniels	492,621	62.1	Daniels	468,548	61.6
Treasurer	Wingfield	445,639	57.5	Shoffner	450,450	59.7
Auditor	Wood	442,349	57.7			
Land Comm.	Wilcox	445,933	58.6			
Att'y General				McDaniel	443,476	58.5

Source: Arkansas Secretary of State, accessed at www.arelections.org/results/33/cand_summary.html.

she had been first lady as she beat Obama 70 to 26 percent. The Illinois senator ran relatively poorly among black voters; the exit polls showed him attracting 74 percent of those votes. The vote in Arkansas was strongly structured by race as 80 percent of the whites supported Clinton.

RACIAL VOTING PATTERNS

Regression estimates of voter preferences in U.S. House races held in presidential years do not reveal extensive racially polarized voting in Arkansas. White and black preferences reported in table 11.3 differ in less than half (three of eight) of the elections for which estimates for both races could be derived. In four contests, white and black majorities lined up behind the Democratic candidate, and in another contest, the African American vote split evenly between the two candidates.

Three estimates suggest that most blacks preferred the Republican candidate. In one instance it is in a district with a GOP incumbent, and the other times it was in a part of Arkansas where blacks had supported Republican Winthrop Rockefeller's gubernatorial campaigns. It is estimated that in House District 2 in 1996 and 2000 the Democratic incumbent failed to attract the bulk of the black vote and won reelection based on white support.[20] All six Democrats who commanded majority support from whites were incumbents.

TABLE 11.3. Estimates of white and black voter support for Democrats in contested Arkansas congressional elections, 1996, 2000, 2004

	Democratic candidate	White	Black	Dem. win?
1996				
Congressional 1	Berry*	51.7	81.8	Yes
Congressional 2	Snyder*	51.6	45.8	Yes
Congressional 3	Henry**	40.6	—	No
Congressional 4	Tolliver**	34.6	46.6	No
2000				
Congressional 1	Berry*	56.9	99.7	Yes
Congressional 2	Snyder*	59.0	48.6	Yes
Congressional 4	Ross**	46.3	87.7	Yes
2004				
Congressional 1	Berry*	64.6	>100.0	Yes
Congressional 2	Snyder*	57.0	50.0	Yes
Congressional 3	Judy**	43.7	—	No

Source: Ecological regression estimates.

*Democratic incumbent candidate.

**Republican incumbent candidate.

The most recent state elections in Arkansas do not reveal racial polarization of the constitutional offices. Regression estimates of white and black voter support for Democrats indicate majority support among both racial groups for Democratic candidates. The black vote is overwhelmingly Democratic, with estimates of support ranging from 80 percent to 100 percent among African Americans, while white voters demonstrated between 53 percent and 84 percent support for Democrats.[21] White support for Republicans was strongest at the top of the ticket and generally fell off down the ballot. None of these contests involved black Democrats.

Arkansas exit polls since 1996 reproduced in table 11.4 reveal racial differences in six of seven recent contests. The African American vote in Arkansas is less cohesive than frequently observed elsewhere—it reaches 90 percent only three times over the course of the data, which includes two presidential elections. In the 1998 gubernatorial election the black vote splits almost evenly with a bare majority supporting the Democratic nominee, Bill Bristow. Governor Huckabee elicited greater support

TABLE 11.4. Black and white voter support for Democratic candidates in Arkansas, 1996–2004

	Contest	Black %	White %
1996	President*	90	49+
	U.S. Senate*	79	43
1998	Governor**	52	38
	U.S. Senate**	73	53
2000	President	84	41
2004	President**	94	36
	U.S. Senate**	96	49

Source: Voter News Service (VNS) exit polls, various years.

*Democratic incumbent candidate.

**Republican incumbent candidate.

+Bill Clinton won a plurality of the white vote as whites gave Bob Dole 41 percent of their vote with 9 percent going to Ross Perot.

among black voters than most Republicans because of his background as a minister.[22] Most whites vote Republican, although in 1998, 53 percent of them helped send Blanche Lincoln to the U.S. Senate. Two years earlier, native son Bill Clinton won a plurality of the white vote. In 2004 when Lincoln won reelection, the exit poll estimates that she took 49 percent of the white vote, although given the error term associated with the poll, it is possible that she was the choice of most white voters. Thus, it could be that black and white preferences differed on as few as three of the seven contests if the actual share of the black vote for Bristow was less than 50 percent and the actual white vote gave Lincoln a majority in 2004.

Democrats did best among whites in the 1996 presidential election and the 1998 and 2004 Senate elections while whites split their support about equally between the parties. Democrats performed worst among whites in the 1998 gubernatorial campaign and the 2004 presidential campaign, when they secured less than 40 percent of white-voter support.

CONCLUSION

African Americans in Arkansas register at rates similar to whites in the state although at lower rates than blacks in Section 5 states. African

American turnout typically trails that for white Arkansans, blacks in the non-South, and, over the last decade, blacks in the Section 5 South. Black office holding increased substantially over the last three decades and especially since 1993, but the number of black legislators has increased little in either chamber since the early 1990s. A brief flurry of black county office holding in the 1970s has been followed by the disappearance of blacks from county office for more than twenty years. Blacks have not succeeded in winning congressional and statewide offices, though Democrats continue to be highly competitive for the white vote, especially when running as incumbents. The failure of blacks to win congressional seats or statewide elections in Arkansas is, at least in part, a product of their small share of the state's population and the relatively small size of the congressional delegation and General Assembly membership.

PART IV

Conclusions

CHAPTER 12

A Comparative Analysis of the Impact of the Voting Rights Act in the South

The consensus is that the Voting Rights Act has been inordinately successful. Virtually no one denies that the political influence of African Americans is dramatically greater today than before the first version of the legislation became law in 1965. But how has progress compared across the South? Who has come furthest?

In order to answer these general questions and to place the detailed descriptions of the previous chapters into a comparative perspective, this section compares the progress of the southern states on several dimensions of voter participation and electoral outcomes. Data on voter registration, voter turnout, and office holding from the local to the national level are aggregated for each state across time, and compared to determine progress in assuring minority voter access and influence. Because African Americans are the predominant minority of interest to the original Voting Rights Act and the most substantial minority group across all eleven southern states, this section focuses on black voting-rights progress.

The raw numbers of political participants and public officials are reported, but in social science there is always more than raw numbers, because raw numbers without context mask important information. In this instance, raw numbers can be deceptive because of differences in the size of the black population and of collegial bodies across states. To develop a metric that will facilitate comparison across states, index numbers are created by dividing the percentage of African Americans in the category of interest by the black share of the state's voting-age population. An index number of 1.0 means that African Americans' share of offices equals their share of the state's voting-age population. Scores in excess of 1.0 indicate that African American officeholders exceed their share of the adult population, while scores below 1.0 indicate a smaller percentage of blacks in office than in the adult population.

It must be noted that states have no obligation to have minorities represented in public office at levels equal to their share of the potential electorate. Indeed, Section 2 of the Voting Rights Act as amended in 1982 includes an explicit proviso disclaiming any obligation to achieve racially proportional representation. That statute states that "nothing in this section establishes a right to have members of a protected class elected in numbers equal to their proportion of the population." Therefore, while we calculate index numbers based upon the concept of proportionality, this does not indicate an expectation that states will achieve proportionality. The degree to which a state approaches proportionality provides a baseline against which to compare performance. Students of electoral systems have long recognized that in single-member district electoral formats as are used in the United States, it is unlikely that a minority will achieve proportionality while the majority usually achieves a larger share of seats than of the electorate.[1] Indeed, the definition of electoral bias used to assess the fairness of a districting arrangement accepts that the majority party will get a share of the seats that exceeds its share of the votes. A system is judged to be free of bias if the bonus that goes to the majority party is roughly equal for either party should it achieve majority status.[2]

Readers may be troubled by inconsistency in the years from which the data used in this chapter come. Where possible, data reflect the 2004 elections. While Census Bureau registration and turnout for 2006 are discussed in the state chapters, the 2004 figures are used in this chapter because, as noted in more than one chapter, participation rates in presidential years exceed those in midterm elections. The differential is especially pronounced in states that choose state and county officials in odd-numbered years. Figures from 2008 would be desirable, but the Census Bureau estimates for that year may not become available until 2010.[3] Figures for local office holding come from the most recent survey done by the Joint Center for Political and Economic Studies, and that enumeration occurred in 2001. Data on African American presence in other offices come from 2005, the point at which individuals elected in 2004 took office.

The individual state chapters presented longitudinal figures on registration and turnout. Since the focus here is on relative rates of participation for blacks and whites, calculations are made using voting-age citizens within the group. Since noncitizens are ineligible to vote, the figures may differ slightly from those reported in appendix B. The white figures are for non-Hispanics.

PROGRESS IN VOTER PARTICIPATION

Throughout this volume we have directed the reader to important data created by the voting-rights legislation, namely the registration and turnout data that the director of the Bureau of the Census is required to collect through post-election surveys. From these surveys come the estimates of the share of voting-age population that registered or turned out to vote presented for each of the eleven southern states in appendix B. As of 2004, more than 60 percent of the adult population in each southern state had registered to vote. Although the trigger mechanism did not specify that a majority of the African American adults should be registered, by 2004, Census Bureau estimates are that most black adults had registered.

Some southern states have substantial numbers of recent immigrants, not all of whom are citizens, and therefore a share of their adult population is ineligible to register. If the registration rates are adjusted to exclude noncitizens, then the Census Bureau estimates for adult black registration range from 60.5 percent in Virginia to 76.2 percent in Mississippi. When the self-reported registration figures for 2004 are compared with the estimates for the early 1960s, prior to the adoption of the Voting Rights Act, it becomes clear that the relative standing of states has changed dramatically. Mississippi, which had the lowest incidence of black registration in the early 1960s, had the highest percentage by 2004. Alabama, which ranked second lowest only to Mississippi, is now second only to Mississippi at the other end of the scale. In contrast, Florida, which had the second-highest

TABLE 12.1. Voter registration

	African Americans								
	Pre-VRA %	Pre-VRA rank	Post-VRA %	Post-1965 VRA rank	2004 %	2004 Rank	White 2004 %	White 2004 rank	Black-white ratio
Alabama	19.3	9	51.6	9	73.2	2	75.3	3	0.97
Arkansas	40.4	4	62.8	3	63.9	10	69.4	9	0.92
Florida	51.2	2	63.6	2	65.1	9	73.0	6	0.89
Georgia	27.4	8	52.6	8	67.5	7	68.5	10	0.99
Louisiana	31.6	7	58.9	6	72.0	4	76.8	1	0.94
Mississippi	6.7	10	59.8	5	76.2	1	73.7	4	1.03
North Carolina	46.8	3	51.3	10	72.1	3	73.3	5	0.98
South Carolina	37.3	6	51.2	11	71.3	5	76.3	2	0.93
Tennessee	69.5	1	71.7	1	65.2	8	64.5	11	1.01
Texas	NA	NA	61.6	4	70.6	6	70.0	8	1.01
Virginia	38.3	5	55.6	7	60.5	11	72.4	7	0.84
Median	39.4		58.9		70.6		73.0		0.97

Sources: Pre– and post–Voting Rights Act figures come from U.S. Commission on Civil Rights, *Political Participation* (Washington, D.C.: U.S. Government Printing Office, 1968), 222–223; the 2004 figures are the percentage of the "black alone or in combination" citizen voting-age population who reported in the Census Bureau survey that they had registered. The white figure is for white non-Hispanic citizens.

rate of black registration in the early 1960s, ranked ninth in 2004. Tennessee, which had the highest percentage of black registrants prior to the Voting Rights Act, ranked eighth.[4]

The median figures at the bottom of table 12.1 provide a measure of change for the eleven-state region. Prior to the adoption of the Voting Rights Act, the median proportion of blacks who had registered stood at 39.4 percent. Just a couple of years after the legislation had been adopted, the median figure had increased to 58.9 percent. In the 2004 Census Bureau survey, the median is 70.6 percent.

Table 12.1 also provides figures on the proportion of the white non-Hispanic citizen voting-age population registered to vote in 2004. The range here is from a low of 64.5 percent in Tennessee up to 76.8 percent in Louisiana. The rank ordering suggests that some states generally have larger shares of their voting-age citizens registered, regardless of race, while in other states the tendency to register is lower. For example,

Alabama had the second-highest percentage of its African Americans registered and ranked third highest for white registrants. Mississippi and Louisiana also do relatively well for both races in terms of registration. On the other hand, Arkansas and Tennessee, the two states not subject to Section 5 of the Voting Rights Act, have relatively small shares of their adult citizens registered regardless of race.[5] Thus the rate of registration may be partially influenced by the ease of registering within a state, outreach efforts, or some other phenomenon beyond the scope of this book.

One way in which to control for differences in registration at the state level is to compare the black rate to the white rate within an individual state by calculating the ratio of black-to-white registration. The figures for that calculation in 2004 appear in the farthest right column in table 12.1. If blacks register at higher rates than whites, then the figure will exceed 1.0 as reported for Mississippi, Tennessee, and Texas. At the other extreme, in Virginia the ratio of black-to-white registration is .84 while in Florida it is .89. The median for the South is .97, indicating a slightly lower proportion of black than white registrants. Mississippi has the highest score, further evidence that the state once most resistant to black registration has now become one of the most open.

Table 12.2 reports on Census Bureau estimates of black and white turnout in the 2004 general election and the total population of the states. Since in addition to blacks and whites, states have Hispanic and Asian citizens, the total figure can actually reside at a number greater or lower than the turnout figures for blacks and whites. As with registration, the two states—Mississippi and Alabama—that most vigorously opposed black participation before enactment of the 1965 Voting Rights Act scored very well in 2004 in the share of their black voting-age population that reported casting ballots. Mississippi ranked first while Alabama placed third. The two states that have never been subject to the preclearance requirement, Arkansas and Tennessee, ranked eleventh and ninth respectively in black turnout. In Mississippi, two-thirds of the black voting-age population cast ballots. Black turnout exceeded 60 percent in three other states. A majority of the black adult citizens voted in every state except Arkansas, where only 49.2 percent went to the polls.

As with registration, turnout may vary by states as both blacks and whites are more likely to vote in some states than others. In seven states

TABLE 12.2. Estimates of voter turnout among citizens in 2004

	Black %	Rank	White %	Rank	Total %	Rank	Black-white ratio	Rank
Alabama	64	3	63.5	5	63.2	4	1.01	3
Arkansas	49.2	11	60.6	7	58.7	8	0.81	10
Florida	54.7	8	65.9	2	64.3	1	0.83	9
Georgia	57.5	7	57.8	9	56.8	10	0.99	5
Louisiana	62.7	4	65.4	3	64.2	2	0.96	6
Mississippi	66.8	1	60	8	61.6	6	1.11	1
North Carolina	64.6	2	61.3	6	61.4	7	1.05	2
South Carolina	59.7	5	65.1	4	63.3	3	0.92	8
Tennessee	52.4	9	55	11	54.6	11	0.95	7
Texas	57.7	6	57.6	10	57.1	9	1	4
Virginia	52.1	10	66.9	1	63	5	0.78	11

Source: Computed from Census Bureau estimates reported in "Voting and Registration of the Total Voting-Age Population, by Sex, Race and Hispanic Origin for States," November 2004.

the proportion of white voting-age citizens who went to the polls exceeds the proportion of blacks. However, in Georgia the difference is less than half a percentage point. In four states black turnout exceeded white turnout, and in Mississippi the difference is 6.8 percentage points. In Texas the difference is only a tenth of a percentage point. Excluding Texas and Georgia, where differences are trivial, white turnout exceeded black turnout in six states while in three states black turnout exceeded white turnout. The range for white turnout as reported in table 12.2 is from 55 percent in Tennessee to a high of 66.9 percent in Virginia.

There are stark differences in the rankings of states in terms of their black and white participation rates. Virginia ranked tenth in terms of black turnout but has the highest rate of white turnout. The other extreme, Mississippi, which had the highest rate of black turnout, ranked eighth in white turnout. Spearman's rho shows no relationship between the two rankings (rho = –.036).

Although there is little relationship between the turnout rates for blacks and whites when all eleven states are considered, in some states patterns are similar. Georgia, for instance, ranks seventh in terms of black turnout and ninth in terms of white turnout. Louisiana, South Carolina, and Tennessee are other states in which the overall ranking for black and white turnout is similar. To assess black turnout in relation to white turnout, a ratio has been computed and ranked, figures that are reported in the last two columns of table 12.2. As noted earlier, black turnout exceeds white turnout in Mississippi, North Carolina, and Alabama. The two races vote at roughly equal rates in Texas and Georgia. The lowest ratio occurs in Virginia, the only state in which black turnout is less than 80 percent of white turnout. The median for these eleven states is .96. Five of the states have ratios between .92 and 1.02. Thus, only in Mississippi is black turnout substantially higher than white turnout, while Florida, Arkansas, and Virginia are states in which black turnout is substantially less than the white participation rate.

The self-reported results in table 12.2 indicate that socioeconomic disparities that some scholars have identified as producing lower rates of participation among blacks than whites do not affect all states in the same manner.[6] Perhaps the differences revealed in table 12.2 stem from variations in get-out-the-vote efforts, local black civic organizations, and so forth as suggested by Tate and Wielhouwer.[7]

The trigger mechanism in various versions of the Voting Rights Act was whether most of the voting-age population in a state had voted. As reported in table 12.2, all southern states saw a majority of their adult citizens go to the polls in 2004. The lowest turnout rate occurred in Tennessee (54.6 percent), a state not subject to preclearance. Seven states had turnout rates above 60 percent; Florida led at 64.3 percent.

PROGRESS IN OFFICE HOLDING

Since passage of the initial Voting Rights Act, the numbers of African American elected officials in the South has grown from a few dozen to almost six thousand as of 2001. Mississippi led the nation with 892 black officeholders, followed by Alabama and Louisiana, each having more than seven hundred. Florida had the fewest African American officeholders with only 243. As table 12.3 shows, in terms of the share of all offices filled by African Americans, Mississippi and Alabama led with approximately 18 percent of their posts filled by blacks. In Louisiana and

TABLE 12.3. African American elected officials, 2001

	Number	%	Index
Alabama	756	17.5	**.709**
Arkansas	502	6.0	.394
Florida	243	4.6	.348
Georgia	611	9.3	.339
Louisiana	705	14.2	.469
Mississippi	892	18.0	.528
North Carolina	491	8.9	.427
South Carolina	534	14.5	.517
Tennessee	540	7.9	.526
Texas	460	1.7	.143
Virginia	246	7.9	.425

Source: Joint Center for Political and Economic Studies.

Note: **Bolded** entry ranks highest on black representativeness.

South Carolina, 14 percent of the officials were black. At the low end are the two states with the most substantial Hispanic populations. In Florida, blacks filled 4.6 percent of the offices while in Texas it was only 1.7 percent.

When the percentage of black officeholders in the state is divided by the black voting-age population, Alabama has the highest index number with the proportion of black officeholders just over 70 percent of the proportion black in the voting-age population. In Mississippi, Tennessee, and South Carolina, the index number exceeds .5. In Louisiana, North Carolina, and Virginia, the index number is greater than .4. Three other states have index numbers between .339 and .394. Texas has the lowest index number at .143. In no state do African Americans hold a share of public offices commensurate with their share of the voting-age population.

State and Legislative Elected Officials

Except in Georgia, few African Americans currently hold statewide offices in the South. Georgia far outstrips any other state with African Americans holding two constitutional offices, serving as attorney general and commissioner of labor. In 2005, a third African American held one of the five seats on the Public Service Commission. The state's Supreme Court had three black members and another three served on the Court of

Appeals, which is also elected statewide. Far behind Georgia comes Texas where the Supreme Court features two African Americans. Six other states each have one African American in a statewide position, while Alabama, Arkansas, and South Carolina have none. The presence of African Americans in statewide offices has varied over time. For a dozen years, the auditor of North Carolina was an African American, but he lost reelection in 2004. Florida once had a black commissioner of education, but he too lost a reelection bid.

All southern states except for Arkansas sent at least one African American to Congress in 2005. As shown in table 12.4, Alabama, Louisiana, Mississippi, South Carolina, and Virginia, among the states initially subject to Section 5 of the Voting Rights Act, each had one African American member of Congress. North Carolina had two and Georgia had four. Texas, which became subject to Section 5 in 1975, had three black representatives, as did Florida, the other southern state impacted by the 1975 Voting Rights Act. Tennessee, which has never had to comply with Section 5, had a black member of Congress in 2005, although, as detailed in the Tennessee chapter, a white won the seat in 2006.

Georgia is the only southern state in which the proportion of black members in its congressional delegation (30.8 percent) exceeds the proportion of black citizens in the voting-age population. While only Georgia has an index number greater than one, in Texas, North Carolina, Mississippi, and Tennessee, African Americans' proportion of the congressional delegation is approximately three-fourths their share of the adult population. In South Carolina, Alabama, and Florida, the index number is between .5 and .6. Of the states with blacks in their congressional delegations, Virginia and Louisiana are at the bottom with scores just under .5.

As of 2005, African Americans hold more than 20 percent of the state legislative seats in four states. Their highest proportion, 27 percent, comes in Mississippi. The other states having more than 20 percent black legislators are Alabama at 25 percent, Louisiana at 22 percent, and Georgia at 21 percent. Just below the 20 percent threshold is South Carolina at 19 percent. North Carolina and Florida have 15 percent black legislators. Among other states subject to Section 5 are Virginia at 11 percent and Texas at just below 9 percent. The two states not subject to Section 5, Arkansas and Tennessee, have approximately one black legislator in every eight lawmakers.

TABLE 12.4. African Americans in congressional, state, and local office

State	Members of Congress		State senators		State house		Supreme courts*	
	%	Index	%	Index	%	Index	%	Index
Alabama	14.3	0.579	22.9	0.927	25.7	1.04	0.0	0.0
Arkansas	0.0	0.0	8.6	0.562	13.0	0.85	0.0	0.0
Florida	7.5	0.563	17.5	**1.316**	15.0	**1.068**	14.3	1.245
Georgia	30.8	**1.12**	19.6	0.713	21.7	0.789	42.9	1.56
Louisiana	14.3	0.472	23.1	0.762	21.9	0.723	14.3	0.472
Mississippi	25.0	0.731	21.2	0.62	29.0	0.863	11.1	0.325
North Carolina	15.4	0.7404	14.0	0.673	15.8	0.76	14.3	0.688
South Carolina	16.7	0.596	17.4	0.621	20.2	0.721	0.0	0.0
Tennessee	11.1	0.74	9.1	0.607	15.2	1.013	25.0	1.667
Texas	9.4	0.79	6.5	0.546	9.3	0.782	22.2	**1.866**
Virginia	9.1	0.489	12.5	0.672	11.0	0.591	14.3	0.769

State	County commissioners**		Mayors**		City councilors**		School boards**	
	%	Index	%	Index	%	Index	%	Index
Alabama	24.2	**0.979**	10.6	0.427	24.2	**0.979**	10.6	0.427
Arkansas	0.0	0.0	6.6	0.434	0.0	0.0	6.6	0.434
Florida	6.7	0.503	3.6	0.269	6.7	0.503	3.6	0.269
Georgia	14.1	0.512	5.4	0.196	14.1	0.512	5.4	0.196
Louisiana	20.0	0.661	11.0	0.362	20.0	0.661	11.0	0.362
Mississippi	25.6	0.749	18.4	**0.539**	25.6	0.749	18.4	**0.539**
North Carolina	19.0	0.913	6.0	0.288	19.0	0.913	6.0	0.288
South Carolina	23.4	0.836	10.6	0.377	23.4	0.836	10.6	0.377
Tennessee	2.3	0.155	0.9	0.06	2.3	0.155	0.9	0.06
Texas	1.3	0.112	3.0	0.248	1.3	0.112	3.0	0.248
Virginia	9.4	0.505	2.2	0.117	9.4	0.505	2.2	0.117

Source: Data compiled by the authors and are for 2005 unless otherwise noted.

Note: **Bolded** entry ranks highest on black representativeness.

**Southern Political Report* (January 30, 2006), 1; for 2006.

**Joint Center for Political and Economic Studies; data are from 2001.

Focusing on the individual chambers, African Americans do better at winning seats in lower chambers where district populations are smaller. The smaller the population, the easier it is to design a district with a black concentration likely to elect an African American, all other things being equal. Across the eleven southern states, the median index number for state houses is .789 while the median senate figure is .672. As reported in table 12.4, Florida and Alabama had the highest house scores at about 1.05. Mississippi has an index number of .86 while the other Section 5 states, except for Virginia, have scores between .72 and .79. Virginia trails the other states with an index score of only .59. In Tennessee, blacks hold a slightly larger proportion of the seats in the lower chamber than their share of the voting-age population. Arkansas, the other state not subject to Section 5, also scores well in black representation in the state house with an index number of .85.

Florida and Alabama also have the highest senate scores. Florida ranks much higher than any other state at 1.316, making it the only state in which the black share of senate seats exceeds the black share in the voting-age population. Alabama ranked second with a score of .927, and Louisiana and Georgia are the only other two states with index scores above .7. Four of the remaining Section 5 states have scores between .62 and .68. Texas and its tiny senate, which makes the drawing of heavily black districts difficult, has the lowest score at .546. The scores for the two non-Section 5 states hover around .6.

Southern states use different methods for selecting the justices on their highest courts. In Alabama, Arkansas, Georgia, Louisiana, Mississippi, North Carolina, and Texas they are elected. In Louisiana justices are elected from districts while in the other states they are elected at large. Florida and Tennessee use a Missouri Plan under which the governor appoints justices who periodically must win a referendum to retain their seats. Virginia justices are also appointed by the governor when the legislature is not in session; if the legislature is in session when a vacancy occurs, then the lawmakers make the selection. In several other states, such as Georgia, Arkansas, and North Carolina, the governor can make interim appointments to the Supreme Court when vacancies occur. In these states the newly appointed justice must run in the next general election. South Carolina justices are selected by the legislature.

In two Section 5 states that elect judges, African Americans hold a larger share of the seats than their proportion of the voting-age population: Texas comes in at 1.866 and Georgia at 1.56 (see table 12.4).[8] The Missouri Plan states also do well. Florida scores 1.256 while Tennessee has an index score of 1.667. In the four other states that have black justices, the index scores range from a high of .769 in Virginia to a low of .325 in

Mississippi.[9] Alabama, South Carolina, and Arkansas had no African Americans serving on their courts of last resort as of 2005.

It has been suggested that minorities are more likely to achieve powerful positions when the selection is made via an appointment rather than a popular election. Moreover, studies of municipal politics have often concluded that blacks are more likely to be elected from districts than at large.[10] The high scores for the states that employ a Missouri Plan where the governor appoints all justices support the appointment hypothesis. Also in line with that hypothesis is Georgia's score. Although justices are elected in Georgia, the current African Americans serving on the two statewide courts were initially tapped by governors to fill interim vacancies. Contrary evidence comes from the states in which the legislature is most likely to name justices, with Virginia ranking fifth while South Carolina ties for tenth and had no black members on its highest court. After the rewrite of Section 2 in 1982, minorities seeking to have a districting plan implemented sued several states that elect judges statewide. Unlike at the municipal level where district elections often produce more black council members than at-large elections, Louisiana, with its district elections of justices, does worse than Texas, Georgia, and North Carolina where justices run statewide.

Texas's African American justices, like every Lone Star statewide officeholder, belong to the GOP. In Georgia, justice elections are nonpartisan, but the Republican governor named the newest African American justice to fill a vacancy. That does not necessarily mean that the justice is a Republican but governors typically fill court vacancies with supporters of their party.

Local Elected Officials

County governments have traditionally been the most important local governmental unit in the South. Southern states have large numbers of counties with Texas (254) and Georgia (159) having more than any other states. Most southern states have between 60 and 120 counties with South Carolina an outlier at the lower end with only 46.

Traditionally many counties elected their commission members at large. However, Section 2 was rewritten in the 1982 Voting Rights Act to encourage challenges to at-large elections if they resulted in minorities having less opportunity to elect their candidates of choice than Anglo voters. As a result, many counties with substantial minority populations incorporated at least some single-member districts. In the wake of those changes, the numbers of African American councilors increased as plaintiffs challenged jurisdictions where they believed a district could be created that would be heavily minority in voting-age population.[11]

According to the most recent enumeration conducted by the Joint Center for Political and Economic Studies in 2001, the results of which appear in table 12.4, the South had 678 African American commissioners. At the upper end, Louisiana had 131 such officials, which in that state are called police jurors, and Mississippi came in second with 105. At the other extreme, Arkansas had no black county commissioners, and in Texas there were only 17.

As table 12.4 shows, the proportion of all commission seats held by African Americans approaches one in four in Mississippi and Alabama. In North Carolina and Louisiana, approximately one-fifth of the commissioners are African Americans while in Georgia the ratio is one in seven. In the other states, fewer than one in ten commissioners is an African American.

In Alabama and North Carolina, African Americans come close to holding a share of commission seats equal to their share of the voting-age population. In South Carolina, the index number exceeds .8 while in Mississippi it approaches .75. At the lower end, in Texas where seventeen black county commissioners are spread across 254 counties, the index number is a lowly .112. The two states that have never been subject to Section 5 ranked last and ninth in their index numbers for county commissioners.

In 2001 the Joint Center for Political and Economic Studies identified 309 African American mayors serving in the South. The largest numbers came in Mississippi (54) and Alabama (46). Virginia had only 5 black mayors and Tennessee just three. Table 12.4 shows that in terms of the share of all municipal mayoral positions filled by African Americans, Mississippi led with 18.4 percent. The other states in which blacks filled at least a tenth of the mayorships in 2001 were Louisiana, Alabama, and South Carolina. In Tennessee, black mayors led fewer than 1 percent of all cities, while in Virginia it was only 2.2 percent. The index numbers show that blacks came closest to holding a proportional share of mayoral offices in Mississippi. But even in the Magnolia State, the proportion of black mayors is barely equal to half the black percentage in the voting-age population. Alabama and Arkansas were the only other states in which the index number exceeds .4. In two other states, the index number is greater than .3. The median value for an index number is .288. In Georgia, Virginia, and Tennessee, the index number is less than .2.

The relative representation of black mayors is substantially below that for county commissioners except in the two states with the lowest scores for county commissioners. Overall the index numbers for mayors are the lowest of any office considered. This may be at least partly attributable to the mayor being a single office within a community while the other positions considered here are collegial offices. Since the mayor's position is a single office filled citywide, it is impossible to create a majority-minority district that would elect a black. The majority in the electorate may be more reluctant to choose a minority for a single office than when the minority member will be part of a board that contains a number of members of the majority.

In 2001, as reported in table 12.4, almost 2,500 southern African Americans served on city councils. The greatest number of black council members, 421, served in Alabama, followed by Mississippi with 362. Most other states had between 200 and 300 black councilors with only Tennessee and Virginia having fewer than 75.

African Americans held more than a quarter of all city council positions in Mississippi and almost a fifth of the council seats in Alabama. In South Carolina, African Americans composed roughly one-sixth of all city councils, while in Louisiana and North Carolina just over 11 percent of the council members were African American in 2001.

Alabama has the highest index number at .807, followed by Mississippi at .756. Three other states have index numbers above .5, and the median value is Florida's .451. Virginia and Tennessee have index numbers below .3.

African Americans held more than 1,000 seats on local boards of education in 2001. The greatest number served in Louisiana, which had 161 and was closely followed by South Carolina with 157. Mississippi, Arkansas, and Georgia each had more than 100 African American school board members. The fewest blacks served in Tennessee and Florida, which had 27 and 16, respectively. Table 12.4 indicates that in four states, more than a fifth of all school board members were African Americans. Next are Georgia and Virginia, where approximately one-tenth of the board members are black. At the low end, blacks hold fewer than 3 percent of the school board seats in Tennessee and Texas.

In Alabama, African Americans hold a share of school board seats almost equal to their percentage of the voting-age population. In South Carolina the index number is greater than .8, and in Louisiana it is above .75. The only other states with index numbers above .5 are Mississippi and Virginia. The median value, .430, comes from North Carolina. The lowest index numbers, which fall below .2, are in Tennessee and Texas. Of states that typically make use of countywide school systems (Florida, Georgia, and Louisiana), two have relatively low index numbers and only Louisiana comes close to having blacks proportionally represented. However, having large numbers of school districts does not necessarily facilitate the election of blacks since Texas, which has the largest number of school districts, ranks last.

AN OVERALL RANKING ON VOTING AND OFFICE HOLDING

Forty years after passage of the Voting Rights Act, southern African Americans have made dramatic gains at both the mass and the elite levels. However, if the objective is proportional representation, that remains an elusive goal more often than not, as would be expected for a system that does not build proportionality into its electoral system. Proportionality has been more frequently achieved at the mass than the elite level. In 2004, blacks registered at higher rates than whites in three southern states and in four voted at higher rates. In all eleven states, blacks registered at rates at least 80 percent of whites, and in all states but Virginia turnout was at least 80 percent of the white rate. Of 110 measures of office holding considered (eleven states across ten dimensions of political participation and office holding), African Americans achieved proportional representation on ten and on another nine garnered index scores between .8 and .99.

Table 12.5 presents the rankings from the dozen criteria that have been reviewed in this chapter. The rankings are summed across categories to yield a total score, and the final column presents a composite ranking.

The differences in index numbers between states on some dimensions are at times small, so one should be careful not to make too much of a state's precise ranking. Therefore, it may make sense to focus on the clustering of states. Alabama and Mississippi emerge as states in which African Americans have been most successful politically. North Carolina stands alone in third place, then Georgia, Louisiana, and South Carolina clump together. Florida lands midway between that cluster and the next couplet, Tennessee and Texas. Virginia and Arkansas cluster together at the end.

A review of mass and elite participation indicates that the two states least hospitable to African American participation prior to passage of the Voting Rights Act in 1965 are now the very ones in which blacks face the fewest obstacles to equality. Across the twelve categories, Mississippi ranks first in black registration and turnout and also on the index number for black mayors. Alabama ranked first in terms of African American elected officials and three local collegial bodies—county commissions, city councils, and school boards. Mississippi ranked second in elected officials and city council members. On none of the dimensions does Mississippi place worse than eighth. Alabama, which scored second in terms of registration, state house members, and senators, fares very poorly in terms of African American representation on its Supreme Court and statewide offices.

Three other states have a first-place ranking on at least one dimension. Florida scores best in terms of black representation in both chambers of its legislature, while Georgia performs best in terms of African American representation in its congressional delegation and in statewide offices. Texas had the best score in African American representation on its Supreme Court.

At the other end of the scale, Arkansas has the lowest composite ranking. It rated last or next to last in terms of registration, turnout, and black representation among members of Congress, state senators, on its Supreme Court, among county commissioners, and in statewide offices. The state that most closely rivaled Arkansas for last place, Virginia, ranked last or next to last in registration, turnout, and black representation among state representatives and mayors.

On the composite ranking, the top six states were ones caught by the trigger mechanism in the initial Voting Rights Act. Florida and Texas, the two states brought in later, placed seventh and ninth respectively on the

TABLE 12.5. Summary of state rankings

	Registration	Turnout	Elected officials	Statewide	Members of Congress	State senators	State representatives	Supreme court	County commission	Mayors	City council	School board	Total score	Composite ranking
Alabama	2	3	1	10	7	2	2	10	1	3	1	1	43	1
Arkansas	10	10	8	10	11	10	5	10	11	2	4	7	98	11
Florida	9	9	9	6	8	1	1	4	8	7	6	9	77	7
Georgia	7	5	10	1	1	4	6	3	6	9	8	8	68	4
Louisiana	4	6	5	6	10	3	9	7	5	5	7	3	70	5
Mississippi	1	1	2	6	5	8	4	8	4	1	2	4	46	2
N. Carolina	3	2	6	6	3	5	8	6	2	6	5	6	58	3
S. Carolina	5	8	4	10	6	7	10	10	3	4	3	2	72	6
Tennessee	8	7	3	6	4	9	3	2	9	11	10	10	82	8
Texas	6	4	11	2	2	11	7	1	10	8	11	11	84	9
Virginia	11	11	7	6	9	6	11	5	7	10	9	5	97	10

composite scale. Arkansas and Tennessee, the states never required to comply with Section 5, ranked last and eighth respectively. Of the states covered by preclearance since 1965, Virginia has the poorest performance; it placed tenth on the composite scale.

There are, of course, many factors that may explain the ranking of the states in terms of openness to African American participation early in the twenty-first century. If one were to focus exclusively on the impact of the Voting Rights Act, one could make the case from these data that not only had the legislation had a tremendous impact, but that the earlier a state became subject to Section 5 the greater that impact. One could even look at the relatively poor rankings of Arkansas and Tennessee and suggest that had these two been made to comply with Section 5 they might now have better scores.

Although the size of the black population in each state was taken into consideration by computing index numbers, African Americans remain more likely to make headway politically when their numbers are larger. There is certainly not a strong one-to-one relationship since Alabama, the state that ranks highest in the composite ranking, places only fifth in terms of the black percentage in its population. Meanwhile, North Carolina ranks third on the composite ranking but sixth in terms of its black percentage. Although the relationship is not perfect, the Spearman's rho between the ranking of the states by their black percentage in the population in 2000 and the composite score is .682.[12] Thus it appears that African Americans tend to win a larger share of offices and to be most likely to participate politically in states in which their presence is greatest.

The rankings here do not indicate that having a substantial Latino population contributes to African American political success. Florida and Texas, the two states with the largest Latino concentrations, ranked in the lower half of the southern states. It has been suggested that having substantial Latino concentrations may contribute to the election of African Americans to the U.S. House of Representatives,[13] but that does not seem to be a factor across the wide range of other offices. It may be a factor in Texas's ranking second on the congressional index since none of its three districts that currently sends an African American to the House has a black majority while each is approximately one-third Latino. But for other districted offices, such as state senators, county commissioners, and school board members, Texas ranks at or near the bottom of the southern states. Thus it does not appear that black-Latino coalitions are uniting to elect African Americans to these collegial bodies. Since Florida's Cuban Americans in Miami tend to be Republicans, they are unlikely to elect African Americans. While members of the Latino population in other parts of the state such as Tampa and Osceloa County are generally Democrats, the impact of a coalition with blacks, if it exists, is not picked up in our data.

There may, of course, be a multitude of other factors that help account for the rankings displayed in individual tables and the composite ranking. Factors such as mobilization efforts, relative strength of the Democratic and Republican parties, leadership within the black community, fundraising, and other elements may all help explain why some states scored better than others.

While undoubtedly there is more that can be done to account for the patterns displayed, it is striking that Ross Barnett's Mississippi and George Wallace's Alabama, less than two generations after those noted opponents to racial progress sought to block the force of history, now have the best composite scores. Indeed, the Deep South states, where lack of racial progress resulted in the imposition of Section 5's preclearance requirement, fill five of the top six ranks on the composite index.

CHAPTER 13

Assessing the Voting Rights Act in Political Context

By guaranteeing minority voter access and facilitating the election of minority officeholders, especially African Americans, the permanent and emergency provisions of the Voting Rights Act have accomplished much. Recognition of the accomplishments of this legislation have spread beyond the United States. As part of an assessment of thirty-six democracies, Arend Lijphart asserts that "universal suffrage was not firmly established in the United States until the passage of the Voting Rights Act in 1965."[1] However, all of these gains occurred not in a vacuum, but in a dynamic political environment. In this setting, black political empowerment accompanied the emergence of the Republican Party as a viable alternative in the South. The implementation of the Voting Rights Act and its subsequent renewals and amendments have coincided with nothing less than a dramatic realignment of southern politics.[2] The one-party Democratic South, bastion of white supremacy and defender of states' rights, started to fall in the 1960s under the combined weight of economic, cultural, and racial pressures that altered both major parties. Four decades of realignment and four decades of implementing voting-rights policy in the South have witnessed heightened minority political participation accompanied by a wholesale movement of white voters to the Republican Party.

Others have detailed the role of race in the movement of southern whites to the GOP,[3] an event anticipated by shrewd politicians in both parties. A year before the VRA became law, Lyndon Johnson observed to Bill Moyers that by signing the 1964 Civil Rights Act, "I think we have just delivered the South to the Republican Party for a long time to come."[4] A similar assessment provided the basis for Richard Nixon's southern strategy.[5]

As a consequence of partisan realignment, the Democratic Party primary has ceased to be the decisive election for statewide offices in the South. As competition has shifted to the general election, party voting has acquired a racial structure. Black voters and Latinos, except for Cuban Americans, overwhelmingly support Democratic candidates, while most white voters favor Republicans. What varies across most states is the intensity of support for Republicans among the white electorate and the range of offices for which whites prefer Republicans.

THE RACE-PARTY-INCUMBENCY STRUCTURE OF SOUTHERN POLITICS

It is partisan realignment that impedes black political success above the local level. Throughout the South, when black candidates lose general elections, they typically lose because they run as Democrats and not because they are minority candidates.

As noted in previous chapters, two factors influence the extent of racial differences in southern voting preferences. Incumbency and candidate race have little impact on black voting preferences, which means that the success of Democratic nominees hinges on the candidates' appeal to whites. Incumbent Democrats attract more white votes than Democrats who are not incumbents. And while nonincumbent Democrats, especially those running statewide, struggle, black challengers often have less appeal for white voters than white challengers.

Democrats' ability to win white support varies across the region. At one extreme, whites have moved so massively to the GOP that even incumbency no longer saves Democrats. This became evident in the 1990s, when voters turned out a number of Democrats serving in Congress and state legislatures. Among positions elected statewide, Republicans held all offices in Texas in 2008; all but one in South Carolina; and twelve of fifteen in Georgia, where only Democratic incumbents survived the 2006 GOP surge. In these states, nonincumbent Democrats fare poorly regardless of their race or ethnicity. Only moderate to conservative Democratic incumbents managed to hold on to congressional seats in the face of the 1994 Gingrich revolution in South Carolina and Mississippi.

At the opposite end of the partisan continuum, in Arkansas and North Carolina, relatively large numbers of whites have joined with black voters to maintain Democratic dominance. In these states, Democrats have held on to the bulk of the statewide and congressional posts, and with some exceptions for the North Carolina house, Democrats have won majorities in the state legislatures.

Virginia offers yet another model. The state followed a pattern similar to Florida, Texas, and South Carolina with whites gradually shifting to the GOP. This enabled Republicans to score a series of statewide victories and later claim majorities in both legislative chambers. Recently, however, Democrats have staged a comeback, winning Virginia's last two gubernatorial and Senate races and regaining a majority in the state senate in 2007. Virginia, along with North Carolina, broke with decades of tradition and voted for Obama. Resurgent Democratic prospects in Virginia and the persistent Democratic strength in North Carolina stem, at least in part, from the in-migration of less conservative whites from outside the South. But even in these states, Democratic victories come despite most white voters favoring Republican nominees.

Louisiana, with its absence of strong party cues in initial primaries, demonstrates the powerful role of that cue in directing black voters toward homogeneity of preferences. In "open" first primary elections when multiple candidates run, the black electorate often fragments, creating instances where Republicans attract black support. Only one-on-one runoffs result in a consistent, homogenous black vote. The white electorate exhibits similar behavior, though it is the presence of a black Democrat on a runoff ballot that prompts the greatest white support for Republicans. Incumbents of both parties scramble the expected racial division of the electorate, and some Democratic incumbents still command white majorities in low-profile contests.

Partisan realignment has consequences not just for the electorate but also for minority officeholders. As more white politicians win office as Republicans, the ranks of Democratic legislators and party leaders, especially the most senior ones, become increasingly black. Movement of whites to the GOP gives black politicians increased institutional clout within state party organizations and in state and national legislatures. As documented in previous chapters, senior black legislators have accrued significant legislative leadership and committee positions, although when Republicans achieve majority status in a legislative chamber, black influence becomes marginalized.

CHALLENGES TO APPRAISING VOTING RIGHTS

In the summer of 2006 Congress renewed the Voting Rights Act for twenty-five more years. The reauthorization legislation extended coverage of the emergency provisions of the Act using the triggers adopted in 1965, 1970, and 1975. The legislation also overturned the Supreme Court change of the preclearance standard that created such controversy in the Georgia and Texas remapping efforts (discussed in chapters 3 and 8, respectively). While Congress resolved questions about whether the legislation should be extended and, if so, whether the triggers should be modified, several other controversies persist.

Time, Change, and Coverage

One issue confronting Congress was whether to adjust the trigger mechanisms included in earlier versions of the Act. Critics, led by southern Republicans, questioned the appropriateness of continuing to rely on participation data from 1964 to 1972 as the basis for requiring federal approval of changes relating to voting through 2030. Those urging change agreed that the unprecedented federal oversight of election activities was justified in 1965 as a temporary expedient method to correct a persistent injustice. As detailed in the previous chapters, by 1970 most African

Americans in Section 5 states had registered to vote, and for decades turnout in presidential elections in covered states has usually involved a majority of the adult citizens. The Norwood Amendment to the 2006 legislation, discussed in the introduction of this volume, would have changed the triggers for federal preclearance. In place of data from elections held decades ago, Norwood proposed relying on the three most recent presidential elections. Jurisdictions in which fewer than half the adult citizens had voted in any of the three most recent presidential elections would have to preclear proposed election changes until voters' participation rates exceeded 50 percent for three consecutive presidential elections. Had the new trigger been implemented, Section 5 coverage would have decreased substantially in Texas, Virginia, Louisiana, Alabama, and Mississippi, while most Georgia and South Carolina jurisdictions would have remained covered. Southern counties and independent cities picked up by the Norwood proposal appear in map 13.1, shaded in gray.

Opponents offered two critiques of Norwood. First, Norwood's trigger would remove coverage from jurisdictions that some voting-rights activists considered problematic in terms of compliance despite increased voter participation and a decline in Justice Department challenges. Application of the Norwood Amendment using turnout data from 2000 to 2004 would have released 340 counties, Alaska, and ten townships of New Hampshire from Section 5 (data for 1996 were not readily available for this analysis, so we rely on a more conservative estimate of exclusion under the Norwood Amendment standard).[6] Of the 340 counties exempted by the Norwood Amendment until such time as their turnout fell below 50 percent of the adult VAP, 43 are in Mississippi, 31 are in Alabama, and 58 are in Virginia, a 55 percent reduction in covered counties in these three states. Of sixty-four Louisiana parishes, fifty-eight would not get picked up. These four states account for more than half of the current Section 5 counties that would no longer be covered. An additional 118 counties come from Texas, though among major urban counties only Tarrant County (Fort Worth) met the Norwood turnout threshold to discontinue Section 5 oversight. In Dallas, Harris (Houston), El Paso, and Bexar (San Antonio) counties and most of the South Valley, Section 5 would continue in place. The excluded counties tend to be in sparsely populated west Texas. Twenty-two of 159 Georgia counties and nine of 46 South

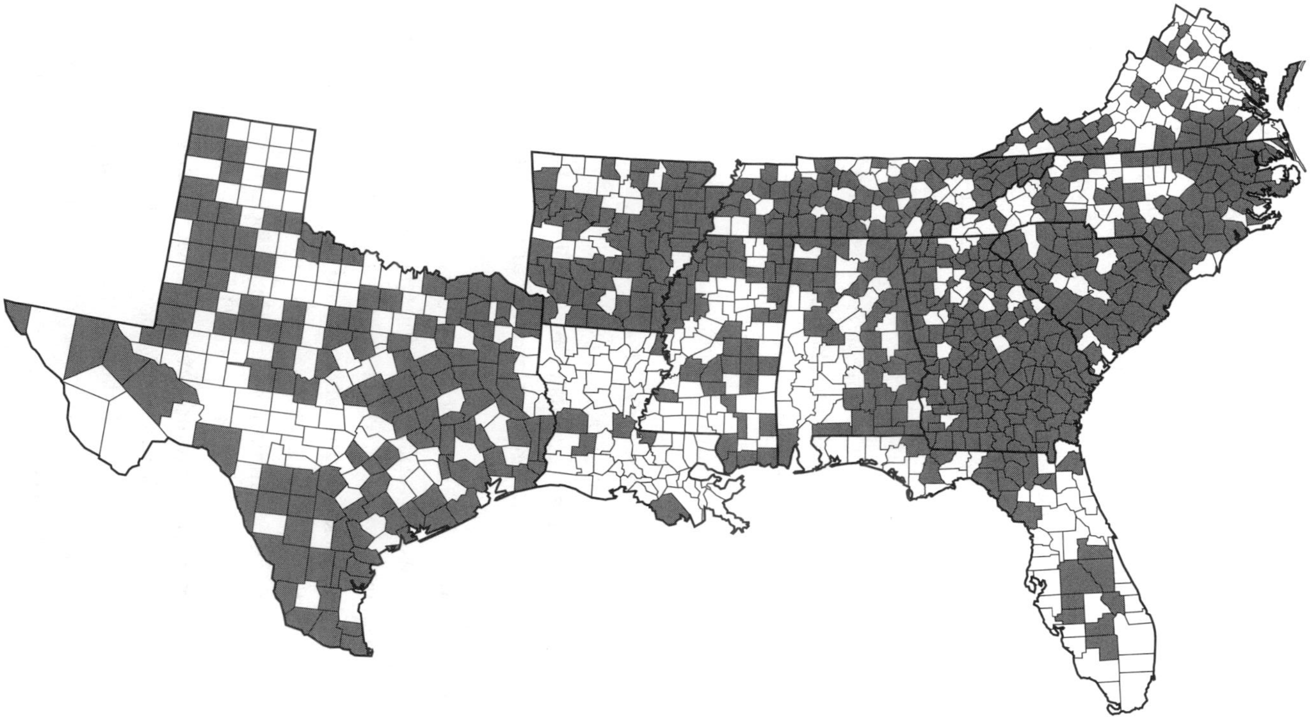

Map 13.1. Possible preclearance coverage using the Norwood Amendment trigger. *Source*: Data compiled by the authors; see also Charles S. Bullock III and Ronald Keith Gaddie, "Good Intentions and Bad Social Science Meet in the Renewal of the Voting Rights Act," *Georgetown Journal of Law & Public Policy* 5 (Winter 2007): 1–27.

Carolina counties are not picked up by the new trigger. Most of the Georgia dropouts are in the Atlanta urban doughnut or outside the Black Belt. Norwood would have extended Section 5 coverage in four of Alabama's 14 Black Belt counties and about half of the rural, majority-black counties of Mississippi. The Norwood Amendment would have continued coverage of 524 Section 5 counties.

The second concern about Norwood focused on the potential expansion of coverage to new jurisdictions. An examination of turnout data from 2000 to 2004 shows how the Norwood Amendment might expand coverage. Norwood's trigger would have imposed Section 5 on 486 counties not previously covered. Of these, 57 are in states already covered in part by Section 5: 12 in California, 18 in Florida, 5 in Michigan, 16 in North Carolina, and 6 in New York State. Another 121 are in Arkansas and Tennessee. The Border States of Kentucky, Missouri, Oklahoma, and West Virginia account for another 155 counties, including many rural Appalachian counties or, in the case of Oklahoma, counties with sizable American Indian populations. In sum, 334 new counties come from former Confederate or Border South states or from current Section 5 states.

Another 21 counties come from New Mexico, where a state court in 2001 and 2002 accepted the presence of racially polarized voting in the southern part of the state and in the areas populated by Navajo and Jicarilla Apache.[7] Of the remaining 131 new, covered counties, 67 are in Indiana and Pennsylvania, where population loss since the census might account for low voting rates. This leaves 64 counties scattered over sixteen states, including very populous counties like rapidly growing Clark County, Nevada (Las Vegas), but also sparsely populated places such as Glacier County, Montana, the home of the Blackfeet Indian Nation and about fourteen thousand residents. Many of the counties that are picked up in the new states with few covered counties host Indian reservations, including counties in Nebraska, Michigan, Idaho, Montana, North Dakota, and Oregon.

The Norwood Amendment would have acknowledged two uncomfortable political truths: the application of Section 5 worked in the South to such an extent that it eradicated the facially neutral legislative rationale that triggered emergency national government preemption of state authority; and beyond the South, the problem of declining participation is growing and this declining participation is evident in nonsouthern areas populated with minorities who have historic concerns about voting rights.

There is a problem with the Norwood Amendment that might have undermined its constitutionality. The original Section 4 trigger and its renewal through subsequent amendments incorporated the historic use of a test or device as a qualification, such as literacy and understanding tests or requirements for English-only ballots. By not incorporating the historic use of tests or devices into the trigger design, the implicit causal factor associated with these now-illegal devices would be absent when determining inclusion, thereby lowering the evidentiary standard for tripping coverage under the emergency preclearance provision.

NAMUDNO: *Warning Shot or Dodging a Bullet?*

A case decided just before this volume appeared in print approached the extension of the extraordinary requirements for preclearance from another perspective. In 2009 the U.S. Supreme Court decided *North Austin Municipal Utility District Number One [NAMUDNO] v. Mukasey,* (later restyled *NAMUDNO v. Holder*) in which a small utility district in Travis County, Texas, sought bailout and was denied.[8] The 1982 extension of the Voting Rights Act supposedly made it easier for jurisdictions to escape Section 5, but in reality very few have exited coverage. The jurisdiction must prove that it has acted (and will continue to act) in good faith in order to reclaim control of its election laws. As of 2008, only seventeen jurisdictions (all in Virginia) had bailed out. *NAMUDNO* focused on two questions, one statutory, the other constitutional. The statutory issue relates to a technical matter: what is a "jurisdiction" under the Voting Rights Act? The constitutional question involves fundamental issues of federalism—specifically the preemption of state authority by the national government; and the scope of evidence and timeliness of wrongdoing necessary to allow the Congress to enforce the Fifteenth Amendment.

Three-judge panels of the D.C. district court hear bailout requests. To bail out from under Section 5 coverage, a jurisdiction must meet many stringent criteria:

> It must show that during the previous 10 years: (A) no "test or device has been used within such State or political subdivision for the purpose or with the effect of denying or abridging the right to vote on account of race or color"; (B) "no final judgment of any court of the United States . . . has determined that denials or abridgments of the right to vote on account of race or color have occurred anywhere in the territory of" the covered jurisdiction; (C) "no Federal examiners or observers . . . have been assigned to" the covered jurisdiction; (D) the covered jurisdiction has fully complied with §5; and (E) "the Attorney General has not interposed any objection (that has not been overturned by a final judgment of a court) and no declaratory judgment has been denied under [§5]" . . . the jurisdiction also has the burden of presenting "evidence of minority participation, including evidence of the levels of minority group registration and voting, changes in such levels over time, and disparities between minority-group and non-minority-group participation" . . . a covered jurisdiction seeking bailout must also meet subjective criteria: it must "(i) have eliminated voting procedures and methods of election which inhibit or dilute equal access to the electoral process; (ii) have engaged in constructive efforts to eliminate intimidation and harassment of persons exercising rights protected [under the Act]; and (iii) have engaged in other constructive efforts, such as expanded opportunity for convenient registration and voting for every person of voting age and the appointment of minority persons as election officials throughout the jurisdiction and at all stages of the election and registration process."[9]

Jurisdictions seeking to escape Section 5 requirements have a substantial burden. In *NAMUDNO*, the lower court denied bailout not because the Municipal Utility District (MUD) failed to satisfy these criteria, but because the MUD did not register voters. NAMUDNO appealed to the high court because the Act imposes no such limitation on bailout. Being a jurisdiction for the purpose of coverage made the MUD one for the purpose of bailout. If it lost on the statutory challenge, the MUD asked the Court to invalidate Section 5.

Disagreements over the need to continue preclearance illuminate the differences in the evaluation of minority-white relations early in the new millennium. The Voting Rights Act renewal celebrated the dramatic improvements in the political status of African Americans and other minorities documented and analyzed in this volume, but it also took place in the context of a changed, two-party South. Opponents of any modification of the VRA triggers view the changes wrought by the Voting Rights Act as tenuous and requiring constant monitoring. They fear that based on the historical precedent of the first Reconstruction, dimming the watchful eye of DOJ would trigger an avalanche of backsliding by an unreconstructed South. Second-generation discriminatory effects are put on par with the insidious evil of Jim Crow in their reading of the South.

Those favoring revising VRA coverage pointed to the same transformed landscape as evidence of changes in white attitudes and the ability of minorities to secure their rights with less federal involvement. The NAMUDNO plaintiff/appellant asserted that the time for national preemption of state and local electoral authority has expired with the passing of the emergency. The plaintiff and supporters filing various amicus briefs pointed to empirical evidence on registration, voting, and minority descriptive representation to challenge the need for continuing federal oversight for another quarter century.[10]

The politics of the Supreme Court also loomed large. Pre-opinion speculation in *NAMUDNO* focused on the role of Justice Anthony Kennedy, and on the patterns of questioning among the justices and how it correlated with the decisions rendered by the Court. Many expected a 5–4 decision with Justice Kennedy holding the swing vote. When *NAMUDNO* came down on June 22, the Court voted 8–1 to reverse the finding of the D.C. district court panel and to remand the case. Chief Justice John Roberts delivered the opinion of the court while the lone partial dissent came from Justice Clarence Thomas. The majority opinion focused entirely on the statutory issue, allowing the Court to avoid the constitutional issues (an application of the doctrine of constitutional avoidance). However, both the majority opinion and the Thomas dissent prompted powerful concerns and cautions regarding the continuing constitutionality of Section 5.

Chief Justice Roberts noted that the MUD sought constitutional relief only if it lost the statutory challenge.[11] Roberts then observed that the larger constitutional questions "attracted ardent briefs from dozens of interested parties, but the importance of the question does not justify our rushing to decide it."[12] Roberts and seven of the brethren demonstrated their own restraint, noting that the "usual practice [of the Court] is to avoid the unnecessary resolution of constitutional questions."[13] In reversing the lower court, the majority found the utility district eligible to seek bailout.

The opinion explored constitutional issues related to Section 5, all the while declining to rule on these issues. Some justices have worried about the constitutionality of Section 5, a concern first articulated by Justice Hugo Black in *Katzenbach* (383 U.S. 358–362), later echoed by Justice John Harlan in *Allen* (393 U.S. 586, note 4) and by Justice Lewis Powell in *City of Rome* (446 U.S. 209–221). Justices Kennedy and Thomas have also indicated concerns about the constitutionality of Section 5, most recently in the *LULAC* decision. Justice Roberts advanced a strong argument for reassessing Section 5's constitutionality:

> Some of the conditions that we relied upon in upholding this statutory scheme in *Katzenbach* and *City of Rome* have unquestionably improved. Things have changed in the South. Voter turnout and registration rates now approach parity. Blatantly discriminatory evasions of federal decrees are rare. And minority candidates hold office at unprecedented levels . . . these improvements are no doubt due in significant part to the Voting Rights Act itself, and stand as a monument to its success . . . the Act imposes current burdens and must be justified by current needs.[14]

Roberts also noted concerns regarding equal sovereignty among the states, guaranteed by the constitution, and brought into question the scope of coverage of the Section 4 trigger:

> a departure from the fundamental principle of equal sovereignty requires a showing that a statute's disparate geographic coverage is sufficiently related to the problem that it targets. . . . The evil that §5 is meant to address may no longer be concentrated in the jurisdictions singled out for preclearance. The statute's coverage formula is based on data that is now more than 35 years old, and there is considerable evidence that it fails to account for current political conditions.[15]

Roberts referenced analysis reported by the American Enterprise Institute, showing that "the racial gap in voter registration and turnout is lower in the States originally covered by §5 than it is nationwide"[16] and also evidence from several amicus briefs filed in support of the MUD. The cautions directed at lawmakers even from supporters of the Act during reauthorization hearings and discussed in this volume, loom large in the majority's opinion. Justice Roberts casts light on an issue well-documented in the journals after the renewal, that "Congress heard warnings from supporters of extending §5 that the evidence in the record did not address 'systematic differences between the covered and the non-covered areas of the United States[,] . . . and, in fact, the evidence that is in the record suggests that there is more similarity than difference.'"[17] The speculation of the Court, when assessing the balance of the evidentiary record against the scope of coverage and impact of the Act on federalism, is circumspect but skeptical:

> The Act's preclearance requirements and its coverage formula raise serious constitutional questions under either test. . . . More than 40 years ago, this Court concluded that "exceptional conditions" prevailing in certain parts of the country justified extraordinary legislation otherwise unfamiliar to our federal system. *Katzenbach,* 383 U.S., at 334. In part due to the success of that legislation, we are now a very different Nation. Whether conditions continue to justify such legislation is a difficult constitutional question we do not answer today. We conclude instead that the Voting Rights Act permits all political subdivisions, including the district in this case, to seek relief from its preclearance requirements.[18]

Justice Thomas, concurring in part and dissenting in part, criticized the circumspect constitutional approach of the majority. The "appeal presents two questions: first, whether appellant is entitled to bail out from coverage under the Voting Rights Act of 1965 (VRA); and second, whether the preclearance requirement of §5 of the VRA is unconstitutional."[19] Thomas was unsatisfied with the majority opinion because it "does not provide appellant with full relief,"[20] making it "inappropriate to apply the constitutional avoidance doctrine in this case. . . . Regardless of the Court's resolution of the statutory question . . . this case raises serious questions concerning the constitutionality of §5 of the VRA. . . . The ultimate relief sought in this case is not bailout eligibility—it is bailout itself."[21] Justice Thomas argues that because the Court cannot afford final relief in the form of bailout, the larger constitutional issue must be decided by the Court.

> To the extent that constitutional avoidance is a worthwhile tool of statutory construction, it is because it allows a court to dispose of an entire case on grounds that do not require the court to pass on a statute's constitutionality. . . . The doctrine of constitutional avoidance is also unavailable here because an interpretation of §4(a) that merely makes more political subdivisions eligible for bailout does not render §5 constitutional and the Court notably does not suggest otherwise.[22]

Thomas is skeptical about the potential for most jurisdictions to make use of the bailout provision, terming it a "distant prospect." At footnote 1, he observes that "all 17 covered jurisdictions that have been awarded bailout are from Virginia . . . and all 17 were represented by the same attorney—a former lawyer in the Voting Rights Section of the Department of Justice [Gerry Hebert]."[23] Of some 12,000 governmental jurisdictions conducting elections within more than nine hundred covered jurisdictions that register voters, only 17 have successfully exited Section 5. Justice Thomas continues, opining that "[w]hatever the reason for this anomaly, it only underscores how little relationship there is between the existence of bailout and the constitutionality of §5."[24]

Beyond this issue of limited success in bailing out, Justice Thomas forcefully takes to task the evidentiary record advanced by Congress for supporting the 2006 renewal:

> [T]he lack of current evidence of intentional discrimination with respect to voting renders §5 unconstitutional. The provision can no longer be justified as an appropriate mechanism for enforcement of the Fifteenth Amendment. . . . The Court has never deviated from this understanding. . . . Congress must establish a "history and pattern" of constitutional violations to establish the need for §5 by justifying a remedy that pushes the limits of its constitutional authority . . . for §5 to withstand renewed constitutional scrutiny, there must be a demonstrated connection between the "remedial measures" chosen and the "evil presented" in the record made by

> Congress when it renewed the Act. . . . The extensive pattern of discrimination that led the Court to previously uphold §5 as enforcing the Fifteenth Amendment no longer exists.[25]

The evidence is inadequate to the task in Justice Thomas's opinion, and the majority opinion also raises questions about the weight of discrimination relative to the constitutional issue. As we will deal with further, below, this issue of data and evidence in context is not merely a technical one for social science, but also a substantive one for lawmakers and judges who make determinations about the law and the constitution based on empirics. Good intentions, it seems, also require impressive and very good data regarding the social biases that are at work.

NAMUDNO opens the way for jurisdictions other than states and counties to seek bailout from Section 5. But, it also illuminates the constitutional vulnerability of the legislation, and in so doing, offers no ready hope for retention in a direct challenge. The lack of a concurrence defending the constitutionality of Section 5 is surprising, and seems to invite additional challenges in the near future. Supporters and opponents of Section 5 await that challenge, likely from one or more southern counties seeking bailout.

Measuring Racially Polarized Voting

Another challenge involves measurement of racially polarized voting. The methods of measuring voting preferences of racial groups are well-established and not subject to debate. But the larger question of the contextual measure of racially polarized voting remains. The concept of racially polarized voting as a source of legal concern arises when white and minority voters have contrary interests,[26] and white voters act to defeat candidates preferred by minority voters. In Democratic Party primaries, the traditional avenue to political empowerment in the South for liberals and conservatives alike,[27] white conservative interests had sought to narrow the franchise and control access to party elections in violation of the Fourteenth and Fifteenth amendments.

Having lost their avenue for expression through the Democratic Party, racial, economic, and eventually social conservatives and some moderates gravitated to the Republican Party in the South,[28] which made general elections the elections of consequence in the region. These contests still pit white and black voters against each other, since they have different partisan preferences. But increasingly throughout the South the racial policy motive for whites has disappeared in structuring their voting.[29] The core political ideologies of blacks and whites are not distributed in the same fashion, and this ideological distribution influences policy preferences, party preferences, and voting behavior.[30] A question for the courts is: do political differences that are racially distributed, but which do not find their basis in racial attitudes or racial motivations, rise to a level of constitutional violation?

Representatives of Choice Versus Candidates of Choice

Both Section 5 and Section 2 of the Voting Rights Act include a term of art used by political science expert witnesses and attorneys: candidate of choice. Section 2 of the Voting Rights Act as amended in 1982 focuses on whether minority voters "have less opportunity than other members of the electorate to participate in the political process and to elect representatives of their choice."[31] In establishing the basis for assessing changes using Section 5, the Supreme Court said that non-retrogression required "that the minority's opportunity to elect representatives of its choice not be diminished, directly or indirectly, by the state's actions."[32] A critical difference exists between the law as written and the term of art as analyzed, and this difference underlies the debate over the application of both Section 2 and Section 5: *candidate* versus *representative*.

A candidate of choice is a candidate, regardless of race or ethnicity, who is the choice of a particular racial or ethnic voting bloc. The threshold for defining candidate of choice is subject to debate, though a minimum standard of a majority preference for *one* candidate from a racial voting bloc has been accepted as sufficient. Epstein and O'Halloran note that "[t]he Supreme Court has made it clear that a candidate of choice need not be a member of any particular minority group. But beyond that, definitions are notoriously vague and hard to apply in specific circumstances so that too often only minority officeholders are considered to be a candidate of choice."[33] The courts have avoided defining a candidate of choice as coming from a particular racial or ethnic group, and the most recent decision dealing with the issue, *Georgia v. Ashcroft*, placed remedies to grant minority access firmly in the realm of simple partisan political outcomes.

One question that remains unanswered: is a representative different from a candidate? On a technical level the answer is no, because an elected candidate becomes a representative. If one thinks of descriptive representation as a prerequisite for successful representation in a racially divided political environment, then a candidate is not necessarily a *representative*, if he or she does not come from the minority community. The community of policy interest is the collection of persons presumed to be the affirmative target of the policy, in this case a minority group receiving legal protection from the implementation of the Act. David Canon illuminated the substantive importance of this distinction in his book *Race, Redistricting, and Representation*,[34] and it is this distinction that continues to merit exploration. The continued implementation of the Voting Rights Act invites that debate.

In Conclusion: Coalition Politics and the "Performance" of Election Laws

The Voting Rights Act initially sought to provide access to the ballot and to ensure that jurisdictions did not throw up new impediments to African American participation. In the late 1960s, the Supreme Court's expansive interpretation broadened the Act's scope. More recently, the Supreme Court in *Georgia v. Ashcroft* offered a different model for assessing the ability of redistricting plans to perform on behalf of minority voters. As noted in the introduction and chapter 3, the *Ashcroft* decision moved away from a fairly narrow model of minority success—majority-minority districts that guaranteed minority control of the election. *Ashcroft* offered an alternative model of coalition districts in which black voters could coalesce with enough whites to control non–majority-minority districts. This approach can result in unintended consequences in both the effort to baseline performance and access for minority voters, and in possible remedies to ensure minority access and non-retrogression.

Congress rejected the *Ashcroft* suggestion of alternative approaches to satisfy Section 5. Did the broadening of solutions also expand the scope of districts protected from retrogression? Before *Ashcroft*, had Section 5 become primarily a vehicle for the pursuit of partisan advantage rather than ensuring minority-group access to the political process? Does a broad definition of the retrogression baseline and remedies draw Section 5 closer to "just politics"?

Republican administrations, specifically the first Bush administration, used the Voting Rights Act to encourage creation of majority-minority districts and to limit the opportunities to create cross-racial coalitions supporting Democrats. White Democrats preferred districts with sizeable (but not majority) minority populations because biracial coalitions could win more seats. The aggressive use of Section 2 of the Voting Rights Act to create majority-minority districts in the early 1990s resulted in electoral maps that helped shift one-third of all southern congressional districts to the GOP over the course of the next three elections. Concentrating the most loyal Democratic voters into the fewest districts possible helped elect Republicans as well as minorities.

Relying on the Equal Protection Clause, courts upheld challenges to several of the new majority-minority districts and this reduced minority concentrations. Ultimately the Supreme Court suggested that as long as jurisdictions justified their actions in partisan rather than racial terms, redistricting plans could probably survive judicial challengers.[35] Maps drawn using the 2000 census resulted in shapes as bizarre as those a decade earlier and allocated minority concentrations with the same care as in the 1990s but without overt acknowledgment of the role race played. After 2000, Democrats sought to maximize the number of districts they could win, a goal endorsed by both the party's black and white legislators. This signalled an abrupt about-face for black legislators who in the past had criticized Democratic plans that distributed black voters to shore up white Democrats, rather than aggregating black population concentrations to enhance the likelihood of black legislators being elected.

A significant difference between 2001 and 1991 was the growing recognition that heightened black participation rates coupled with increased numbers of whites willing to support black candidates meant that African Americans could win in districts with lower black concentrations. The success of black candidates in the whiter districts drawn after the courts invalidated the racially gerrymandered 1990s districts showed that such heavy black-voter concentrations were unnecessary. Following the 2000 census, some legislatures reduced black percentages in minority districts to barely half the voting-age population. In the 1980s, the Department of Justice and courts often demanded that a district be at least 65 percent black in its total population in order to enable African Americans to elect their preferences.[36] In the 1990s DOJ reinforced black aspirations and required maximizing the number of districts likely to elect minorities. A decade later, neither DOJ nor minority groups pushed for the creation of additional districts designed to elect minorities, and the Supreme Court articulated a new standard for assessing compliance with Section 5. Despite plans lowering black concentrations, the number of African Americans serving in southern legislatures has continued to grow.[37]

Assuming that minority-representation guarantees can be achieved through biracial coalitions, another question arises: can minority candidates and candidates of choice be elected from districts with minority VAP percentages at or below 50 percent? In an analysis embraced by Georgia's Legislative Black Caucus, David Epstein estimated that a black candidate had a 50–50 chance of winning in a district where the black voting-age population was 44.3 percent.[38] In order for an African American to have an "even chance" at winning a 44.3 percent black voting-age population district, assuming equal rates of black and white turnout with 90 percent minority-voter cohesion, a candidate of choice needs 18.1 percent of the Anglo vote to win. To have an even chance at winning a 40 percent minority VAP district requires 23.3 percent of the Anglo vote. And, to have an even chance at winning with 30 percent minority VAP and 90 percent cohesion requires 32.8 percent of the Anglo vote. These thresholds for white crossover voting increase as the rate of minority turnout falls. A review of the tables in this volume showing racial voting patterns demonstrates that these thresholds are often met in most Section 5 states in major elections.

On the other hand, by overturning the *Ashcroft* attempt to reduce minority concentrations, even when the minority community approves such redistribution, Congress endorsed ratcheting up minority percentages in heavily minority districts with each round of redistricting. An obvious consequence of that approach is to reduce the number of districts where minorities acting alone or in collaboration with white voters can elect candidates preferred by the minority electorate.

In renewing the VRA, Congress sided with the DOJ in favoring districts with higher concentrations of minorities. The Supreme Court, beginning with *Shaw v. Reno* in 1993, has issued rulings that reduce minority concentrations and encourage the development of cross-racial coalitions. While lowering the minority percentage in a district involves some risk for minority candidates, coalitions that elect Democrats promote the likelihood of legislatures controlled by Democrats, which, in turn, increase the potential for policy outputs preferred by minority voters. The Supreme Court's discussion of coalitional possibilities in *Ashcroft* indicates the extent of change among southern white voters. At the time of the adoption of the VRA, so few whites would vote for a black candidate, regardless of the individual's qualifications, that only in districts in which minorities dominated the electorate could a minority candidate hope for success. Now minority voters control Democratic primaries in majority-white jurisdictions when whites participate in the Republican primary. Once nominated, minority candidates can win if they fashion a coalition as noted above.

The initial goals of the VRA—removing barriers to black registration and turnout—have long since been attained. The more recent goal of facilitating the election of candidates preferred by minority voters has also achieved great success. The remaining concern is whether in the absence of the federal oversight authorized by Section 5 subject jurisdictions would unravel the advances of the last two generations. The potential for that happening seems slight. Suit can be brought under Section 2, a tool used extensively in jurisdictions far beyond the sixteen states wholly or partially covered by Section 5.

In the context of redistricting, and it is this activity that has most frequently drawn the relatively few DOJ objections of recent years, the political situation militates against backsliding. As noted repeatedly in this volume, Republicans benefit from drawing majority-minority districts so that GOP-controlled legislatures will gladly pump up minority percentages in selected districts. Any temptation by Democrats to crack minority concentrations in order to maximize the numbers of districts likely to elect white Democrats would face tough sledding in southern legislatures given the size of their black caucuses. In 2008, in the lower chambers of six southern states, along with three upper chambers, at least 40 percent of Democrats were black, and in both Texas chambers most Democrats were either Hispanic or black. The chambers in which fewer than 40 percent of Democrats were minorities include Arkansas and Tennessee, states not under Section 5. North Carolina and Virginia, two other states with lower percentages of blacks among Democratic legislators, voted for Obama.

Of course, redistricting, while among the highest profile activities subject to Section 5, is but one type of change that must be submitted to DOJ. Would backsliding be a problem in other areas reviewed by DOJ? This question can never be answered definitively in jurisdictions that remain subject to Section 5. One indication of the potential for bad behavior by Section 5 jurisdictions may come with the new administration. Will the Justice Department in a Democratic administration led by the nation's first African American attorney general find more objectionable activities than its recent predecessors? Will the Obama Justice Department deny more plans to move voting sites, to annex land, to change conditions under which elections are held, or to change candidate qualifications? Should that occur, it might indicate lingering bad faith by officials in covered jurisdictions.

The data examined in this volume indicate that context is important when dealing with the issue of voting rights. Certainly, in the application of Section 2 of the Voting Rights Act in Noxubee County, Mississippi (see chapter 1), context does matter. A higher degree of intent is necessary to establish voting-rights violations involving discrimination against white voters. The threshold is higher because history was kinder to privileged whites. Context too matters in dealing with issues of discrimination toward black voters.

It is increasingly difficult to distinguish a racial vote from a party vote in the South. Most elections, at least above the local level and especially in the absence of a Democratic incumbent, are racially polarized, regardless of the race of the candidates or the role of race as an issue in campaigns. This is because whites vote for Republicans and African Americans massively prefer Democrats. Is it appropriate to ascribe sinister motives to voters who make a choice governed by partisanship? Perhaps, but to do so raises the concept of party and free association to an uncomfortable level of scrutiny, with white partisanship preference assumed to be discriminatory behavior.

Partisan bias is permissible under the Constitution, as long as a superior principle is not violated in the process—electoral systems that discriminate by party are evidently permissible if they do not violate equal protection and racial equality standards.[39] The movement of elections of consequence in the South out of the Democratic Party primary and to the general election moves the location of the assessment of both the value of the vote and where we measure racially polarized voting. The consequence of that movement is that racial polarization continues to be found in a variety of elections because of the preference for Republicans among southern, Anglo voters.

Finally, context matters in determining the nature of the evidence to be considered in making law. Much as it is increasingly difficult to distinguish a racial vote from a party vote in a general election, it is also important to remember that a racial vote does not rise to the level of unconstitutional discrimination, and that the evidence that warrants overturning just politics under our constitutional system must be compelling. In his *NAMUDNO* dissent, Justice Thomas echoes many witnesses and scholars noted throughout this volume—that the evidence of problems was thin compared to the continued scope of the federal intervention. According to Justice Thomas:

> when reenacting §5 in 2006, Congress evidently understood that the emergency conditions which prompted §5's original enactment no longer exist. . . . Instead of relying on the kind of evidence that the Katzenbach Court had found so persuasive, Congress instead based reenactment on evidence of what it termed "second generation barriers" constructed to prevent minority voters from fully participating in the electoral process. . . . Congress relied upon evidence of racially polarized voting within the covered jurisdictions. But racially polarized voting is not evidence of unconstitutional discrimination . . . is not state action . . . and is not a problem unique to the South. . . . The other evidence relied on by Congress, such as §5 enforcement actions, §§2 and 4 lawsuits, and federal

> examiner and observer coverage, also bears no resemblance to the record initially supporting §5, and is plainly insufficient to sustain such an extraordinary remedy.[40]

In sum, evidence of "second generation barriers" cannot compare to the prevalent and pervasive voting discrimination of the 1960s. And, it stands up poorly to evidence of dramatically declining federal intervention, growth in minority office holding, voter participation, and the emergence of a politics where the South and the rest of the nation are more alike than different.

Epilogue

The 2008 Presidential Election

If the polls are right, if it don't rain and the creek don't rise, the winner of the presidential election is sure to be Lyndon Baines Johnson.
RICHARD COHEN, NOVEMBER 4, 2008

I ain't got time to die 'cause I've got to see a black president.
ANN NIXON COOPER, AGE 106, TO THE CABLE NEWS NETWORK, NOVEMBER 6, 2008

The 2008 presidential campaign ended with the election of the first African American president of the United States. Barack H. Obama, a forty-seven-year-old first-term senator from Illinois, won 53 percent of the national popular vote and 365 votes in the Electoral College. It is impossible to overstate the historical significance of his election, and also impossible to conclude a volume on the triumph of voting rights in the South without addressing this event.

PATH TO NOMINATION

The Voting Rights Act was critical to the election of President Barack Obama. Since the 1971 McGovern-Frasier reforms brought primaries to the fore in choosing the Democratic Party's presidential nominee, the South has played a critical role, and the Obama campaign owes a substantial portion of its delegate margin in 2008 to the impressive wins in the Section 5 states.

South Carolina, always so important in recent Republican presidential nomination fights, was the first southern state to hold a (sanctioned) presidential primary in 2008. Coming off the narrow loss of the New Hampshire primary to Hillary Clinton, Obama needed a South Carolina win to demonstrate consolidated support among black voters thought to be susceptible to Clinton's candidacy. The racially charged campaign environment ended with a 55 percent victory by Obama, driven largely by a 78 to 19 percent margin among Palmetto State blacks.

In subsequent primaries in the other Section 5 states, Obama racked up similarly dominant victories, taking 61 percent of the primary vote in Mississippi; 56 percent in Alabama; 66 percent in Georgia; 57 percent in Louisiana; 64 percent in Virginia (including a majority of white votes); and 56 percent in North Carolina. Black voters constituted majorities or near majorities of Democratic voters in all of these primaries except Virginia.

Obama only lost southern primaries in Florida (where he did not campaign in the renegade primary); Tennessee, where he lost by 14 points but took 77 percent of the black vote; and Arkansas (losing 70 to 26). In Texas, Obama narrowly lost the popular vote but won the caucus portion of the delegate selection process and thereby garnered most of the delegates.

Barring the impressive showing of Obama in these primaries, he likely would not have been positioned to claim the superdelegate support needed to nail down the nomination. Almost unprecedented black voter turnout and cohesion allowed Obama to claim 60.7 percent of the primary delegates in the nine southern Section 5 states, but just 49.4 percent of the delegates from other states. Obama's entire delegate margin was provided, on balance, by the nine southern Section 5 states. The impressive showing of Obama in the constituencies of black superdelegates such as John Lewis (D-Ga.) and Stephanie Tubbs Jones (D-Ohio) increased pressure on those delegates to move their support from uncommitted or Clinton to Obama. Tubbs Jones resisted the pressure, while Lewis gave in to his constituency. Observed the Cleveland congresswoman, in defense of her Georgia colleague, "I say shame on anyone who's engaged in that conduct, to put that kind of pressure on John Lewis. . . . I'm not trying to be a martyr. I think Senator Clinton is the best candidate. And the beauty of the United States of America is you have the right to have your opinion, and I have the right to my opinion."[1]

GENERAL ELECTION SUCCESS

The Obama victory is stunning in its scope and magnitude. The Democratic nominee secured the largest percentage of the vote by a Democratic presidential candidate since 1964, and had the second-highest vote percentage ever for a Democratic nonincumbent behind Franklin Delano Roosevelt's 57.4 percent in 1932. Senator Obama won Electoral College votes in every region and became the first Democrat ever to sweep New England, the industrial Midwest, and the Pacific Coast. He was also the first nonsouthern Democrat to win any southern state since John Kennedy. The Obama-Biden ticket also ran stronger among white voters nationwide than any Democratic presidential ticket in forty years.

In the South, Barack Obama commanded 46.7 percent of the two-party presidential vote, or about eighteen million of thirty-eight million ballots cast. Even more impressive, however, was that the Obama-Biden ticket won fifty-five Electoral College votes by taking Florida, North Carolina, and Virginia. These three states, all covered at least in part by Section 5 of the Voting Rights Act, delivered on behalf of the Democratic nominee. For Virginia it was a monumental event, as the state last went for a Democratic presidential candidate in 1964. North Carolina had not voted for a Democratic nominee since 1976 when it narrowly backed Jimmy Carter. Florida had sided with the Democrats in 1964, 1976, and again in 1996 before shifting narrowly back to Republicans in 2000 and 2004.

These three southern victories can be ascribed to two factors: unified bloc voting by black voters combined with some crossover support by a minority of whites. As indicated in table E.1, the Obama-Biden ticket received almost unanimous support from black voters. According to Voter News Service (VNS) exit polls, between 92 percent and 98 percent of African American voters supported the Democratic ticket. These percentages reflect levels of support seen for other black candidates running in the South but rank at the high end of support for white Democrats. Among white voters, the Democratic ticket posted its strongest support in Florida (42 percent), Virginia (39 percent), and North Carolina (35 percent), with support weakest among whites in Mississippi (11 percent), Alabama (12 percent), and Louisiana (14 percent). All of the Rim South states except Texas offered at least 30 percent support to Obama while no Deep South state showed more than 26 percent white support for the Democratic candidate. In Texas and Florida, Obama ran strong with Latinos: Obama posted figures consistent with Democrats in general in Texas and performed better than prior Democrats among Florida Latinos.

Comparison of the Obama-Biden ticket to major statewide races on the ballot in the South indicates some minor penalty for Obama compared to other Democrats, though the differences are highly contextual. The Section 5 states of Alabama, Georgia, Mississippi, South Carolina, Texas, and North Carolina had incumbent Republican U.S. senators on the ballot. In those six states, Obama ran, on average, 6 points ahead of the Democratic challengers among black voters and trailed Democratic challengers by less than 1 point among white voters. One Republican incumbent (Elizabeth Dole) lost while another (Saxby Chambliss) was thrown into a runoff after failing to attain the majority required by Georgia law. Both of these candidates benefitted from the heightened black turnout mobilized by Obama.

In Louisiana, Democratic incumbent Mary Landrieu ran 2 points ahead of Obama among blacks and 19 points ahead among whites in winning reelection to the U.S. Senate. In Virginia's open seat, former governor Mark Warner ran a point ahead of Obama among blacks and 17 points ahead among whites to win, while in Mississippi's special election, former Democratic governor Ronnie Musgrave ran 6 points behind Obama among blacks but 7 points ahead among whites in a losing effort. North Carolina's open gubernatorial election featured Democratic lieutenant governor Beverly Perdue, who ran 2 points behind Obama among blacks and 1 point ahead of him among whites. In Texas, Barack Obama ran better among Hispanics than Democratic U.S. Senate nominee Rick Noriega.

The 2008 election shows variable effects by the Obama candidacy on black-voter mobilization. Exit poll estimates indicate that the Deep South

TABLE E.1. Vote share and racial support for southern Democratic candidates in 2008

	Total %	Black %	White %	Latino %
Obama-Biden				
Alabama	39	98	12	
Arkansas	39.7	94	30	
Florida	51.2	96	42	57
Georgia	46.7	98	23	
Louisiana	42.1	94	14	
Mississippi	43.1	98	11	
N. Carolina	50.1	97	35	
S. Carolina	45.3	96	26	
Tennessee	42.1	94	34	
Texas	44.1	98	26	63
Virginia	52.3	92	39	
U.S. Senate				
Alabama (R-I)	37	90	11	
Arkansas (D-I)	100	—	—	
Florida		No Senate Contest		
Georgia (R-I)	47	93	26	
Louisiana (D-I)	52	96	33	
Mississippi Regular (R-I)	38	94	8	
Mississippi Special (R-I)	45	92	18	
N. Carolina (R-I)	53	96	39	
S. Carolina (R-I)	42	87	26	
Tennessee (R-I)	32	72	26	
Texas (R-I)	43	89	27	61
Virginia (Open)	64	93	56	
Governor				
N. Carolina (Open)	50	95	36	

Source: Voter News Service (VNS) exit polls and election returns compiled by the authors.

Note: R-I indicates Republican incumbent; D-I indicates Democratic incumbent.

states led in black share of turnout. However, those same states also showed the most starkly polarized electorates in terms of black-versus-white preferences for president (see table E.2).

When one uses linear regression—one of the techniques we describe in appendix A and that we use throughout the volume—to test the relationship between white vote shares of down-ticket candidates for U.S.

TABLE E.2. Proportion black, white, and Latino in the 2008 electorate

	Turnout share		
	Black	White	Latino
Alabama	29	65	4
Arkansas	12	83	3
Florida	13	71	14
Georgia	30	65	3
Louisiana	29	65	4
Mississippi	33	62	4
N. Carolina	23	72	3
S. Carolina	25	71	3
Tennessee	12	84	2
Texas	13	63	20
Virginia	20	70	5

Source: Voter News Service (VNS) exit polls and election returns compiled by the authors.

Senate and governor and the Obama performance among whites, while controlling for incumbency in the contest, the following patterns emerge: First, the fit is good (adjusted $R^2 = .73$). In the absence of incumbency and assuming no support among whites for Obama, white Democrats got 1.82 percent of the white vote as indicated by the constant. Second, each percentage point gain for Obama among whites translated into a 1.16 point gain for the down-ticket Democrats (all of whom except for the challengers to Jeff Sessions [R-Ala.] and Thad Cochran [R-Miss.] are white). Put another way, a white electorate that voted 50 percent for Obama voted 59.8 percent for a down-ticket white Democrat. Third, the presence of an incumbent Republican diminished Democratic vote share among whites by –5.66 points, while a Republican incumbent enhanced the white vote share by +5.66 points. A 1 point gain in black vote share for Obama translated into a 1.18 point gain for down-ticket whites, but the substantial negative intercept (–21.41) indicates that in a black electorate where everyone voted for Obama, white down-ticket candidates still ran about 3.4 points behind.[2]

There is an indication at a very high level of aggregation that Obama's white vote share is structured by the presence of large, active black voting populations. Regressing the Obama white vote share in the South onto the percent of the voter turnout that is African American and Latino, respectively, indicates that Obama receives 52.4 percent of the vote when there are no minority voters (the intercept).

Every one-point increase in the share of the electorate that is black results in a 1.12 point decrease in the white vote for Barack Obama. A .29 point decrease is indicated for every point increase in the Latino share of the electorate, though the relationship is not statistically significant.[3]

Exit poll data from 2004 and 2008 indicate that Barack Obama ran behind John Kerry among white voters in five southern states: Alabama (–12.1 percent), Arkansas (–6.1 percent), Florida (–4.3 percentage points), Louisiana (–9.8 percentage points), and Mississippi (–4.9 percentage points). Obama ran ahead of the 2004 ticket among whites in North Carolina (+8.2 percentage points), South Carolina (+5 percentage points), Virginia (+7.4 percentage points), and Texas (+0.8 percentage points). He ran even with Kerry among whites in Tennessee and Georgia.

The Obama candidacy prompted turnout and also restored cohesion to southern black voters. The gains in the original Section 5 states are varied, from +3.8 percentage points in Louisiana, +4.7 percentage points in Virginia, +4.8 percentage points in Alabama, and +5.1 percentage points in Mississippi to double-digit gains in Georgia (+10 percentage points) and North Carolina (+12 percentage points). The other two Section 5 states show gains also (Florida, +5 percentage points; Texas, +15.5 percentage points). The non–Section 5 states vary, with just a +0.6 percentage point gain in Arkansas and a +29 percentage points gain in Tennessee.

Regardless of the gains among blacks in cohesion and turnout or the decline of support among whites, Obama outperformed Kerry in all of the Section 5 states except Louisiana (–0.1 percentage point). The gains in the total vote in the Deep South states are modest: Alabama, +2.2 percentage points; Mississippi, +3.3 percentage points; South Carolina, +4.4 percentage points; and Georgia, +5.3 percentage points. In the longest-covered Section 5 states of the Rim South the gains are larger, with +6.5 percentage points in North Carolina and +6.8 percentage points in Virginia. The experiences of Texas and Florida, states brought under Section 5 in 1975, fall closer to the Deep South than Rim South members of the class of 1965, with +4.1 percentage points in Florida and +5.9 percentage points in Texas.

The Obama-Biden ticket continues the sorting of the parties' presidential vote in the South on rural-urban and black-white dimensions (see map E.1, with Obama-carried counties shaded in gray). The pattern of counties carried by the Obama campaign will seem familiar to any casual observer of southern political geography—Obama, like Kerry and Gore before him, won the South Florida urban centers; the urban core counties of the Deep South, North Carolina, and Texas; the south Rio Grande valley; suburban Virginia; urban Memphis; and, finally, an arc of old Black Belt counties from Tidewater Virginia to the Mississippi Delta.

CONCLUSION

The Obama-Biden ticket got more Electoral College votes from the South than any Democratic Party ticket since Jimmy Carter in 1976. As in 1992 and 1996, the success in the South was not critical to the election outcome. Subtract the fifty-five southern electoral votes won by Obama or the thirty-nine and fifty-one electoral votes for the two Clinton tickets from their national totals and the Democrats still prevail. However, these southern successes indicate an enhancement of tremendous value, because the competitiveness of the Democratic ticket carried the fight to a region generally lost to Democrats.

Two generations removed from the attack at the Edmund Pettus Bridge, a black Democratic candidate won more southern electors than any nonsouthern Democrat since Kennedy, and more than any Democrat since Jimmy Carter. The pattern of success is consistent with the analysis offered in this volume. Mobilized black voters when combined with a sufficient minority of white voters can prevail in southern elections, even in support of black candidates. Black and white candidates are largely undistinguishable in the nature of the coalitions they fashion, though sometimes the lack of distinction is to the decided disadvantage of Democratic candidates. The politics of the South are still the most polarized, and the prospects for major-office success for blacks most constrained in Mississippi, Louisiana, and Alabama. The degree of racial

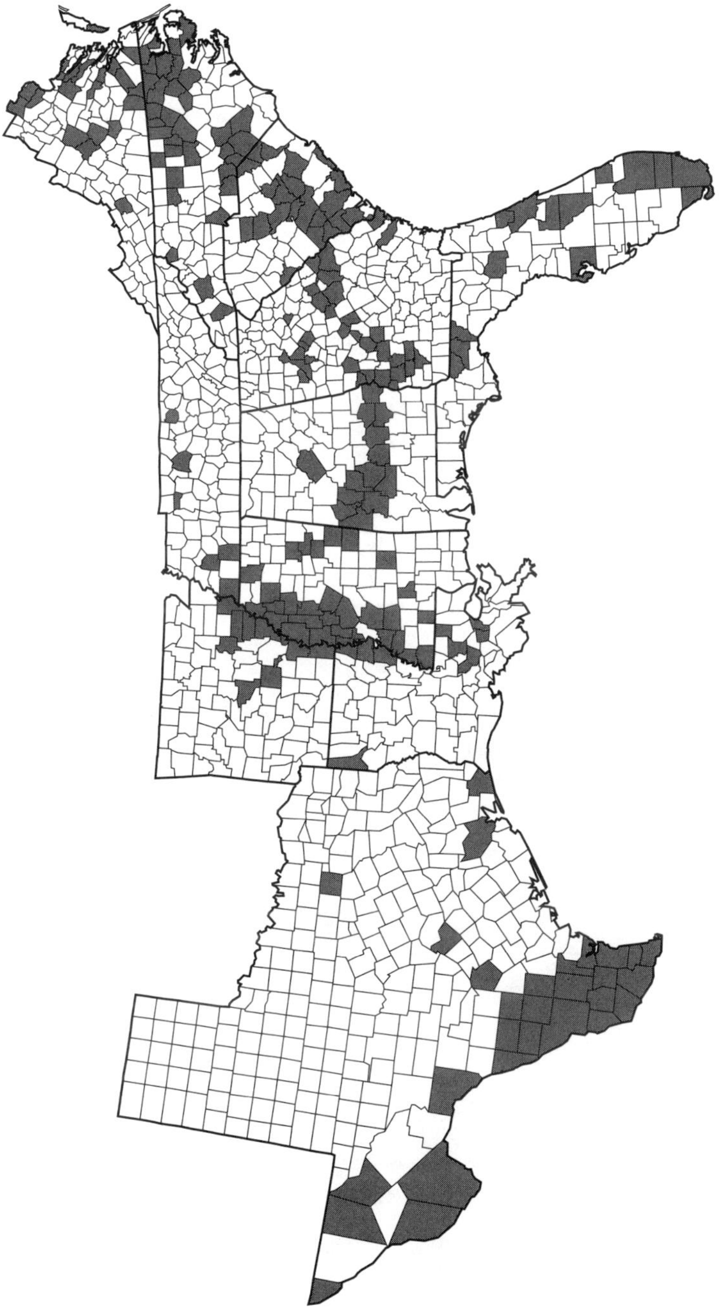

Map E.1. Counties won by Obama-Biden in 2008.

polarization in the 2008 presidential campaign rivals any contest in this analysis. Meanwhile, in Virginia, Florida, North Carolina, and Georgia, success or near-success came because Obama increased black participation and cohesion while also running at par or ahead of average for Democrats among white voters.

Appendix A

Analytic Methods for Estimating Racial Voting Patterns

Three techniques are used by voting scholars and expert witnesses to estimate racial voting patterns: homogenous precinct analysis, ecological regression, and ecological inference (the King technique). The latter two are used in this study, though explanation of all three is included here to provide a proper evolutionary description of the techniques.

Homogenous precinct analysis entails identifying voter precincts that are largely homogenous; the standard definition of homogenous is that 90 percent or more of the voting-age population (VAP) in the constituency or district is of one ethnic or racial group. The vote shares for candidates in these precincts are then computed, under the assumption that most of the votes for the prevailing candidate come from the overwhelming ethnic or racial majority in those districts.

Bivariate ecological regression (BERA, or Goodman's regression technique) is the most common technique used since the 1980s. And, when dealing with voting by more than one minority group, the multiple-regression technique (MERA) is applied. In such an analysis, the dependent variable—proportion of the voting-age population casting ballots for some candidate "A"—is regressed onto an independent predictor (or predictors): the proportion of the voting-age population for each respective minority population of interest, such as the proportion that is black and proportion that is Hispanic, respectively. Often the regression is weighted by the number of voters in each precinct, to give greater consideration in the analysis to cases where there are more voters in ascertaining minority preferences. To ascertain the level of support for some candidate A among a particular ethnic or racial group, the following computation is performed: Assume that the ethnic/racial populations controlled for as independent variables in the regression analysis are percent black VAP and percent Hispanic VAP. This makes percent Anglo + VAP (Anglo plus any other ethnic category, such as Asians) the null or control category. It therefore follows that level of voter turnout for candidate A among Anglo voters is the intercept for the regression equation, assuming 0 percent Hispanic VAP and 0 percent Black VAP. Those zeroes, multiplied by the values of the slope coefficients for black VAP and Hispanic VAP respectively, result in an estimated value of the dependent variable at 100 percent Anglo. To estimate the level of turnout for that candidate A among black voters, multiply the value of the coefficient for black VAP by 100 (for 100 percent black VAP), the coefficient for Hispanic VAP by 0 (0 percent Hispanic VAP), and then add the products to the value of the intercept. The result is the expected turnout among black VAP for candidate A. The value for turnout for the candidate among Hispanic VAP is similarly computed, but in this instance the value of the Hispanic coefficient is multiplied by 100 and the value of the coefficient of black VAP is multiplied by 0, then the product is added to the intercept. The estimated levels of turnout for each candidate in each population are summed to produce a total level of turnout for the population. The level of turnout for each candidate within a group is then divided by the total level of turnout for that group. The product is the estimated share of the racial or ethnic group vote cast for the candidate in question. Comparison of these estimates across different groups is the basis for identifying cohesion (voting together) across ethnic and racial groups.

The *ecological inference (EI)* technique estimates the relationship between minority population concentrations and voter participation and voter preferences in aggregated units, such as precincts, in order to determine the extent of group participation and voter polarization among groups. In so doing, it extends beyond the ecological regression method to consider the potential, realistic bounds on the range of preference within a group. The EI method extends beyond linear regression techniques to correct for potential errors arising from the use of the linear regression.[1] Specifically, King's EI technique considers the relative weight of number of individuals aggregated into a data point (such as potential voters within a precinct), and also the bounds of possible, realistic outcomes. For example, linear regression can produce logically impossible estimates of voter participation for a group, such as turnout less than 0 percent, or support for a candidate in excess of 100 percent within a given group. King's EI estimations control for these logical bounds in order to produce estimates of turnout and candidate support that yield non-impossible results. A practical approach to this method was advanced by Harvard's Gary King and is described in detail in his 1997 book, *A Solution to the Ecological Inference Problem.*[2]

Appendix B

Voter Registration and Turnout by Race and Ethnicity

Table B.1. Voter registration data by race and ethnicity

	1980	1982	1984	1986	1988	1990	1992	1994	1996	1998	2000	2002	2004	2006
Alabama														
Black	62.2	57.7	71.4	75.4	68.4	65.3	71.8	66.3	69.2	74.3	72.0	67.6	72.9	71.8
White	73.3	70.2	77.2	74.3	75.0	74.9	79.3	73.3	75.8	74.1	74.5	73.7	73.8	73.0
Non-Hispanic White										74.5	74.9	74.2	74.9	74.5
Arkansas														
Black	62.6	63.3	71.2	62.5	68.0	50.8	62.4	56.0	65.8	51.8	60.0	62.0	63.7	57.5
White	67.4	65.3	70.8	63.5	67.9	62.6	67.8	61.0	64.5	65.9	59.5	62.9	67.1	65.0
Non-Hispanic White										66.3	60.5	64.4	69.4	68.4
Florida														
Black	58.2	50.3	57.3	61.3	57.7	53.3	54.7	47.2	64.6	50.4	52.7	47.9	52.6	50.3
White	64.1	60.8	64.1	59.9	64.3	59.5	64.5	57.6	67.8	61.1	62.5	60.7	64.7	58.1
Latino	33.7	25.3	33.2	35.5	37.7	32.3	35.0	22.7	36.7	35.8	37.1	39.1	38.2	32.2
Non-Hispanic White										67.0	69.2	66.6	71.8	66.3
Georgia														
Black	59.8	51.9	58.0	55.3	56.8	57.0	53.9	57.6	64.6	64.1	66.3	61.6	64.2	57.9
White	67.0	59.7	65.7	60.4	63.9	58.1	67.3	55.0	67.8	62.0	59.3	62.7	63.5	62.1
Non-Hispanic Whites										63.1	61.0	65.3	68.0	67.9
Louisiana														
Black	69.0	68.5	74.8	71.9	77.1	72.0	82.3	65.7	71.9	69.5	73.5	73.5	71.1	66.9
White	74.5	67.5	73.2	71.4	75.1	74.1	76.2	72.7	74.5	75.2	77.5	74.2	75.1	73.2
Non-Hispanic White										75.6	78.0	75.6	76.6	75.0
Mississippi														
Black	72.2	75.8	85.6	75.9	74.2	71.4	78.5	69.9	67.4	71.3	73.7	67.9	76.1	72.2
White	85.2	76.9	81.4	77.3	80.5	70.8	80.2	74.6	75.0	75.2	72.2	70.7	72.3	69.2
Non-Hispanic White										75.8	72.6	72.1	73.6	70.7

Table B.1. Voter registration data by race and ethnicity (*continued*)

	1980	1982	1984	1986	1988	1990	1992	1994	1996	1998	2000	2002	2004	2006
N. Carolina														
Black	49.2	43.6	59.5	57.1	58.2	60.1	64.0	53.1	65.5	57.4	62.9	58.2	70.4	61.1
White	63.7	62.5	67.0	65.8	65.6	63.6	70.8	63.9	70.4	65.6	67.9	63.1	69.4	65.9
Non Hispanic White										66.9	71.5	66.2	73.2	71.1
S. Carolina														
Black	61.4	53.3	62.2	58.8	56.7	61.9	62.0	59.0	64.3	68.0	68.6	68.3	71.1	67.8
White	57.2	54.5	57.3	56.4	61.8	56.2	69.2	62.6	69.7	67.9	68.2	66.2	74.4	60.2
Non-Hispanic White										68.0	69.8	68.2	75.5	63.5
Tennessee														
Black	69.4	67.1	78.5	73.0	74.0	68.5	77.4	70.0	65.7	64.8	64.9	54.1	63.9	53.5
White	66.9	68.5	70.2	65.0	64.4	63.3	63.4	63.9	66.3	63.9	61.9	62.3	62.6	63.8
Non-Hispanic White										63.9	62.8	65.2	64.1	65.9
Texas														
Black	56.4	56.6	65.3	66.6	64.2	60.0	63.5	58.5	63.2	62.1	69.5	65.1	68.4	62.4
White	61.4	59.4	66.0	58.2	66.5	61.1	66.1	59.7	62.7	59.7	61.8	57.7	61.5	59.7
Latino	39.3	43.2	45.2	43.1	45.5	40.0	42.9	39.2	42.7	39.7	43.2	39.1	41.5	40.0
Latino Citizens										56.2	60.0	56.2	58.8	58.1
Non-Hispanic Black										64.4	69.4	66.2	NA	NA
Non-Hispanic White										69.4	71.8	70.2	73.6	71.5
Virginia														
Black	49.7	53.6	62.1	66.5	63.8	58.1	64.5	51.1	64.0	53.6	58.0	47.5	57.4	52.0
White	65.4	60.8	63.7	63.3	68.5	61.9	67.2	63.6	68.4	63.5	67.6	64.1	68.2	65.5
Non-Hispanic White										64.7	69.1	66.7	71.6	69.8

Table B.1. Voter registration data by race and ethnicity (*continued*)

	1980	1982	1984	1986	1988	1990	1992	1994	1996	1998	2000	2002	2004	2006
Original Seven State Median														
Black	61.4	53.6	62.2	66.5	63.8	61.9	64.5	59.0	65.5	68.0	68.6	67.6	71.1	66.9
White	67.0	62.5	67.0	65.8	68.5	63.6	70.8	63.9	70.4	67.9	68.2	66.2	72.3	66.9
Non-South														
Black	60.6	61.7	67.2	63.1	65.9	58.4	63.0	58.3	62.0	58.5	61.7	57.0	63.3	53.6
White	69.3	66.7	70.5	66.2	68.5	64.4	70.9	65.6	68.1	63.9	65.9	63.0	68.5	64.2
Non-Hispanic White									72.2	68.2	70.3	67.8	74.3	69.7
Latino	35.5	33.9	39	33.2	32.4	30.4	32.9	29.1	33.8	31.9	32.7	30.6	33.4	32.1

Source: U.S. Census Bureau data.

Table B.2. Voter turnout data by race and ethnicity

	1980	1982	1984	1986	1988	1990	1992	1994	1996	1998	2000	2002	2004	2006
Alabama														
Black	48.9	41.2	54.8	55.2	52.4	45.7	58.1	53.5	54.3	51.6	57.2	43.3	63.9	47.8
White	59.2	52.0	62.8	52.5	58.4	52.7	65.9	64.3	56.3	51.6	60.8	50.7	62.2	49.6
Non-Hispanic White										51.9	61.1	51.3	63.1	50.5
Arkansas														
Black	50.8	47.7	56.9	43.3	49.6	34.5	46.4	34.5	50.6	31.1	52.2	44.0	49.4	34.0
White	58.6	54.3	61.5	47.9	57.3	48.2	60.7	43.1	52.1	45.0	49.0	46.1	58.6	46.2
Non-Hispanic White										45.4	50.5	47.3	60.8	48.7
Florida														
Black	50.3	30.4	43.2	42.4	40.8	37.4	46.3	30.0	40.5	33.4	42.3	33.0	44.5	33.5
White	56.5	43.1	55.5	47.5	57.1	44.9	57.9	46.2	52.7	40.6	53.8	44.8	58.4	39.7
Latino	29.3	18.6	29.1	28.0	34.1	22.8	30.5	20.1	29.0	22.9	31.4	27.4	34.0	18.0
Non-Hispanic White										44.8	59.8	49.5	64.0	46.7
Georgia														
Black	43.7	32.5	45.9	37.3	42.4	42.3	47.1	30.9	45.6	40.2	51.6	38.5	54.4	38.6
White	56.0	40.7	55.3	40.5	53.2	42.6	58.7	38.3	52.3	36.8	48.3	41.4	53.6	42.2
Non-Hispanic White										37.6	49.6	43.0	57.4	46.2
Louisiana														
Black	60.1	32.0	66.4	55.8	61.5	55.9	71.5	30.9	60.9	46.0	63.2	46.9	62.1	36.1
White	65.6	23.6	64.7	57.5	67.5	50.2	68.3	35.6	62.6	35.7	66.4	51.0	64.0	40.9
Non-Hispanic White										36.2	67.3	52.1	65.2	41.6
Mississippi														
Black	59.5	50.8	69.6	40.2	60.3	32.5	61.9	41.7	48.8	40.4	58.5	40.2	66.8	50.5
White	70.9	52.4	69.2	45.8	64.2	35.8	69.4	46.2	59.3	40.7	61.2	43.6	58.9	38.8
Non-Hispanic White										41.1	61.9	44.6	60.0	39.7

Table B.2. Voter turnout data by race and ethnicity (*continued*)

	1980	1982	1984	1986	1988	1990	1992	1994	1996	1998	2000	2002	2004	2006
N. Carolina														
Black	38.8	30.4	47.2	39.1	46.6	48.1	54.1	28.3	48.7	38.2	47.6	42.2	63.1	31.8
White	55.9	41.7	59.1	47.1	55.2	49.9	62.4	38.4	56.4	40.5	55.9	43.5	58.1	40.0
Non-Hispanic White										41.5	58.9	45.7	61.5	43.4
S. Carolina														
Black	51.3	38.9	51.4	42.0	40.7	44.6	48.8	38.7	49.9	42.8	60.7	48.7	59.5	48.9
White	51.7	37.0	47.9	41.3	52.3	42.0	61.6	49.4	56.2	48.8	58.7	45.1	63.4	41.2
Non-Hispanic White										49.3	60.0	46.4	64.3	43.5
Tennessee														
Black	56.9	50.8	64.7	46.0	57.9	35.3	62.9	38.5	56.0	39.0	52.6	39.8	51.3	38.5
White	56.7	46.6	56.7	43.8	50.7	29.7	54.8	44.5	52.8	35.8	52.3	45.8	53.5	45.6
Non-Hispanic White										36.0	53.3	48.0	54.8	47.2
Texas														
Black	40.7	37.8	51.2	39.8	47.0	38.7	50.1	33.1	47.1	35.5	57.5	44.3	55.8	35.3
White	52.7	40.6	55.5	37.5	55.2	42.5	57.2	39.4	46.7	33.5	48.1	35.0	50.6	34.3
Latino	29.7	26.8	32.7	23.6	33.2	22.5	33.1	18.9	27.9	15.3	29.5	19.1	29.3	17.5
Latino Citizens										21.8	41.0	27.4	41.6	25.4
Non-Hispanic Black										36.7	57.8	45.1	NA	NA
Non-Hispanic White										42.4	57.9	45.7	63.4	44.4
Virginia														
Black	42.9	44.3	55.0	42.5	47.7	32.0	59.0	33.8	53.3	23.8	52.7	27.2	49.6	34.6
White	58.3	46.2	57.8	36.8	61.1	39.6	63.4	50.4	58.5	32.4	60.4	37.8	63.0	47.7
Non-Hispanic White										33.3	61.8	39.6	66.2	51.0

TABLE B.2. Voter turnout data by race and ethnicity (*continued*)

	1980	1982	1984	1986	1988	1990	1992	1994	1996	1998	2000	2002	2004	2006
Original Seven States														
Black	48.9	38.9	54.8	42.0	47.7	44.6	58.1	33.8	49.9	40.4	57.2	42.2	62.1	38.6
White	58.3	41.7	59.1	45.8	58.4	42.6	63.4	46.2	56.4	40.5	60.4	44.8	62.2	41.2
Non-South														
Black	52.8	48.5	58.9	44.2	55.6	38.4	53.8	40.2	51.4	40.4	53.1	39.3	56.7	38.0
White	62.4	53.1	63.0	48.7	60.4	48.2	64.9	49.3	57.4	45.4	57.5	44.7	61.8	48.0
Non-Hispanic Whites										48.6	61.6	48.6	67.3	52.5
Latino	29.8	25.8	32.8	23.8	26.8	20.5	27.4	20.8	26.3	21.4	26.8	18.2	28.2	21.3
Nationwide														
Latino Citizens										32.8	45.1	30.4	47.2	32.3

Source: U.S. Census Bureau data.

Notes

ACKNOWLEDGMENTS

1. Ronald Keith Gaddie and Charles S. Bullock III, "From *Ashcroft* to *Larios*: Recent Redistricting Lessons from Georgia," *Fordham Urban Law Journal* 34 (April 2007): 997–1048.

2. Charles S. Bullock III and Ronald Keith Gaddie, "Voting Rights Progress in Georgia," *New York University Journal of Legislation and Public Policy* 10 (Spring 2007), 1–49.

3. Charles S. Bullock III and Ronald Keith Gaddie, "Good Intentions and Bad Social Science Meet in the Renewal of the Voting Rights Act," *Georgetown Journal of Law & Public Policy* 5 (Winter 2007), 1–27.

INTRODUCTION

1. Numan V. Bartley and High D. Graham, *Southern Politics and the Second Reconstruction* (Baltimore: Johns Hopkins University Press, 1976).

2. Richard Scher and James Button, "Voting Rights Act: Implementation and Impact," in *Implementation of Civil Rights Policy,* ed. Charles S. Bullock III and Charles Lamb (Belmont, Calif.: Wadsworth, 1984).

3. V. O. Key, Jr., *Southern Politics in State and Nation* (New York: Knopf, 1949).

4. James H. Street, *James Street's South* (New York: Doubleday, 1955), 1–3.

5. W. J. Cash, *The Mind of the South* (New York: Knopf, 1941).

6. John Dollard, *Caste and Class in a Southern Town* (New Haven, Conn.: Yale University Press, 1937).

7. Key, *Southern Politics,* 2.

8. Contemporary to Key, Cortez A. M. Ewing argued for a ten-state South, excluding unreconstructed Tennessee from Key's eleven because of the enduring two-party competition of the Volunteer State, a competitiveness absent from the rest of the South in the first part of the twentieth century. Cortez A. M. Ewing, *Primary Elections in the South* (Norman: University of Oklahoma Press, 1953). A more inclusive South emerges from the work of H. D. Price, who argued for a six-category typology to define the South, which produced gradations of "southernness." This typology was based largely on historic race relations and politics. H. D. Price, *The Negro in Southern Politics: A Chapter in Florida History* (New York: New York University Press, 1957). In addition to the states identified by Key, Price's work incorporates those states identified by others as "Border South" states: West Virginia, Maryland, Kentucky, Missouri, Delaware, and Oklahoma. John H. Fenton, *Politics in the Border States* (New Orleans: Hauser, 1957).

9. William C. Havard, ed., *The Changing Politics of the South* (Baton Rouge: Louisiana State University Press, 1972); Bartley and Graham, *Second Reconstruction,* 1976; Earl Black and Merle Black, *Politics and Society in the South* (Cambridge, Mass.: Harvard University Press, 1987); Black and Black, *The Vital South* (Cambridge, Mass.: Harvard University Press, 1992); Black and Black, *The Rise of Southern Republicans* (Cambridge, Mass.: Harvard University Press, 2002); Alexander P. Lamis, ed., *Southern Politics in the 1990s* (Baton Rouge: Louisiana State University Press, 1999); Joseph A. Aistrup, *The Southern Strategy Revisited* (Lexington: University of Kentucky Press, 1996); David Lublin, *The Republican South* (Princeton, N.J.: Princeton University Press, 2003); Jack Bass and Walter de Vries, *The Transformation of Southern Politics* (New York: Meridian, 1976).

10. J. Morgan Kousser, *The Shaping of Southern Politics: Suffrage Restriction and the Establishment of the One-party South, 1880–1910* (New Haven, Conn.: Yale University Press, 1974).

11. Ibid.

12. Literacy tests were eventually adopted in the seven states covered by Section 5 of the original Voting Rights Act of 1965, in this order: Mississippi, 1890; South Carolina, 1895; North Carolina, 1900; Alabama, 1901; Virginia, 1902; Georgia, 1908; and Louisiana, 1921.

13. Key, *Southern Politics.*

14. *Williams v. Mississippi,* 170 U.S. 213 (1898).

15. Key effectively documents the collapse of the southern electorate in chapters 25–29 of *Southern Politics.* We recommend his expansive treatment of the data on late nineteenth- and early twentieth-century participation. See also Kousser, *Shaping of Southern Politics,* chapters 1 and 2 and especially page 12.

16. Laughlin McDonald, *A Voting Rights Odyssey: Black Enfranchisement in Georgia* (New York: Cambridge University Press, 2003), 41.

17. *Guinn v. United States,* 238 U.S. 347 (1915).

18. *Smith v. Allwright,* 321 U.S. 649 (1944). Fort Bend County, Texas, sought to maintain the practice subsequent to *Smith v. Allwright* by creating a private association that conducted a "preprimary" to select candidates for the Democratic nomination and to exclude black voters. The Supreme Court overturned this practice in 1953 (*Terry v. Adams,* 345 U.S. 461). The white primary was present in every southern state except Tennessee. In five of the ten states with the white primary (Florida, Georgia, Louisiana, Mississippi, and Texas), efforts were made to put the primary beyond the law. See O. Douglas Weeks, "The White Primary: 1944–1948," *The American Political Science Review* 42 (1948): 500–510.

19. Dan T. Carter, *The Politics of Rage* (New York: Simon & Schuster, 1995), 97–104.

20. O. Douglas Weeks, "The White Primary: 1944–1948," *The American Political Science Review* 42 (1948): 510n19.

21. Harrell R. Rodgers, Jr., and Charles S. Bullock III, *Law and Social Change* (New York: McGraw-Hill, 1972), 25.

22. Ibid., 27.

23. Robert Mann, *The Walls of Jericho* (San Diego: Harcourt, Brace and Co., 1996), 448.

24. A somewhat analogous approach had been taken to improve housing stock. Urban renewal projects razed structures deemed beyond salvage. To secure federal money for urban renewal, local governments had to implement housing codes designed to prevent existing buildings from deteriorating.

25. Quoted in Walter Isaacson and Evan Thomas, "Pondering the Voting Rights Act," *Time,* May 11, 1981.

26. Federal authorities had learned from the minimal pace of school desegregation. When the VRA was passed, many southern schools remained as segregated as before *Brown v. Board of Education,* and where segregation was not total, no more than token desegregation had taken place. Following a course of massive resistance, southern states enacted numerous laws to bolster their segregated schools and then exhausted every opportunity for appeal before countenancing the first cracks in the wall separating black and white children.

27. *Harper v. Board of Elections,* 303 U.S. 663 (1966).

28. *The Voting Rights Act . . . the First Months* (Washington, D.C.: U.S. Commission on Civil Rights, 1966), 23.

29. U.S. Commission on Civil Rights, *Political Participation* (Washington, D.C.: U.S. Government Printing Office, 1968), 223.

30. *Georgia v. United States,* 411 U.S. 526 (1973).

31. Rodgers and Bullock, *Law and Social Change,* 25.

32. Abigail M. Thernstrom, *Whose Votes Count? Affirmative Action and Minority Voting Rights* (Cambridge, Mass.: Harvard University Press, 1987), chapter 4.

33. *The Voting Rights Act . . . the First Months,* 23.

34. Both the 1970 and 1975 triggers applied to Yuba County, California, and Bronx and Kings counties, New York.

35. *South Carolina v. Katzenbach,* 383 U.S. 301 (1966).

36. *City of Boerne v. Flores,* 521 U.S. 507 (1997).

37. Senate Judiciary Committee, "Response of Richard H. Pildes, Sudler Family Professor of Constitutional Law, NYU School of Law, to Written Questions from Senator Arlen Specter Supplement to Original Testimony Before Senate Judiciary Committee on May 16, 2006," for hearing on *The Continuing Need for Section 5 Preclearance,* submitted June 16, 2006; Senate Judiciary Committee, "Testimony of Professor Samuel Issacharoff, NYU School of Law, on the Reauthorization of Section 5 of the Voting Rights Act," for hearing on *An Introduction to the Expiring Provisions of the Voting Rights Act,* May 9, 2006; Senate Judiciary Committee, "Testimony of Professor Nathaniel Persily, University of Pennsylvania School of Law, before the United States Senate Committee on the Judiciary on *Understanding the Benefits and Costs of Section 5 Pre-Clearance,*" submitted May 16, 2006; Senate Judiciary Committee, "Testimony of Professor Richard L. Hasen, William H. Hannon Distinguished Professor of Law, Loyola Law School, Senate Judiciary Committee Legislative Hearing on *An Introduction to the Expiring Provisions of the Voting Rights Act and Legal Issues Relating to Reauthorization,*" May 9, 2006.

38. Rep. Melvin Watt, floor statement to the U.S. House of Representatives, July 13, 2006; press release of Watt's office at http://watt.house.gov/pressreleases_2007.asp?ARTICLE5353=3265.

39. Rep. James Sensenbrenner, floor statement to the U.S. House of Representatives, July 13, 2006, *Congressional Record,* H 5144.

40. Sen. Jeff Sessions, floor statement to the United States Senate, July 20, 2006, *Congressional Record,* July 20.

41. Ibid.

42. Sen. Barack Obama, floor statement to the United States Senate, July 20, 2006.

43. *Congressional Record,* July 13, 2006, H 5162.

44. Ibid.

45. Ibid., H 5150.

46. Nathaniel Persily, "The Promise and Pitfalls of the New Voting Rights Act," *The Yale Law Journal* 117, no. 2 (2007): 105–183.

47. Senators John Cornyn (R-Tex.) and Tom Coburn (R-Okla.) did include a substantial minority report in the Judiciary Committee's reporting of the act's renewal. This report incorporated the caveats of those witnesses who argued for modification of the act.

48. *City of Mobile v. Bolden,* 446 U.S. 55 (1980).

49. Ibid.

50. Walter Isaacson, "Pondering the Voting Rights Act," *Time,* May 11, 1981. Accessed at www.time.com/time/magazine/article/0,9171,949120,00.html.

51. Ibid.

52. *Shaw v. Reno,* 509 U.S. 630 (1993).

53. *Miller v. Johnson,* 515 U.S. 900 (1995).

54. *Beer v. United States,* 425 U.S. 130 (1976).

55. *Reno v. Bossier Parish School Board,* 520 U.S. 471 (1997).

56. Paul R. Abramson and William Claggett, "Race-related Differences in Self-Reported and Validated Turnout," *Journal of Politics* 46 (1984): 719–739.

CHAPTER 1: MISSISSIPPI

1. Key, *Southern Politics,* 5.

2. Ibid.

3. According to the 1860 census, a majority of the populations of Mississippi and South Carolina were Africans held in bonded servitude. By 1900, only South Carolina and Mississippi reported majority-black populations. By the 1930 census, only Mississippi remained majority black.

4. Key, *Southern Politics,* 229.

5. Ibid., 229–253.

6. During Freedom Summer, hundreds of college students came to Mississippi to work on voter registration projects.

7. Jere Nash and Andy Taggart, *Mississippi Politics* (Jackson: University Press of Mississippi, 2006), 16.

8. See, for example, James W. Silver, *Mississippi: The Closed Society* (New York: Harcourt, Brace and World, 1963).

9. Kousser, *Shaping of Southern Politics,* 241.

10. *Allen v. State Board of Elections,* 393 U.S. 544 (1969).

11. *Allen v. State Board of Elections,* 393 U.S. 544 (1969).

12. U.S. Commission on Civil Rights, *Political Participation,* 244–247.

13. Ibid.

14. Ibid.; see also William T. Harbaugh, "If People Vote Because They Like To, Then Why Do So Many of Them Lie?" *Public Choice* 89 (1996): 63–76.

15. *Allen v. State Board of Elections,* 393 U.S. 544 (1969).

16. Robert McDuff, *The Voting Rights Act and Mississippi, 1965–2006,* RenewtheVRA.org (2006), 10.

17. *National Roster of Black Elected Officials* (Washington, D.C: Metropolitan Applied Research Center, 1969).

18. McDuff, *Voting Rights Act and Mississippi,* 10.

19. Ibid., 11.

20. The 1962 black percentage comes from ibid., 8.

21. *Wesberry v. Sanders,* 366 U.S. 1 (1964).

22. For a discussion of the politics and motivations behind the changes in the Mississippi congressional plans, see Frank R. Parker, *Black Votes Count* (Chapel Hill: University of North Carolina Press, 1990), 41–51.

23. Ibid.

24. Allen Ehrenhalt, ed., *Politics in America, 1984* (Washington, D.C.: Congressional Quarterly, 1983), 835.

25. Michael Barone and Grant Ujifusa, *The Almanac of American Politics, 1988* (Washington, D.C.: National Journal, 1987), 655.

26. David T. Canon, *Race, Redistricting and Representation* (Chicago: University of Chicago Press, 1999), 93–142

27. Mississippi had two Democrats until Travis Childers won a special election called to replace Roger Wicker (R), who had been appointed to replace Sen. Trent Lott (R).

28. Michel Barone with Richard E. Cohen, *The Almanac of American Politics, 2006* (Washington, D.C.: National Journal, 2005), 950–952.

29. Parker, *Black Votes Count*, describes in chapter 4 the legal battle that preceded a districting plan that opened the way for the big jump in blacks serving in the House.

30. The pathbreaking Clark was able to challenge for Congress while extending his legislative career due to Mississippi's odd-year election calendar.

31. David A. Breaux, Stephen D. Shaffer, and Hilary B. Gresham, "Mississippi: Emergence of a Modern Two-Party State," in *The New Politics of the Old South*, 3rd ed., ed. Charles S. Bullock III and Mark J. Rozell (Lanham, Md.: Rowman and Littlefield, 2007), 110.

32. Ibid.

33. Byron D'Andra Orey, "Black Legislative Politics in Mississippi," *Journal of Black Studies* 30 (July 2000): 802.

34. Breaux et al., "Mississippi: Emergence," 105.

35. Ibid., 107.

36. The only successful Democrat was the incumbent attorney general. Another former Democratic incumbent, Lester Spell, switched parties and won 51 percent of the vote in a three-way contest.

37. McDuff, *Voting Rights Act and Mississippi*, 11.

38. Ibid.

39. *Allen v. State Board of Elections*, 393 U.S. 544 (1969).

40. See for example, Pamela S. Karlan, "Testimony of Professor Pamela S. Karlan, Stanford Law School, on the Continuing Need for Section 5 Preclearance," *Election Law Journal* 5 (2006): 338.

41. Walter Isaacson, "Pondering the Voting Rights Act," *Time*, May 11, 1981.

42. Sen. Patrick Leahy (D-Vt.), *Congressional Record*, July 20, 2006, S 8008.

43. Luis Ricardo Fraga and Maria Lizet Ocampo, "The Deterrent Effect of Section 5 on the Voting Rights Act: The Role of More Information Requests," presented at the symposium Protecting Democracy: Using Research to Inform the Voting Reauthorization Debate, Washington, D.C., February 9, 2006.

44. *United States v. Ike Brown*, 4:05-CV-33-TSL-LRA (U.S. Federal Court for the Southern District of Mississippi, 2007).

45. For an example of a white southern boss voting a white electorate in a similar manner in a Black Belt county, see Jimmy Carter, *Turning Point: A Candidate, a State, and a Nation Come of Age* (New York: Times Books, 1993), 74–101.

46. Jack Tapper and Avery Miller, "Reverse Racism?" *ABC World News Today*, December 28, 2006.

47. *Gingles v. Thornburg*, 2764.

48. *United States v. Ike Brown*, 102.

49. Ibid.

50. Allan J. Lichtman, "Racial Bloc Voting in Mississippi Elections: Methodology and Results," prepared for *Martin v. Allain*, SAJ 84-0708 (W), February 1987.

51. As of 1987, Anderson was the only black judicial candidate to have carried the white vote. *Martin v. Allain*, 658 F. Supp. 1183, 1194 (S.D. Miss. 1987).

52. The 2002 white vote for Sen. Thad Cochran reached 89.2 percent, but no Democrat faced him. His sole opponent, who represented the Reform Party, managed only 15.4 percent of the vote.

53. In 2005, Taylor had the most conservative voting record of any House Democrat and was the only Democrat who voted conservatively more often than liberally. "The Centrists," *National Journal* 38 (February 25, 2006): 28–29.

54. Breaux et al., "Mississippi: Emergence," 101.

55. Ibid., 102.

56. Ibid.

57. Ibid.

58. A useful table that demonstrates the relative shares of black and white votes needed appears in Earl Black and Merle Black, *The Rise of Southern Republicans* (Cambridge, Mass.: Belknap Press, 2002), 30, and also in a Cartesian graphic format in Earl Black and Merle Black, *Politics and Society in the South* (Cambridge, Mass.: Harvard University Press, 1989), 141.

59. Because of the presence of a third-party candidate, Ronnie Musgrove secured a nine thousand–vote advantage but failed to win the majority that is required under Mississippi law. As a consequence, the actual decision of who would be the state's new governor was made by the state house, which, with its overwhelming Democratic majority, fell in line behind its party nominee. Had the state representatives voted as their districts did, the election would have remained a standoff since Musgrove and the Republican Mike Parker each carried sixty-one house districts.

60. A similar argument is made with regard to Democratic successes in holding on to congressional seats. The argument is that Democrats who have strong local ties having been born and gone to school in the area were able to win against Republican challengers, while Democrats who had moved to the area as adults

were much more vulnerable. For this argument, see Byron Shafer and Richard Johnston, *The End of Southern Exceptionalism* (Cambridge: Harvard University Press, 2006), 149–154.

61. Breaux et al., "Mississippi: Emergence," 112. Orey, whose analysis ends with 1988, is less sanguine that Breaux and his colleagues, although Orey does note some successes for the Black Caucus. Orey, "Black Legislative Politics," 804–812.

62. In keeping with the theme introduced earlier in this chapter that suggested that Mississippi presents the extreme example of "southernness," some of the findings reported by a 1960s study help explain the higher levels of black participation in the Magnolia State. Matthews and Prothro reported that, "If southern Negroes could translate their existing level of political interest in participation in the same fashion as whites do, there would be a 19–20 percentage-point increase in the proportion of Negroes who vote or participate beyond voting!" (268–269). Moreover, Matthews and Prothro found that for a third of the African Americans who had registered to vote, an important motivation was to "be a citizen" or "to be a man." This consideration motivated only 13 percent of the white voters. We would expect that these factors cited by Matthews and Prothro would have a greater impact in Mississippi than elsewhere in the South. Donald R. Matthews and James Prothro, *Negroes in the New Southern Politics* (New York: Harcourt, Brace and World, 1966).

CHAPTER 2: ALABAMA

1. Quoted in Dan T. Carter, *The Politics of Rage* (New York: Simon and Schuster, 1995), 96.

2. Peyton McCrary, Jerome A. Gray, Edward Still, and Huey L. Perry, "Alabama," in *Quiet Revolution in the South*, ed. Chandler Davidson and Bernard Grofman (Princeton: Princeton University Press, 1994), 65.

3. Ibid., 44.

4. The best estimate of the length of the Alabama Constitution is 360,000 words, or about three and a half times longer than this volume.

5. Key, *Southern Politics*, 632.

6. U.S. Commission on Civil Rights, *Political Participation*, 226–227.

7. Charles V. Hamilton and Stokely Carmichael, *Black Power* (New York: Vintage, 1967).

8. Patrick R. Cotter, "Alabama: From One Party to Competition, and Maybe Back Again," in *The New Politics of the Old South*, 3rd ed., ed. Charles S. Bullock III and Mark J. Rozell (Lanham, Md.: Rowman and Littlefield, 2007), 77.

9. Alabama black turnout also exceeded the white non-South figure in 2004, but the disparity reverses once Hispanics are removed.

10. Cotter, "Alabama: From One Party."

11. *Dillard v. Crenshaw County*, 640 F. Supp. 1347 (N.D. Ala. 1986). Much of the material in the remainder of this paragraph comes from James Blacksher, Edward

Still, Nick Quinton, Cullen Brown, and Royal Dumas, "Voting Rights in Alabama 1982–2006," RenewtheVRA.org (July 2006), 13–14.

12. Edward Still, "Cumulative Voting and Limited Voting in Alabama," in *United States Electoral Systems: Their Impact on Women and Minorities*, ed. Wilma Rule and Joseph F. Zimmerman (New York: Greenwood Press, 1992), 183–196.

13. Blacksher et al., "Voting Rights in Alabama," 23.

14. Hastings Wyman, "Diversity in Dixie: A Special Report," *Southern Political Report* (September 2001).

15. Ford's frustrations with the Democratic Party prompted him to join the GOP in 2003. Charles E. Menifield, Stephen D. Shaffer, and Brandi J. Brassell, "An Overview of African American Representation in Other Southern States," in *Politics in the New South: Representation of African Americans in Southern State Legislatures*, ed. Charles E. Menifield and Stephen D. Shaffer (Albany: State University of New York Press, 2005), 160.

16. Blacksher et al., "Voting Rights in Alabama," 6.

17. Ibid., 8.

18. Ibid., 18.

CHAPTER 3: GEORGIA

1. Laughlin McDonald, Michael B. Binford, and Ken Johnson, "Georgia," in *Quiet Revolution in the South 101*, ed. Chandler Davidson and Bernard Grofman (Princeton, N.J.: Princeton University Press, 1994).

2. Kousser, *Shaping of Southern Politics*, 239.

3. Key, *Southern Politics*, 620.

4. *Smith v. Allwright*, 321 U.S. 649 (1944); several southern states attempted creative mechanisms to retain the white primary. Georgia finally gave up the fight in 1946, after the state lost its effort to defend the white primary in an inferior federal court in *Chapman v. King*, 154 F.2d 460 (5th Cir. 1946).

5. William Anderson, *The Wild Man from Sugar Creek* (Baton Rouge: Louisiana State University Press, 1975), 219–222.

6. Key, *Southern Politics*, 126.

7. Ibid., 636.

8. U.S. Commission on Civil Rights, *Political Participation*, 238 (figures presented for nonwhites and whites; almost all Georgia nonwhites in the 1960s would be African American).

9. Ibid., 238 (excludes four mountain counties that in 1960 had fewer than ten nonwhite residents of voting age).

10. Ibid., 15, 222–223.

11. Ibid.

12. The exception is Chattahoochee County, which contains much of Fort Benning, many of whose soldiers are not Georgia residents. Section 5 can be

over-inclusive when a county contains a large number of military personnel who do not vote locally.

13. Georgia State Elections Division, www.sos.georgia.gov/elections (accessed January 31, 2007).

14. William T. Harbaugh, "If People Vote Because They Like To, Then Why Do So Many of Them Lie?," *Public Choice* 89 (October 1996): 63–64.

15. As reported in the voter turnout table in appendix B, the Census Bureau estimated that 57.4 percent of non-Hispanic whites and 54.4 percent of blacks voted in the 2004 election. It should be noted that the Census Bureau estimates use the voting-age population as the denominator for the calculations while the turnout figures reported in table 3.2 use registration as the denominator.

16. *National Roster of Black Elected Officials* (Washington, D.C.: Metropolitan Applied Research Center, 1969).

17. The Joint Center Staff, *Black Elected Officials* (Washington, D.C.: The Joint Center for Political and Economic Studies, 1969–2001 inclusive).

18. Currently the twenty-nine–member New York delegation and the fifty-three–member California delegation have four African American representatives each.

19. *Miller v. Johnson*, 515 U.S. 900, 917–22 (1995); Letters from John R. Dunne, Assistant Attorney General to Mark M. Cohen, Georgia assistant attorney general, January 21, 1992, and March 20, 1992.

20. *Miller v. Johnson*, 515 U.S. 900, 903, 924, 928 (1995).

21. Ibid., 916–17.

22. David G. Savage, "Despite Redistricting Dispute, Black Lawmakers Win Reelection," *Los Angeles Times*, Nov. 9, 1996, 10.

23. Cynthia A. McKinney, Op-Ed., *A Product of The Voting Rights Act*, Washington Post, November 26, 1996, A15.

24. Unlike other states, Georgia's governors have teams of three people in each chamber who act as the governor's floor leaders, responsible for introducing the governor's bills and shepherding them through the chamber.

25. Peter W. Wielhouwer and Keesha M. Middlemass, "Black Representation in Georgia," in *Politics in the New South*, ed. Charles E. Menifield and Stephen D. Shaffer (Albany: State University of New York Press, 2005), 85.

26. Ibid., 103.

27. African Americans had unsuccessfully run statewide prior to Benham's appointment. In 1968 Maynard Jackson challenged Sen. Herman Talmadge. While Jackson managed only a quarter of the vote in the Democratic primary, this launched a career that saw him become the first African American mayor of a major southern city. He led Atlanta for three terms, and since his initial victory in 1973, blacks have served as mayors of Atlanta without interruption.

28. Georgia is unique in requiring a majority vote in the general election. Burgess led in the initial round, but like most incumbents forced into a runoff, came up short in the runoff.

29. Judicial elections in Georgia are nonpartisan.

30. Expert report of David Epstein, *Georgia v. Ashcroft*, 195 F. Supp. 2d 25 (D.D.C. 2002) (No. 01-2111), 16–17.

31. Ibid.

32. Affidavit of Charles Walker, *Georgia v. Ashcroft*, 195 F. Supp. 2d 25 (D.D.C. 2002) (No. 01–2111), 12.

33. *Georgia v. Ashcroft*, 195 F. Supp. 2d 25, 72 (2002).

34. *Georgia v. Ashcroft*, 539 U.S. 461, 472, 490 (2003).

35. Rhonda Cook, "Attorney General's Authority Upheld," *Atlanta Journal-Constitution*, September 5, 2003, A1.

36. Affidavit of John Lewis, *Georgia v. Ashcroft*, 195 F. Supp. 2d 25 (D.D.C. 2002), 18.

37. Ibid., 15–16.

38. Direct Testimony of Robert Brown, *Georgia v. Ashcroft*, 195 F. Supp. 2d 25 (D.D.C. 2002), 8.

39. Ibid., 26–27.

40. Ibid., 29–30.

41. Charles S. Bullock III, "A Deep Look at What the Primary and Runoff Results Tell Us," *Insider Advantage Georgia,* October 9, 2006, http://insideradvantagegeorgia.com/restricted/2006/September%2006/9-12-06/Charles%20Bullock.php.

42. Affidavit of Charles Walker, *Georgia v. Ashcroft*, 195 F. Supp. 2d 25 (D.D.C. 2002), 22–23.

43. Post-trial brief of the state of Georgia, *Georgia v. Ashcroft,* C.A. No. 01–2111 (EGS) (D.C., DC 2002), 2.

44. Fraga and Ocampo, "Deterrent Effect of Section 5 of the Voting Rights Act."

45. *Georgia v. Reno,* 881 F. Supp. 7 (D.D.C. 1995).

46. *Miller v. Johnson,* 515 U.S. 900 (1995).

47. Fraga and Ocampo, "Deterrent Effect of Section 5 of the Voting Rights Act," tables 6 through 9.

CHAPTER 4: LOUISIANA

1. Kousser, *Shaping of Southern Politics*, 55.

2. Ibid., 241.

3. Key, *Southern Politics*, 626.

4. U.S. Commission on Civil Rights, *Political Participation*, 242–243.

5. Pearson's simple correlation, where 0 indicates no relationship between two variables where an absolute value approaching 1 indicates nearly perfect correlation between two variables.

6. Key, *Southern Politics*.

7. The exit polls of the total votes in Louisiana show black voters constituting 49 percent of the Democratic participants with whites casting 46 percent of the votes.

8. The share of voters in statewide contests who are African American in the last decade are: 1998, 29.9 percent; 1999, 22.6 percent; 2000, 26.6 percent; 2002, 25.9 percent; 2003, 26.2 percent; 2004, 27.2 percent; 2006, 23.8 percent; 2007, 23.6 percent; and the 2008 presidential-preference primary, 39.7 percent.

9. Hale Boggs won his first election to the House in 1940 but failed to be renominated for a second term. After serving in World War II, Boggs regained the congressional seat in 1946 and held it until his death in 1972.

10. Ronald Keith Gaddie and Charles S. Bullock III, "Voter Turnout and Candidate Participation Effects of Affirmative-Action Districting," in *Southern Parties and Elections: Studies in Regional Change*, ed. Robert Steed, Laurence Moreland, and Tod Baker (Tuscaloosa: University of Alabama Press, 1997); Richard L. Engstrom and Jason F. Kirksey, "Race and Representation Districting in Louisiana," in *Race and Redistricting in the 1990s*, ed. Bernard Grofman (New York: Agathon, 1998), 237–241.

11. Engstrom and Kirksey, "Race and Representation," 253.

12. Michael Barone and Grant Ujifusa, *The Almanac of American Politics 1994* (Washington, D.C.: National Journal, 1993), 534.

13. *Shaw v. Reno*, 509 U.S. 630 (1993).

14. *Hays v. Louisiana*, 839 F. Supp. 1188 (W.D. La. 1993).

15. *Hays v. Louisiana*, 862 F. Supp. 119 (W.D. La. 1994).

16. *United States v. Hays*, 515 U.S. 737 (1995).

17. Engstrom and Kirksey, "Race and Representation," 263.

18. Ibid., 244.

19. Ibid., 234–235.

20. The BESE was created in the 1973 constitutional reform as part of an effort to provide separate administration for primary and secondary education, and higher education respectively. The board has eleven members, eight elected from single-member districts and three at-large members appointed by the governor. Until 1991, elected BESE members shared the same district lines as congressional incumbents, but the reduction of the Louisiana congressional delegation by one in reapportionment led to the crafting of distinct BESE districts.

21. Foster, a state legislator, changed political party the day of filing.

22. Fields had garnered 19 percent of the vote to trail Republican Foster with 26 percent and to lead former governor Buddy Roemer, who had 16 percent.

23. Michael Barone and Grant Ujifusa, *The Almanac of American Politics 1998* (Washington, D.C.: National Journal, 1997), 621.

24. Scott Dyer, "The politics of race is 1995 trump card," *The Advocate*, November 9, 1995, B9.

25. See, for a discussion of the David Duke phenomenon, John C. Kuzenski, Charles S. Bullock III, and Ronald Keith Gaddie, eds., *David Duke and the Politics of Race in the South* (Nashville: Vanderbilt University Press, 1995); and Douglas Rose, ed., *David Duke and the Politics of Race* (Chapel Hill: University of North Carolina Press, 1993).

26. Analysis of the District 2 primary, won by black incumbent Bill Jefferson, is omitted due to data problems encountered in merging Orleans Parish precinct data with state election board returns. Inconsistent precinct identifiers for Orleans Parish prevented merging about half of all precinct election data with precinct registration and turnout data.

27. Fraga and Ocampo, "Deterrent Effect of Section 5 of the Voting Rights Act."

28. *Beer v. United States*, 425 U.S. 130 (1976).

29. John R. Dunne, "Remarks of John R. Dunne," *Cardozo Law Review* 14 (1993): 1128.

30. *Reno v. Bossier Parish School Board*, 428 U.S. 320 (1999).

CHAPTER 5: VIRGINIA

1. Twenty-fourth Amendment; and *Harper v. Virginia State Board of Elections*, 383 U.S. 663 (1966).

2. Key, *Southern Politics*, 20.

3. Thomas R. Morris and Neil Bradley, "Virginia," in *Quiet Revolution in the South*, ed. Chandler Davidson and Bernard Grofman (Princeton: Princeton University Press, 1994), 298.

4. U.S. Commission on Civil Rights, *Political Participation*, 222–223.

5. Key, *Southern Politics*, 20.

6. These calculations exclude two counties in which the 1960 census showed fewer than ten nonwhite adults.

7. *Shaw v. Reno*, 509 U.S. 630 (1993). The Virginia challenge came in *Moon v. Meadows*, 952 F. Supp.1141 (E.D.Va. 1996).

8. Ronald Keith Gaddie, "An Evaluation of Racial Polarization and the Election of Minority Legislative Candidates of Choice in the Vicinity of Virginia Congressional Districts 3 and 4," prepared for *Hall v. Commonwealth*, June 2003.

9. Ibid.

10. McEachin, a longtime Douglas Wilder ally from Henrico County, defeated delegate Floyd H. Miles in the June 2005 Democratic primary.

11. Warner had been considered a rising star in the Virginia Democratic Party for more than a decade. Initially his name surfaced as a possible candidate for Democrat Jim Moran's northern Virginia congressional seat, and then in 1996 he unsuccessfully challenged incumbent U.S. senator John Warner. See Thomas A. Kazee, ed., *Who Runs for Congress?* (Washington, D.C.: CQ Press, 1994).

12. CBS News/The New York Times, "CBS News/New York Times Virginia Gubernatorial Election Exit Poll," ICPSR study number 9494, released May 1991 (Ann Arbor, Mich.: Interuniversity Consortium for Political and Social Research).

13. Charles S. Bullock III and Ronald Keith Gaddie, *An Assessment of Voting Rights Progress in California* (Washington, D.C.: American Enterprise Institute Policy Series, 2006).

14. www.cnn.com/ALLPOLITICS/1997/11/06/poll/#archive (accessed October 1, 2005).

15. The results for the 2001 Virginia statewide elections were, for governor: Mark Warner (D), 984,177 (52.16 percent), Mark Early (R), 887,234 (47.03 percent); for lieutenant governor, Tim Kaine (D), 925,974 (50.35 percent), J. K. Katzen (R), 883,886 (48.06 percent); for attorney general, Don McEachin (D), 736,431 (39.92 percent), J. W. Kilgore (R), 1,107,068 (60.01 percent). Source: www.sbe.state.va.us/web_docs/election/results/2001/nov2001/html/index.htm.

16. On Warner's personal campaign contribution, see Michael Barone with Richard E. Cohen, *The Almanac of American Politics 2006* (Washington: National Journal, 2005), 1710.

17. The results for the 2005 Virginia statewide elections were, for governor: Tim Kaine (D), 1,025,942 (51.72 percent), J. W. Kilgore (R), 912,327 (45.99 percent); for lieutenant governor, L. L. Byrne (D), 956,906 (49.32 percent), W. T. Bolling (R), 979,265 (50.47 percent); for attorney general, R. C. Deeds (D), 970,563 (49.95 percent), R. F. McDonnell (R), 970,886 (49.96 percent). Source: www.sbe.state.va.us/web_docs/election/results/2005/nov2005/html/index.htm.

18. One important difference that contributes to Scott's stronger showing in 1992 than 1986 is that in the earlier contest he faced a well-entrenched, well-funded incumbent, while in 1992 the district had no incumbent. In 1986, Bateman spent almost 75 percent more than Scott. In Scott's 1992 victory, he outspent his lackluster Republican challenger by a margin of thirty to one. Campaign finance data come from Michael Barone and Grant Ujifusa, *The Almanac of American Politics 1988* (Washington: National Journal, 1987), 1225, and Michael Barone and Grant Ujifusa, *The Almanac of American Politics 1994* (Washington: National Journal, 1993), 1315.

19. Gaddie, "Evaluation of Racial Polarization."

20. Gary King, *A Solution to the Ecological Inference Problem* (Princeton, N.J.: Princeton University Press, 1997). King's technique can be used with measures of the racial makeup to estimate voter participation and candidate preferences by race when using aggregated units, such as precincts or counties.

21. Lisa R. Handley, "Liability Issues in *Moon v. Meadows*" (September 4, 1996). *Moon v. Meadows*, 952 F. Supp. 1141 (ED Va. 1997).

22. Joel Turner, "Democrat Tim Kaine Wins Lieutenant-Governor; Analysts Say Mark Warner's Gubernatorial Victory Boosted Kaine's Position," *The Roanoke Times*, November 7, 2001, A-16.

23. Michael Hardy, "Candidates Playing to Perceptions," *Richmond Times-Dispatch*, November 4, 2001, C-4.

24. Gaddie, "Evaluation of Racial Polarization."

25. In all of the fourteen except for Senate District 16 in 1991, a majority of blacks opposed a majority of whites.

26. Gaddie, "Evaluation of Racial Polarization," 3.

27. Gaddie, "Evaluation of Racial Polarization," 4.

28. These data come from Fraga and Ocampo, "Deterrent Effect of Section 5 of the Voting Rights Act."

29. www.usdoj.gov/crt/voting/sec_5covered.htm (accessed December 6, 2006).

CHAPTER 6: SOUTH CAROLINA

1. Key, *Southern Politics*, 130.

2. Ibid, 131.

3. Ibid, 130.

4. *Smith v. Allwright* , 321 U.S. 649 (1944).

5. Key, *Southern Politics*, 627.

6. Robert W. Oldendick, "Gender and Race in South Carolina," *New Voices in the Old South*, ed. Todd A. Shields (Tallahassee: Florida State University, 2008), 66.

7. The irony of this event is that, prior to 1948, Strom Thurmond was characterized as a political moderate who had the support of the NAACP in his bid for governor. John Gunther, *Inside U.S.A.* (New York: Harper and Brothers, 1947), 726.

8. Kari Fredrickson, *The Dixiecrat Revolt and the End of the Solid South, 1932–1968* (Chapel Hill: University of North Carolina Press, 2001), chapter 4.

9. The Deep South states are Alabama, Georgia, Louisiana, Mississippi, and South Carolina.

10. U.S. Commission on Civil Rights, *Political Participation*, 252–253.

11. One of these, Clarendon County, was the site of one of the challenges to separate-but-equal policies in school assignments that became part of *Brown v. Board of Education*.

12. The count for Georgia excludes mountain counties with fewer than ten black adults.

13. U.S. Commission on Civil Rights, *Political Participation*, 222–223.

14. Willie M. Leggette, "The South Carolina Legislative Black Caucus, 1970 to 1988," *Journal of Black Studies* 30 (July 2000): 841–842.

15. Carol M. Swain, *Black Faces, Black Interests* (Cambridge, Mass.: Harvard University Press, 1993), 145–159.

16. David T. Canon, *Race, Redistricting, and Representation* (Chicago: University of Chicago Press, 1999), 135.

17. W. E. B. Du Bois, *Black Reconstruction in America 1860–1880* (New York: Free Press, 1999).

18. Leggette, "South Carolina Legislative Black Caucus," 842.

19. Menifield et al., "An Overview of African American Representation," 169–170.

20. Key, *Southern Politics*, 151.

21. Charles S. Bullock III and Ronald Keith Gaddie, "Changing from Multi-Member to Single-Member Districts: Partisan, Racial, and Gender Impacts," *State and Local Government Review* 25 (1993), 155–163.

22. Leggette, "South Carolina Legislative Black Caucus," 852–857.

23. According to the Voter Research and Surveys exit poll in the 1990 South Carolina gubernatorial election:

	Theo Mitchell-D	Carroll Campbell-R	*n*
White	14.5	81.1	1,412
Black	63.7	24.0	438

Source: See Voter Research and Surveys, 1990. "Voter Research and Surveys General Election Exit Poll: State Files, 1990." Computer file. (New York, N.Y.: Voter Research and Surveys [producer]; Ann Arbor, Mich.: Inter-university Consortium for Political and Social Research [distributor], 1991).

24. The results for Democratic candidates running statewide in South Carolina in 2002 were: U.S. Senate, 44.85 percent; governor, 47.1 percent; lieutenant governor, 46.5 percent; secretary of state, 43.1 percent; attorney general, 44.5 percent; comptroller, 45.4 percent; commissioner of agriculture, 49.5 percent. Candidates for secretary of state and attorney general are African Americans. Data obtained from South Carolina Election Board Web page, www.scvotes.org.

25. Hastings Wyman, "Democrats Aim for Gubernatorial Gains," *Southern Political Report*, April 15, 2005, 5.

26. James W. Loewen, "Racial Bloc Voting in South Carolina," unpublished manuscript, August 13, 1987.

27. Ibid., 5–6.

28. Ibid., 15.

29. Ibid., 6.

30. House Committee on the Judiciary, "Testimony of James H. Loewen before the Subcommittee on Civil and Constitutional Rights of the Committee on the Judiciary of the House of Representatives, extension of the *Voting Rights Act*," May 19, 1981, Part I, 271.

31. Ibid., 271.

32. Ibid., 276.

33. Ibid., 273.

34. Estimates for the Clyburn contests are from Charles S. Bullock III and Richard E. Dunn, "The Demise of Racial Districting and the Future of Black Representation," *Emory Law Journal* 48 (Fall 1999): 1209–1253. White support for Clyburn was, by year (OLS/EI): 1992, 22.7/ 29.5; 1994, 25.7/ 32.1; 1996, 30.3/ 35.7; 1998: 32/ 37.1. Black support for Clyburn was, by year (OLS/EI): 1992, 100/ 96.2; 1994, 100/ 95; 1996, 100/ 95.2; 1998: 100/ 99. Clyburn was incumbent in 1994, 1996, and 1998.

35. Charles S. Bullock III and Richard E. Dunn, "The Demise of Black Districting and the Future of Black Representation," *Emory Law Journal*, 48 (Fall 1999): 1248.

36. Leigh Strope, "Hodges Wins in Upset," Associated Press, November 3, 1998.

37. David Epstein and Sharyn O'Halloran, "A Social Science Approach to Race, Redistricting, and Representation," *American Political Science Review* 93 (March 1999): 189.

38. Cited in Orville Vernon Burton, "Legislative and Congressional Districting in South Carolina," in *Race and Redistricting in the 1990s*, ed. Bernard Grofman (New York: Agathon Press, 1998), 297.

39. Fraga and Ocampo, "Deterrent Effect of Section 5 of the Voting Rights Act," table 9.

CHAPTER 7: NORTH CAROLINA

1. Kousser, *Shaping of Southern Politics*, 239.

2. William R. Keech and Michael P. Sistrom, "North Carolina," in *Quiet Revolution in the South*, ed. Chandler Davidson and Bernard Grofman (Princeton, N.J.: Princeton University Press, 1994), 190.

3. The covered counties, largely located in the eastern part of the state, are Anson, Beaufort, Bertie, Bladen, Camden, Caswell, Chowan, Cleveland, Craven, Cumberland, Edgecombe, Franklin, Gaston, Gates, Granville, Greene, Guilford, Halifax, Harnett, Hertford, Hoke, Jackson, Lee, Lenoir, Martin, Nash, Northampton, Onslow, Pasquotank, Perquimans, Person, Pitt, Robeson, Rockingham, Scotland, Union, Vance, Washington, Wayne, and Wilson.

4. Key, *Southern Politics*, 205.

5. Jack Bass and Walter de Vries, *The Transformation of Southern Politics* (New York: Meridian, 1977), 219.

6. Paul Luebke, *Tar Heel Politics, 2000* (Chapel Hill: University of North Carolina Press, 1998).

7. William D. Snider, *Helms and Hunt: The North Carolina Senate Race, 1984* (Chapel Hill: University of North Carolina Press, 1985).

8. U.S. Commission on Civil Rights, *Political Participation*, 222–223.

9. The use of presidential-year elections for state office contributes to a lack of midterm participation in North Carolina.

10. Keech and Sistrom, "North Carolina."

11. *Thornburg v. Gingles*, 478 U.S. 30 (1986).

12. *Beer v. United States*, 425 U.S. 130 (1976).

13. *Shaw v. Reno*, 509 U.S. 630 (1993).

14. *Shaw v. Hunt*, 517 U.S. 899 (1996).

15. *Cromartie v. Hunt*, No. 4: 96-CV-104-BO (3) (E.D. N.C., 1998).

16. *Hunt v. Cromartie*, 526 U.S. 541 (1999).

17. *Cromartie v. Hunt*, No. 4: 96-CV-104-BO (3) (E.D. N.C., 2000).

18. *Easley v. Cromartie*, 532 U.S. 234 (2001).

19. Bernard Grofman, Lisa Handley, and David Lublin, "Drawing Effective Minority Districts: A Conceptual Framework and Some Empirical Evidence," *North Carolina Law Review* 79 (2000), 1384–1430.

20. Luebke, *Tar Heel Politics, 2000*, 157.

21. *Thornburg v. Gingles*, 478 U.S. 30 (1986).

22. Menifield et al., "An Overview of African American Representation," 165.

23. Quoted in Luebke, *Tar Heel Politics, 2000*, 182–183.

24. Michael Barone, Grant Ujifusa, and Douglas Matthews, *The Almanac of American Politics, 1980* (New York: E. P. Dutton, 1979), 649.

25. Paul Luebke, *Tar Heel Politics: Myth and Realities* (Chapel Hill: University of North Carolina Press, 1990), 118.

26. Richard Engstrom, "Racial Differences in Candidate Preferences in North Carolina Elections," report in *Shaw v. Reno.*

27. Fraga and Ocampo, "Deterrent Effect of Section 5 of the Voting Rights Act."

CHAPTER 8: TEXAS

1. Richard W. Murray, "Richard W. Murray Report," submitted in *Del Rio v. Perry*, 2001, 12; see also Robert Brischetto, David R. Richards, Chandler Davidson, and Bernard Grofman, "Texas," in *Quiet Revolution in the South: The Impact of the Voting Rights Act, 1965–1990*, ed. Chandler Davidson and Bernard Grofman (Princeton, N.J.: Princeton University Press, 1994).

2. Quoted in Nina Perales, Louis Figueroa, and Criselda G. Rivas, "Voting Rights in Texas, 1982–2006," renewtheVRA.org, June 2006, 8.

3. *Nixon v. Herndon*, 273 U.S. 536 (1927).

4. *Nixon v. Herndon*, 273 U.S. 536 (1927); *Nixon v. Condon*, 286 U.S. 73 (1932).

5. *Grovey v. Townsend*, 295 U.S. 45 (1935).

6. *Smith v. Allwright*, 321 U.S. 649 (1944).

7. *Terry v. Adams*, 345 U.S. 461 (1953).

8. Key, *Southern Politics*, especially chapters 27 and 28. See also Brischetto et al., "Texas"; and Jerry L. Polinard, "Expert Report of Jerry L. Polinard Regarding Congressional Redistricting Plan 1374C," submitted in *Sessions v. Perry*, 2003, 5. *Sessions v. Perry*, 298 F. Supp. 2d 451 (E. D. Tex. 2004).

9. Kousser, *Shaping of Southern Politics*, 239.

10. Abigail M. Thernstrom, *Whose Votes Count?* (Cambridge, Mass.: Harvard University Press, 1987), 48–62.

11. U.S. Commission on Civil Rights, *Political Participation*, 222–223.

12. Brischetto et al., "Texas," 270.

13. Ibid., 270

14. Nina Perales, Luis Figueroa, and Criselda G. Rivas, "Voting Rights in Texas, 1982–2006," RenewtheVRA.org (June 2006), 5.

15. Ibid.

16. Douglas D. Abel and Bruce I. Oppenheimer, "Candidate Emergence in a Majority Hispanic District: The 29th District in Texas," in *Who Runs for Congress? Ambition, Context and Candidate Emergence*, ed. Thomas A. Kazee (Washington, D.C.: Congressional Quarterly, 1994), 45–66.

17. Murray, "Murray Report," 12.

18. Allan J. Lichtman, "Report of Allan J. Lichtman on Voting Rights Issues in Texas Congressional Redistricting," submitted in *Sessions v. Perry*, 2003, 52–53.

19. Richard L. Engstrom, "Report: G.I. Forum v. Texas," submitted in *Sessions v. Perry*, 2003.

20. Hastings Wyman, "Update on Four Congressional Races," *Southern Political Report*, November 20, 2006, 6.

21. Extensive data demonstrate that an incumbent who leads in the primary but is forced into a runoff loses more often than challengers or candidates for open seats who lead in the first primary. Charles S. Bullock III and Loch K. Johnson, *Runoff Elections in the United States* (Chapel Hill: University of North Carolina Press, 1992), chapter 2.

22. Richard Murray, "An Analysis of the Impact of Texas Congressional District Plan 01374C on Congressional Districts 18 and 30," submitted in *Sessions v. Perry*, 2003, 13.

23. Eddie Bernice Johnson testimony in *Sessions v. Perry*.

24. Murray, "Impact of Texas Congressional District Plan," 12.

25. Ibid., 9.

26. Michelle G. Briscoe, "Cohesiveness and Diversity Among Black Members of the Texas State Legislature," in *Politics in the New South: Representation of African Americans in Southern State Legislatures*, ed. Charles E. Menifield and Stephen D. Shaffer (Albany: State University of New York Press, 2005), 142.

27. An F-statistic tests for significant differences in the mean on one variable across two or more categories of cases. In this case, the variable is Democratic vote share, and the categories are black, white, and Latino candidates.

28. The result of the regression is: Expected Democratic Vote = 45.48 + (–2.06 × Time Counter) + (5.05* × African American) + (.54 × Hispanic); Adjusted-R-Squared = .38; $N = 66$; $*p < .01$, two-tailed test.

29. Murray, "Impact of Texas Congressional District Plan," 10.

30. Murray, "Murray Report," 10.

31. Polinard, "Expert Report," 5.

32. Initially Green was not the candidate of choice of Latino voters. However, as he gained seniority, he also gained Latino support and, as noted earlier, has been their candidate of choice in recent elections.

33. See Ronald Keith Gaddie, "Supplement #3," submitted in *Del Rio v. Perry*, 2001; results of that analysis are below (black candidate in **bold**, Latino candidate in *italics*):

	Tarrant County			Harris County			Dallas County		
	% Black	% Hispanic	% Anglo	% Black	% Hispanic	% Anglo	% Black	% Hispanic	% Anglo
1998 Agriculture Comm.									
De Leon	17.8	77.8	33.3	51.4	73.7	7.7	23.4	80.8	36.3
Patterson	82.2	22.2	66.7	48.6	26.3	92.3	76.6	19.2	63.8
1998 Att'y General									
Kelly	2.5	18.7	18.8	13.7	38.2	30.8	1.8	9.7	7.8
Mattox	23.8	>100	>100	19.1	>100	>100	34.1	100	88.7
Overstreet	73.7	< 0	< 0	67.2	< 0	< 0	64.1	< 0	3.5
2000 Constable 3 (Harris County only)									
Jones	26.9	—	>100						
Clowers	13.6	—	23.1						
Pappilion	52.5	—	< 0						

34. The data presented are consistent with the finding of a three-judge federal panel in 2001, that African American and Hispanic voters do not coalesce in Democratic primaries: "The Latino and African American plaintiffs thus present competing positions, reflecting a political reality that they are competitors in the political process. This competition finds expression in an absence of cohesive voting between Latinos and African Americans at the point in which it is meaningfully measured, the Democratic primaries." See *Balderas v. Perry*, 6:01-CV-158 (2001), 12.

35. Charles S. Bullock III and Susan A. MacManus, "Voting Patterns in a Tri-Ethnic Community: Conflict or Cohesion: The Case of Austin, Texas, 1975–1985," *National Civic Review* 79 (January-February, 1990): 5–22.

36. Jonathan N. Katz, "Report on Texas Congressional Redistricting: Minority Opportunities and Partisan Fairness," submitted in *Del Rio v. Perry*, 2001.

37. Six Democrats escaped GOP opposition, while in two other contests Katz's EI models did not converge.

38. EI estimates for 1996 to 2000 in Congressional District 24 are:

	Black	Anglo	Hispanic
1996	0.919	0.453	0.995
1998	0.773	0.466	0.989
2000	0.795	0.521	0.843

Source: Estimates are from Jonathan N. Katz, "Report on Texas Congressional Redistricting: Minority Opportunities and Partisan Fairness," submitted in *Del Rio v. Perry*, 2001.

39. As a write-in candidate, Gibbs attracted 42 percent of the vote. In the election to fill the remainder of DeLay's term in the 109th Congress, Gibbs's name appeared on the ballot and she won. Lampson was not a candidate for the remainder of the term.

40. Perales et al., "Voting Rights in Texas," 16.

41. *Reno v. Bossier Parish School Board*, 528 U.S. 320 (1999).

42. Fraga and Ocampo, "Deterrent Effect of Section 5 of the Voting Rights Act."

43. Ibid., 5.

CHAPTER 9: FLORIDA

1. Kousser, *Shaping of Southern Politics*, 239.

2. U.S. Commission on Civil Rights, *Political Participation*, 230–231.

3. Ibid., 222–223.

4. Dario V. Moreno and Kevin A. Hill, "Expert Report on South Florida's Congressional Districts 17, 18, 21, and 25," submitted in *Martinez v. Bush*, 234 F. Supp. 2d 1275 (S.D. Fla. 2002).

5. "2004 Primary Election Profiles," National Association of Latino Elected Officials; press release at www.naleo.org/press_releases/TXProfile_03-04fin.pdf (accessed July 20, 2004).

6. Phil Duncan, ed., *Politics in America, 1992* (Washington, D.C.: Congressional Quarterly Press, 1991), 341.

7. Sometimes called the "Cuban Kennedys," the Diaz-Balarts also count among their numbers a successful investment banker (Rafael) and a highly regarded TV broadcaster (Jose) who broadcasts for Telemundo and the Miami NBC affiliate.

8. 509 U.S. 630 (1993).

9. The challenge to Florida's 3rd Congressional District came in *Johnson v. Mortham*, 915 F. Supp. 1529 (N.D. Fla. 1995).

10. The 2001 redistricting changed the district's shape.

11. Michael Barone and Grant Ujifusa, *The Almanac of American Politics 1994* (Washington, D.C.: National Journal, 1993), 323.

12. The first Hispanic to serve in the Florida legislature was Fernando Figueredo of Key West, who represented Monroe County in 1885. See Allen Morris, *The Florida Handbook, 1989–1990* (Tallahassee: Peninsular Publishing, 1989), 149.

13. In 1980, Dade County voters approved an anti-bilingual ordinance. It was subsequently overturned by the Dade commission in 1993.

14. The last of the Reconstruction blacks to serve in the Florida legislature were George A. Lewis and John R. Scott, Jr., who represented Duval County (Jacksonville) in 1889. Carrie Meek was the first black woman to serve in the state senate. In 1983 Meek and Arnette Girardeau from Jacksonville desegregated the senate.

15. Hatchett biography found at www.floridasupremecourt.org/about/gallery/hatchett.html (accessed October 1, 2005).

16. Latino VAP data on the dozen state house districts:

District:	47	55*	56	57	58*	59*	60	61	62	63	67	68
Latino VAP:	15.7	8.4	11.4	12.6	38.4+	13.6†	9.7	7.4	12.3	8.9	6.1	5.4

Source: Data obtained from Hillsborough County Supervisor of Elections, at www.votehillsborough.org.

*Elected a Democrat; +50.1 percent black VAP; †52 percent black VAP.

17. Letter from Ralph D. Boyd to Sen. John McKay and Rep. Tom Feeney, July 1, 2002, 3.

18. Estimates reported in table 9.7 show Collier Latinos overwhelmingly rejecting Diaz-Balart in favor of his Democratic opponent.

19. Dario V. Moreno and Kevin A. Hill, "Expert Report on South Florida's Congressional Districts 17, 18, 21, and 25," submitted in *Martinez v. Bush,* 234 F. Supp. 2d 1275 (S.D. Fla. 2002), 1.

20. Harold Meyerson, "The Rising Latino Tide in Florida and Texas," *American Prospect,* November 18, 2002, www.prospect.org/print/V13/21/meyerson-h.html (accessed November 19, 2002).

21. Ibid., 19–28. See also Kevin A. Hill and Dario V. Moreno, "A Community of a Crowd? Regional and Ethnic Block Voting in the Florida Legislature, 1989–1996." Typescript. Florida International University, Miami, Fla. 33199 (www.fiu.edu/~khill/florida.htm).

22. *Martinez v. Bush,* 234 F. Supp. 2d 1275 (S.D. Fla. 2002).

23. Moreno and Hill, "Expert Report," figs. 6–14 and pgs. 33–36.

24. Report of Ronald Keith Gaddie, "Expert Report," submitted in *United States v. Osceola County,* 6: 05-CV-1053-Orl-31 DAB (M.D. Fla. 2006), and Theodore S. Arrington, "Expert Report," submitted in *United States v. Osceola County,* 6: 05-CV-1053-Orl-31 DAB (M.D. Fla. 2006).

25. Dario V. Moreno and Kevin A. Hill, "Expert Report on South Florida's Congressional Districts 17, 18, 21, and 25," submitted in *Martinez v. Bush,* 234 F. Supp. 2d 1275 (S.D. Fla. 2002); estimates of voter turnout by ethnicity appear below:

	1998			2000		
	Hispanic	Black	Anglo	Hispanic	Black	Anglo
Broward	40	39	51	53	60	67
Collier	10	28	50	31	62	76
Dade	46	40	52	74	64	75
Monroe	39	16	51	50	65	75

26. Jonel Newman, "Voting Rights in Florida 1982–2006," RenewtheVRA.org, March 2006, 4.

27. Fraga and Ocampo, "Deterrent Effect of Section 5 of the Voting Rights Act."

28. In her capacity as secretary of state, Harris certified George W. Bush to be the winner of Florida's critical Electoral College votes.

CHAPTER 10: TENNESSEE

1. Sharon D. Wright, "The Tennessee Black Caucus of State Legislators," *Journal of Black Studies* 31 (September 2000): 5.

2. Kousser, *Shaping of Southern Politics*, 239.

3. Ibid., 118.

4. Key, *Southern Politics*, 74–75. The Crump machine sought to register and control the sizeable black vote of Memphis in an effort to dominate statewide elections; see also David M. Tucker, *Memphis Since Crump* (Knoxville: University of Tennessee Press, 1980).

5. U.S. Commission on Civil Rights, *Political Participation*, 222–223.

6. Tennessee's poll tax was implemented in an arbitrary fashion. Estimates of the impact of the poll tax on voter participation from 1870 to 1940 indicate that a black adult was three times more likely than a white adult to be denied access to the ballot because of the use of the poll tax; see Ronald Keith Gaddie, "Testing Some Key Hypotheses of Voter Turnout," presented at the annual meeting of the Southern Political Science Association, Atlanta, Ga., November 2000.

7. U.S. Commission on Civil Rights, *Political Participation*, 223.

8. The seven states are Alabama, Georgia, Louisiana, Mississippi, North Carolina, South Carolina, and Virginia.

9. While we question the reliability of the sample for registration estimates in 2002 and 2006, the black turnout estimates for these years are in line with midterm figures for earlier years.

10. Michael Barone, Grant Ujifusa, and Douglas Matthews, *The Almanac of American Politics 1978* (New York: E. P. Dutton, 1977), 806.

11. Menifield et al., "An Overview of African American Representation," 172.

12. Ibid, 171–172.

13. Wright, "Tennessee Black Caucus," 16–17.

14. Richard E. Cohen, "Down the Middle," *National Journal* 38 (February 25, 2006): 60.

15. The CNN Web site has exit poll results at www.cnn.com/ELECTION/2006/pages/results/states/tn/s/ (accessed December 1, 2006).

16. Sharon D. Wright, *Race Power and Political Emergence in Memphis* (New York: Garland Publishing, 2000), 106.

17. Ibid., 91.

18. Travis Loller, "Senate Votes Ford Out," *Nashville Tennessean*, www.tennessean.com/apps/pbcs.dll/article?AID=/20060420/NEWS0201/604200396 (accessed February 28, 2007).

19. Naifeh garnered an estimated 58.9 percent of the white vote in the Haywood County portion of house District 81, while Wilder pulled 54.2 percent of the white vote in the Haywood County portion of senate District 26.

20. A similar pattern has been observed for congressional candidates in the South; see Byron E. Shafer and Richard Johnston, *The End of Southern Exceptionalism* (Cambridge, Mass.: Harvard University Press, 2006).

CHAPTER 11: ARKANSAS

1. Faubus would attempt a political comeback, but the emergence of the black electorate and the decline of race as a salient issue thwarted his ambitions. See Alexander Lamis, *The Two-Party South* (London: Oxford University Press, 1988).

2. Kousser, *Shaping of Southern Politics*, 239.

3. Key, *Southern Politics*, 637.

4. Ibid.

5. U.S. Commission on Civil Rights, *Political Participation*, 222–223.

6. The Rim South, sometimes referred to as the Peripheral South, consists of Arkansas, Florida, North Carolina, Tennessee, Texas, and Virginia.

7. U.S. Commission on Civil Rights, *Political Participation*, 223.

8. The extraordinarily low rates of black registration reported for 1990 and 1998 may result from sampling problems. Note that the levels of black registration in the elections just before and just after those years are substantially higher. Consequently, for these low estimates to be accurate would mean that a substantial share of the black electorate dropped off the voter rolls but then signed up again or was replaced by new black registrants within the next two years.

9. The seven states are Alabama, Georgia, Louisiana, Mississippi, North Carolina, South Carolina, and Virginia.

10. Janine A. Parry and William Miller, "African Americans in the Arkansas General Assembly: 1972–1999," in *Politics in the New South: Representation of African Americans in Southern State Legislatures*, ed. Charles E. Menifield and Stephen D. Shaffer (Albany: State University of New York Press, 2005), 34.

11. Parry and Miller, "African Americans in the Arkansas General Assembly," 21.

12. Ibid., 22–23.

13. Ibid., 24–40.

14. Kerry L. Haynie, *African American Legislators in the American States* (New York: Columbia University Press, 2001), 50–51.

15. On political incorporation see Rufus P. Browning, Dale Rogers Marshall, and David H. Tabb, *Protest Is Not Enough* (Berkeley: University of California Press, 1984), especially chapters 1 and 2. For a description of how Haynie operationalizes incorporation in a state legislature, see *African American Legislators in the American States*, 66–68.

16. Haynie, *African American Legislators*, 69.

17. The Arkansas term limits are two four-year terms for senators and three two-year terms for representatives.

18. Haynie, *African American Legislators*, 69.

19. Perry and Miller, "African Americans in the Arkansas General Assembly," 36.

20. These regression estimates are made using county-level data. Potential problems are the small number of counties in District 2 (eight for the 1996 and 2000 elections) and the distribution on the independent variable. The range in the black population is from 1 to 43 percent, so that the estimate for preferences in a 100 percent black county involves a great deal of extrapolation.

21. Ecological regression estimates of support for statewide Democratic candidates in 2006:

	Black voters	White voters
Governor	.81	.53
Lt. Governor	.80	.56
Att'y General	.83	.57
Sec'y of State	>1.00	.62
Treasurer	>1.00	.58
Auditor	.99	.84

Source: Data compiled by the authors.

22. Personal communication from Professor Gary Wekkin, March 16, 2007.

CHAPTER 12: A COMPARATIVE ANALYSIS OF THE IMPACT OF THE VOTING RIGHTS ACT IN THE SOUTH

1. Douglas Rae, *The Political Consequences of Electoral Laws* (New Haven, Conn.: Yale University Press, 1971); Arend Lijphart, *Patterns of Democracy: Government Forms and Performance in Thirty-Six Countries* (New Haven: Yale University Press, 1999), see especially chapter 8; David M. Farrell, *Electoral Systems: A Comparative Introduction* (New York: Palgrave, 2001), see especially chapter 7.

2. Andrew Gelman and Gary King, "Estimating Incumbency Advantage without Bias," *American Journal of Political Science* 34 (1990): 1142–1164.

3. The Census Bureau did not release its report on the 2006 election until 2008.

4. For all of these comparative analyses we rely on Spearman's rho to test for significant changes in terms of black voter progress across the South. Spearman's rho calculates the similarity or dissimilarity of two rank orderings. The Spearman's rho computed using the pre-Voting Rights Act ranking and the 2004 ranking from table 12.1 is –.406. This indicates a degree of reversal in the rank orderings of the two different periods of time although the relationship is not statistically significant ($p = .12$, one-tailed test).

5. The Spearman's rho of .636 ($p = .018$, one-tailed test) calculated between the 2004 rankings for blacks and whites shows a striking similarity between the relative registration rates of the two races across the eleven states.

6. Angus Campbell, Philip Converse, Warren Miller, and Donald Stokes, *The American Voter* (New York: J. Wiley and Sons, 1960); Sidney Verba and Norman Nie, *Participation in America* (New York: Harper and Row, 1972); Sidney Verba, Norman Nie, and J. Kim, *Participation and Political Equality* (New York: Cambridge, 1978); Raymond Wolfinger and Steven Rosenstone, *Who Votes?* (New Haven, Conn.: Yale University Press, 1980); Jan E. Leighley and Jonathan Nagler, "Class Bias in Turnout: The Voters Remain the Same," in *American Political Science Review* 86 (1992): 725–736; Jan E. Leighley and Jonathan Nagler, "Individual and Systemic Influences on Turnout: *Who Votes?* 1984," *Journal of Politics* 54 (1992): 718–740.

7. Katherine Tate, "Black Political Participation in the 1984 and 1988 Presidential Elections," *American Political Science Review* 85 (1991): 1159–1176; Peter W. Wielhouwer, "Releasing the Fetters: Parties and the Mobilization of the African American Electorate," *Journal of Politics* 62 (2000): 206–222.

8. States would invariably have higher index scores if the denominator reflected the size of the pool of potential justices rather than the voting-age population. Service on a state's highest court requires not simply that one be an adult but that one also be an attorney. It is highly likely that African Americans constitute a smaller share of the bar than of the voting-age population.

9. The *Southern Political Report* (2006) shows North Carolina not having a black justice but governor Mike Easley subsequently named an African American to a vacancy.

10. Richard L. Engstrom and Michael McDonald, "The Election of Blacks to City Councils," in *American Political Science Review* 75 (June 1981): 344–354.

11. Chandler Davidson and Bernard Grofman, eds., *Quiet Revolution in the South* (Princeton, N.J.: Princeton University Press, 1994).

12. $p = .021$, one-tailed test.

13. David Lublin, *The Paradox of Representation* (Princeton, N.J.: Princeton University Press, 1997).

CHAPTER 13: ASSESSING THE VOTING RIGHTS ACT IN POLITICAL CONTEXT

1. Arend Lijphart, *Patterns of Democracy* (New Haven, Conn.: Yale University Press, 1999), 52.

2. For a recent overview of the potential sources of the southern realignment, see Alan I. Abramowitz and Kyle L. Saunders, "Ideological Realignment in the U.S. Electorate," *Journal of Politics* 60(3): 634–652; Kyle L. Saunders and Alan I. Abramowitz, "Ideological Realignment and Active Partisans in the American Electorate," *American Politics Research* 32(3): 285–309; Charles S. Bullock III, Donna R. Hoffman, and Ronald Keith Gaddie, "The Consolidation of the Southern White Vote," *Political Research Quarterly* 58: 231–243; Charles S. Bullock III, Donna R. Hoffman, and Ronald Keith Gaddie, "Regional Variations in the Realignment of American Politics, 1944–2004," *Social Science Quarterly* 87: 494–518; Earl Black and Merle Black, *The Rise of the Southern Republicans* (Cambridge, Mass.: Belknap, 2002).

3. Earl Black and Merle Black, *Politics and Society in the South* (Cambridge, Mass.: Harvard University Press, 1989); Black and Black, *The Rise of the Southern Republicans*, 2002; Alexander Lamis, *The Two-Party South* (New York: Oxford University Press, 1986); Charles S. Bullock III and Mark Rozell, eds., *The New Politics of the Old South* (Boulder: Rowman and Littlefield, 1998/2002/2006). But see also David Ian Lublin, *The Republican South: Democratization and Partisan Change* (Princeton, N.J.: Princeton University Press, 2007). Lublin directs readers to the prominent role of social and economic forces beyond race that helped propel the rise of the southern Republicans.

4. Robert Dallek, *Lyndon B. Johnson: Portrait of a President* (2005), 170.

5. Reg Murphy and Hal Gulliver, *The Southern Strategy* (New York: Scribner, 1971).

6. Data used in this section were compiled by the authors with the assistance of the staffs of Rep. Charles Norwood (R-Ga.) and Rep. Lynn Westmoreland (R-Ga.).

7. See *Jepsen v. Vigil-Giron*, CV-2001-2177, 2d Judicial Circuit of New Mexico.

8. The Northwest Austin Municipal Utility District Number One was created in 1987 to deliver basic city services to part of Travis County, Texas. The district has a five-member board and it conducts elections, but the "MUD" does not engage in voter registration. All of Texas is subject to Section 5 (see chapter 8).

The MUD applied for bailout, and asked that the constitutionality of Section 5 be reconsidered if it were denied bailout. The case was designed to test the constitutionality of Section 5.

9. Opinion of Justice Thomas, dissenting, *NAMUDNO v. Holder*, 557 U.S. ___ (2009), at 3–4.

10. Among the parties filing briefs in support of the *NAMUDNO* were the limited-government groups the Mountain States Legal Foundation, The Pacific Legal Foundation Center For Equal Opportunity and Project 21, the Southeastern Legal Foundation, Georgia governor Sonny Perdue, Abigail Thernstrom, and the Goldwater Institute. Alabama governor Bob Riley's filing was in support of neither party but appeared sympathetic toward the plaintiff-appellant's perspective.

11. Opinion of the Court, Justice Roberts, *NAMUDNO v. Holder*, 557 U.S. ___ (2009), at 1.

12. Ibid., 2.

13. Ibid.

14. Ibid., 7.

15. Ibid.

16. Ibid., 8–9.

17. Ibid., 9.

18. Ibid., 16–17.

19. Thomas, J. dissent, at 1.

20. Ibid.

21. Ibid., at 1–2.

22. Ibid., 3.

23. Ibid., 5, note 1.

24. Ibid.

25. Ibid., 15.

26. A collection of essays from the University of Arkansas's Diane D. Blair Center documents the consistent economic policy differences between blacks and whites in several southern states. See Todd G. Shields and Shannon G. Davis, eds., *The New South Consortium: The Status of Women and Minorities in the New South* (Tallahassee: FSU Institute of Government, 2008).

27. See, for example, Key, *Southern Politics;* Alexander Heard, *A Two-Party South* (Chapel Hill: University of North Carolina Press, 1952).

28. Black and Black, *The Rise of the Southern Republicans,* 2002; Lublin, *The Republican South*, 2007.

29. Black and Black, *The Rise of the Southern Republicans*.

30. Abramowitz and Saunder, "Ideological Realignment and Active Partisans"; Shields and Davis, *The New South Consortium*.

31. Pub. L. No. 97–205, 96 Stat. 134, at 42 U.S.C. § 1973(a) (1982).

32. *Bush v. Vera*, 517 U.S. 952, 983 (1996); see also Samuel Issacharoff, "Is Section 5 of the Voting Rights Act a Victim of Its Own Success?" *Columbia Law Review* 104 (2005): 1717.

33. David Epstein and Sharyn O'Halloran, "Measuring the Electoral and Policy Impact of Majority-Minority Voting Districts," *American Journal of Political Science* 43 (2): 369.

34. David T. Canon, *Race, Redistricting, and Representation: The Unintended Consequences of Black Majority Districts* (Chicago: University of Chicago Press, 1999).

35. *Easley v. Cromartie,* 532 U.S. 234 (2002).

37. Although DOJ claims that it never had a 65 percent rule, that was its threshold in *Busbee v. Smith,* 549 F. Supp. 494 (D.D.C. 1982) and is referenced in other court opinions of the period; see also *United Jewish Organizations of Williamsburgh v. Carey,* 430 U.S. 144 (1977).

37. The replacement of African American members of Congress in Memphis and New Orleans by a white Democrat and a Vietnamese-American Republican, respectively, is not due to reducing black concentrations in these districts.

38. Expert report of David Epstein, *Georgia v. Ashcroft,* 195 F. Supp. 2d 25 (D.D.C. 2002) (No. 01-2111), 16–17; David Epstein and Sharyn O'Halloran, "Measuring the Electoral and Policy Impact of Majority-Minority Voting Districts," *American Journal of Political Science* 43 (1999): 367–95.

39. See, for example, *Vieth v. Jubelirer,* 541 U.S. 267 (2004), on partisan gerrymandering; *Cox v. Larios,* 542 U.S. 947 (2004), on population equality and partisan gerrymandering; and *Easley v. Cromartie,* 532 U.S. 234 (2001), for racial gerrymandering under the beard of partisan gerrymandering.

40. Thomas, J. dissent, at 17–18.

EPILOGUE: THE 2008 PRESIDENTIAL ELECTION

1. Shailagh Murray, "For Black Superdelegates, Pressure to Back Obama," *Washington Post,* March 3, 2008: A1.

2. Estimate of total, black, and white vote shares for southern Democratic U.S. Senate and gubernatorial candidates in 2008:

	Total vote	Black vote	White vote
Intercept	–30.86	–21.41	1.82
Obama %	1.72**	1.18	1.16**
Incumbency	3.15	4.54*	5.66
Adjusted R^2	.62	.18	.73
N	11	11	11

Source: Analysis conducted by the authors.

*$p < .05$

**$p < .01$

3. The response of the Obama share of the white vote to the size of the African American and Latino share of turnout:

	White vote share
Intercept	52.41**
African American %	–1.12**
Latino %	–.29
Adjusted R^2	49
N	11

**Significant at a .01 level, two-tailed test.

APPENDIX A: ANALYTIC METHODS FOR ESTIMATING RACIAL VOTING PATTERNS

1. Goodman's ecological regression method, a linear regression technique, is commonly accepted in the federal courts. See *Thornburg v. Gingles,* 478 U.S. 30 (1986); see also Allan Lichtman, "Correlation, Regression, and the Ecological Fallacy: A Critique," *Journal of Interdisciplinary Studies* 104 (1974): 622–633.

2. Gary King, *A Solution to the Ecological Inference Problem* (Princeton, N.J.: Princeton University Press, 1997).

Index

Adams, Oscar, 70
Aistrup, Joseph A.: *The Southern Strategy Revisited*, 382n9
Alabama, 58–77; African Americans as judges, 70–72, 77, 338–339; African Americans as local officials, 64–66, 77, 332, 335–339; African Americans in Congress, 66–67, 149, 331, 339; African Americans in state legislature, 67–69, 77, 148–149, 306, 331–333, 338–339; African Americans in statewide offices, 70–72, 77, 338–339; Birmingham, 58, 67; black population of, 67–68, 329–340; Civil Rights Movement in, 18, 58–60, 366; Constitution of 1901/Boswell Amendment, 59, 388n4; Dallas County, 60–61; in Democratic primary of 2008, 360; *Dillard v. Crenshaw County*, 65–66; Edmund Pettus Bridge incident in Selma, 18, 60, 366; federal monitoring/DOJ objections in, 76–77, 161, 217; federal registrars in, 12, 60, 77; Greene County, 60; Hale County, 77; Jefferson County, 60; literacy test in, 59, 382n12; Lowndes County, 60; Marengo County, 60; Mobile, 20–21; Montgomery, 58–59, 67; Montgomery County, 60; vs. nonsouthern states, 56, 64, 77; obstacles for black voters in, 9–10, 17, 59, 327, 338, 340–341, 382n12; vs. other southern states, 59, 65, 67, 77, 166, 217, 306, 325–341, 346, 348, 360, 362–368; Perry County, 60; preclearance requirement/Section 5 of VRA in, 76–77, 331, 346, 348, 404n8; racial voting patterns in, 71–77, 363–364, 366; redistricting in, 66–68; registration of blacks in, 12, 17, 59–63, 77, 79, 166, 254, 325–327, 338–339, 374; registration of whites in, 60, 61–62, 326–327, 374; school desegregation in, 30; States' Rights Party in, 166; Supreme Court of, 70,

Alabama (*continued*)
72, 74–75, 77, 332–334, 338–339, 407n8; turnout of blacks in, 61, 63–64, 77, 327–329, 339, 365, 377, 388n9; turnout of whites in, 61, 63, 77, 328–329, 377, 388n9; in 2008 presidential election, 362–365, 368; United Citizens Party in, 172; University of Alabama, 30, 59; Wilcox County, 60. *See also* Democratic Party, in Alabama; Republican Party, in Alabama
Alaska: Alaska Natives, 13, 223; and minority-language provision, 223; preclearance requirement in, 14, 346
Alexander, Rodney, 131
Allen, George, 151, 162
Almanac of American Politics, 121
Alvaredo, Maria Luis, 240, 242
Analytical methods: ecological inference (EI) analysis, 101–102, 155–160, 181–183, 211–213, 232, 234, 245–249, 370–371, 401nn37–38; ecological regression/ordinary least squares (OLS) analysis, 24, 51–52, 75–76, 99, 101–102, 128–130, 132, 137, 153–160, 181–183, 212–216, 232, 234, 298–299, 318, 363–364, 369–370, 406n20; homogeneous precinct (HP) analysis, 207, 232, 234, 369; Spearman's rho, 328, 340, 406n4, 407n5
Anderson, Gary, 42–44, 52
Anderson, Reuben, 44, 49, 387n51
Arizona: and minority-language provision, 223; preclearance requirement in, 14
Arkansas, 304–320; African Americans as candidates for statewide offices, 316–317, 320, 339; African Americans as judges, 316, 338, 339; African Americans as local officials, 310–311, 332, 335–336, 338–339; African Americans in Congress/candidates for Congress, 311–312, 320, 338–339; African Americans in state legislature, 149, 306, 312–316, 320, 331–333, 338–339, 356; black population of, 304; Chicot County, 307; Civil Rights Movement in, 304–305; Crittenden County, 307; in Democratic primary of 2008, 360; General Assembly, 149, 306, 312–316, 320; Lee County, 307; as not subject to Section 5 of VRA, 25, 304–305, 307, 309, 313, 319–320, 327, 331, 333, 335, 339, 348, 356, 365, 405n9; obstacles for black voters in, 305–307; vs. other southern states, 297, 305, 306, 307–310, 313, 315–316, 319–320, 326–341, 344, 346, 348, 356, 360, 363–367; Phillips County, 307; poll tax in, 305, 307; racial voting patterns in, 317–319, 363–364, 406n20; redistricting in, 312–316; registration of blacks in, 306–309, 319, 326–327, 338–339, 374, 405n8; registration of whites in, 306–309, 319, 326–327, 374; school desegregation in, 304–305; vs. states outside the South, 308; St. Francis County, 307; Supreme Court of, 316, 332–334, 338–339, 407n8; term limits in, 315, 405n17; turnout of blacks in, 309–310, 319–320, 327–329, 338–339, 365, 377; turnout of whites in, 309–310, 320, 328–329, 377; in 2008 presidential election, 363–365; white primaries in, 305–306. *See also* Democratic Party, in Arkansas; Republican Party, in Arkansas
Asian Americans, 223
At-large election systems: vs. cumulative voting, 66; vs. limited voting,

66; and *Thornburg v. Gingles*, 197, 203–207, 230, 398n11; vs. single-member district systems, 20–21, 32, 38, 41, 64–66, 87, 197, 334–335
Attorneys, African American, 9

Baker, Richard, 127
Baker, Thurbert, 95–97, 107
Ballance, Frank, 201–202, 214, 218
Barber, Mac, 105
Barbour, Haley, 54
Barnes, Roy, 93–94
Barnett, Ross, 340–341
Barone, Michael, 39–40, 121, 392n12
Bartley, Numan: *Second Reconstruction*, 382n9; on VRA, 4
Bass, Jack, 191; *The Transformation of Southern Politics*, 382n9
Bateman, Herb, 153, 394n18
Beasley, David, 185
Bell, Chris, 236
Benavides, Pete, 241
Benham, Robert, 94, 390n27
Benjamin, Steve, 177, 185
Bentsen, Kent, 243
Beyer, Donald, 150–151
Bilbo, Theodore, 6, 30
Bishop, Sanford, 89–90, 101, 296
Black, Earl and Merle: *Politics and Society in the South*, 382n9, 387n58; *The Rise of Southern Republicans*, 382n9, 387n58; *The Vital South*, 382n9
Blackmon, Barbara, 42–43, 52
Blacksher, James: "Voting Rights in Alabama," 388n11
Blue, Dan, 207
Boggs, Hale, 121, 392n9
Boggs, Lindy, 121
Boissiere, Lambert, III, 125, 132
Bolling, W. T., 394n17
Bond, Julian, 89
Bonilla, Henry, 232–234, 247, 249
Bowles, Erskine, 209
Boyd, Ralph D., 402n17
Bradley, Tom, 150–151, 297
Breaux, David A., 53, 388n61
Breaux, John, 126
Bredesen, Phil, 299–302
Bristow, Bill, 318
Brooke, Edward, 36
Brown, Corrine, 263
Brown, Cullen: "Voting Rights in Alabama," 389n11
Brown, Ike, 46–47
Brown, Robert, 91, 98
Bryant, Phil, 43
Bullard, Larcenia, 272, 278
Bumpers, Dale, 305
Burgess, David, 95, 103–105, 109–110, 391n28
Bush, George H. W., 353
Bush, George W., 52–53, 131, 265, 274, 281, 403n28
Bustamante, Albert, 231–232, 246
Butterfield, G. K., 201–202, 210, 218
Byrd, Harry, 141–142
Byrne, L. L., 394n17

California: African Americans in Congress, 390n18; Hispanics as local officials in, 231; and minority-language provision, 223; preclearance requirement in, 14, 348, 383n34; Yuba County, 383n34
Campbell, Bill, 209
Campbell, Carroll, 177, 396n23
Campbell, Ralph, 209, 211–212, 214
Candidates of choice: among blacks, 21–22, 38–39, 112, 134, 137, 139, 147, 155, 159–160, 203–207, 212, 218, 236, 247, 272, 319, 335, 354–355; among Hispanics, 232, 234, 236, 251, 269, 271–272, 274, 276, 281, 400n32; vs. representatives of choice, 351–352;

Candidates of choice (*continued*)
and Section 2 of VRA, 21–22, 203–207, 334–335
Canon, David, 40; *Race, Redistricting, and Representation,* 352
Cao, Ahn "Joseph," 123
Carmichael, Stokely, 60
Carter, Jimmy, 54, 88, 361, 366
Carter, Karen, 122–123
Casas, Roberto, 264
Cash, W. J.: *The Mind of the South,* 5–6
Castor, Kathy, 270
Castro, Fidel, 267, 273
Chambliss, Saxby, 362
Cherry, Gwen, 265
Childers, Travis, 386n27
Chiles, Lawton, 267–268
Civil Rights Act of 1957, 8–9
Civil Rights Act of 1960, 9
Civil Rights Act of 1964, 10, 31
Civil Rights Movement, 9–10, 18, 311; in Alabama, 18, 58–60, 366; in Arkansas, 304–305; in Mississippi, 30, 41, 385n6; in Virginia, 141
Civil War, 6, 8, 141, 164
Clark, Jim, 59
Clark, Robert, 40, 41, 48–49, 386n30
Clayton, Eva, 201–202, 210–212, 214, 218
Clement, Bob, 299
Clinton, Bill, 40, 100, 103, 115, 305, 319
Clinton, Hillary, 71, 119, 180, 297–298, 316–317, 360, 361
Cloverdell, Paul, 103
Clyburn, James, 173–174, 181–184, 397n34
Cobb, Sue Bell, 71
Coburn, Tom, 384n47
Cochran, Thad, 36–37, 45, 49, 54, 364, 387n52
Cohen, Mark M., 390n19
Cohen, Steve, 293–294
Coleman, James, 11
Coleman, Marshall, 150
Coleman, Ron, 245
Colorado, 267
Congress, African Americans in: Alabama, 23, 25, 66–67, 149, 331, 339; Arkansas, 311–312, 320, 338–339; Florida, 263–264, 268, 281, 331–332, 339; Georgia, 22, 87–91, 98–101, 107, 109–110, 149, 293, 331–332, 338–339; Louisiana, 120–123, 149, 331–332, 339; Mississippi, 39–40, 56, 149, 331–332, 339; North Carolina, 15–16, 149, 198–203, 218, 331–332, 339; South Carolina, 149, 172–174, 181–184, 188, 331–332, 339; Tennessee, 292–294, 302, 331–332, 339; Texas, 87, 149, 235–237, 250–251, 293, 331–332, 339–340; Virginia, 146–147, 331
Congress, Hispanics in: Florida, 261–264, 271–272, 281; Texas, 231–235, 250–251
Congressional Black Caucus, 67
Connor, Bull, 58
Cook, Ralph, 70, 72, 77
Cooper, Clarence, 94
Corker, Bob, 296–297, 300, 302–303
Cornyn, John, 384n47
Cotter, Patrick, 64
Crist, Charlie, 274–275
Crump, Edward: political machine in Memphis, 286, 404n4
Curry, Darrell, 182

Davis, Arthur, 67, 75–76
Davis, Jefferson, 58
Davis, Jim, 274–275
DeBerry, Lois, 295
Deeds, R. C., 394n17
De la Garza, Kika, 231

Delaware, 5, 382n8
DeLay, Tom, 249, 401n39
De Leon, Ernesto, 246, 400n33
Democratic Party: in Alabama, 67, 68–77, 172, 389n15; in Arkansas, 305–306, 312, 314–320, 344; convention of 1964, 30–31; in Florida, 263–264, 267–268, 270, 272–278, 281–282, 340, 402n18; in Georgia, 68, 78–79, 87–91, 93, 95, 100, 102–107, 109–110; incumbent candidates, 43–44, 49–50, 51–52, 54–55, 57, 67, 71, 73, 74–75, 90, 101, 103, 105, 110, 124, 127, 153, 156, 162–163, 177–178, 182–186, 211–215, 218, 232, 235–236, 245, 249, 251, 270, 298–302, 305, 317–320, 343–345, 363, 405n20; in Louisiana, 112, 117, 119, 121–123, 125–137, 139–140, 344–345, 392n7; McGovern-Frasier primary reforms, 359–360; in Mississippi, 30–31, 36–37, 39–44, 46–57, 172, 386n27, 386n36, 387n53, 387nn59–60; in North Carolina, 191–192, 199, 202–203, 207–216, 218, 344; in South Carolina, 68, 165–166, 172–184, 188–189, 396n24; and states' rights, 342–343; in Tennessee, 292–303, 382n8, 409n19; in Texas, 79, 222, 231–236, 238–240, 246, 249, 251–252, 401n34, 401n37; 2008 primary, 44, 71, 106, 117, 119, 180, 188, 297–298, 316–317, 359–361; in Virginia, 146, 147, 150–160, 162–163, 344, 394n11; white primaries, 8, 59, 78–79, 111, 141, 165, 190, 222, 305–306, 350. *See also* Carter, Jimmy; Clinton, Bill; Clinton, Hilary; Johnson, Lyndon B.; Kennedy, John F.; Kerry, John; Obama, Barack
Dent, Hayes, 40
Deukmejian, George, 151
De Vries, Walter, 191; *The Transformation of Southern Politics*, 382n9
Diaz-Balart, José, 402n7
Diaz-Balart, Lincoln, 262, 402n7
Diaz-Balart, Mario, 262, 264, 271–272, 278, 402n7, 402n18
Diaz-Balart, Rafael, 402n7
District of Columbia District Court, 11, 13, 32; *Busbee v. Smith*, 409n18; *Georgia v. Reno*, 108, 391n45
Dixon, Irma, 124–125, 132
Doggett, Lloyd, 232, 234
Doggett, Teresa, 244
Dole, Elizabeth, 362
Dollard, John, 6
Duke, David, 126
Dumas, Royal: "Voting Rights in Alabama," 389n11
Dunne, John R., 390n19
Dyer, Scott, 126

Early, Mark, 394n15
Easley, Michael, 208, 210, 212, 407n9
Edison Media Research, 151
Edwards, Chet, 249
Edwards, Edwin, 125–126, 140
Edwards, John, 209
Eisenhower, Dwight, 305–306
Ellis, Rodney, 238
England, John, 70–72
Engstrom, Richard, 210–211, 233
Epstein, David, 96, 98, 187, 351–352, 354
Espy, Mike, 39, 48–49
Everett, Robinson, 199–200
Evers, Charles, 37
Evers, Medgar, 30
Ewing, Cortez A. M.: *Primary Elections in the South*, 382n8
Exit polls, 95, 280, 404n15; and racial voting patterns, 24, 74, 100, 103, 297, 300, 318–319, 362–65, 396n23;

Exit polls (*continued*)
for 2008 presidential election, 362–365, 392n7

Faubus, Orval, 304–305, 405n1
Feeney, Tom, 402n17
Fenton, John H.: *Politics in the Border States,* 382n8
Fernandez, Alvaro, 273
Fields, Cleo, 123, 132; as Congressman, 121–122, 127–128, 139; as gubernatorial candidate in 1995, 125–126, 134–135, 140, 392n22
Fifteenth Amendment, 4, 6, 17, 20, 350
Figueredo, Fernanco, 402n12
Figures, Michael, 69
Figures, Vivien, 69
Fitch, Milton, 207
Five Tribes, 6
Florida, 253–281; African Americans as judges in, 267, 332–333, 339; African Americans as local officials, 260–262, 282, 332, 336–337, 339; African Americans in Congress, 263–264, 268, 281, 331–332, 339; African Americans in state legislature, 148, 265–266, 269–270, 272, 281, 331–333, 338–339, 402n14; African Americans in statewide offices, 267–268, 331, 339; Broward County, 255, 270, 273–274, 277, 403n25; Collier County, 254–255, 265, 268–269, 270–274, 276–277, 282, 402n18, 403n25; Cuban Americans in, 255, 261–264, 267, 272–276, 278, 281, 402n7; Cubans vs. other Latinos in, 273–276, 282, 340, 343, 402n18; Dade County, 255, 263–264, 269–271, 273–274, 276–277, 282, 402n13, 403n25; in Democratic primary of 2008, 360; Duval County, 402n14; 18th Congressional District, 264, 272; federal monitoring/DOJ objections in, 270–271, 278, 280; Gadsden County, 254; Hardee County, 254–255, 265, 268–269, 272; Hendry County, 265, 268–269, 271–273; Highlands County, 273; Hillsborough County, 254–255, 265, 268–270, 277–279, 402n16; Hispanic population, 25, 255, 268–278, 340; Hispanics as judges, 270; Hispanics as local officials, 260, 270, 282; Hispanics as senators, 267, 274; Hispanics in Congress, 261–264, 271–272, 281; Hispanics in state legislature, 264–266, 269–271, 278, 281–282, 402n12; Hispanics in statewide office, 267; and *Johnson v. Mortham,* 402n9; Lafayette County, 254; Liberty County, 254; Manatee County, 270; Martin County, 263; and *Martinez v. Bush,* 274, 403n22, 403n25; and minority-language provision, 223, 255; Monroe County, 254–255, 265, 269, 271–274, 276–277, 282, 403n25; multiple ballot boxes in, 253; obstacles for black voters in, 253; Osceola County, 276, 340, 403n24; vs. other southern states, 253–254, 294, 307, 325–333, 336–341, 344, 348, 360–368; Palm Beach County, 263; Pinellas County, 270; poll tax in, 253; population of, 253, 255; preclearance requirement/Section 5 of VRA in, 14, 25, 253–255, 264–265, 268–273, 277–278, 280, 282, 331, 338–339, 348, 365–366; racial voting patterns in, 271, 273–278, 282, 363–364, 368; redistricting in, 22, 262–264, 266, 268, 270–271, 402n10; registration of blacks in, 23, 254, 256–257, 259–260,

280–282, 307, 325–327, 339, 374; registration of Hispanics in, 23, 256–260, 265, 280, 282, 374; registration of whites in, 23, 256, 259–260, 326, 374; secretary of state data for, 254, 258–260, 280–281, 327; 17th Congressional District, 264; and *Shaw v. Reno,* 263; vs. states outside the South, 256–258, 280–281; St. Lucie County, 263; Supreme Court of, 267, 332–333, 339, 407n8; 3rd Congressional District, 263, 264; turnout of blacks in, 23, 257–258, 276, 281–282, 328–329, 339, 365, 377, 403n25; turnout of Hispanics in, 23, 257–258, 276, 280–282, 329, 403n25; turnout of whites in, 23, 258, 276, 281, 328, 377, 403n25; 21st Congressional District, 264; 23rd Congressional District, 264; 25th Congressional District, 264, 272, 276, 278; in 2008 presidential election, 361–366, 368; Union County, 254; and *United States v. Osceola County,* 403n24; white primaries in, 383n18. *See also* Democratic Party, in Florida; Republican Party, in Florida

Folsom, "Little Big Jim," Jr., 74

Forbes, Randy, 146

Ford, Aubrey, 70–72

Ford, Harold, 292–293, 298

Ford, Harold E., Jr., 293, 296–300, 302–303

Ford, Jake, 294

Ford, Joe, 293

Ford, John, 300–301

Ford, Johnny, 70, 389n15

Ford, Ophelia, 300–301

Fordice, Kirk, 54

Foster, Mike, 125–126, 392nn21–22

Fourteenth Amendment, 4, 350; Equal Protection Clause, 22, 90, 200, 222, 353

Fowler, Wyche, 88–89, 99

Fraga, Luis Ricardo, 138, 395n28

Frankel, Lois, 263

Franklin, Webb, 49

Freedom Riders, 58

Freeman, Denise, 100–101

Frist, Bill, 293

Frost, Martin, 235, 249

Frye, Henry, 210

Galifianakis, Nick, 209

Gantt, Harvey, 208–209, 211–212

Garcia, Hector, 233

Georgia, 78–110; African Americans as judges, 94, 330–334, 339; African Americans as local officials, 87–88, 332, 335–337, 339, 390n27; African Americans in Congress, 22, 87–91, 98–101, 107, 109–110, 149, 293, 331–332, 338–339; African Americans in state legislature, 87, 91–94, 107, 109–110, 149, 316, 331–333, 339; African Americans in statewide offices, 19, 94–95, 103–106, 109–110, 330, 338–339; Atlanta, 80, 89, 98, 348, 390n27; Baker County, 80; Chattahoochee County, 80, 389n12; Constitution of 1945, 78; Court of Appeals, 330–331, 334; in Democratic primary of 2008, 360; Fayette County, 80; federal monitoring/DOJ objections in, 90, 96–99, 107–108, 121; 5th Congressional District, 87–89, 99; General Assembly, 79, 90–94, 96; *Georgia v. Ashcroft,* 19–20, 96–98, 107, 352–355, 409n20; and *Georgia v. Reno,* 108, 391n45; governor's leadership team in, 93, 390n24; Hispanics in, 83–84; literacy test in, 8, 78–79,

Georgia (*continued*)
382n12; Marion County, 80; and *Miller v. Johnson*, 22, 90, 108, 390n19, 391n46; obstacles for black voters in, 7, 19, 78–80; vs. other southern states, 68, 79, 107–108, 293, 326, 330–341, 344, 346, 348, 360, 363–368, 395n12; poll tax in, 7, 78; pre-clearance requirement/Section 5 of VRA in, 45, 90, 96–99, 107–108, 121, 345–346, 348, 404n8, 405n9; racial voting patterns in, 89, 95, 97–107, 109, 363–364, 368; redistricting in, 90–91, 93, 96–99, 108, 345; registration of blacks in, 19, 23, 79–86, 98, 109, 166, 254, 326, 339, 374; registration of whites in, 23, 79–81, 83–84, 86, 98, 109, 326, 374; secretary of state data for, 85–86, 109; vs. states outside the South, 83, 85; Supreme Court of, 94, 330–334, 339, 407n8; turnout of blacks in, 23, 80–81, 84–86, 98, 109, 328, 339, 365, 377, 390n15; turnout of whites in, 23, 80–81, 84–86, 98, 109, 328, 377, 390n15; in 2008 presidential election, 362–364, 368; white primaries in, 78–79, 383n18, 389n4. *See also* Democratic Party, in Georgia; Republican Party, in Georgia
Gibbs, Shelly Sekula, 249, 401n39
G. I. Forum, 233
Gilmore, James, III, 151
Gingrich, Newt, 344
Girardeau, Arnette, 266, 402n14
Givens, Louella, 125
Goldwater, Barry, 31
Gonzales, Henry, 231, 237
Gonzalez, Raul A., 239, 241
Good character tests, 11, 59, 286
Gore, Al, 71, 264–265, 270, 298–299, 301–303, 366
Graham, Frank, 191
Graham, High D.: *Second Reconstruction*, 382n9
Grandfather clauses, 7–8, 78
Green, Al, 235–236
Green, Gene, 232, 246, 400n32
Green, Jimmy, 209
Gresham, Hilary B., 53, 388n61
Grofman, Bernard, 207
Guerrero, Lena, 241

Hackett, Richard, 298
Handley, Lisa, 153–156
Harris, Joe Frank, 94
Harris, Katherine, 275, 281, 403n28
Hastings, Alcee, 263, 268
Hatch, Orrin: on Section 2 of Voting Rights Act, 21
Hatchett, Joseph, 267, 402n15
Havard, William C.: *The Changing Politics of the South*, 382n9
Haynie, Kerry, 314–315
Helms, Jesse, 191–192, 208–209
Help America Vote Act of 2002, 83–84
Henriquez, Bob "Coach," 269
Herenton, W. W., 298
Hill, Kevin A., 255, 272, 274, 276–277
Hilliard, Earl, 67, 75–76
Hinson, Jon, 37
Hispanics: with Anglo surnames, 228–29; citizen vs. noncitizens, 224, 226, 232; Cuban Americans, 255, 261–264, 267, 272–276, 278, 281, 343, 402n7; and extension of VRA in 1975, 13–14; and poll taxes, 223; in presidential election years, 227, 243, 257, 265, 362–364; Puerto Ricans, 273, 276; registration of, 63, 224–226, 228–229, 250–251, 256–260, 265, 280, 282, 374–376; relationship to African American political success, 340; turnout of, 25, 62, 64, 227–228, 243, 250–251, 257–258, 265,

276, 280–282, 328–329, 362–364, 379, 403n25
Hodges, Jim, 178, 185
Holcomb, Charlie, 239
Holloway, Clyde, 123, 127
Holmes, Alvin, 69
Hood, Jim, 43, 52
Hoover, Herbert, 285
Huckabee, Mike, 315, 318–319
Huckaby, Jerry, 127
Humphrey, Hubert, 165, 306
Hunt, Jim, 192, 208–209
Hutchinson, Tim, 316

Idaho, 348
Ieyoub, Richard, 134
Illinois: African American senators from, 17; Butternut counties, 5
Indiana: Butternut counties, 5; and Section 5 of VRA, 348
Indian Territory, 6
Ingraham, John, 209
Irvin, Tommy, 105

Jackson, Jesse, 95, 202
Jackson, Maynard, 390n27; on VRA, 3
Jamerson, Douglas, 267–268
Jefferson, William: as Congressman, 120–123, 125, 127–130, 393n26; as gubernatorial candidate in 1999, 126, 134–135, 140
Jewell, Jerry, 314
Jim Crow laws, 47
Jindal, Bobby, 130
John, Chris, 126
Johnson, Eddie Bernice, 235, 237, 245, 247
Johnson, Keith, 125
Johnson, Leroy, 91
Johnson, Linda, 125
Johnson, Lyndon B.: campaign of 1964, 30–31, 223; and Civil Rights Act of 1964, 10, 31, 343; on the South and Republican Party, 343; and Texas, 221; and Voting Rights Act of 1965, 3–4, 10, 24, 221
Johnston, Bennett, 126
Johnston, Richard, 388n60
Joint Center for Political and Economic Studies, 23, 37, 145, 230, 325, 332, 335
Jordan, B. Everett, 209
Jordan, Barbara, 235, 237, 293
Joyner, Arthenia, 270
Judges, African Americans as: in Alabama, 70–72, 77, 338–339; in Arkansas, 316, 338–339; in Florida, 267, 332–333, 339; in Georgia, 94, 330–334, 339; in Louisiana, 332, 334, 339; in Mississippi, 37–39, 44, 49, 332, 339; in North Carolina, 209–210, 332, 334, 339, 407n9; in Tennessee, 296, 332–333, 339; in Texas, 239, 244, 252, 331–334, 338–339; in Virginia, 333–334
Judges, Hispanics as: in Florida, 270; in Texas, 239, 244

Kaine, Tim, 151, 156, 394n15, 394n17
Katz, Jonathan, 246–249, 401n37
Katzen, J. K., 394n15
Katzenbach, Nicholas, 10
Kennedy, Edward M.: on VRA, 3
Kennedy, John (Louisiana), 126
Kennedy, John F.: election campaign of 1960, 8–10, 361, 366; letter to Coretta Scott King, 9–10; policies regarding civil rights, 9–10
Kentucky, 6, 148, 348, 382n8
Kerry, John, 105, 293, 299, 303, 365, 366
Kershaw, Joe Lange, 265
Key, V. O., Jr.: on Arkansas, 306; on black population concentrations, 113; black-threat hypothesis of, 164;

Key, V. O., Jr. (*continued*)
on definition of the South, 6, 382n8; on Mississippi, 29–31; on North Carolina, 191; on the poll tax, 223; on South Carolina, 164; on southern politics and blacks, 29–31; *Southern Politics in State and Nation,* 5, 29, 382n15; on Tennessee, 286; on Virginia, 142; on white supremacy, 29
Kilgore, J. W., 394n15, 394n17
King, Gary: *A Solution to the Ecological Inference Problem,* 369, 371, 394n20
King, Martin Luther, Jr., 9–10, 59
Kirk, Claude, 305
Kirk, Ron, 242–243
Knight, John, 69
Kousser, Morgan, 31, 111, 286
Ku Klux Klan, 58, 126
Kuykendall, Dan, 293

Lamb, Charles: on VRA, 4
Lamis, Alexander P.: *Southern Politics in the 1990s,* 382n9
Lampson, Nick, 249, 401n39
Lander, Jim, 178, 185
Landrieu, Mary, 125–126, 362
Lee, Howard, 202, 209–211
Lee, Sheila Jackson, 235
Leggette, Willie M., 172
Leland, Mickey, 245–246
Lewis, George A., 402n14
Lewis, John, 18, 60, 88–89, 100–101, 360–361; on changes in Georgia, 97–98
Lichtman, Allan, 48–49, 232, 234
Lijphart, Arend, 342
Lincoln, Blanche, 319
Linguistic minorities, 13–14, 16–17, 25, 190, 223, 255
Literacy test, 10–14, 223, 253, 305, 349; in Alabama, 59, 382n12; in Georgia, 8, 78–79, 382n12; in Louisiana, 111, 382n12; in Mississippi, 7, 31, 382n12; in North Carolina, 190, 382n12; in South Carolina, 165, 382n12; in Tennessee, 285–286; in Virginia, 141, 382n12
Local officials, African Americans as, 19–21, 25; in Alabama, 64–66, 77, 332, 338–339; in Arkansas, 310–311, 332, 339; city councilors, 21, 36–38, 87, 108, 270, 332, 334–336, 338–339; county commissioners, 32, 246, 332, 334–336, 338, 340; at county level, 32, 64–65, 120, 144–145, 172, 197–198, 230, 246, 260–261, 292, 311, 334–336, 338, 340; in Florida, 260–262, 282, 332; in Georgia, 87–88, 332, 339, 390n27; in Louisiana, 111, 119–120, 332, 339; mayors, 20, 37, 45–46, 70, 121, 125, 151, 202, 208–209, 243, 298, 302, 332, 335–336, 338–339, 390n27; in Mississippi, 32, 36–39, 45–46, 56–57, 332, 338–339; at municipal level, 20–21, 36–38, 45–46, 64–65, 70, 87, 108, 119–121, 125, 144–145, 151, 172, 197–198, 202, 208–209, 230–231, 243, 260, 270, 281, 292, 298, 302, 310–311, 332, 334–336, 338–339, 390n27; in North Carolina, 197–198, 332, 335–337, 339; school board members, 21, 37–38, 64–65, 77, 87, 111, 119–121, 124–125, 132–133, 145, 172, 292, 332, 336–340; in South Carolina, 172–173, 332, 335–337, 339; in Tennessee, 291–292, 302, 332, 335–337, 339; in Texas, 229–231, 332, 335, 337, 339–340; in Virginia, 144–145, 335–338
Local officials, Hispanics as, 231, 270, 282; in Florida, 260, 270, 282; in Texas, 231
Loewen, James W., 180–182, 186–187

Lott, Trent, 52–53, 386n27
Louisiana, 111–140; African Americans as judges, 332, 334, 339; African Americans as local officials, 111, 119–120, 332, 335–337, 339; African Americans as statewide candidates, 125–126, 133–134, 139–140, 339; African Americans in Congress, 120–123, 149, 331–332, 339; African Americans in state legislature, 111, 123–124, 149, 331–333, 339; African Americans on Board of Elementary and Secondary Education (BESE), 124–125, 131–133, 138, 392n20; African Americans on Public Service Commission (PSC), 124–125, 131–133; Bossier Parish, 138; Caddo Parish, 112; Claiborne Parish, 112; in Democratic primary of 2008, 360; Evangeline Parish, 112; federal monitoring/DOJ objections in, 108, 123, 137–139; federal registrars in, 12, 112–113; 4th Congressional District, 121–122, 127, 149; Franklin Parish, 113; and *Hays v. Louisiana,* 122, 392nn14–15; Hurricane Katrina, 117; literacy test in, 111, 382n12; Morehouse Parish, 113; obstacles for black voters in, 111; open primary system in, 116, 119, 133, 140, 344–345; Orleans Parish, 393n26; vs. other southern states, 111, 121, 137, 326–327, 330–341, 346, 360, 362–368; poll tax in, 111; preclearance requirement/Section 5 of VRA in, 108, 123, 137–139, 331, 346, 404n8, 405n9; racial voting patterns in, 112, 126–137, 139–140, 363–364, 366; redistricting in, 22, 121–123, 137–139; registration of blacks in, 12, 23, 111–115, 117–118, 139, 326–327, 339, 374; registration of whites in, 23, 114, 326–327, 374; Richland Parish, 113; secretary of state data for, 118–119; vs. states outside the South, 116; States' Rights Party in, 166; Supreme Court of, 332–334, 339, 407n8; Tensas Parish, 112; turnout of blacks in, 23, 111, 115–119, 126, 139, 328–329, 339, 365, 377, 392n8; turnout of whites in, 23, 115–117, 119, 328–329, 377; in 2008 presidential election, 362–366, 368; West Feliciana Parish, 112–113; white primaries in, 111, 383n18
Lublin, David: *The Republican South,* 382n9
Lucas, Jeanne Hopkins, 207
Lucas, Louise, 146–147, 153–154, 156
Lucio, Eduardo, 239
Luebke, Paul, 192, 202–203

Mabus, Ray, 54
Mack, Connie, 268
Majette, Denise, 105
Marshall, Jim, 91
Martinez, Bob, 267
Martinez, Mel, 267, 274
Maryland, 382n8
Matthews, Donald R., 388n62
Mattingly, Mack, 103
McCrery, Jim, 127
McDonnell, R. F., 394n17
McEachin, Don, 147, 151–152, 156–157, 393n10, 394n15
McGee, Ben, 312
McKay, John, 402n17
McKinney, Cynthia, 89–90, 101
McLemore, Lester Burl, 37
Meek, Carrie, 263–264, 266, 402n14
Meek, Kendrick, 264
Melton, Harold, 94
Mettetal, Nolan, 55–56
Mexican American Legislative Caucus, 237

Michaux, Mickey, 202, 210–211
Michigan: and minority-language provision, 223; preclearance requirement/Section 5 in, 14, 348
Middlemass, Keesha M., 94
Miles, Floyd H., 393n10
Miller, Les, 270
Miller, William, 314
Miller, Yvette, 94
Miller, Zell, 94, 100, 103
Minorities, linguistic, 16–17, 25, 190, 223, 255, 349
Mirabal, Margaret, 242
Mississippi, 29–57; African Americans as judges, 37–39, 44, 49, 332, 339; African Americans as local officials, 32, 36–39, 45–46, 56–57, 332, 335–339; African Americans as senators, 36; African Americans in Congress, 39–40, 56, 149, 331–332, 339; African Americans in state legislature, 41–42, 55–56, 57, 149, 331–333, 339; African Americans in statewide offices, 42–44, 339; black population of, 29, 385n3; Bolivar County, 48; Civil Rights Movement in, 30, 41, 385n6; Claiborne County, 33; Constitution of 1890, 7, 31, 78; Court of Appeals, 44; Delta district, 39, 49, 56; in Democratic primary of 2008, 360; federal monitoring/DOJ objections in, 45–46, 108, 137, 250; federal registrars in, 12, 33; Grenada, 46; Hinds County, 33; Holmes County, 32–33; Humphreys County, 32; Kilmichael, 45–46; LaFlore County, 33; literacy test in, 7, 31, 382n12; Madison County, 33, 48; *Martin v. Allain*, 387nn50–51; Mound Bayou, 38; Noxubee County, 46–48, 356; obstacles for black voters in, 7, 10, 30–32, 36, 45–46, 56, 240–241, 327, 338; obstacles for white voters in, 46–48; vs. other southern states, 45, 59, 65, 77, 166, 250, 288–291, 302, 325–341, 344, 346, 360, 362–368, 385n3; poll tax in, 7, 31; preclearance requirement/Section 5 of VRA in, 45–46, 108, 137, 250, 331, 346, 348, 404n8, 405n9; in presidential election of 1964, 30–31; in presidential election of 2008, 44; racial voting patterns in, 40–42, 44, 48–57, 363–364, 366, 387n52; during Reconstruction, 36; redistricting in, 39–41; registration of blacks in, 12, 31–36, 56, 79, 166, 288–289, 325–327, 338–339, 374; registration of whites in, 33–34, 325–327, 374; residency requirement in, 7, 31; slavery in, 385n3; state flag referendum, 53; vs. states outside the South, 34–36; States' Rights Party in, 166; support for Obama in, 44; Supreme Court of, 44, 332–334, 339, 407n8; Tunica County, 33; turnout of blacks in, 34–36, 56, 290–291, 327–329, 338–339, 365, 377, 388n62; turnout of whites in, 34–36, 56, 328–329, 377, 388n62; in 2008 presidential election, 362–366, 368; United Citizens Party in, 172; and *United States v. Ike Brown*, 46–48, 387n44, 387n48; Warren County, 32; White Citizens Councils in, 30; white primaries in, 383n18; white supremacy in, 30; Winstonville, 38. *See also* Democratic Party, in Mississippi; Republican Party, in Mississippi
Mississippi Freedom Democratic Party (MFDP), 30–31, 36–37
Mississippi State University, 53
Missouri, 6, 348, 382n8
Missouri Plan, 267, 333–334

Mitchell, Theo, 177, 396n23
Molina, J. R., 242
Montana: Glacier County, 348
Moore, Mike, 52
Morales, Dan, 239, 241
Morales, Victor, 241, 243
Moran, Jim, 394n11
Moreno, Dario V., 255, 272, 274, 276
Morial, Marc, 121, 125
Morrell, Arthur, 126, 137
Moseley, Ken, 174
Motor Voter Act of 1993, 83–84
Moyers, Bill, 343
Murray, Richard, 221–222, 236, 243
Musgrove, Ronnie, 43, 52, 362, 387n59

Naifeh, Jimmy, 302, 404n19
National Association for the Advancement of Colored People (NAACP), 30
National Association of Latino Elected Officials, 260
Native Alaskans, 223; and extension of VRA in 1975, 13
Native Americans, 223, 348; and extension of VRA in 1975, 13
Nebraska, 348
Nelson, Bill, 274–275
Nevada, Clark County, 348
New Hampshire: Democratic primary of 2008, 360; and Section 5 of VRA, 346
New Jersey, 5
Newman, DeQuincey, 175
New Mexico: Hispanics as local officials in, 231; and *Jepsen v. Vigil-Giron*, 408n7; and Section 5 of VRA, 348
Newton, Demetrius, 69
New York City: preclearance requirement in, 14; Puerto Rican registration in, 14
New York State: African Americans in Congress, 390n18; Bronx County, 383n34; Hispanics in, 14, 22; Kings County, 383n34; and minority-language provision, 223; redistricting in, 22; and Section 5 of VRA, 348
Nixon, Richard, 306; southern strategy of, 343
Noriega, Rick, 362
North Carolina, 190–218; African Americans as judges, 209–210, 332, 334, 339, 407n9; African Americans as local officials, 197–198, 332, 335–337, 339; African Americans in Congress, 15–16, 149, 198–203, 218, 331–332, 339; African Americans in state legislature, 149, 203–208, 218, 331–332, 339, 356; African Americans in statewide offices, 208–210, 331; black population of, 340; Court of Appeals, 210; *Cromartie v. Hunt/Easley v. Cromartie*, 200–201, 398n15; in Democratic primary of 2008, 360; federal monitoring/DOJ objections in, 121, 160–161, 198–201, 217; 1st Congressional District, 201–202, 210–212, 214–215, 218; Greensboro, 192; Guilford County, 192; Harnett County, 217; literacy test in, 190, 382n12; and minority-language provision, 223; multi-seat districts in, 203–207; obstacles for black voters in, 190; vs. other southern states, 167, 190–192, 217–218, 326, 328–332, 334–341, 344, 348, 356, 360–368; poll tax in, 8, 190; preclearance requirement/Section 5 of VRA in, 25, 121, 160–161, 190–193, 197–201, 217, 348, 397n3, 404n8, 405n9; racial voting patterns

North Carolina (*continued*)
in, 191, 202, 210–216, 218, 363–364, 368; redistricting in, 22, 191, 198–203, 206, 217; registration of blacks in, 23, 167, 192–197, 218, 326, 339, 374; registration of whites in, 192–197, 218, 326, 374; 2nd Congressional District, 202–203, 210–211; and *Shaw v. Hunt*, 200, 398n14; and *Shaw v. Reno*, 122, 199–201; State Board of Elections data, 192, 195–197; Supreme Court of, 209–210, 332–333, 339, 407nn8–9; and *Thornburg v. Gingles*, 197, 203–207, 398n11; turnout of blacks in, 23, 194–197, 218, 328–329, 339, 365, 377; turnout of whites in, 23, 194–197, 328–329, 377; 12th Congressional District, 15–16, 22, 122, 199–202, 211–212, 214–215; in 2008 presidential election, 344, 356, 361–366, 368. *See also* Democratic Party, in North Carolina; Republican Party, in North Carolina
North Dakota, 348
Norwood, Charlie, 14–15, 100, 346–349, 408n6

Obama, Barack: African American support for, 360–366, 409nn2–3; vs. Carter, 366; in Democratic primary, 44, 71, 106, 117, 119, 180, 297–298, 316–317, 359–361; on extension of Voting Rights Act, 17–18; vs. Gore, 366; vs. Kerry, 365–366; in Presidential election, 95, 259, 344, 356, 361–368; as Senator, 17–18; and superdelegates, 360–361
Ocampo, Maria Lizet, 138, 395n28
O'Connor, Sandra Day, 201; on Georgia's 12th Congressional District, 22; on North Carolina's I–95 district, 199–200
Office holding by African Americans: in Alabama, 329–330, 338; in Arkansas, 320, 330, 339; in Florida, 329–330, 339; in Georgia, 330–331, 339; in Louisiana, 329–330, 339; in Mississippi, 329–330, 338–339; in North Carolina, 330, 339; progress in, 19, 23–24, 56–57, 77, 109–110, 161–163, 188, 217–218, 250–252, 281–282, 302, 320, 323–325, 329–341, 353–354; in South Carolina, 330, 339; in Tennessee, 330, 339; in Texas, 330, 339; in Virginia, 330, 339. *See also* Congress, African Americans in; Judges, African Americans as; Local officials, African Americans as; State legislatures, African Americans in; Statewide offices, African Americans in
O'Halloran, Sharyn, 187, 351–352
Oklahoma, 5–6, 148, 348, 382n8
Oregon, 348
Orey, Byron D'Andra, 42
Ortiz, Solomon, 231
Overstreet, Morris, 239, 241, 246, 400n33

Parker, Frank, 39, 41–42
Parker, Mike, 387n59
Parks, Rosa, 58–59
Parry, Janine A., 314
Patterson, Grady, 186
Patterson, John, 59
Peabody, Endicott, 36
Peeler, Bob, 185
Pelosi, Nancy: on extension of Voting Rights Act, 18–19
Pennsylvania, 348
Pepper, Claude, 261
Perdue, Beverly, 362
Perdue, Sonny, 94, 97
Perot, Ross, 103

Perry, Matthew, 174
Persily, Nathaniel, 19
Peterman, Frank, 270
Phipps, Herbert, 94
Pickering, Chip, 50–51
Pickett, Owen, 153, 155–156
Polinard, Jerry, 243
Poll tax, 5, 11–12, 59, 78, 253, 285–286; in Arkansas, 305, 307; in Florida, 253; in Georgia, 7, 78; in Louisiana, 111; in Mississippi, 7, 31; in North Carolina, 8, 190; in South Carolina, 165; in Tennessee, 285–286, 404n6; in Texas, 221–223, 286; in Virginia, 141
Presidential election years: 1928, 285; 1952, 306; 1956, 306; 1960, 8, 9–10, 361, 366; 1964, 30–31, 63, 142, 166, 190, 223, 286, 306, 361; 1968, 63, 306; 1976, 54, 170, 361, 366; 1980, 144, 227, 310; 1984, 63, 170, 310; 1988, 63, 95, 170, 227, 257, 310; 1992, 100, 103, 115, 193, 275, 290, 310, 366; 1996, 63, 86, 193, 257, 275, 290, 310, 319, 361, 366; 2000, 63, 71, 131, 170–171, 183, 193, 264–265, 270, 274–275, 281, 298–299, 301–303, 310, 361, 366; 2004, 34, 54, 63–64, 73, 86, 105, 170–171, 196, 209, 228, 275, 293, 299, 303, 310, 319, 337, 361, 365–366; 2008, 71, 95, 106, 117, 150, 178, 196, 259, 344, 356, 361–368, 409nn2–3; African American turnout during, 17, 36, 83, 84, 86, 115–116, 170–171, 179, 188, 194–196, 228, 265, 290, 309, 310, 324, 327–329, 337, 360, 409nn2–3; Hispanic turnout during, 227, 243, 257, 265, 362–364
Price, H. D.: *The Negro in Southern Politics*, 382n8
Progress since Voting Rights Act, 4–5, 25, 349–350; electoral outcomes, 19, 23–24, 56–57, 77, 109–110, 161–163, 188, 217–218, 250–252, 281–282, 302, 320, 323–325, 329–341, 353–354; voter registration, 17, 19, 22–23, 56, 77, 109, 139, 161, 188, 251, 280–281, 319, 323, 325–327, 337–341, 345–346, 406n4; voter turnout, 17, 19, 22–23, 56, 77, 109, 139, 161, 188, 251, 280, 302, 320, 323, 325–329, 337–341
Property-ownership requirements, 8, 59, 78
Proportionality between elected officials and voting-age population: in Alabama, 77, 148–149, 330, 331–332, 334, 336–337; in Arkansas, 149, 332, 334, 336; in Florida, 148–149, 264, 269–270, 331–333, 337; in Georgia, 149, 331–333, 336–337; in Kentucky, 148–149; in Louisiana, 149, 330, 332, 337; in Mississippi, 56–57, 149, 330–332, 334, 336–337; in North Carolina, 149, 218, 330, 331–332, 337; in Oklahoma, 148–149; in South Carolina, 149, 188, 330–332, 334, 337; in Tennessee, 149, 295, 302, 330–333, 336–337; in Texas, 149, 330–333, 337; in Virginia, 148–149, 161–162, 330, 332–334, 336–337; and Voting Rights Act of 1982, 21, 324
Prothro, James, 388n62
Pryor, David, 305
Pryor, Mark, 316

Quinton, Nick: "Voting Rights in Alabama," 389n11

Racial voting patterns, 23–25, 353–355; in Alabama, 71–77, 363–364, 366; Cubans vs. other Latinos in Florida, 273–276, 282, 343; in Florida, 271, 273–278, 282, 363–364, 368; in Georgia, 89, 95, 97–107, 109, 363–364, 368; in Louisiana, 112, 126, 127–137,

Racial voting patterns (*continued*) 139–140, 363–364, 366; in Mississippi, 40–42, 44, 48–57, 363–364, 366, 387n52; in North Carolina, 191, 202, 210–216, 218, 363–364, 368; as polarized, 46–49, 76, 99–100, 127, 147, 155, 158–160, 180–181, 205–207, 247, 298, 317–318, 348, 350–351, 356–357, 363, 366–368, 370, 408n8; in South Carolina, 178–187, 363–364; in Texas, 240, 243–251, 363–364, 400n33, 401n34, 401n38; and *Thornburg vs. Gingles,* 204–207; in 2008 presidential election, 361–366, 368; in Virginia, 147, 150–160, 162–163, 363–364, 368, 395n25
Randolph, Ned, 127
Raymond, Richard, 241
Reconstruction, 4, 6–7, 8, 36, 174, 221–222, 402n14
Redistricting, 32, 352–356; in Alabama, 66–68; in Arkansas, 312–316; in Florida, 262–263, 264, 266, 268, 270–271, 402n10; in Georgia, 90–91, 93, 96–99, 108, 345; in Louisiana, 121–123, 137–139; in Mississippi, 39–41; in North Carolina, 191, 198–203, 206, 217; in South Carolina, 172–173, 175–176, 188; in Tennessee, 295; in Texas, 231–236, 238, 249–251, 345; in Virginia, 146–147, 153, 161
Reeves, Tate, 43–44
Reform Party, 50, 387n52
Registration of African Americans in the South: Alabama, 12, 17, 59–63, 77, 79, 166, 254, 325–327, 338–339, 374; Arkansas, 306–309, 319, 326–327, 338–339, 374, 405n8; and Civil Rights Act of 1957, 8–9; data on, 22–24; by federal registrars, 12, 33, 60, 77, 112–113, 166; Florida, 254, 256–257, 259–260, 280–282, 307, 325–327, 339, 374; Georgia, 19, 79–86, 98, 109, 166, 254, 326, 339, 374; Louisiana, 12, 111–115, 117–118, 139, 326–327, 339, 374; Mississippi, 12, 31–36, 56, 79, 166, 288–289, 325–327, 338–339, 374; North Carolina, 167, 192–197, 218, 326, 339, 374; number registered, 8–10, 12, 22–25; progress regarding, 17, 19, 22–23, 56, 77, 109, 139, 161, 188, 251, 280–281, 319, 323, 325–327, 337–341, 345–346, 406n4; vs. registration of blacks outside the South, 34, 56, 62, 83, 85, 114, 117, 143, 168, 188, 193–194, 226–227, 257, 281, 288–289, 308–309; vs. registration of Hispanics in the South, 225, 256–257, 259–260, 282; vs. registration of Hispanics outside the South, 376; vs. registration of whites in the South, 33–34, 60–62, 79–84, 98, 109, 114, 166, 167, 192–196, 197, 218, 224–226, 256, 259–260, 286–288, 306–309, 326–327, 337, 376, 407n5; vs. registration of whites outside the South, 34, 62–63, 114–115, 376; South Carolina, 165–171, 188, 326, 339, 374; Texas, 224–227, 250–251, 326–327, 339, 374; Virginia, 141–143, 161, 325–327, 338, 374; women vs. men, 81–82
Registration of Hispanics in the South: Florida, 256–260, 265, 280, 282, 374; vs. Hispanics outside the South, 226, 251, 256–257, 280; Texas, 224–226, 228–229, 250–251, 375
Republican Party: in Alabama, 66–69, 71–75, 77; in Arkansas, 305–306, 312, 314–319; and extension of VRA, 345–346; in Florida, 261–262, 264, 267–268, 270–271, 273–278, 281–282,

285, 340, 402n18; in Georgia, 68, 78, 92–93, 101, 105–106, 109–110, 334; incumbent candidates, 43, 49–52, 57, 73, 75–76, 87, 103, 106, 122, 131, 140, 151, 162, 177, 184–186, 208, 247, 277, 293, 298–299, 301, 312, 316–319, 344–345, 362–364, 394n18, 399n21; in Louisiana, 112, 123, 125–137, 139–140, 344–345, 409n19; in Mississippi, 36–37, 42–44, 48–57, 207, 344; in North Carolina, 192, 199, 202, 208–209, 212, 285; in South Carolina, 68, 174–175, 177–180, 184, 186, 188–189, 344; in Tennessee, 285, 293–294, 296–297, 300, 302–303, 382n8; in Texas, 221–222, 231–235, 239, 244, 247, 249, 251–252, 285, 334, 344; in Virginia, 150–153, 158, 160, 162, 285, 344, 394n18; and Voting Rights Act of 2006, 15, 17, 345–346; white support for, 342–344, 351, 353, 355–357. *See also* Bush, George H. W.; Bush, George W.; Nixon, Richard
Residency requirements, 7, 31, 59
Reyes, Ben, 231–232, 246
Reyes, Silvestre, 232
Richardson, Bill, 228
Rivera, David, 271, 277–278
Rockefeller, Winthrop, 305, 316–317
Rodriguez, Ciro, 234
Roemer, Buddy, 392n22
Roosevelt, Franklin Delano, 361
Ros-Lehtinen, Ileana, 261–262, 272
Ruffin, John, 94
Ruoff, John, 187

Salazar, Ken, 267
Sanchez, Tony, 242–243
Sanders, Henry "Hank," 69
School desegregation, 30, 141, 304–305, 383n26; *Brown v. Board of Education*, 191, 383n26, 395n11
Schwegmann, John, 124
Scott, David, 89–90
Scott, John R., Jr., 402n14
Scott, Robert, 146, 152–155, 163, 394n18
Sears, Leah, 94
Senators: African Americans as, 17–18, 36; Hispanics as, 267, 274
Sensenbrenner, James: on extension of Voting Rights Act, 16
Sessions, Jeff, 364; on VRA, 17
Shafer, Byron, 388n60
Shaffer, Stephen, 53, 388n61
Sharp, John, 243
Sheffield, Ron, 316
Shelby, Richard, 74
Shows, Ronnie, 49–51
Siegelman, Don, 70, 73–74
Sisisky, Norman, 146, 153
Smith, Judy, 312
Smith, Willis, 191
South, the: Deep South states, 166, 395n9; defined, 5–6, 382n8; in Democratic primary of 2008, 359–361; economic conditions, 5–6; obstacles for black voters in, 4–13; in presidential election of 2008, 361–368; Reconstruction in, 4, 6–8, 36, 174, 221–222, 402n14; Rim South, 306, 405n6; and secession, 6, 58, 285; segregation in, 5–6; as target of VRA, 4, 10–12, 24–25; tenant farming in, 5
South Carolina, 164–189; African Americans as local officials, 172, 173, 332, 335–337, 339; African Americans as statewide candidates, 177–180, 339; African Americans in Congress, 149, 172–174, 181–184, 188, 331–332, 339; African Americans in state legislature, 149, 174–177, 188, 306, 331–332, 339;

South Carolina (*continued*)
black population of, 164–165, 385n3; Clarendon County, 166, 395n11; Democratic primary in 2008, 360; federal monitoring/DOJ objections in, 187–188; federal registrars in, 166; literacy test in, 165, 382n12; McCormick County, 166–167; multiple ballot boxes in, 165, 253; obstacles for black voters in, 164–166, 174; vs. other southern states, 68, 164, 166–167, 253, 306, 326, 328–332, 334–341, 344, 346, 348, 360, 363, 364–367, 385n3, 395n12; poll tax in, 165; preclearance requirement/Section 5 of VRA in, 187–188, 331, 346, 348, 404n8, 405n9; racial voting patterns in, 178–187, 363–364; redistricting in, 172–173, 175–176, 188; registration of blacks in, 23, 165–171, 188, 326, 339, 374; registration of whites in, 23, 166–168, 188, 326, 374; Richland County, 175; 6th Congressional District, 172–173, 181–184; slavery in, 385n3; and *Smith v. Allwright*, 165; States' Rights Party in, 165–166, 174; Supreme Court of, 332–334, 339, 407n8; turnout of blacks in, 23, 168–172, 188, 328–329, 339, 377; turnout of whites in, 23, 171–172, 188, 328–329, 377; in 2008 presidential election, 362–365; United Citizens Party in, 172; white primaries in, 165
South Dakota: and minority-language provision, 223; preclearance requirement in, 14
Southern Manifesto, 191
Southern Political Report, 69, 332
Spaulding, Kenneth, 202, 210–211
Spell, Lester, 44, 386n36
Spence, Floyd, 174
Spratt, John, 182–184
State legislatures, African Americans in, 23, 25, 354; Alabama, 67–69, 77, 148–149, 306, 331–333, 338–339; Arkansas, 149, 306, 312–316, 320, 331–333, 338–339, 356; Florida, 148, 265–266, 269–270, 272, 281, 331–333, 338–339, 402n14; Georgia, 87, 91–94, 107, 109–110, 149, 316, 331–333, 339; Louisiana, 111, 123–124, 149, 331–333, 339; Mississippi, 41–42, 55–57, 149, 331–333, 339; North Carolina, 149, 203–208, 218, 331–332, 339, 356; South Carolina, 149, 174–177, 188, 306, 331–332, 339; Tennessee, 149, 295, 302, 331–333, 339, 356; Texas, 149, 237–239, 251, 331–333, 339, 356; Virginia, 147–149, 161–162, 331, 333, 338, 356
State legislatures, Hispanics in: Florida, 264–266, 269–271, 278, 281–282, 402n12; Texas, 237–239, 251, 356
Statewide offices, African Americans as candidates for: in Arkansas, 316–317, 320, 339; in Louisiana, 125–126, 133–134, 139–140, 339; in South Carolina, 177–180, 339; in Texas, 239–243, 246, 250–252, 339
Statewide offices, African Americans in, 23, 25; in Alabama, 70–72, 77, 338–339; in Florida, 267–268, 331, 339; in Georgia, 19, 94–95, 103–106, 109–110, 330, 338–339; in Mississippi, 42–44, 339; in North Carolina, 208–210, 331; in Tennessee, 295–298, 339; in Virginia, 141, 149–152, 162
Statewide offices, Hispanics as candidates for: in Florida, 267; in Texas, 239–244, 246, 250–252

Still, Edward: "Voting Rights in Alabama," 388n11
Street, James, 5
Student Nonviolent Coordinating Committee, 60
Superdelegates in 2008 Democratic primary, 360–361

Tallon, Robin, 173
Talmadge, Eugene, 78–79
Talmadge, Herman, 390n27
Tanner, John, 301–302
Tate, Katherine, 329
Taylor, Gene, 49–51, 55, 387n53
Tejeda, Frank, 231
Tennessee, 285–292; African Americans as judges, 296, 332–333, 339; African Americans as local officials, 291–292, 302, 332, 335–337, 339; African Americans in Congress, 292–294, 302, 331–332, 339; African Americans in state legislature, 149, 295, 302, 331–333, 339, 356; African Americans in statewide offices, 295–298, 339; in Democratic primary of 2008, 360; Fayette County, 286–287; Haywood County, 286–287, 301–302, 404n19; literacy test in, 285–286; Memphis, 286, 298, 366, 404n4, 409n19; as not subject to Section 5 of VRA, 25, 285–286, 291, 302, 304, 327, 329, 331, 333, 335, 339, 348, 356, 365; obstacles for black voters in, 285–288; vs. other southern states, 150, 285–286, 290–291, 293–297, 302, 304, 307, 326–333, 335–341, 348, 356, 363–367; poll tax in, 285–286, 404n6; racial voting patterns in, 294, 297–302, 363–364; redistricting in, 295; registration of blacks in, 285–288, 307, 326–327, 339, 374; registration of whites in, 286–287, 326–327, 374; Shelby County, 298–299; vs. states outside the South, 288–291; Supreme Court of, 296, 332–333, 339, 407n8; turnout of blacks in, 286, 289–290, 302, 327–329, 339, 365, 377, 404n9; turnout of whites in, 289–290, 328–329, 377; in 2008 presidential election, 363–366; white primaries in, 287. *See also* Democratic Party, in Tennessee; Republican Party, in Tennessee
Terry, Mary Sue, 151
Texas, 221–252; African Americans as judges, 239, 244, 252, 331–334, 338–339; African Americans as local officials, 229–231, 332, 335, 337, 339, 340; African Americans as statewide candidates, 239–243, 246, 250–252, 339; African Americans in Congress, 87, 149, 235–237, 250–251, 293, 331–332, 339–340; African Americans in state legislature, 149, 237–239, 251, 331–333, 339, 356; and *Balderas v. Perry*, 248; Bexar County, 346; Dallas County, 246, 346, 400n33; and *Del Rio v. Perry*, 234, 248, 399n1; in Democratic primary of 2008, 360; Dream Ticket, 243, 252; El Paso County, 346; federal monitoring/DOJ objections in, 108, 137, 250; Fort Bend County, 222, 305, 382n18; and *Grovey v. Townsend*, 222; Harris County, 235–236, 246, 346, 400n33; Hispanic population of, 25, 221, 223, 228–229, 236, 330; Hispanics as judges, 239, 244; Hispanics as local officials, 231; Hispanics as statewide candidates, 239–244, 246, 250–252; Hispanics in Congress, 231–235, 250–251; Hispanics in state legislature,

Texas (*continued*)
237–239, 251, 356; Jaybird Party in, 222, 305; and *LULAC v. Perry*, 235; and minority-language provision, 223; and *Nixon v. Herndon/Nixon v. Condon*, 222; obstacles to black voters in, 221–222; vs. other southern states, 141, 223–224, 250, 293, 297, 305, 307, 326–335, 337–341, 344, 346, 356, 360, 362, 363–367; poll tax in, 221–223, 286; preclearance requirement/Section 5 of VRA in, 13, 25, 45, 108, 137, 223–224, 231, 235, 250–251, 331, 338–339, 345–346, 349, 365–366; racial voting patterns in, 240, 243–251, 363–364, 400n33, 401n34, 401n38; redistricting in, 22, 231–236, 238, 249–251, 345; registration of blacks in, 224–227, 250–251, 326–327, 339, 374; registration of Hispanics in, 224–226, 228–229, 250–251, 375; registration of whites in, 224–226, 307, 326–327, 374; and *Sessions v. Perry*, 234, 400n23; and *Smith v. Allwright*, 222; vs. states outside the South, 231; Supreme Court of, 239, 244, 252, 331–333, 338–339, 407n8; Tarrant County, 246, 346, 400n33; and *Terry v. Adams*, 222, 383n18; and *Thornburg v. Gingles*, 230; Travis County, 349–350; turnout of blacks in, 227–228, 243, 250–251, 328–329, 339, 365, 377; turnout of Hispanics in, 227–228, 243, 250–251, 328–329; turnout of whites in, 227–228, 377; in 2008 presidential election, 362–366; white primaries in, 78, 141, 383n18. *See also* Democratic Party, in Texas; Republican Party, in Texas
Theodore, Nick, 185
Thompson, Bennie, 40, 49, 51
Thompson, M. E., 79
Thurmond, J. Strom, 165–166, 174, 395n7
Thurmond, Michael, 95
Till, Emmett, 30
Tillman, "Pitchfork Ben," 6, 165
Timmons-Goodson, Patricia, 210
Tinker, Nikki, 294
Truman, Harry S., 165
Tubbs Jones, Stephanie, 360–361
Tuck, Amy, 43, 55
Turnout of African Americans in the South, 23–25, 345–346, 354; Alabama, 61, 63–64, 77, 327–329, 339, 365, 377, 388n9; vs. blacks outside the South, 35–36, 56, 64, 77, 116–117, 144, 169, 195, 218, 228, 258, 281, 290, 309, 320; data on, 33–36; Georgia, 80–81, 84–86, 98, 109, 328, 339, 365, 377, 390n15; vs. Hispanics in the South, 250–251, 257–258, 276, 281–282; vs. Hispanics outside the South, 379; Louisiana, 111, 115–119, 126, 139, 328–329, 339, 365, 377, 392n8; Mississippi, 34–36, 56, 290–291, 327–329, 338–339, 365, 377, 388n62; North Carolina, 194–197, 218, 328–329, 339, 365, 377; in presidential election years, 17, 36, 83–84, 86, 115–116, 170–171, 179, 188, 194–196, 228, 265, 290, 309–310, 324, 327–329, 337, 360, 409nn2–3; progress regarding, 17, 19, 22–23, 56, 77, 109, 139, 161, 188, 251, 280, 302, 320, 323, 325–329, 337–341; relationship to socioeconomic disparities, 329; South Carolina, 168–172, 188, 328–329, 339, 377; Texas, 227–228, 243, 250–251, 328–329, 339, 365, 377; in 2008 presidential election, 361–366, 409nn2–3; Virginia, 142–144, 147,

161, 328, 329, 337–338, 365, 377; vs. whites in the South, 34–36, 56, 61, 63, 80–82, 84–85, 98, 115–117, 119, 143–144, 147, 161, 171–172, 188, 194–197, 227–228, 258, 276, 281–282, 289–290, 309–310, 319–320, 327–329, 337, 379, 409nn2–3; vs. whites outside the South, 35–36, 64, 379, 388n9; women vs. men, 80–82
Turnout of Hispanics in the South: Florida, 257–258, 276, 280–282, 329, 403n25; vs. Hispanics outside the South, 228, 251, 258, 280; in presidential election years, 227, 243, 257, 265, 362–364; Texas, 227–228, 243, 250–251, 328, 329
Twenty-fourth Amendment, 11

Ujifusa, Grant, 39–40, 121, 392n12
Understanding test, 11, 59, 78, 141, 286, 305, 349
United Citizens Party, 172
University of Arkansas: Diane D. Blair Center, 408n8
University of Mississippi, 30
Uribe, Hector, 241
U.S. Census Bureau data: for 2006 vs. 2004, 324; for Alabama, 61–67, 374, 377; for Arkansas, 307–310, 314, 374, 377; exclusion of Hispanics for white registration and turnout, 34–35, 62–63, 83–84, 114–116, 143–144, 167–169, 193, 195, 225–227, 288, 290, 308–309, 374–375, 377–379, 388n9; exclusion of noncitizens, 325; for Florida, 256–258, 280–281, 374, 377; for Georgia, 83–86, 109, 374, 377, 390n15; for Louisiana, 113–115, 117, 374, 377; for Mississippi, 33–36, 325, 374, 377; for North Carolina, 193–197, 207, 218, 375, 378; post-election participation surveys by, 23, 325; for South Carolina, 167–172, 188, 375, 378; for Tennessee, 287–291, 375, 378; for Texas, 221, 224–228, 237, 243, 251, 375, 378; for Virginia, 142–144, 325, 375, 378
U.S. Commission on Civil Rights, 8, 112, 254, 286, 288, 307, 389n8; data on Alabama, 60–61; data on Mississippi, 32, 33; data on Texas, 224
U.S. Department of Justice: and Alabama, 76–77, 161, 217; attorney general, 11–12, 32; and Florida, 270–271, 278, 280; and Georgia, 90, 96–99, 107–108, 121; in Kennedy administration, 9–10; and Louisiana, 108, 123, 137–39; and Mississippi, 45–46, 108, 137, 250; and North Carolina, 121, 160–161, 198–201, 217; in Obama administration, 356; Section 2 incorporated into Section 5 reviews by, 21–22, 138–139, 199, 250, 312, 353–355; and South Carolina, 187–188; and Texas, 108, 137, 250; and Virginia, 160–161, 217
U.S. federal courts (lower): *Balderas v. Perry*, 401n34; *Busbee v. Smith*, 409n18; *Chapman v. King*, 389n4; District of Columbia District Court, 11, 13, 32, 108, 391n45, 409n18; *Georgia v. Reno*, 108, 391n45; *Gingles v. Thornburg*, 47, 387n47; *United States v. Ike Brown*, 46–48, 387n44, 387n48
U.S. Supreme Court: *Allen v. State Board of Elections*, 32, 36, 45, 385n15, 386n39; *Beer v. United States*, 22, 138–139, 199, 398n12; *Brown v. Board of Education*, 191, 383n26, 395n11; *Bush v. Vera*, 351, 408n14; and candidates of choice, 203–207, 351–352; *City of Boerne v. Flores*,

U.S. Supreme Court (*continued*) 384n36; *City of Mobile v. Bolden*, 19–21; *Cox v. Larios*, 409n21; and DOJ interpretation of Section 2 of VRA, 20–22, 47, 139, 250, 353–355; *Easley v. Cromartie*, 200–201, 353, 398n18, 409n17, 409n21; *Georgia v. Ashcroft*, 19–20, 96–98, 107, 352–355, 409n20; *Georgia v. United States*, 383n30; *Grovey v. Townsend*, 222, 399n5; *Guinn v. United States*, 382n17; *Harper v. Virginia Board of Elections*, 383n27, 393n1; *Hunt v. Cromartie*, 200, 298n17; *LULAC v. Perry*, 235; *Miller v. Johnson*, 22, 90, 153, 345, 390n19, 391n46; and Mississippi Constitution of 1890, 7, 78; *NAMUDNO v. Mukasey*, 349–350; *Nixon v. Condon*, 222, 399n4; *Nixon v. Herndon*, 222, 399n3; *Reno v. Bossier Parish School Board*, 22, 139, 250, 393n30, 401n41; *Shaw v. Hunt*, 200, 398n14; *Shaw v. Reno*, 22, 122, 146, 153, 199–201, 263, 355, 384n52, 398n13; *Smith v. Allwright*, 78, 111–112, 165, 222, 287, 382n18, 389n4, 399n6; *South Carolina v. Katzenbach*, 15, 383n35; *Terry v. Adams*, 222, 382n18, 399n7; *Thornburg v. Gingles*, 197, 203–207, 230, 398n11, 398n21, 410n1; *United Jewish Organizations of Williamsburgh v. Carey*, 409n18; *United States v. Hayes*, 392n16; *Vieth v. Jubelirer*, 409n21; *Wesberry v. Sanders*, 39; and white primaries, 8, 59, 78, 165, 222, 287, 389n4; *White v. Regester*, 205–206; *Williams v. Mississippi*, 382n14; *Zimmer v. McKeithen*, 205–206

Valentine, Tim, 202
Van de Putte, Leticia, 239
Virginia, 141–163; African Americans as judges, 333–334; African Americans as local officials, 144–145, 335–338; African Americans in Congress, 146–147, 331; African Americans in state legislature, 147–149, 161–162, 331, 333, 338, 356; African Americans in statewide offices, 141, 149–152, 162; apology for slavery in, 141; and bailout provision in Voting Rights Act of 1982, 14, 161, 349; Civil Rights Movement in, 141; in Democratic primary of 2008, 360; election of statewide officials in odd-numbered years, 144; federal monitoring/DOJ objections in, 160–161, 217; 4th Congressional District, 146–147, 156–157; and *Hall v. Commonwealth*, 154–155; Henrico County, 393n10; independent candidates in, 158, 160; independent cities in, 142, 161; literacy test in, 141, 382n12; and *Miller v. Johnson*, 153; and *Moon v. Meadows*, 153–154; Northampton County, 161; obstacles for black voters in, 141; vs. other southern states, 141–143, 145, 147–150, 160–162, 217, 294, 297, 307, 325–341, 344, 346, 356, 360–368; poll tax in, 141; preclearance requirement/Section 5 of VRA in, 14, 160–161, 217, 331, 339, 346, 349, 404n8, 405n9; racial voting patterns in, 147, 150–160, 162–163, 363–364, 368, 395n25; redistricting in, 22, 146–147, 153, 161; registration of blacks in, 141–143, 161, 325–327, 338, 374; registration of whites in, 142–143, 161, 307, 326–327, 374; school desegregation in, 141; and

Shaw v. Reno, 146, 153; vs. states outside the South, 144, 150–151; Supreme Court of, 333–334; 3rd Congressional District, 146–147, 153, 155–157, 163; turnout of blacks in, 142–144, 147, 161, 328–329, 337–338, 365, 377; turnout of whites in, 143–144, 147, 161, 328–329, 337, 377; in 2008 presidential election, 344, 356, 361–366, 368. *See also* Democratic Party, in Virginia; Republican Party, in Virginia
Vitter, David, 131
Vitter, John, 126
Voter Education Project (VEP): and Arkansas, 307; and Texas, 224
Voting Rights Act of 1965: and attorney general, 11–12, 32; and District Court for the District of Columbia, 11, 13, 32; and election data, 14–15, 19, 22–24; extensions of, 4, 13–20, 45–46, 223, 250, 254, 342, 345–352; and federal registrars, 12, 33, 60, 77, 112–113, 166; and intent to discriminate, 20–21; and Lyndon Johnson, 3–4, 10, 24, 221; and Obama election, 359–368; permanent parts of, 4, 20; Section 2, 5, 17, 20–24, 46–48, 64–65, 87, 138–139, 146, 197, 199, 203–207, 250, 282, 313, 324, 334–335, 351–356; Section 4, 11, 79, 217, 221, 254, 286, 306, 349; Section 5/preclearance requirement, 5, 11–22, 24, 32, 45–46, 63–64, 76, 79, 90, 96–97, 107–108, 121, 137–139, 142, 148, 160–162, 187–188, 190–193, 197–201, 217, 223–224, 231, 235, 250–251, 253–255, 264, 268–273, 277, 310, 312, 338–339, 341, 345–349, 351–356, 360, 365–366, 382n12; the South as target of, 4, 10–12, 24–25; sunset provisions of, 4, 13, 350
Voting Rights Act of 1970, 13, 142, 223–224, 345, 350, 383n34
Voting Rights Act of 1975, 345, 350, 383n34; and Florida, 254–255, 331; and linguistic minorities, 13–14, 25, 190, 223; and North Carolina, 190; and Texas, 250–251, 331
Voting Rights Act of 1982, 16, 250, 350; amendment of Section 2 in, 19–21, 87, 324, 334–335, 349, 351; bail out provision in, 14, 161, 349; and intent to discriminate, 20–21; and *Mobile v. Bolden*, 19–21; and *Thornburg v. Gingles*, 197, 203–207
Voting Rights Act of 2006, 14–20, 22, 45–46, 345–350; Norwood Amendment, 14–15, 346–349

Wade, Rick, 177–178, 185
Walker, Champ, 90–91
Walker, Charles, 91, 96, 106
Wallace, George, 9, 30, 59, 63, 306, 340–341
Walley, James Shannon, 55
Warner, John, 394n11
Warner, Mark, 147, 151–152, 156, 162, 362, 394n11, 394n15
Warren, Earl, 15, 32
Washer, Dale Barbara, 50
Washington, Harold, 202
Watt, Melvin, 201–202, 211–212, 214; on extension of Voting Rights Act, 15–16
Webb, Jim, 162
Weber, Ronald, 152–154
Weeks, O. Douglas, 383n18
Wekkin, Gary, 406n22
West, Royce, 239
Westmoreland, Lynn, 408n6; on extension of Voting Rights Act, 19
West Virginia, 348, 382n8
White, George H., 3, 16

White Citizens Councils, 30
White primaries: in Arkansas, 305–306; in Florida, 383n18; in Georgia, 78–79, 383n18, 389n4; in Louisiana, 111, 383n18; in Mississippi, 383n18; in South Carolina, 165; in Tennessee, 287; in Texas, 78, 141, 383n18; and U.S. Supreme Court, 8, 59, 78, 165, 222, 287, 389n4
White supremacy, 29, 30, 165
Wicker, Roger, 50–51, 386n27
Wielhouwer, Peter W., 93–94, 329
Wilder, Douglas, 149–150, 154–157, 297, 393n10
Wilder, John, 296, 302, 404n19
Williams, Faye, 123
Wright, Fielding, 166
Wright, Sharon, 295, 298
Wyman, Hastings, 69–70

Yanez, Linda, 242
Young, Andrew, 87–88, 99, 235, 293

Zaffirini, Judith, 239

Also by Charles S. Bullock III and Ronald Keith Gaddie

(ed. with John C. Kuzenski) *David Duke and the Politics of Race in the South* (Nashville, 1995)

Elections to Open Seats in the U.S. House (Lanham, Md., 2000)

Georgia Politics in a State of Change (New York, 2009)

Also by Bullock

(comp. with Robert T. Golembiewski and Harrell R. Rodgers, Jr.) *The New Politics: Polarization or Utopia?* (New York, 1970)

(ed. with Harrell R. Rodgers, Jr.) *Black Political Attitudes; Implications for Political Support* (Chicago, 1972)

(with Harrell R. Rodgers, Jr.) *Law and Social Change: Civil Rights Laws and Their Consequences* (New York, 1972)

(with Harrell R. Rodgers, Jr.) *Racial Equality in America: In Search of an Unfulfilled Goal* (Pacific Palisades, Calif., 1975)

(with Harrell R. Rodgers, Jr.) *Coercion to Compliance* (Lexington, Mass., 1976)

(with James E. Anderson and David W. Brady) *Public Policy and Politics in America* (North Scituate, Mass., 1978)

(with James E. Anderson and David W. Brady) *Public Policy in the Eighties* (Monterey, Calif., 1983)

(with Susan A. MacManus and Donald M. Freeman) *Governing a Changing America* (New York, 1984)

(ed. with Charles M. Lamb) *Implementation of Civil Rights Policy* (Monterey, Calif., 1984)

(with Loch K. Johnson) *Runoff Elections in the United States* (Chapel Hill, N.C., 1992)

The Partisan, Racial, and Gender Makeup of Georgia County Offices (Atlanta, 1993)

(with Frederick W. Cubbage and Jay O'Laughlin) *Forest Resource Policy* (New York, 1993)

(ed. with Mark J. Rozell) *The New Politics of the Old South* (Lanham, Md., 1998, 2003, 2007)

Also by Gaddie

(with James L. Regens) *The Economic Realities of Political Reform* (Cambridge and New York, 1995)

(with James L. Regens) *Regulating Wetlands Protection* (Albany, 2000)

Born to Run (Lanham, Md., 2004)

(with James L. Regens) *The Economic Realities of Political Reform* (Cambridge and New York, 2005)